CONVERSION TABLES

Measurements for weights, lengths, and liquids have been

OVEN TEMPERATURES

FAHRENHEIT	225°	250°	275°	300°	325°	350°	375°	400°	425°	450°
CELSIUS	110°	120°	140°	150°	160°	180°	190°	200°	220°	230°

WEIGHTS

IMPERIAL	METRIC
½ oz	15 g
1 oz	30 g
4 oz (¼ lb)	125 g
6 oz	185 g
8 oz (½ lb)	250 g
12 oz (¾ lb)	375 g
14 oz	440 g
1 lb (16 oz)	500 g
1½ lb	750 g

LENGTHS

IMPERIAL	METRIC
¼ in	5 mm
½ in	1 cm
1 in	2.5 cm
6 in	12 cm
12 in	30 cm

SPOON MEASURES

IMPERIAL	METRIC
¼ tsp	1.125 ml
½ tsp	2.5 ml
1 tsp	5 ml
1 tbsp	15 ml

BODY TEMPERATURE

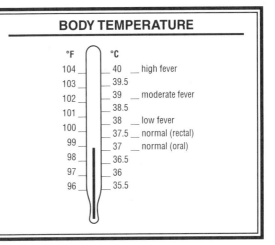

°F	°C	
104	40	high fever
103	39.5	
102	39	moderate fever
101	38.5	
100	38	low fever
99	37.5	normal (rectal)
98	37	normal (oral)
97	36.5	
96	36	
	35.5	

SPEED

IMPERIAL	METRIC
30 mph	50 km/h
40 mph	60 km/h
50 mph	80 km/h
55 mph	90 km/h
60 mph	100 km/h

LIQUIDS

IMPERIAL	METRIC
¼ cup	60 ml
⅓ cup	80 ml
½ cup	125 ml
⅔ cup	160 ml
¾ cup	180 ml
1 cup	250 ml

STRENGTHEN YOUR IMMUNE SYSTEM

STRENGTHEN YOUR IMMUNE SYSTEM

Boosting the body's own healing
powers in the fight against disease

Reader's Digest

The Reader's Digest Association
(Canada) Ltd., Montreal

CANADIAN PROJECT STAFF

Editor
Robert Ronald

Designer
Cécile Germain

Copy Editor
Gilles Humbert

Production Manager
Holger Lorenzen

Production Coordinator
Susan Wong

Editorial Administrator
Elizabeth Eastman

Researcher
Jeremy Derksen

Medical Consultant
Mark Berner, M.D., Montreal

Books and Home Entertainment
Vice President
Deirdre Gilbert

Art Director
John McGuffie

U.S. PROJECT STAFF

Project Editor
Susan Carleton

Senior Designer
Susan Welt

Production Technology Manager
Douglas A. Croll

Editorial Manager
Christine R. Guido

Contributing Editor
Kimberly Ruderman

Reader's Digest Health and Science Books
Associate Editorial Director
Marianne Wait

ISBN 0-88850-754-2

Address any comments about *Strengthen Your Immune System* to:
    Editor, Books and Home Entertainment
    c/o Customer Service, Reader's Digest
    1125 Stanley Street, Montreal, Quebec H3B 5H5

For information about this and other Reader's Digest products, or to request a catalog, please call our 24-hour Customer Service hotline at 1-800-465-0780.

You can also visit us on the World Wide Web at: www.readersdigest.ca.

Printed in Canada

02 03 04/3 2 1

NOTE TO OUR READERS
The information in this book should not be substituted for, or used to alter, medical therapy without your doctor's advice. For a specific health problem, consult your physician for guidance.

CREATED BY
The Harold Press, L.L.C.

Publisher and Editorial Director
Nuna Alberts

Executive Editor
Diane Umansky

Contributing Editor
Nikky Barnes

Writers
Elisa Agostinho, Mary Dolan,
Beth Howard, Robin Latham,
Annetta Miller, Barbara Tunick,
Jan Sheehy, Karyn Siegel-Maier

Recipe Development
Shari Citron, R.D.

Exercise Development
Eric Ludlow, M.S.T., A.T.C., C.S.C.S.

Copy Editors
Amy Burrous, Miranda Spencer

Researchers
Catherine Grillo, Maud Kernowski,
Milada Rehakova

Indexer
Milada Rehakova

DESIGN DIRECTION BY
Nina Scerbo Design, Inc.

Director, Design and Photography
Nina Scerbo

Photo Production
Sylvia Lachter

Assistant Photo Editor
Leslie Ohori

Art Assistants
HyeJoong Ryu,
Tammy Schoenfeld,
Julide Aksiyote, James Kim

MEDICAL BOARD OF ADVISORS

Chief Medical Adviser
M. Eric Gershwin, M.D.
Professor and Chief, Division of
Rheumatology, Allergy, and Clinical
Immunology, University of
California at Davis School of
Medicine

Advisers
Sonia Ancoli-Israel, Ph.D.
Director, Sleep Disorders Clinic,
VA San Diego Healthcare System

Mark Blumenthal
Executive Director, American
Botanical Council, Austin, Texas;
Editor and Publisher of *HerbalGram*

Hyla Cass, M.D.
Assistant Clinical Professor of
Psychiatry, University of California,
Los Angeles School of Medicine

Paul A. Lachance, Ph.D.
Director, Nutraceutical Science
Institute, Department of Food
Science, Cook College,
Rutgers University, New Brunswick,
New Jersey

Andy Liu, M.D.
Training Program Director and
Assistant Faculty Member in
Pediatric Allergy & Clinical
Immunology, National Jewish
Medical and Research Center,
Denver

Tedd Mitchell, M.D.
Medical Director, Cooper Clinic
Wellness Program, Dallas

Ramesh Raghavan, M.D.
Research Fellow, Pediatric Pain
Program, University of California,
Los Angeles School of Medicine

Cynthia Thomson, Ph.D., R.D.
Assistant Professor of Public
Health, University of Arizona,
Arizona Cancer Center, Tucson

Contents

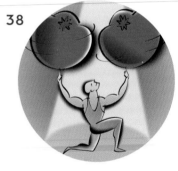

About This Book

When we think about all the organs and systems that function together to keep us alive, we often overlook the immune system. Without this complex, far-flung network of specialized tissues and cells, though, everything else would shut down.

How does the immune system fit in with such basic life processes as breathing, digestion, and metabolism? Because its main agents (white blood cells) are dispersed throughout the body instead of anchored in one place like organs, the answer is somewhat elusive. It doesn't follow a well-defined cycle the way eating, digestion, and energy storage do. And it has a host of different functions, many of which remain unexplained.

Not surprisingly, then, the notion that individuals can have any effect on their immune responses is fairly new. Until a few years ago, the prevailing medical view was that chance alone determined whether a particular germ or toxic exposure would make you sick.

Now, though, there's abundant evidence that each of us can do a number of relatively simple things to boost our immunity. Our food choices, exercise habits, sleep schedules—even our thoughts and feelings—affect our immune function in many surprising ways.

This book will help you take advantage of the most recent findings on building up your natural resistance to disease and infection. Every chapter summarizes the latest research linking diet, herbs, exercise, sleep, mental outlook, and risk reduction to enhanced immunity. Hundreds of tips show how you can put this information into practice. For instance, there's a delicious week-long menu plan (recipes included) packed with immune-boosting nutrients, a detailed guide to herbs that enhance immunity, and a unique total body tune-up appropriate for all fitness levels. The book closes with an easy-to-follow 12-week action plan for optimum immunity.

They're all here—the facts and research to motivate you and the step-by-step instructions to start you on the road to better health for life.

A Message from
M. Eric Gershwin, M.D.

In just the last 20 years, research into the workings of the immune system has really taken off. It wasn't until the 1980s that the medical community recognized the importance of the body's sophisticated defense network.

In the 1950s, for example, removing the tonsils was standard procedure for children who frequently got colds. Today, we know that the tonsils are one of the first lines of defense against respiratory disease. Similarly, doctors not so long ago prescribed antibiotics for just about anyone who had a sore throat. Now we're aware that overusing antibiotics does a serious disservice to the immune system, making us more vulnerable to illness by killing weak microbes and letting strong ones flourish.

When I teach medical students about the immune system, I like to compare it to a car. Just as some cars can log well over 100,000 miles and never break down, some people's immune systems perform at their peak year after year. The lucky owners of reliable cars spend very little on repairs; the fortunate people with strong immunity rarely get sick.

But even a new car can develop one problem after another. Constant car trouble often stems from lack of routine maintenance—oil and filter changes, fluid-level checks, and other standard upkeep.

The same is true of some people who always seem to be sick: Their eating habits are poor, they rarely sleep enough, and they neglect routine preventive care. In other words, they're lax about maintenance.

Unlike cars, though, our immune systems have evolved into complex networks over hundreds of thousands of years. That's why a quick fix such as an immune booster in a bottle isn't likely to have much impact. But we can harness our bodies' innate desire to be well by following the instructions in this book.

Let's hope that all your colds are minor ones. Be aware, however, that as Hippocrates supposedly said,

"Even hypochondriacs get sick." Eternal youth and perpetual health unfortunately don't exist. But the small miracle of feeling good and experiencing joy almost every day is well within our reach!

M. Eric Gershwin, M.D.

Immunologist M. Eric Gershwin, M.D., the chief consultant for this book, is professor of medicine and chief of the Division of Rheumatology, Allergy, and Clinical Immunology at the University of California, Davis School of Medicine.

CHAPTER 1

All Systems Go!

Germs: You do everything you can to avoid them, but harmful bacteria, viruses, and molds are relentless in their attempts to invade and infect your body. Strengthen your immune system —the body's awesome shield against these enemies—and your chance of staying healthy, robust, and vigorous will soar.

Your Amazing Fighting Forces

These days, it's increasingly common for doctors and patients alike to rely on pills and other pharmaceutical potions to cure whatever medical problems they encounter.

Because of this quick-fix mentality, we often neglect what may be the most effective curative of all: the immune system. When your immune system is strong enough to do its job properly, odds are that you are healthy. But when it stumbles, foreign agents—including bacteria, viruses, parasites, fungi, even cancer cells—may gain a foothold inside you.

Recognition and response.

It may sound melodramatic, but it's true: Your immune system saves your life every day. A vast network of white blood cells, chemicals, and organs working together, it recognizes millions of potentially harmful invaders and destroys them before they injure healthy cells, deplete the body's nutrients, or damage vital organs.

Perhaps the reason we don't think much about the immune system is that it is so complex. Unlike other major players in the body—the heart and the lungs, for example—it's not a single organ. It's more like a relay team that passes the job of protection from player to player, each responsible for further weakening any pathogen (disease-causing organism) that crosses its path.

This network of players cooperates to get its mission of resistance and restoration done, so focusing on just one member of the team won't give you much of a sense of what's going on—you need an overall view.

COLORIZED ELECTRON MICROGRAPHS reveal samples of the bacteria that threaten the finely tuned balance of our health. CLOCKWISE, FROM LEFT TO RIGHT: *Staphylococcus* can produce skin abscesses; *Clostridium* infects food and releases toxins that damage the nervous system; *Listeria*, often acquired in contaminated dairy products, may affect almost any organ; harmful strains of *Streptococci* most commonly inflame the throat, but some produce flesh-eating disease.

That's the purpose of this first chapter: to take you on a brief tour of the immune system so you can get a feeling for how it all fits together and, most important, gain a better understanding of what you can do to help it do its job better.

PROTECTION ON THE SURFACE: Healthy skin helps keep harmful microbes out of the body.

The First Line of Defense

As soft and as vulnerable as your bare skin may feel, it's tough enough to serve as the body's primary armor against roving bacteria and viruses. What makes it so well suited to its protective role is the layer of dead cells that form the top part of the skin, the epidermis. Although thinner than plastic wrap, this layer is composed of a protein called keratin, which is difficult to break down. As a result, it's impossible for most infectious agents to penetrate the skin, except when it is unhealthy or damaged.

Even before germs land on the skin, they are often stopped by hairs, which help to keep out dirt and microorganisms. Germs that do manage to get past the hairs land on a film of sweat and oil, laced with acidic chemicals and beneficial bacteria that together hold back hostile organisms. Some immune cells also stand guard. For example, Langerhans' cells lie in the epidermis waiting to ingest unwelcome microbes and alert other immune-team players that more attackers may be on the way.

A blanket of protection. Vulnerable areas such as the eyes are protected in a similar fashion by mucous membranes, skinlike surfaces coated with secretions that fight germs. These membranes are generally found at natural openings in the body, including the eyes, nose, mouth, and reproductive tract—places unprotected by the skin. The thick, sticky film produced by mucous membranes traps yeasts, viruses, bacteria, dirt particles, pollen grains, fungus spores, and most anything else that tries to enter through the openings. The mix of mucus and debris that accumulates in oral and nasal cavities is

---

VITAL STATISTICS: SKIN

1 millimeter – 2 millimeters
Average thickness of the skin

19 – 34 days
Life span of skin cells

2 square meters
Area covered by skin on the average adult

10,000
Number of "good" bacteria inhabiting every square centimeter of skin

965 kilometers
About how much hair most people grow in a lifetime

50,000 a minute
Rate at which dead cells flake and fall off the body

---

then swallowed, whereupon stomach acid and pancreatic enzymes destroy most of the germs, or they are carried out of the body by such actions as coughing or sneezing. The mucous membranes lining every part of the respiratory tract get additional help from cilia, which are tiny hairlike projections that snag particles and sweep them toward the nearest exit—that is, the nostrils or mouth. For the most part, these outermost layers of protection are able to guard the body.

God Bless the Sneeze

A sneeze. A scratch. A tear. Typically, these reflexes barely register on your consciousness, or, if they do, it's as an annoyance. In reality, however, each is an unconscious action that, in its own way, provides essential protection against disease-causing microbes or toxins before they can do harm.

◆ **Scratching** is a natural reaction to itching, which is triggered by tiny receptors (called nociceptors) in the skin's nerve endings. The job of these receptors is to warn you that something—for example, a mosquito—is putting pressure on your skin, and send the command: "Get rid of it!"

◆ **Coughing** helps clear mouth, throat, and lung tissues of foreign invaders, such as molds, pollen, dust mites, and pet dander, as well as microbe-laden mucus. In fact, coughing is such an important defense mechanism that, although you may not notice it, you normally cough once or twice an hour. The irony: Respiratory infections may be spread by droplets of pathogens put in the air by a cough.

SNEEZING helps rid the body of disease-inducing invaders.

Quick Tip

When you feel a sneeze coming on, try not to suppress it: Preventing that 160 km/h blast of air from escaping may cause a nasty infection by forcing germs and viral particles up into the Eustachian tubes, which lead to the middle ear.

◆ **Sneezing** is like coughing but directed through the nose. When, for example, dust blows in your face, nerve cells in the nose signal the brain to expel it. We also sneeze to get rid of microbes that multiply in the nasal passageways, say, as the result of a cold or the flu.

◆ **Vomiting** occurs when harmful substances in the stomach or duodenum (the upper segment of the small intestine) are identified by receptors in the walls of the digestive tract. The brain signals the digestive tract to stop, reverse itself, and squeeze the stomach's contents past the muscle that separates it from the esophagus, up and out through the mouth.

◆ **Tearing** keeps the surface of the eyes moist and sterile, thanks to lysozyme, an enzyme in tears that destroys bacteria by dissolving a chemical bond in the cell membrane, causing the cell wall to collapse. Tears also protect the eye when dust or debris irritate it: Tear production increases until the fluid overflows the eyelids and washes away the irritant. Crying, a natural response to stress, flushes away certain harmful chemicals produced by anxiety.

Despite this impressive range of barriers, reflexes, and chemicals, dangerous invaders do occasionally manage to penetrate the body. Fortunately, a second line of defense stands ready to attack.

A closer look at…microbes

Everywhere you go, you run the risk of encountering one or another of the germs that can make you sick. These bugs are transmitted through air, food, water, insects, and contaminated objects, such as hands or doorknobs.

BACTERIA

They may look harmless even under the most powerful microscopes, but these single-celled organisms can cause big problems when they invade our bodies, reproduce rapidly, and excrete toxic by-products. Bacterial infections range from cat-scratch fever to plague (Black Death). But not all bacteria are bad; some, in fact, help keep us healthy.

RIGHT: *Salmonella,* **magnified 11,759 times**

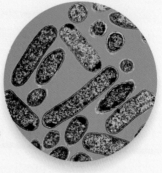

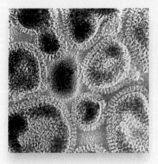

VIRUSES

Made of nothing more than a strand of genetic material (DNA or RNA), viruses are so simple that they aren't even considered living things. Yet they can trigger illness by overtaking the genetic machinery of cells within the body. Once in command, they direct those cells to produce more viruses, which, if not stopped, may overwhelm vital organs.

LEFT: *Influenza Type A,* **magnified 285,750 times**

PARASITES

Any organism that survives by living off a host is a parasite. Parasites able to latch onto humans vary from tiny single-celled creatures, such as the protozoan *Giardia lamblia,* to 9-meter-long tapeworms. These nasty creatures can induce a range of health problems, including rashes, fever, nausea, cramps, diarrhea, and miscarriage. Many of the most common parasites are transmitted through food and water.

RIGHT: *Giardia lamblia,* **magnified 1,979 times**

MOLDS

Airborne spores of these simple plants can cause a variety of infections when they are inhaled into the lungs or gain a foothold in other dark, warm places, such as the mouth, vagina, or skin folds. Although these infections tend to strike people with compromised immune systems, some types are more widespread: A Mayo Clinic study, for example, pegged molds as the cause of many chronic sinus infections.

LEFT: *Aspergillus* **(common bread mold), magnified 514 times**

Equipped for Battle

Sometimes invaders slip past our first line of defense, the physical barrier of skin and mucous membranes, and into the bloodstream and organs.

When they do, our second line of defense, the innate immune system—a complex army of specialized molecules and white blood cells—is there to greet them. Without a doubt, you've seen your innate immune system in action. Think back to a time when you stumbled, fell, and scraped your knee. Dirt, bacteria, or viruses may have entered your body through the break in the skin. Within a few hours, the area had become red and swollen, sure signs that your innate immune system had kicked in. But exactly what players had leapt to your defense?

Antigens
The signalers.
The first and most important function of the immune system is to determine what is foreign and what is not. Antigens provide the clues. These molecules cover the surface of every cell—whether it is native to the body or an invader—acting as the cell's calling card. If the cell belongs to the body, the calling card is engraved with the message "Self!"—in other words, "I belong here; do not attack." If, however, the cell belongs to an invader, such as a bacterium that came in through the scrape on your knee, the calling card reads "Foreign!" This sounds the signal for the immune system to attack.

Antibodies
The tag team. After an antigen is detected, the immune system's ground troops—many millions of white blood cells called leukocytes—mobilize to fight the invader. Alongside them are lymphocytes, an elite force of specialized white blood cells that have especially important jobs. In the case of the B-lymphocytes, or B-cells, that task is to custom-make proteins called antibodies, which recognize and bind to a particular invader. A given antibody matches an antigen much as a key matches a lock. Once attached to the invader, these antibodies serve as tags that signal other immune cells to swarm and engulf, kill, or quickly remove the offending substance.

Remarkably, once B-cells have encountered a specific germ, they can remember it if it invades again. This enables them to launch a much quicker, more intense, and more effective attack against that germ years, even decades later. That so-called "adaptive" immune response is the reason why you

---

Thwarting Microbial Invaders

Once you injure your skin, it can no longer act as the barrier that it's supposed to be. So how do you treat a minor cut to ensure that it doesn't open the door to trouble?

1 Let it bleed a bit. **This helps the cut clean itself of pieces of dirt and debris. Do not use alcohol, iodine, or mercurial solutions; these strong disinfectants can damage tissue.**

2 If you have a gentle cleanser, **such as mild, unscented soap, mix it with water, preferably lukewarm. Otherwise, liberally flood the cut with plain water alone, then rinse. Pat dry gently with sterile gauze or a clean cloth.**

3 Encourage clotting **by pressing down for five minutes on the washed cut with clean gauze, cloth, or if necessary, your bare hand. Release the pressure slowly. There is generally no need to apply an antibacterial ointment.**

4 Check to be sure that your immunization against tetanus is up to date. **You need a booster every ten years to protect against this serious bacterial infection, which can be introduced by any wound and often causes a fatal neurological reaction marked by lockjaw.**

IMMUNE SYSTEM ALL-STARS

A healthy body teems with many millions of different white blood cells that work together to scout out and destroy bacteria and viruses. Because white blood cells are so vital to the immune response, they are used as the key measure of immune system health. If your doctor remarks that you have a "strong immune system," it generally means that a count of the different white blood cells in a sample of your blood was well within the normal range: about 4,000 to 11,000 cells per microliter of blood. More precise tests can determine the number of specific types of white blood cells, such as T-cells, in the blood.

are much less susceptible to certain infections, such as the measles or chicken pox, after you've had them once. It also is the basis for vaccines, which introduce small amounts of an antigen into the body to prime the immune system for subsequent attacks. The eradication of smallpox through the immunization of millions of people is one of modern medicine's greatest successes.

Breast's benefits. Antibodies belong to a family of large molecules called immunoglobulins, of which there are several—immunoglobulin M, G, A, E, and D. Each type plays a different role in the immune defense strategy. (Whenever you see an abbreviation like IgE or IgG in a medical document, it refers to an antibody.) During pregnancy, many copies of IgG, an antibody that helps guard against systemic infections like the flu, pass from the mother to her unborn child through the placenta, providing the first immunity from disease. However, other antibodies—most notably IgA, which plays a major role in shielding the mucous membranes from harm—are available to the baby only through colostrum, the mother's first milk. Because of the abundance of IgA and other protective substances in mothers' milk, the Canadian Paediatric Society and several other major health organizations take very strong pro-breastfeeding positions.

T-Cells

The generals. A variety of T-cells organize and direct other white blood cells in the fight against infection. The immunity controlled by T-cells is known as cellular immunity to differentiate it from the disease resistance conferred by antibodies. There are two types of T-cells.

◆ **Helper T-cells,** sometimes referred to as CD4 T-cells, respond to certain antigens and secrete cytokines, soluble proteins that help other types of immune system cells, such as B-cells, respond to and get rid of invaders.

◆ **Cytotoxic T-cells,** or CD8 T-cells, kill cells infected with viruses or other germs. This prevents such pathogens from replicating and so stops infection's spread.

Phagocytes

The germ eaters. If you are an invader, the last thing you want to encounter is a phagocyte—a third type of immune cell that gobbles up everything unwanted, from dust to viruses. Phagocytes come in two types: neutrophils, which circulate in the blood and enter tissues that have become infected, and macrophages, which dwell in healthy tissues and lie in wait for invaders to show up. The name macrophage literally means "big eater," and eat big they certainly do, capturing,

Interesting!

Antigens, the molecules that let the immune system distinguish "self" from "foreign" cells, are at the root of most problems with organ transplants. Sitting atop the cells of new donor tissues, antigens trigger the "foreign" alarm, revving the immune cells to reject the transplanted tissue or organ. Drugs are needed to suppress this response.

engulfing, and breaking down microorganisms. Macrophages are versatile warriors that can also secrete cytokines, which direct large numbers of other immune cells, including neutrophils, to an infected area. Once on the scene, neutrophils are fierce but short-lived warriors. They die at the battle scene, forming pus.

Natural Killer Cells

The specialists. Unlike B- and T-cells, these large, circulating immune system cells (often referred to as NK-cells) are filled with toxic granules that help them kill their targets on contact. The "natural" part of their name comes from the fact that, unlike T-cells, which must mature before they can become killers, NK-cells have the ability to kill from the moment they are formed. Viral infections stimulate production of NK-cells, which often hold down the fort until cytotoxic T-cells can arrive. NK-cells also kill certain tumor cells, so they help prevent cancer.

Other immune cells, granulocytes, also contain toxic granules that mainly fight parasites.

Other players. T-cells and macrophages (as well as other cells outside the immune system) also manufacture many other chemicals that play key roles in defending the body. These include interferons, which have antiviral and anticancer properties, and interleukins, many of which fight cancers as well. Some of these substances are now being made in large quantities through genetic engineering and used to treat patients with cancer, blood disorders, autoimmune disorders, and immunodeficiency diseases (including AIDS), as well as in those receiving bone-marrow transplants.

The Reason We Get Sick

If the immune system is such a wonder, why do we ever get sick? The simplest explanation is that often there is a lapse between the time a microbe enters the body and the time the immune system conquers it. In the interim, the invader can make its mark, killing cells and spewing toxins. In fact, the toxins germs produce as they multiply are responsible for most of the symptoms of some infections, such as the sore throat caused by a toxin from the *Streptococcus* bacterium. Once an invader is stopped, the body takes time to recover, so symptoms can linger.

Interesting!

More than 200 known viruses cause colds—and the number of those cold-causing viruses is always growing. That's because viruses are constantly changing their genetic makeup, begetting new forms the immune system does not recognize. The result: Children average some six to ten colds a year; adults, two to four.

UNCOMMON KNOWLEDGE
Too Clean May Be Bad

Antibacterial soaps, antibacterial toothpaste, antibacterial cutting boards—potent germ-destroying products are popping up everywhere. Unfortunately, using them could leave you and your family more vulnerable to infection. These products do a good job of killing off most germs, but a few—because of genetic mutations—survive and multiply. The result? A new generation of bacteria with inbred resistance to antibacterial compounds. Cleaning the old-fashioned way—using plain soap and water on the body and a weak bleach solution on the countertop—works fine for preventing illness. Antibacterial products are a good idea mainly when caring for someone whose immune system is compromised.

The Stages of Infection

How sick you become when a microbe invades depends largely on how strong a defense your immune system can launch. If a key component of your immune system is weak, the threat posed by an invader is greater. Once a germ begins to take hold and multiply—the incubation period—an infection is under way. Depending on the pathogen, this may take a few days (as with a cold) or many years (as with HIV, the virus that causes AIDS). People are often infected without knowing it, which is one reason contagious diseases can so easily be spread.

The symptomatic period is marked by the appearance of noticeable signs of the illness—fever, for one. When an infection is overwhelming, as is often the case with HIV, "opportunistic" infections may take hold, such as thrush, an oral yeast infection caused by *Candida albicans,* which the body normally can easily keep from gaining a foothold. Once the immune system gains the upper hand (sometimes aided by medication), the recovery period begins.

BEYOND MICROBES: OTHER CAUSES OF DISEASE

When it comes to illness, infectious agents are not always to blame.

Deficiencies

result from too little of one or more essential nutrients. Vitamin C deficiency is the cause of scurvy, a now-rare disease marked by bleeding problems and tooth loss.

Malfunctions

are triggered by glitches in an organ or regulating gland. Diabetes, for one, occurs when the pancreas produces too little of the hormone insulin or other organs become less responsive to insulin. This results in high blood sugar levels and a host of other problems.

Degenerative Diseases

weaken or destroy body parts and can be brought on by wear and tear, injury, overuse, or age. Osteoarthritis, for example, results from deterioration of the cartilage that forms a cushion between joint parts.

QUIZ: CAN YOUR IMMUNE SYSTEM USE HELP?

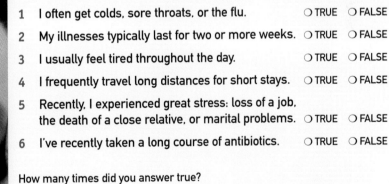

1 I often get colds, sore throats, or the flu. ○ TRUE ○ FALSE

2 My illnesses typically last for two or more weeks. ○ TRUE ○ FALSE

3 I usually feel tired throughout the day. ○ TRUE ○ FALSE

4 I frequently travel long distances for short stays. ○ TRUE ○ FALSE

5 Recently, I experienced great stress: loss of a job, the death of a close relative, or marital problems. ○ TRUE ○ FALSE

6 I've recently taken a long course of antibiotics. ○ TRUE ○ FALSE

How many times did you answer true?
NONE The chances that your body is functioning at or near peak immunity are excellent. Taking advantage of well-researched immune boosters will help ensure good health and vigor.
ONE OR MORE Your immune system may be flagging. Fortifying it should enable your body to more aggressively fight disease and may even help prevent a wide range of life-threatening conditions like heart disease and cancer.

An Inside Look at the Immune System

Our immune system is made up of a complicated network of organs with the power to manufacture, store, and aid the team of white blood cells that fights off disease. Each individual player is in constant communication with the others via nerves, hormones, and the brain. In a way, this continual conversation joins them into one collective organ; if even one player slacks off or brings its full force to bear at the wrong time— or in the wrong place—the whole protective system can falter. It's an amazing, high-wire balancing act, and these are the players that keep it all in synchrony.

NOT SO FAST!

Once routinely removed during childhood, the **tonsils** and **adenoids** have gained new respect as important infection fighters. Forming a ring in the back of the throat, these tissues become inflamed as they fill with white blood cells in response to an infection (viral or bacterial) or an allergic reaction. The tonsils can be seen as reddish lumps, one on either side, at the base of the tongue. The adenoids, which can't be seen without a special mirror, sit at the back of the nose.

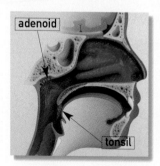

adenoid

tonsil

Bone marrow, at the core of certain long bones, such as the upper arm bone, produces B-cells, natural killer cells, phagocytes, and immature T-cells through a process called hematopoiesis.

The **lymph vessels** comprise a special circulation system throughout the body that carries lymph, a yellowish liquid, around the body. Lymph accounts for about a quarter of the total weight of the immune system and is rich in the B-cells and T-cells that battle infection.

Small, bean-shaped **lymph nodes** are found throughout the lymph system and cluster where lymph vessels converge in the neck, chest, armpits, abdomen, and groin. Each node contains a mesh that filters the lymph to remove antigens. Each node also serves as a hub where white blood cells gather until called to action. When the body is fighting an infection, the lymph nodes can swell to the point where you can easily feel them.

The **thymus,** a gland behind the breastbone, is where baby T-cells multiply and, in a process called T-cell "education," learn to target specific antigens. Scientists once thought that the thymus shuts down in early adulthood after producing a lifetime's worth of T-cells. Now it is clear that the gland stays functional far longer.

The **liver,** located at the top of the abdominal cavity and in front of the stomach, is not technically part of the immune system. But it is a vital partner that helps protect the body by transforming harmful chemicals like poisons, pesticides, and environmental pollutants into harmless products, which can then be removed from the body in bile or urine. Other ways toxins and waste are excreted are through the intestines (as feces) and the skin (as sweat).

The **spleen,** a fist-sized organ just above the abdomen, is another place where white blood cells congregate before being deployed. It also is the spot where some immune cells are activated and where worn-out blood cells and foreign materials are filtered from the blood. The spleen is not an essential organ, however. Still, having it removed or losing it to sickle cell disease makes a person more vulnerable to infection.

Peyer's patches, oval lumps of tissue similar to the tonsils and adenoids in their function and composition, are found on mucous membranes lining the small intestine.

What Else Can Go Wrong

Zealous about protecting the body from danger, the immune system nonetheless sometimes makes mistakes. For instance, it may misidentify harmless substances as dangerous ones or tag the body's own tissues as foreign. Researchers are still trying to find reliable ways to bring these out-of-control immune responses back in line. Here is an overview of what can happen when things go wrong.

Allergies

Sensitive to a fault. The most commonplace immune-system error is the allergic reaction, which pops up in as many as 7 million, or more than one in five, Canadians. In allergic reactions, the immune system gets mixed up and starts confusing safe substances with harmful ones. The result: Things that pose no threat of disease—such as mold, weeds, food, grasses, feathers, dust mites, pollen grains, or flakes of dog or cat skin—become fearsome enemies that throw the immune system into high gear.

Although rarely fatal, allergies are chronic and costly. Experts estimate that 3 million to 4 million workdays are lost annually by North Americans who must stay home to nurse their misery. Many more allergy sufferers, including children, manage to go to school or work, but they may underperform at daily tasks because their symptoms or medications make it so difficult to stay alert and concentrate.

Once is often enough. Allergies are tricky things. In a susceptible person, the first exposure to a particular allergy-causing substance, or allergen, may set the stage for a lifetime of annoyance—but not always, so allergies can develop at any age. What's more, the first time an allergen triggers an immune reaction, no symptoms appear. Instead, the body becomes sensitized to the allergen, so its white blood cells manufacture antibodies against it. This causes the immune cells to sense the allergen's presence if it returns days,

MANY COMMON ALLERGENS are inhaled: pet dander—dry flakes of dog or cat skin, urine, or saliva—and pollen grains (ABOVE) from trees, grasses, weeds, or flowers.

The Path of an Allergic Reaction

1 Allergens—pollen grains, for example—enter the body **through the eyes, nose, or mouth. The grains land on mucous membranes,** where they are detected by T-cells and mistakenly identified as harmful.

2 Excited T-cells signal B-cells **to produce IgE antibodies, which then latch onto the pollen** and tag it foreign.

3 The IgE antibodies bind to certain cells **in the skin and airways. Now primed for the** next exposure to the same type of pollen, these cells will quickly release histamine and other inflammatory chemicals.

4 Tissues swell. **The nose is stuffed, the palate itchy. Eyes turn watery and red.** Sneezing may ensue. These classic symptoms, ranging from mild to severe, will reappear with every future encounter with similar pollen grains.

even years, later. When that happens, the immune system responds with overkill. A cascade of irritating chemicals is released, and any or all of the familiar allergy symptoms appear—sneezes, coughs, wheezes, or hives. In rare cases, the reaction leads to anaphylactic shock, a life-threatening attack characterized by the swelling of body tissues, including the throat, and a sudden fall in blood pressure. People who know that they are at risk for anaphylactic shock, which goes hand-in-hand with allergies to certain medications, insect stings, and foods, can carry kits that include adrenaline to counter its symptoms.

All in the family. The answer to the question, "Are allergies inherited?" is very often, "Yes." If your mother or father has allergies, chances are you will, too. But an inherited tendency, called atopy, is rarely the whole story. A lot depends on which allergens you encounter in life and on other factors, such as the age at which you are exposed to an allergen. It's very possible for a person to come from a long line of allergy-prone ancestors and remain allergy-free forever. Or the reverse can happen: No one in your family has ever sneezed in response to a cat, for example, but the moment you step into a cat owner's home, you can't stop achooing.

HEALTH HINT

Immunotherapy

If medications don't provide relief from allergy symptoms, immunotherapy—injections of small amounts of the substance you are allergic to—is an option. Be aware, however, that its routine use for allergy sufferers is controversial since the shots are costly. Many patients do not respond even after years of therapy.

One thing is clear: Allergies and allergy-induced asthma are on the rise. In fact, some 2 million Canadians over 12 years of age suffer from asthma. The disease is the leading cause of hospitalization for children. One factor in the increase is the widespread construction of tightly sealed, energy-efficient homes in which built-up irritants may activate full-blown allergic responses that might otherwise have been avoided. If your office is similarly airtight, it may provoke the same kind of reaction.

Psychological factors may contribute to allergies, too. Stress and the emotions it causes have long been thought to trigger allergic attacks or make symptoms worse. Also, someone who is anticipating an allergic reaction to a particular substance will, quite often, have the expected reaction—even when the substance is a fake. For example, hypnotized subjects sometimes develop a rash to ordinary ivy after being told that it is poison ivy.

Masqueraders. Some people who think they have allergies are simply sensitive to such substances as cigarette smoke and paint fumes, which can irritate airways and cause look-alike symptoms. Even stepping into cold air can trigger wheezing. Or respiratory symptoms may be due to a chronic cold, not chronic allergies. The best bet: See a doctor if your symptoms are long lasting.

Autoimmune Diseases

Misguided attacks. One revelation of modern immune research was the discovery of a connection among several chronic diseases previously thought to be unrelated. Although the conditions—lupus, multiple sclerosis, and others—involve many different organs and tissues, it became clear that they share a bond: In each case, the body makes antibodies and/or T-cells that are directed against its own tissues. This immune-system disaster typically ravages the body in three main ways:

1. As a direct attack on an organ, such as the skin (which occurs in psoriasis, for example)

2. As a domino effect—for instance, when lupus causes inflammation in the kidneys that directly leads to kidney damage

3. As a response that starts in one spot, then spreads. The swelling of rheumatoid arthritis first affects joints but can move to other tissues.

What allows the immune system to run amok this way is a mystery. It seems many factors—from viruses to certain drugs to sunlight—may play a role. Heredity appears to be a strong influence, but, oddly, when these disorders cluster in families, they can surface as different illnesses. A mother may have lupus; her daughter, juvenile diabetes; and her grandmother, rheumatoid arthritis. Although "autoimmune disease" refers to more than 80 illnesses, only a few affect lots of people:

◆ **Hashimoto's thyroiditis.** Continued attack by the immune system destroys the thyroid gland, an organ that helps control the body's metabolism, leading to an underproduction of thyroid hormone. Luckily, the deficiency can be made up with medication. Graves' disease, another autoimmune thyroid problem, has the opposite effect: The gland produces too much of the hormone.

◆ **Lupus.** This disorder (systemic lupus erythematosus) can involve inflammation of different tissues and organs, such as the joints, skin, kidneys, and even the brain, in different people.

◆ **Rheumatoid arthritis.** The immune system attacks the tissue that lines and cushions joints—most often in the knees, wrists, and hands—causing scarring within the joint that eventually disables one in ten sufferers.

◆ **Multiple sclerosis.** A disorder in which the immune system methodically destroys myelin, the coating that protects nerve fibers of the eye, brain, and spinal cord. For some reason, people who grow up in tropical climates are much less likely to suffer from the disease.

Cancer

One name, many illnesses. Cancer is not a single disease, but instead is many different ones linked by the way they begin—when an errant cell from any part of the body starts multiplying without rhyme or reason.

Cell multiplication is not normally a problem. It's a necessary process; cells must divide often, splitting one after another in an orderly way, to provide the constant supply of new cells that the body requires for growth, maintenance, and repair. But some-

A Women's Issue...

Scientists don't know for sure why, but the vast majority of autoimmune diseases occur in women.

FEMALE/MALE RATIOS

Disease	Ratio
Hashimoto's thyroiditis	50:1
Systemic lupus erythematosus	9:1
Antiphospholipid syndrome	9:1
Sjögren's syndrome	9:1
Primary biliary cirrhosis	9:1
Autoimmune hepatitis	8:1
Graves' disease	7:1
Rheumatoid arthritis	4:1
Scleroderma	3:1
Juvenile diabetes	2:1
Multiple sclerosis	2:1

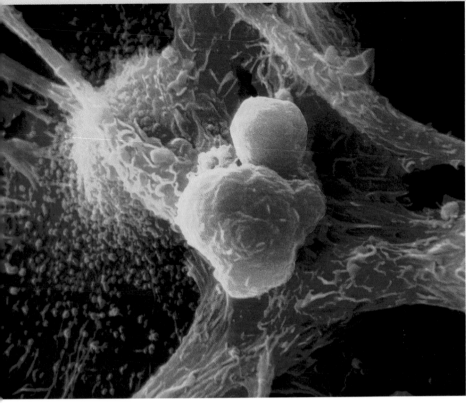

A MACROPHAGE (PURPLE) engulfs a cancer cell (YELLOW), killing it with toxins.

times a cell begins multiplying out of control for no good purpose and with no restraint, creating a mass of tissue called a tumor.

Fortunately, not all tumors are cancerous. If they are benign, the extra cells will stay in one place, generally posing no threat. But if they are malignant, the extra cells may break away, enter the bloodstream or lymph system, and land some place far from their origin, where they multiply anew, growing and pressing upon, invading, or destroying other tissues. This spread is called metastasis, and the type of cancer that arises from it depends on the type of cell that initially went haywire.

When good cells go bad. For healthy cells to turn into cancerous ones, there must be damage to a cell's DNA, the long coils of genetic material that contain the complete instructions for cell function. For example, uncontrolled cell division can occur if p53, a tumor-suppressor gene whose job is to regulate cell division, is inactivated by changes or mutations in the sequence of protein building blocks that compose it. How can such important processes go amiss? Sometimes, the trouble starts with an inherited genetic defect that predisposes certain cells to make a mistake when dividing.

But experts estimate that heredity is directly responsible for only about 35 percent of cancers. Many times, cancer reflects the toll of aging; everyday wear-and-tear affects cells, just as it does the rest of the body, which is why cancer is more common among older people. Convincing research also suggests that DNA may be altered by repeated exposure to environmental triggers, including certain chemi-

> "The immune system is the body's doctor, our own personal physician that cures and protects us from a panoply of diseases."
> —ROBERT S. DESOWITZ, M.D. / MICROBIOLOGIST

cals, metals, gases, radiation, viruses, harmful compounds in foods or in tobacco smoke, or as the result of physical inactivity and other lifestyle factors. About 4 percent of the cancer cases seen in one study, for instance, were found to be linked to high alcohol use. Less than 1 percent were related to insufficient physical activity, and about 1 percent more appeared to be linked to excessive weight gain.

Luckily, when a cell goes berserk, it doesn't always keep multiplying unchecked. It may repair itself, stop multiplying and die, or be attacked and eliminated by patrolling immune cells. Unluckily, a potential cancer cell can sometimes slip past the immune defenses quite easily for a very simple reason: Unlike viruses and bacteria, cancer cells are not easily recognized as the enemy. They're family—our own cells gone astray.

The power to prevent. Just as important as the continuing discovery of the factors that can cause cancer is the advancing knowledge of what can be

REGULAR EXERCISE lowers cancer risk. To a smaller extent, lack of exercise raises risk.

done to prevent it. Already, research has shown that many different nutrients and behaviors can help maintain critical elements of the immune system at robust levels. Adopting changes and making choices that will help stave off cancer cuts down on the workload of your immune system and makes it easier for your body to recognize and dispose of any errant cells that do develop—before they can spread.

As daunting as cancer can be, medical advances offer much hope. Decades of research have yielded many steps forward in the detection and treatment of cancer, as well as in the measures we can all take to prevent it. The result: Apart from lung cancer deaths in women, cancer mortality rates for Canadian men and women have been declining for several years. Medical journals are bringing us closer to a clear understanding of cancer's causes and cures.

Better understanding of the immune system holds out great promise for more victories in the fight against cancer. Scientists are exploring several different ways to direct the immune system's power against cancerous cells using bioengineered immune system products. In addition, vaccines against some types of cancer are in the offing. (See next page.)

GOOD QUESTION!
What does "immunocompromised" mean?

People who are immunocompromised—most often, the elderly and those with chronic illnesses, such as advanced heart disease—get sick more easily and often more severely than others. The reason: They have one or more defects in their natural defense mechanisms that put them at higher risk for infection.

On the horizon...cancer treatments

Borrowing some of their strategies directly from the immune system, researchers have recently developed several experimental therapies that, used alone or in combination, promise to revolutionize cancer care in the coming years. In the pipeline:

MONOCLONAL ANTIBODIES

Scientists, using biotechnology, took a cue from the natural immune system to create these artificial molecules. Like antibodies that seek out and destroy invading microorganisms, monoclonal antibodies seek out tumor cells and latch onto their surfaces, then shut them down. Some are armed with radioactivity or other toxins that are inserted into tumors to annihilate them. RIGHT: **Molecular model of a monoclonal antibody**

GENE THERAPY

For this approach, scientists are using viruses as their model. The theory is this: Since disease-causing viruses insert their own genetic material into a cell's DNA, why can't harmless viruses be used to enter and repair a cell by carrying unflawed DNA into it? Mapping the human genome has advanced this technology; there have already been promising studies in cancer patients. LEFT: **DNA in a vial to be used for gene therapy**

VACCINES

These preparations are used to stimulate or replenish a patient's immune system by injecting substances known as biological response modifiers. These molecules help fight disease by, for example, nudging certain white blood cells to go after tumor cells more aggressively. The immune system needs this extra push because it may not detect cancer cells, which arise from normal body cells and therefore may not send the alarm. RIGHT: **T-cells (YELLOW) attacking a cancer cell (RED), magnified 28,000 times**

ANTI-ANGIOGENESIS DRUGS

One reason that a tumor can spread so wildly and dangerously is that it produces protein molecules called growth factors that stimulate angiogenesis, the growth of blood vessels. The aim of this therapy, now being tested in clinical trials, is to use compounds that shrivel the blood-vessel lifelines, causing the tumor to shrink and eventually disappear. The hope is that anti-angiogenesis drugs will have few side effects since adults don't normally need to produce new blood vessels. LEFT: **Blood capillary, magnified 700 times**

HIV/AIDS

Not so long ago, people didn't give much thought to their immune systems. Then AIDS came along. In the early 1980s, reports of the first cases of this intractable disease, caused by the then-unknown human immunodeficiency virus, or HIV, provided the wake-up call. Although there have always been immunodeficiency diseases, in the past most were the result of rare inherited disorders or inadvertent side effects of drug treatments, such as chemotherapy.

Not so with HIV. Spread primarily through sexual contact or infected blood products, HIV turned out to be a relentless insurgent, ravaging the immune systems of most people who came in contact with it. Over time, by destroying the cells that direct the rest of the immune system (the helper T-cells or T-4 cells), HIV makes it harder and harder for an infected body to fight off certain cancers and infections. As the disease progresses, bacteria, viruses, and other microbes that would rarely harm a healthy person can turn into severe, sometimes fatal, infections.

Technically, a diagnosis of HIV infection becomes an AIDS diagnosis only after blood tests show that an infected person has fewer than 200 helper T-cells per microliter of blood. (Healthy adults usually have 1,000 or more T-cells per microliter of blood.) Many of the 35 million people worldwide now infected with HIV are so debilitated, they can't hold steady jobs or even do household chores. Some of them

VIRUSES come in a variety of shapes and sizes. The spherical HIV (ABOVE) uses the protein protrusions that make up its outer layer to attach itself to a healthy T-cell. Once the virus is attached, the strand of genetic material at its core takes over the newly infected cell's genes and uses them to replicate itself.

experience periods of intense, life-threatening illness followed by periods of normal functioning. But a few patients with HIV show no outward evidence of infection at all, even 18 years or so after contracting the virus. Protease inhibitors, a new class of anti-HIV drugs, have also increased life expectancy and reduced illness episodes for many AIDS patients.

What the future holds. Scientists now are trying to find out how long-term survivors manage to delay the disease year after year. On other fronts, a flurry of research is focusing on creating the next generation of antiviral drugs, including "fusion inhibitors" that cripple HIV's ability to attach to and disable white blood cells. Although there are no absolute answers or solutions yet, the fervent desire to stop the rapid spread of HIV has shed

---

UNCOMMON KNOWLEDGE
Why It's Called AIDS

Acquired: It is caused by a virus that gains a foothold in the body.
Immune Deficiency: It is marked by the inability of the body's natural defenses to fight off disease.
Syndrome: It triggers a cluster of symptoms.

Making Sex Safer

Viruses are easily spread by sexual activity, a reason why about 12 million new cases of sexually transmitted diseases (STDs)—including HIV/AIDS, chlamydia, and human papillomavirus—are diagnosed annually. Also, at least one in five Canadians has a chronic STD, like herpes, that may require constant attention by the immune system to ward off outbreaks, which can occur at any time.

Women are highly vulnerable to STDs and their complications (infection, infertility, pregnancy problems, even cancer) because their moist internal anatomy promotes the growth of microbes. These steps can protect you and your partner.

1. Always use latex or polyurethane condoms during intercourse. Either offers a protective barrier against HIV and other STDs. Avoid sheepskin condoms, which have tiny pores that viruses and bacteria can penetrate. Scrutinize the label before purchasing. It will say if the condom protects against STDs. Always heed the expiration date, and even if it hasn't passed, don't use a condom if it seems sticky or brittle.

2. Don't rely on other types of birth control to protect you from STDs. The pill, Norplant, and Depo-Provera offer no protection against these diseases. Diaphragms and cervical caps provide some protection to the cervix, uterus, and fallopian tubes, but not the vagina. IUDs may actually increase the risk for STDs and pelvic inflammatory disease because when they're inserted into the cervical canal, bacteria may be introduced into the uterus and then spread through the reproductive tract.

3. For safer oral sex, place a dental dam (a latex square used in dental procedures) over the genitals.

4. Tell your doctor about your sexual history and behavior, and disclose any symptoms as soon as you notice them.

5. Get tested for STDs, which often are symptomless, before undergoing any surgical procedure, especially one involving the urinary or reproductive tracts.

6. Avoid douches, which can push infectious agents into the upper genital tract.

much light on the secrets of the immune system—knowledge that is already helping to prolong life and promote health for all, not just those with HIV.

Other Viral Threats

Of course, HIV is not the only viral infection to avoid. Viruses cause a wide range of other illnesses, from respiratory infections like the common cold to life-threatening meningitis. Apart from the symptoms they produce, some viruses can be factors in the development of other noninfectious conditions. For example, hepatitis, a common and contagious illness caused by one of several different viruses—hepatitis A, B, C, D, or E—infects the liver, sometimes resulting in severe disease that can progress to noncontagious cirrhosis or liver cancer.

Some other types of cancer are triggered by viruses. Studies show, for example, that women who have been exposed to certain strains of the human papillomavirus (HPV)—which causes genital warts—have a greatly increased risk of cervical cancer. Yet another cancer that is linked to a virus is T-cell leukemia. The best way to increase your immunity is by receiving vaccines against common viruses you may encounter, such as flu, measles, and hepatitis A and B. Turn the page for an immunization guide.

Vaccines: An Educated Defense

When it comes to great medical achievements, there have been few as important as the discovery by a daring 18th-century English doctor, Edward Jenner, of the technique known as vaccination—artificially creating immune defenses (antibodies) to prevent infection.

Operating on a hunch, Jenner took pus from a sore caused by cowpox—a similar but much milder relative of lethal smallpox—and scratched it into the arm of a healthy boy. Despite subsequent, repeated exposure to smallpox, the boy avoided the disease. Jenner never knew exactly why his risky experiment worked, but today we do. When tiny amounts of weakened or inactive bacteria or viruses are introduced into the body, the bits of foreign material stimulate white blood cells to produce antibodies, making it easier for the body to fight off any subsequent invasion by a similar organism. Now, vaccines developed on principles Jenner brought to light protect against a host of once terrible scourges, some of which have only recently been conquered.

Vaccines available today are highly reliable, and most Canadian children routinely receive them. Adult immunization, however, is a frequently overlooked part of health care, even though the benefits can be enormous. One U.S. study found that giving flu shots to health-care workers in elder-care facilities cut the death rate for patients by 60 percent. Other research found that immunization against hepatitis B can decrease the occurrence of liver cancer.

ADULT VACCINATIONS

Depending on their circumstances, adults often need more of these shots than they suspect.

RECOMMENDED VACCINE	HOW OFTEN
INFLUENZA Protects against the flu, which can be fatal, especially in the elderly.	Every year in October or November.
PNEUMOCOCCAL (PPV) Guards against pneumonia and blood infections caused by *Pneumococcus* bacteria.	Once, at or after age 65—additional shots not recommended, except for people at high risk.
HEPATITIS B (HEP-B) Prevents infection that can cause liver failure.	Three shots over a 6–18-month period.
HEPATITIS A (HEP-A) Shields against liver inflammation caused by the HEP-A virus.	Two doses, 6–18 months apart.
TETANUS, DIPHTHERIA (TD) Prevents lockjaw and an infection of the throat that can damage the heart and lungs.	After a primary series of three shots (usually in childhood), boosters every 10 years.
MEASLES, MUMPS, RUBELLA (MMR) Prevents three contagious viral infections that may cause birth defects or death.	Two doses separated by at least one month (usually given during childhood).
VARICELLA ZOSTER Protects against chicken pox.	Two doses within four weeks.
POLIO Prevents an infection that can lead to paralysis.	Two doses, one to two months apart, followed by a third dose six months to one year later—if not given in childhood.

SOURCE: **Adapted from recommendations of Health Canada.**

GET IT IF YOU...

- Are age 50 or older, or if you have certain chronic medical problems, live in a nursing home, or care for someone who is chronically ill.
- Are a health-care worker who comes in contact with chronically ill people.

- Are age 65 or older.
- Suffer from kidney failure, have a chronic cardio-respiratory disease, or are an organ transplant recipient.
- Lost your spleen or are immunocompromised for other reasons, regardless of your age.

- Are an unvaccinated adolescent; have had a sexually transmitted disease and/ or multiple sexual partners; a homosexual or bisexual male; use illicit injectable drugs; or are a firefighter, police officer, health-care worker, long-term resident of a health-care facility, or a worker with the developmentally disabled.
- Plan to travel internationally to countries where the disease is prevalent.

- Plan to travel outside Canada, except to the United States, northern and western Europe, New Zealand, Australia, or Japan.
- Have chronic liver disease, use illicit injectable drugs, or work as a food handler.

- Haven't had one within the last 10 years.

- Are an adult born after 1970 and are uncertain whether you were vaccinated.
- Belong to a high-risk group, including health-care workers, students entering college, and international travelers.

- Have never had chicken pox, especially if you frequently come in close contact with very young children or anyone who is seriously ill.
- Plan to travel internationally.

- Are traveling to the developing countries of Africa (all regions), Asia (East and Southeast), the Middle East, the Indian subcontinent, or most of the former Soviet Union.

AVOID IF YOU ARE...

- Severely allergic to eggs.

- Severely allergic to eggs.
- Pregnant or may become pregnant within three months.
- Have an immune disorder other than HIV infection.

- Pregnant or may become pregnant within one month.
- Are immunocompromised.

Troublemakers to Avoid

Most of the time, the immune system wins in the long run. But the strength of its response—which determines how well or ill you may feel—depends on many things, including a host of environmental factors that are difficult to avoid in modern life, especially in cities.

These hazards can rarely, by themselves, break down your defenses. Your hereditary makeup—the genes that encode the function of every cell in your body—has a great deal to do with your susceptibility to harm from the environment. Age, too, may increase your vulnerability. Wear and tear on the organs that produce immune cells can weaken the natural protection against invading organisms.

There's not much you can do to change your genes or your age—yet. Scientists are working on it! But there is evidence that strengthening your body's defenses in other ways will enhance your natural immune powers. First on the list is sidestepping these commonly encountered immunosuppressants whenever possible.

Tobacco Smoke

Whether you are inhaling it right from the burning stick or as an innocent bystander, tobacco smoke reduces the effectiveness of your immune system. (Of course, it also raises your risk of heart disease, cancer, and other ills.) For one thing, it wreaks havoc on T-cells lining the lungs, gradually making them less and less responsive to invading microbes and increasing your susceptibility to respiratory infections. Also, macrophages in lung tissue become far less capable of destroying viruses, bacteria, and cancer cells, and their ability to communicate with other immune players is drastically diminished.

Tobacco smoke also stimulates the production of antibodies that trigger allergic reactions, which may explain why smokers experience more allergies than nonsmokers do. The more heavily

SECONDHAND TOBACCO SMOKE is a class A carcinogen, responsible for more than 4,000 cases of lung cancer in North American nonsmokers each year. All smoke can contain carcinogens.

and longer you smoke, the weaker your immune system becomes. Good news: Studies show that the immune system begins to return to normal within a few months after you quit.

Air Pollution

Lighter-than-air particles that float in smog can settle deep in your lungs and raise levels of harmful free radicals, letting dust and inhaled chemicals go unchecked and causing genetic mutations that can lead to cancer. Polluted air can also increase production of IgE antibodies, making the body more sensitive to allergens.

Short of moving to a pristine wilderness, it can be hard to avoid smog, especially if you live in a large metropolitan area. To limit your exposure:

◆ **Stay indoors** as much as possible when smog levels are highest, usually during the afternoon hours, peaking about 2:00 P.M.

◆ **Avoid exercising outdoors** during morning and evening rush hours, especially in places near traffic.

◆ **Don't spend too much time in any poorly ventilated indoor place** where chemicals are being used (such as beauty salons and gas stations) or where new materials, such as carpets, have recently been installed.

UNCOMMON KNOWLEDGE

Car Exhaust Chokes Immunity

Exhaust contains toxic chemicals. Animal studies suggest that one of them, benzoapyrene, triggers cell mutation and decreases immune function over time by lowering production of IgM, the first antibody produced by the immune system in response to viruses. Other research shows that exhaust can lower the amount of interferon (an immune-system messenger chemical) made by macrophages, reducing resistance to viral infection. City dwellers who find it hard to avoid the spew of tailpipes may get some protection by taking supplements of antioxidant vitamins (C, E, and others).

EXERCISE outdoors if you like, but time it to avoid exhaust from traffic-choked roads.

{ "To be or not to be isn't the question. The question is how to prolong being." }

—TOM ROBBINS / NOVELIST

Sunlight

Whether or not you spend enough time in the sun to burn, ultraviolet (UV) rays can create precancerous cells in the skin and suppress the action of special macrophages called Langerhans' cells, found in the upper layers of the skin. In other words, sunlight can both set the stage for cancer and limit the body's ability to fight off the disease. Wearing protective clothing—a wide-brimmed hat and light but tightly woven garments that you can't see through—along with an effective sunblock can protect you.

Choose a product with an SPF (sun protection factor) of 15 or more that contains titanium dioxide, zinc oxide, or Parsol 1789 (avobenzone), all of which deflect or chemically absorb UV rays.

Products spiked with vitamins C and E are promoted with the promise of providing extra protection. In general, antioxidants help disarm free radicals—damaging molecules that form after exposure to sunlight. If you try a vitamin-laced sunscreen, apply it liberally (it takes about a quarter of a 120-ml bottle to cover an adult's body), giving extra attention to often overlooked spots: the front and back of the neck, under the chin, on the backs of the knees,

under and around the armpits, and on the tops of the feet. Be sure to shield your lips with a dark-colored lipstick or a lip balm containing a sun-blocking agent.

HEALTH HINT

Slather It On

It pays to apply sunscreen every day throughout the year. Chemicals in the lotion bind to the skin's top layers. Using it daily can actually increase your resistance to sun damage, as can moisturizers and foundation that contain sunscreen.

Antibiotics

Sometimes aggressive bacteria reproduce so quickly and spew out so many toxins so fast that they may damage the body irreversibly before the immune system gets the danger under control. To prevent this, doctors prescribe antibiotics—penicillin, tetracycline, sulfa drugs, and the like—to stop the infection in its tracks.

But there's a problem: Antibiotics lose effectiveness over time. If even a few of the targeted bacteria have a mutation that lets them survive the medication, they go on to produce offspring with the same mutation that also can survive that antibiotic. This new strain of bacteria reproduces, making it more likely that the infection will recur or spread easily. New antibiotics, targeting the new bacteria, must be developed; once they're used, the cycle begins again. New research shows that antibiotics also may suppress immunity. Scientists have discovered, for instance, that tetracycline inhibits the ability of phagocytes to engulf

---

Antibiotic Advice

Only a doctor can determine whether it is appropriate to skip an antibiotic. If one is prescribed, keep these basic guidelines in mind:

1 Take the full course of treatment. Stopping the drug early because you feel better will allow any bacteria still alive inside you to multiply and possibly rekindle the infection.

2 Never save antibiotics for later use. A doctor should evaluate you each time you may be sick enough to need antibiotics.

3 Antibiotics have no effect on viruses, but they do kill bacteria—and not just the ones making you sick. Use yogurt or acidophilus supplements to help restore beneficial bacteria quickly.

ARE YOU BURN-BOUND?

Several medications, cosmetics, and fragrances may make your skin more vulnerable to sunburn, raising the risk of damage to skin-cell DNA and suppressing special immune cells in the skin. Bright summer sun is not the only thing to avoid; winter daylight or artificial ultraviolet light sources, such as tanning booths or even the purple haze emitted by mosquito zappers, can trigger reactions, too. Here is a partial list of products to watch out for.

PRODUCT	SUN-RELATED SIDE EFFECT	TO AVOID TROUBLE
ANTIBIOTICS	Some antibiotics increase the likelihood of damage to your skin.	If you're beach-bound, tell your doctor; perhaps an alternative medication is available. Also, wear a hat and tightly woven fabrics.
ANTI-INFLAMMATORY DRUGS	Prescription arthritis drugs and common painkillers, such as ibuprofen or ketoprofen, may make the skin more vulnerable to burning, even in a short time.	Avoid self-prescribing over-the-counter painkillers; ask your doctor about alternatives with less potential for causing photosensitivity.
ANTIDEPRESSANTS, TRANQUILIZERS	If you have fair skin or a family history of skin cancer, these drugs may add to your already increased risk of skin damage.	Take extra sun-protection precautions. If you have a reaction even to slight sun exposure, ask your doctor to recommend an alternative.
MOISTURIZERS	Common ingredients in moisturizers, including retinol, vitamin A, and alpha-hydroxy acids, may make skin burn more easily.	Try not to use these products on sunny days or choose only those that contain a sunblock with an SPF of 15 or higher.
PERFUMES	Certain ingredients, including oils made from musk, sandalwood, bergamot, citrus, and vanilla, can be chemically changed by the sun, triggering an allergic rash—and increasing the chance of hyperpigmentation (age spots). Even scents in soaps and shaving cream can be a problem.	Leave off the scented stuff when the sun is shining brightly.
ST. JOHN'S WORT	May make more than just your skin sensitive to the sun. Research suggests it may also raise the risk of developing cataracts.	Wear sunglasses, and if you are using St. John's wort to treat winter depression, ask your doctor before combining the herb with light-box therapy.
SUNSCREENS	Surprisingly, sunscreens that contain PABA, benzophenones, cinnamates, oxybenzone, 6-acetoxy-2, or 4-dimethyl-m-dioxane make some people more reactive to UV rays.	Check ingredients before applying and consider using a self-tanning preparation under your sunscreen to create a chemical reaction that provides additional protection.

and destroy bacteria. Other antibiotics slow production of antibodies and reduce T-cell activity.

Take antibiotics wisely. Does this mean that you should avoid them at all costs? Of course not. Antibiotics are rightly credited with saving countless lives; used appropriately, they could one day save yours. But taking them unnecessarily may increase your risk of disease. What's more, because antibiotics are so powerful in the short term, they make it easy to forget that illnesses are not all bad. Some minor infections provide a chance for the immune system to get a good workout and power up to even greater fighting potential against future threats.

How You Can Make a Difference

Can you really strengthen your immune system so that you'll feel better and be better equipped to fight off infections, nip cancer in the bud, and stay healthy to a ripe, old age?

Fifteen years ago, most scientists would have laughed at the idea. Back then, everyone thought of the immune system as the body's formidable but independent fighting force, impervious to any influence short of intense exposure to radiation or lethal, antibiotic-resistant bacteria. The notion that seemingly minor changes in what you eat, how you spend your leisure time, or the amount of sleep you get each night might alter the complex dynamics of the immune system seemed ludicrous.

Having seen in this chapter just how complicated and finely tuned our immune systems are, almost anyone would be similarly skeptical. How could your actions possibly affect the invisible world of antibodies, T-cells, B-cells, and phagocytes, to name only a few of the major players that make up the immune system?

Even as research immunologists have been mapping the multilayered terrain of the body's vital and mysterious guardian band, scientists approaching the immune system from a different angle have been making practical observations about things that help and hinder it in its work.

In the next six chapters, we'll be detailing their findings, which strongly suggest that steering clear of factors that dampen immunity is only half the equation. It's not enough just to avoid the wrong foods. To strengthen your immune system, you need to eat the right foods (see Chapter 2, "The Miracle of Food"). Similarly, staying on an even emotional keel may protect you from the immunosuppression linked to depression (see Chapter 6, "The Mind-Body Connection"), but seeking out positive experiences and cultivating your capacity for joy just might give your disease-fighting mechanisms a special added boost.

A New Attitude

Taking proactive measures to strengthen your immune system might sound daunting, given how many other tasks we're already trying to balance in today's revved-up, 24-hour society. In reality, though, the new findings about lifestyle and immune-system robustness are quite encouraging: They make clear that little things really do mean a lot, that it's definitely worthwhile to take that brisk walk around the block, eat one more scoop of nutrient-rich fruit salad, and carve out extra time for relaxing with the people who make you happiest.

Fortunately, the body is wonderfully regenerative. By making and sticking with a few simple changes, you can coax your internal army of white blood cells into fighting shape in just a few months, as detailed in Chapter 8, "Your 12-Week Action Plan."

One of the many ironies of medical progress is this: As knowledge of the body's intricate workings grows more detailed, evidence that individuals can improve their health by doing simple, low-tech things like exercising becomes more and more compelling. The immune system, startlingly complex yet surprisingly responsive to outside factors we can control, illustrates this paradox perfectly.

GOOD QUESTION!
Can strengthening the immune system turn back the clock?

Most people over 70 have weakened immune function. Some, however, are blessed with the robust immune systems and the low illness rates of young adults. These fortunate few are also likely to surpass average life expectancy. Their gift is partly the result of lucky genes, but avoiding things that damage immunity in the elderly—nutrient deficiencies, in particular—plays a role as well. So the answer to the question? Yes.

{ "Today's broader definition of health goes beyond the absence of disease or injury to include vitality—a zest for living." }

—KATHYRN L. OLSON, M.D. / OBSTETRICIAN-GYNECOLOGIST

CHAPTER 2

The Miracle of Food

"Your food shall be your remedy." These words, written by Hippocrates more than 2,000 years ago, still hold true. What's changed is the science behind the statement. Every day, researchers are gathering groundbreaking insights into the connection between nutrition and a strong immune system.

You Are What You Eat

Expert opinion is unanimous: The single most important thing we can do to prevent disease is to eat more fruits, vegetables, beans, nuts, and whole grains. Not only do these foods contain compounds that influence the makeup of our cells and enhance cell-to-cell communication, most are great sources of antioxidants—chemicals that benefit our health by neutralizing harmful molecules called free radicals.

Current theory holds that cancer, heart disease, stroke, and other ills of aging result from damage to cells by free radicals, oxygen molecules that are unstable because they have an extra electrical charge, or electron. (Electrons usually come in pairs.)

In small numbers, free radicals help fight infection. In large amounts, however, they may harm tissue and DNA in a process called oxidative stress. In order to "steal" an electron, they may attack cell membranes, making a hole through which bacteria or viruses can enter. Once inside the cell, free radicals may attack chromosomes, rewriting or destroying genetic information. If this damage goes unrepaired, healthy cells may turn cancerous, and existing cancer cells may multiply even faster.

Ironically, most free radicals are generated by the body itself during ordinary metabolism. They are also produced by air pollution, radiation, pesticide residues, and other assaults on the environment.

What does this have to do with nutrition? Plenty. By studying large populations, scientists have learned that people who eat an ample share of fruits and vegetables experi-

FRUITS AND VEGETABLES are the most flavorful, economical, and nutrient-dense foods around. Plus, they are packed with vital plant chemicals that can measurably improve your immune response.

Interesting!

Many factors can contribute to the development of cancer, including poor eating habits. In fact, a high-fat, high-calorie diet now is thought to be as harmful as smoking, triggering up to 75 percent of colorectal cancer cases and 50 percent of breast cancer cases.

ence less oxidative stress. It turns out that fruits and vegetables contain hundreds of substances called phytochemicals. If you don't know how to pronounce that word (FIGH-toe-chemicals), you're not alone. As recently as 20 years ago, nutritional gurus never mentioned phytochemicals, many of which hadn't even been discovered. Everyone assumed that all the body needed from food was fat, protein, carbohydrates, vitamins, minerals, trace elements, and water.

Since then, a dizzying array of studies has shown that these compounds play essential roles in maintaining health. Some phytochemicals reduce oxidative stress; others dampen inflammation, detoxify contaminants and pollutants, and activate enzymes that block unbridled cell division. Still others make it easier for nutrients to pass in and out of cells.

Can eating an apple a day actually keep the doctor away? It can help. Studies make clear that the more phytochemicals you consume, the lower your risk for disease will be. Eating the minimum five servings of fruits and vegetables each day, for example, can lower your risk of cancer by 20 percent. Eating more will benefit you more. At a Colorado research center, an ongoing study of 80 women at high risk for breast cancer found that those who ate 10 servings of fruits and vegetables a day for two weeks experienced significant reductions in cancer-associated cell damage. A group of breast-cancer survivors in a similar University of Arizona study showed comparable improvements.

Reaping food's benefits. Of course, you can't benefit from the remarkable disease-fighting powers of phytochemicals if you don't consume enough of them. The typical Western diet is short on foods rich in these nutrients. Recently, a major survey of eating habits in North America found that a whopping 25 percent of the "vegetables" respondents reported

> **VITAL STATISTICS: FOOD**
>
> **1.5 kilograms**
> Amount of garlic the average Canadian consumes each year
>
> **14 percent and 23 percent**
> Percentage of Canadian women who were overweight in 1991 and 2001
>
> **22 percent and 34 percent**
> Percentage of Canadian men who were overweight in 1991 and 2001
>
> **13–18 grams**
> Amount of fiber most Canadians eat each day
>
> **25–40 grams**
> Amount of fiber scientists say Canadians should eat daily for optimal health
>
> **10,000**
> Phytochemicals found so far in plant-based foods

GARLIC helps fight infections, earning it the nickname "poor man's antibiotic."

eating each day consisted of peeled, deep-fried white potatoes. Although an order of fries won't kill you, it's not exactly what Canada's Food Guide to Healthy Eating had in mind when they recommended five to ten servings a day.

If fitting in more vegetables, fruits, and grains sounds too difficult or unappealing, keep reading. It's easier—and tastier—than you think. How do blueberry pancakes strike your fancy? Or pizza with tomato sauce? Both contain immune-boosting nutrients you'll read about in this chapter. You'll find answers to such questions as:

◆ **What foods offer the biggest immune-boosting bang for your buck,** and what well-documented health benefits do they provide?

◆ **How do vitamins, minerals, and micronutrients** affect the body's ability to fend off disease?

◆ **How can you prepare healthy meals** without spending a lot of time or money?

All the handy tips, shortcuts, and menus that follow will help you use food to stay well.

Immune-Boosting Foods

One of the first things you need to know about your immune system is this: The forces that defend you against infection and other illnesses cannot wage their best battle without being well nourished.

Because eating too few of the right nutrients can weaken your body and allow germs and disease to gain a foothold, a good diet is the first and most important way to stay well. That's plain old common sense. But it's also been scientifically proven. Researchers now know that B-cells, T-cells, phagocytes, and natural killer (NK) cells can't do their best at quashing cancer cells and dangerous invaders such as viruses and bacteria without strong backup from the vitamins, minerals, fiber, and phytochemicals found in healthful foods.

The latest proof: An American study found that women in their older years (ages 60 to 80) with good eating habits had immune function just as sound as that of younger women aged 20 to 40. This confirmed what several earlier studies had already suggested—that while genetic and environmental factors may do their part to gradually chip away at immune function, much of the decline often seen with advancing age is probably preventable with good nutrition.

You'd be surprised how many chronic health problems start small and snowball into something more serious mainly because of a bad diet. Nutrient deficiencies that stem from poor eating habits can dampen the immune response and open the door to illness. In a vicious cycle, being sick creates an increased need for immune-boosting foods.

The arsenal of health-protective compounds in food can enhance immune functioning in measurable ways—for example, by increasing the number of white blood cells when the body is most vulnerable to infection. If this fact carries a ring of "boring, rigid diet," put your fears to rest. When it comes to eating, we've all had our fill of "no" and "never." Instead, this chapter is about choices. After reading up on the many flavor-packed foods with documented health-enhancing potential, you'll realize how easy it is to devise an immune-boosting diet you'll love.

Foods versus supplements.

Why bother with good-for-you foods when you can simply pop a pill? While supplements have their place, by far the easiest, most effective, and least expensive way to heighten your body's ability to fight disease is to eat a diet rich in immune-stimulating nutrients. These include vitamins and minerals as well as many other compounds—including ones that haven't even been discovered yet.

One important discovery made by scientists investigating the disease-fighting powers of foods is that nutrients are absorbed better from food than from pills. It also turns out that foods work synergistically—that is, their health benefits are greater when they are eaten together. For instance, tomatoes, chilies, and garlic—the classic salsa ingredients—deliver more potent health-protective

---

And the Winners Are...

Which fruits and vegetables are the best disease fighters? Those that score highest in a new antioxidant analysis called ORAC, short for Oxygen Radical Absorbance Capacity. Top scores belong to:

FRUIT/SCORE
(raw, 100 grams)

Fruit	Score
Prunes	5,770
Blueberries	2,400
Strawberries	1,540
Raspberries	1,220
Oranges	750
Red Grapes	739

VEGETABLE/SCORE
(raw, 250 ml)

Vegetable	Score
Kale	1,770
Spinach	1,260
Brussels sprouts	980
Broccoli florets	890
Red peppers	710
Onions	450

Source: USDA

Dietary superstars.

A varied diet replete with fruits and vegetables is the overall goal, but you'll want to take extra care to fill your plate with the following "superfoods." These nutritional powerhouses are amazing sources of immune-boosting phytochemicals and should be top on your shopping list.

If you haven't been eating these foods to date, don't be discouraged. It's never too late to start reaping their benefits. *Bon appétit!*

powers when they are eaten in combination than when they are eaten alone. This finding reinforces the fact that supplements can never replicate the benefits of a varied diet.

Another reason not to rely solely on supplements: Research shows that you can get too much of certain immune boosters, including the antioxidant vitamin E, by taking supplements. An overload of these nutrients might actually suppress immunity, making you more vulnerable to illness.

Besides helping your body fight infection, eating more immune-boosting foods will give you a number of other health advantages. The dietary habits that strengthen immunity also reduce the risk of heart disease, stroke, and diabetes. A diet based on plant foods, with only limited amounts of meat, dairy, and other high-fat foods, is particularly effective in reducing the risk of cancer. For added health protection, maintain a balance of calorie intake and physical activity.

TOMATOES are rich in vitamins, low in fat and calories, and packed with fiber and potassium.

Tomatoes

Need proof of the healing power of food? Look no further than the humble tomato, which has earned more high scores than any other menu item in studies of cancer-fighting foods. Along with a rich supply of vitamin C, tomatoes are loaded with lycopene. This powerful antioxidant gives them their luscious red pigment, and it has been convincingly shown to defend the body against cancer. Tomatoes are second only to carrots as a source of beta-carotene, a member of the carotenoid family of phytochemicals (see page 48). They are also excellent sources of the flavonoids quercetin and kaempferol, which inhibit the growth of cancer cells.

◆ **The proof.** In a review of 72 studies published in the *Journal of the National Cancer Institute*, Harvard Medical School researcher Edward Giovannucci, M.D., concluded that men who consumed tomatoes and tomato-based products were less likely to develop prostate cancer. Similar studies suggest that high levels of lycopene inhibit lung, pancreatic, and digestive tract cancers, as well as reduce the likelihood of heart disease.

Women reap benefits from lycopene, too. When researchers measured lycopene levels in breast-tissue samples from 109 women, those with higher levels of the nutrient were found to be less likely to develop breast cancer. More direct cancer-fighting benefits came to light when University of Milan researchers put healthy young women on a tomato-free diet for three weeks, followed by three weeks of a tomato-rich diet. The results: On the tomato-rich diet, the levels of lycopene in the women's blood increased, while the free-radical damage to the DNA in their lymph cells dropped by about 33 percent.

◆ **Put tomatoes to work.** Because lycopene is fat-soluble, it is more accessible to the body when the foods that contain it are prepared and eaten with a small amount of fat. In other words, pizza slathered with tomato sauce is preferable to tomatoes sliced raw and tossed in a salad. Hard to believe? In one study, volunteers ate either a mock pizza made of bread, tomato paste, and corn oil or a pile of fresh tomato slices without oil. Several hours after the meal, the pizza eaters' blood levels of lycopene were two and a half times higher than those of the salad eaters. Similarly, when University of California at Los Angeles researchers put prostate cancer patients on a high-fiber diet that included small amounts of fat and 180 ml of tomato-vegetable juice a day, they detected a "highly significant increase" of lycopene and other phytochemicals in the patients' blood.

THE BEST KIND OF BLUES. The pigments that color blueberries also protect cells against oxidation.

Blueberries

Anthocyanins, the pigments that give blueberries their stunning deep color, have potent immune-stimulating properties. Because they are antioxidants, anthocyanins protect capillaries (tiny blood vessels) from oxidative damage. In doing so, they promote brisk blood flow through the circulatory channels many immune cells travel to reach parts of the body that need their help. Protection against oxidation also helps ensure good circulation of lymph, the fluid that carries immune cells through its own system of channels.

Moreover, blueberries are rich in concentrated tannins, astringent substances also found in tea. According to researchers at Rutgers University in New Jersey, these tannins prevent E. coli bacteria from sticking to the cells that line the urinary tract and causing infection. Scientists think that tannins block the growth of the part of the bacteria that gives the bugs their adhesive property. Tannins also contain compounds called catechins. Studies suggest that catechins shield us against some types of cancer.

◆ **The proof.** When researchers at the Jean Mayer USDA Human Nutrition Center on Aging at Tufts University in Massachusetts measured the levels of

{ "No illness which can be treated by diet should be treated by any other means." }

—MOSES MAIMONIDES / PHYSICIAN AND PHILOSOPHER (1135-1204)

antioxidants in 40 different fruits and vegetables, blueberries came out near the top. In fact, a 100-gram serving of fresh blueberries supplies enough antioxidants to almost double the average Canadian's daily intake.

◆ **Put blueberries to work.** The Rutgers research suggests that a daily fistful of blueberries (or cranberries, their cousins) will go a long way toward preventing urinary tract infections and promoting good overall health. Use fresh berries to add texture to cold chicken or shrimp salads. Or add them fresh, frozen, or dried to pancake or muffin batters.

Don't like blueberries? Other berries, including raspberries, blackberries, and strawberries, deliver many of the same cancer-fighting phytochemicals. Like blueberries, they're loaded with fiber (all those tiny seeds) and ellagic acid, shown in early studies to inhibit the development of cancer. This may explain, in part, why Harvard School of Public Health research involving 1,271 people found that strawberry lovers were less likely to develop cancer than those who rarely ate the fruit.

These enzymes destroy carcinogens (cancer-causing substances) and free radicals before they can attack healthy cells.

Second, cruciferous vegetables are loaded with indole-3-carbinol (I3C), a phytochemical shown to inhibit the growth of estrogen-responsive cancer cells in the breast. In fact, researchers are now examining the feasibility of putting I3C in a pill to combat breast cancer.

◆ **The proof.** When scientists fed rats hearty servings of broccoli for a few days, then exposed them to a potent compound that induces breast cancer, the broccoli eaters were half as likely to develop tumors as animals on standard feed. And the broccoli eaters that did develop cancer ended up with fewer and smaller tumors.

◆ **Put broccoli to work.** Regardless of how you prepare cruciferous vegetables, eating them is good for you. But if you want to rev up your body's disease-fighting abilities fast, look a little further down the family tree to broccoli sprouts. Scientists have found that, gram for gram, these tender shoots can contain up to 20 times more sulforaphane than mature broccoli. In other words, 30 grams of sprouts yields as

Broccoli

This cruciferous vegetable is regarded as the number-one anticancer food, and with good reasons. The first is sulforaphane, a chemical that occurs naturally in broccoli and other vegetables of the cruciferous family—kale, cabbage, cauliflower, bok choy, brussels sprouts, and mustard or turnip greens. Sulforaphane stimulates the body's production of substances called Phase II detoxification enzymes.

UNCOMMON KNOWLEDGE

For Mature Palates Only

If you snubbed broccoli as a child, it may be time to try it again. There's a good chance you'll enjoy its flavor now. Studies of flavor perception show that the taste buds lose some of their sensitivity to bitterness with age. So some good-for-you foods that you couldn't tolerate in your youth—including brussels sprouts, spinach, cabbage, and grapefruits—may be downright tasty later in life. A U.S. study involving 329 women aged 21 to 85 found that those in the oldest group (aged 54 to 85) were the least sensitive to the bitter taste of a laboratory compound similar to the phytochemicals that can make vegetables bitter and fruits tart. As a result, the older women were more likely to enjoy the immune-stimulating benefits linked to consumption of a wide variety of fruits and vegetables than were the younger women.

much protective power as 600 grams of cooked broccoli! Purchase broccoli sprouts only from established produce dealers—not roadside stands—and wash them thoroughly before eating. (A few outbreaks of foodborne illness have been linked to sprouts grown in unsanitary water.) Store broccoli sprouts in the refrigerator and use them by the expiration date. Low-calorie and fat free, they're great in sandwiches and salads.

Garlic

Garlic fans adore the bulb's pungent flavor, and so should health seekers. Several of the same chemicals that contribute to garlic's intense flavor also appear to help block cancer by preventing the formation of some carcinogens that damage DNA. Garlic may also trigger increased production of the immune-system chemicals interleukin-2,

> ### Quick Tip
>
> After chopping garlic, let it sit on the counter for about 15 minutes before cooking. This allows ample time for its various health-protective substances to form. Heat stops this important process, notes garlic researcher John Milner, Ph.D., of the Pennsylvania State University.

tumor necrosis factor, and interferon gamma—the same substances used in immune-system-based cancer therapies.

◆ **The proof.** Fresh garlic juice can kill various microorganisms. Small studies have hinted at its effectiveness in promoting human health. Some studies even suggest that eating lots of chopped garlic may lower the risk of colon and stomach cancer by up to 35 percent and 50 percent respectively. The reduction in stomach cancer among garlic eaters suggests that the tasty bulb contains compounds that stop the growth of ulcer-causing *Helicobacter pylori* bacteria, since gastric ulcers have been identified as a strong risk factor for stomach cancer.

◆ **Put garlic to work.** How much garlic do you need to eat to harness its healing powers? Generally, benefits have been observed in people who eat 5 to 18 grams (about two to six cloves) of raw or lightly

QUIZ: ARE YOU GETTING ENOUGH PHYTOCHEMICALS?

1	I often flavor foods with fresh garlic or onions.	○ TRUE	○ FALSE
2	I usually use olive, canola, or flaxseed oil.	○ TRUE	○ FALSE
3	I regularly drink tomato juice or eat pizza, tomato-based soups, or pasta with marinara sauce.	○ TRUE	○ FALSE
4	I prefer whole fiber-filled fruits over fruit juices.	○ TRUE	○ FALSE
5	I eat four servings or more each day of nonstarchy vegetables like broccoli, spinach, or carrots.	○ TRUE	○ FALSE
6	I drink one or two cups of tea without milk daily.	○ TRUE	○ FALSE

How many times did you answer true?

FOUR OR MORE Congratulations! Besides preventing disease, the way you're eating should leave you energized and feeling terrific. Keep it up.

THREE OR LESS You're falling behind on phytochemicals. To reap their benefits, try making one small dietary change—say, drinking a glass of tomato juice each day. Once you've made it a habit, give yourself a high five and make another change.

THE AMAZING KIWI

New Zealand's fuzzy fruit, the kiwi, is an excellent source of antioxidants, phytochemicals, and fiber. Each kiwi has more vitamin C per milliliter than an orange, more potassium than a banana, and more fiber than bran flakes. Kiwi also is a perfect fast-food snack—simply cut one in half and scoop out the fruit with a spoon. One kiwi equals 40 to 50 calories.

cooked garlic a week. (Overcooking can destroy the beneficial enzymes.) Add garlic to stir-fries; toss it in sauces, stews, and soups; or opt instead for its close cousins—shallots, onions, chives, or leeks. Be leery of garlic pills; the products available vary greatly. Some, in fact, contain few active ingredients. Also, although some folk remedies involve applying crushed garlic directly to the skin, don't. It can be strong enough to cause severe irritation.

Citrus Fruits

Grapefruits, oranges, tangerines, lemons, and limes are excellent sources of the plant form of vitamin C, ascorbic acid. As a component of food, this nutritional superstar has a myriad of immune functions, including enhancing the movement of phagocytes, boosting NK cell activity, and building and maintaining mucous membranes and collagen, a tissue that plays a vital role in wound healing.

Vitamin C is also required for the manufacture of hormones that help the body deal with stress, and it helps convert toxins to water-soluble substances that can be excreted by the body. But it's just one of more than 100 phytochemicals that citrus fruits contain. Oranges and grapefruits are also loaded with naringenin, which, according to some researchers, works against HIV infection and tumor formation. The oil in citrus rinds contains limonene, which researchers think helps enzymes deactivate cancer-causing substances in the body. Limonene may also encourage tumors to slow down cell division.

◆ **The proof.** Contrary to popular claims, vitamin C can't cure the common cold or make cancer patients live longer. Even so, its importance for health can't be disputed. Many studies have found an unmistakable correlation between low blood levels of vitamin C and increased risk of cancer, especially cancer of the esophagus, mouth, pancreas, and stomach. Just by adding a small amount of lemon peel to their diets, participants in a study at the University of Arizona appear to have lowered their incidence of skin cancer by as much as 34 percent.

◆ **Put citrus fruits to work.** Most animals manufacture their own vitamin C, but humans have lost their ability to do so. Since the body doesn't store the vitamin (any excess is eliminated through the urine), get a little bit every day. (There's no benefit to taking large doses of supplements.) To benefit from limonene, add a twist of citrus peel to your beverage.

Carrots

Carrots and other fruits and vegetables with a deep orange color (mangoes, cantaloupe, and sweet potatoes, for example) contain large amounts of nutrients called carotenoids, some of which the body converts to vitamin A. Many studies have demonstrated that vitamin A reduces the incidence and severity of infectious illnesses by helping to keep the mucous membranes healthy and intact. Vitamin A also hikes antibody response and increases white blood cell proliferation.

People with high blood levels of beta-carotene have lower odds of developing cancer and heart disease. Not long ago, however, widely reported studies suggested that taking beta-carotene supplements could increase the risk of lung cancer in smokers. It turned out that the people in the study were smokers *and* heavy drinkers. When the data were corrected for alcohol effects, the connection between beta-carotene and lung-cancer disappeared.

LENTINAN, an immune-stimulant in shiitakes, is also sold in extract form.

◆ **The proof.** In a U.S. study, taking 15 to 60 mg of carotenoids daily was linked to improved immune function, especially in older people. Another study, conducted in Canada, showed that downing 16 mg of carotenoids along with small doses of 17 other nutrients every day for a year boosted immune function and cut infectious illnesses by half in healthy elderly people. Researchers have found that men taking the equivalent of about 6 mg of beta-carotene a day (the amount in one medium carrot) over 25 years had a 28 percent lower risk of death from all causes compared with men who ate very little beta-carotene. Another study found significantly greater NK cell activity in men who took 50 mg of beta-carotene every other day for 12 years than in those who took a placebo.

◆ **Put carrots to work.** Aim to eat about 250 ml of cooked carrots a day. As with all vegetables, cooking softens the cell walls so that you absorb more of what the plant has to offer.

Shiitake Mushrooms

Traditional Chinese herbalists claim that shiitake mushrooms, a mainstay of Asian cuisine and medicine for thousands of years, protect the immune system by activating "Qi"—the life force. Although there's no way to verify that claim, it's clear that the mushrooms do contain disease-fighting substances. An example: lentinan, a string of sugar molecules that helps the body resist and fight off cancer by stimulating the production of T-cells, macrophages, and NK cells. In combination with conventional drugs, lentinan has been found to help heart-bypass patients fight off infections.

UNDERSTANDING NUTRIENTS

Antioxidants

Substances that protect against free radicals, the molecules that attack cells and can damage DNA

Essential Fatty Acids

Used to manufacture and repair cell membranes and to produce prostaglandins, which exert effects throughout the body. EFAs must be obtained from food sources, hence they are called "essential"

Isoflavones

Found chiefly in soy foods, these compounds can alter the action of true estrogens in the body

Phytochemicals

Plant molecules that may prevent and/or suppress disease in the human body

Phytonutrients

Biologically active substances that are needed to sustain life, such as ascorbic acid and beta-carotene, the plant forms of vitamins C and A

DISEASE-FIGHTING PHYTOCHEMICALS

"Eat your vegetables!" Your mother may have been so insistent that her voice still rings in your ears whenever you leave a carrot on your plate. But she had good reason: There's mounting evidence that the phytochemicals in vegetables and fruits help ward off disease. Scientists have begun to study the compounds listed below, and it seems there's more reason than ever to listen to Mom.

PHYTOCHEMICAL	POTENTIAL BENEFIT	GOOD SOURCES
ELLAGIC ACID	Known to inhibit carcinogen-induced tumors in lung, liver, skin, and esophageal tissues. May have other cancer-preventive properties.	Berries, including blueberries and strawberries
EPIGALLOCATECHIN-3-GALLATE (EGCG)	Shown to kill both animal and human cancer cells in laboratory experiments.	Green tea
FRUCTOOLIGO-SACCHARIDES	Shield the colon by stimulating the growth of beneficial bacteria and inhibiting the growth of harmful bacteria. May be helpful to people on antibiotics or chemotherapy.	Jerusalem artichokes
GENISTEIN	Appears to reduce colon, breast, and ovarian cancer risk by limiting the effect of estrogen on these tissues.	Legumes, soy milk, tofu
INDOLE-3-CARBINOL	Blocks some types of breast cancer by altering the response of cells to the hormone estrogen.	Broccoli, cauliflower, kale
ISOTHIOCYNATES	Trigger the production of protective enzymes that may block cancer development.	Watercress
LENTINAN	Stimulates the immune response. Is used in Japan to treat patients with cancer and HIV infection.	Shiitake mushrooms
LIMONENE	Inhibits a key protein that facilitates the growth of cancer cells. Has shown particular value in preventing breast, liver, and lung cancer.	Grated citrus rind, mint, kumquats, caraway and celery seeds
LYCOPENE	Fights free radicals in the body and has been shown to inhibit DNA oxidation, which can lead to some cancers.	Tomatoes (especially juice), watermelon, pink grapefruit
QUERCETIN	Inhibits the growth of the bacterium that causes most stomach ulcers. Also protects against cataracts.	Apples, berries, tomatoes, red grapes, pea pods
SAPONINS	Help kill disease-causing protozoa, such as Giardia, in the digestive tract. Also appears to have cholesterol-lowering activity in humans.	Soybeans
STEVIOSIDE	A calorie-free sweetener that may aid weight loss by cutting cravings for sweets. It is made from a sugar molecule in the leaf of stevia, a South American plant in the chrysanthemum family.	Supplements sold in health-food stores
SULFORAPHANE	A potent booster of Phase II detoxification enzymes, which protect healthy cells against disease.	Broccoli, cauliflower, kale
ZINGERONE	Deactivates free radicals that can cause tissue damage and inflammation.	Ginger

Source: Nutraceutical Science Institute, Rutgers University, New Jersey.

{ "If most of the fat in your diet is of the healthy variety, there's no need to focus on having a low-fat diet." }

—WALTER WILLET, M.D. / NUTRITION RESEARCHER, HARVARD SCHOOL OF PUBLIC HEALTH

◆ **The proof.** Japanese officials approved shiitake mushrooms as an anticancer drug in 1985 after doctors there reported that some stomach and colon cancer patients lived longer when they took purified lentinan during chemotherapy. Other research found that when HIV patients took lentinan along with the anti-HIV drug didanosine, their T-cell activity rose for up to 38 weeks, versus only 14 weeks for those given didanosine alone. Ongoing trials are testing lentinan to see if it will rev up T-cells when combined with another drug. Other research suggests that shiitakes can lower blood cholesterol and help prevent blood clots.

◆ **Put shiitakes to work.** Studies point to 85 grams of fresh shiitake mushrooms or ten grams of dried shiitake as the smallest daily dose to affect health. Other medicinal mushrooms that should have a place on the immune-enhancing plate include maitake. (See page 94.)

OILS AND OTHER FATS are not entirely bad. Recent studies confirm, for example, the health-protective effects of monounsaturated olive oil.

The Truth About Fats

Years of reports on the danger of eating a high-fat diet have led to a widely held but mistaken belief that fat is useless and even dangerous, something that should be avoided whenever possible. In truth, cutting out all the fat in your diet wouldn't be healthy. Fat contains essential acids needed for energy and to aid the absorption of fat-soluble nutrients, such as vitamin A. Dietary fat also delivers the building blocks for hormone-like compounds called prostaglandins, essential for regulating blood pressure, nervous system function, inflammatory response, and fertility.

Important as fat may be, not all fats have equal immunity-boosting and health-promoting properties. Saturated fats of animal origin, including those in lard, butter, bacon, whole milk, and marbled steak, increase the risk of many cancers. High consumption of these fats clearly raises the risk of heart disease. Trans-fats, the man-made fats in most margarines and packaged foods (listed as hydrogenated or partially hydrogenated oil on the label), have the same effects as saturated fats. And even polyunsaturated oils, such as sunflower, are unhealthy in large amounts. Too much fat of any kind increases the production of cell-damaging free radicals.

Olive Oil

Where, then, should you get the fat your body needs? As long as you don't overindulge, olive oil appears to be a healthy choice. The evidence comes from studies of disease rates in Italy and Greece, two countries with low rates of colon and breast cancer, which are common in North America. This reduced cancer risk may be due in part to the popularity of olive oil.

Oil pressed from olives is the predominant fat in the Italian and Greek diet, also known as the Mediterranean diet. What's behind the oil's magic? It contains polyphenols that activate the Phase II enzyme system, which turns hazardous substances into water-soluble compounds that can be excreted through urine or bile. The scientific literature suggests an association between impaired detoxification and certain diseases, including cancer, Parkinson's disease, and chronic fatigue syndrome. Olive oil contains mostly monounsaturated fats, which are more stable than other fats and less likely to form cancer-causing compounds.

◆ **The proof.** In animal studies, squalene, a com-

> **PROTEIN is essential for immune health— and no food is a better source than fish.**

pound found in all olive oils, has been shown to improve immune function and inhibit cell changes and enzymes that encourage cancer development. Recent work reported in the journal *Gut* suggests that olive oil may prevent colon cancer.

◆ **Put olive oil to work.** Extra virgin oil has the highest content of polyphenols and therefore delivers the greatest potential health benefits.

Protein's Purpose

As beneficial as a plant-based diet can be for overall immune function, it doesn't eliminate the need to eat some protein-packed foods. A constant supply of high-quality protein—from fish, beans, and other sources—is necessary for cell growth and repair. In fact, proteins are the building blocks that make up the immune system. Antibodies, for example, are proteins. The protein-deficient diet common among older people plays a large role in their high rate of immune deficiency.

What's "Extra" Virgin, Anyway?

"Extra virgin" olive oil refers to the fruity oil from the first pressing of the olives. No chemicals, high heat, or other potential corrupters have been introduced. Extra virgin olive oil has the lowest acidity (less than 1 percent) and best flavor of all olive oils. Virgin olive oil, also from the first pressing, has higher acidity (about 2 percent) and a mellower taste. Pure "classic" olive oil is a combination of the two. Keep in mind:

1. Olive oil spoils, so buy only as much as you'll use within three months. Also, heed the expiration date if there is one. You don't need to refrigerate olive oil. But do store it out of sunlight and away from heat.

2. Applied to the skin after sun exposure, virgin olive oil may protect against cell damage due to ultraviolet radiation, according to a study by researchers at Kobe University School of Medicine in Japan.

Saltwater Fish

These fish have a dual role in immunity. They provide not only protein, but also special fatty acids called omega-3s. Studies suggest that omega-3s offer magnificent protection against several cancers by suppressing cancer cell growth and metabolism. Research also indicates that fish oils can regulate immune function, mainly by cutting the production of inflammatory compounds and raising the production of anti-inflammatory ones.

◆ **The proof.** Clinical trials have found that omega-3 oils help reduce acute inflammation, which occurs as part of the immune response. Omega-3s activate parts of the immune system that rein in attack cells to stop them when their job is done. They have also been used to reduce organ transplant rejection and treat some autoimmune disorders.

◆ **Put fish to work.** Fish, which cooks to perfection in minutes, is the ultimate convenience food. Eating 110 grams of saltwater fish daily is a great way to meet half your protein needs. Sardines, herring, mackerel, and bluefish are all good protein and omega-3 sources. The rest should come from other high-protein foods, such as beans.

Beans

In addition to being the least expensive source of protein, beans (also called legumes) are loaded with protease inhibitors, compounds that may impede the spread of cancer cells. Soybeans are also rich in isoflavones, shown to diminish prostate cancer risk and, perhaps, to cut breast cancer risk by counteracting the tumor-promoting influence of estrogen.

LEGUMES OR BEANS, such as soybeans (GREEN) and anasazi beans (RED AND WHITE), are edible seeds that develop in pods.

◆ **The proof.** Molecular studies suggest that beans have a range of properties that contribute to their anti-cancer actions. For example, genistein, found in yellow split peas, lima beans, and soy beans, inhibits two enzymes that play a role in transforming normal cells into cancerous cells. Researchers are looking at other ways in which soy affects the immune system.

PLAIN, NONFAT yogurt is a good source of beneficial bacteria, the kind that often gets wiped out when you take a course of antibiotics.

◆ **Put beans to work.** Aim to eat a 120-ml serving daily. Dried beans, with the exception of split peas and lentils, must be soaked before cooking. Scout your grocery for Indian curries made with lentils. Look, too, for hummus, a Middle Eastern dip made with chickpeas. And choose Mexican entrées prepared with black or kidney beans.

Yogurt

It may come last, but it's definitely not least. Yogurt is described by many as the ultimate health food. The live bacteria in protein-rich yogurt endow this fermented dairy product with more, and more potent, immune-enhancing substances than any other food. By attaching themselves to mucous membranes that line the intestines and reproductive tract, the beneficial bacteria in yogurt crowd out disease-causing germs that would otherwise take up residence. And some bacteria in yogurt produce acids that kill other bacteria, including *Clostridia,* a family of germs that causes tetanus, botulism, and other diseases.

◆ **The proof.** The *American Journal of Gastroenterology* reports that *Lactobacillus bulgaricus* helps protect the gastrointestinal tract by stimulating immune cells. A six-month University of California study found that eating 500 ml of yogurt a day quadrupled levels of virus-fighting gamma interferon produced by white blood cells, enhancing the body's ability to ward off colds. Also, the *Annals of Internal Medicine* reported that women with recurrent yeast infections had one-third as many flare-ups during a six-month period in which they ate 230 grams of yogurt a day as during another six months without yogurt.

◆ **Put yogurt to work.** Read the label to make sure the product contains "active" or "living" yogurt cultures. Also check the expiration date. If yogurt sits too long on the shelf, millions of its good bacteria may die from the acidic environment.

HERBS AND SPICES COUNT, TOO

When used generously in cooking, many herbs and spices pack enough antioxidant power to help protect your health. For detailed information on the powers of some 3,000 herbs, check out the phytochemical database at www.ars-grin.gov/duke.

HERB/SPICE	POTENTIAL BENEFIT
BASIL	Reportedly stimulates the immune system to produce more disease-fighting antibodies. Has also been shown to suppress tumor growth and help kill intestinal parasites. Use in tomato sauces or on poultry and fish.
CAYENNE	Contains capsaicin, a fiery oil that increases blood circulation and acts as a decongestant by opening airways and facilitating drainage. May reduce the risk of pneumonia. Use on pizza and in sauces.
CILANTRO	Also called coriander, it is rich in coriandrol, which, in animal studies, combats liver cancer by protecting the DNA in healthy cells from attack by aflatoxins—potent "natural" carcinogens—in moldy bread, peanuts, and other foods. Use in place of parsley, and in salsa, guacamole, and curries.
MINT	Long heralded for its ability to calm stomach upsets, mint now is earning a reputation as an anticancer agent, thanks to an abundance of the antioxidant limonene. Besides using mint in tea, try it for flavoring yogurt, fruit salad, carrots, and peas.
OREGANO	This traditional Italian spice has a robust flavor and the benefits of more than a dozen antioxidants, including carvacrol and thymol, which research has found are effective in combating bacteria, such as *E. coli*, *Salmonella* and *Staphylococcus*.
ROSEMARY	Rosmarinic acid and about a dozen other free-radical-zapping compounds in rosemary activate several of the Phase II detoxification enzymes that help the body rid itself of potentially harmful substances. Use rosemary to flavor poultry dishes and bread dough or to season vegetables.
TURMERIC	The spice that gives curry its bright orange-yellow color, turmeric contains large amounts of a compound called curcumin. Animal studies show that curcumin is a powerful antioxidant that may inhibit stomach and colon cancers. Very preliminary research with 18 HIV-positive patients suggests that high doses (2,000 mg daily) may block a protein secreted by HIV-infected cells that hastens the development of AIDS.

Source: Nutraceutical Science Institute.

Copenhagen took a long-term look at the drinking habits of more than 13,000 men and about 11,500 women and discovered that people who drank wine—rather than beer, hard liquor, or no alcohol—had lower mortality rates than did those who drank no wine at all. It's important to note, though, that while all of the wine drinkers lived longer, those who drank large amounts faced a higher risk of death than those who stuck to no more than three glasses a day.

RED WINE AND DARK CHOCOLATE have several scientifically proven health benefits, so it's fine to enjoy them—in moderation.

Which wine is best? Research shows that one antioxidant in wine, resveratrol, is particularly protective, and some wines have more of this compound than others. Pinot Noir contains twice as much as Merlot, Cabernet Franc, or Cabernet Sauvignon.

Good Guys in Disguise

Healthy eating is more fun if you add in small indulgences—and in this arena there's great news: Some treats that you'd never expect to find on a list of "good" foods could actually benefit your health. Before you forgo a glass of wine with your meal or an after-dinner chocolate, take a look at what you might be missing.

Red Wine

It's long been reported that having a glass of red wine with dinner can help prevent heart disease. Now it's clear that light to moderate wine consumption offers even more benefits. A study team at the Institute of Preventive Medicine in

Dark Chocolate

Chocolate contains some of the same disease-fighting antioxidants as red wine, fruits, and vegetables. In fact, a 40-gram bar of dark chocolate offers about the same amount of antioxidant protection as a 150-ml glass of Cabernet. Tests conducted in Japan on human blood samples found that antioxidants extracted from chocolate suppressed cell-damaging chemicals and boosted immune function. More recently, the *British Medical Journal* reported that people who regularly eat chocolate live up to a year longer than those who avoid it altogether. The study, which examined health records of 7,841 men, found that individuals who ate modest amounts of chocolate candy bars—from one to three a month—had a 36 percent lower risk of death than those who abstained.

A closer look at...foods to cut back on

These foods seem harmless enough, but they have few if any nutritional benefits and lots of drawbacks you may not recognize. In large amounts, they may contribute to reduced immune system function. Think twice (thrice!) before reaching for the following.

PREPARED SALAD DRESSING

A little salad dressing can be a good thing, but ladling it on adds so many calories and so few nutrients that you bankrupt what would otherwise be a vitamin- and fiber-rich meal. Stick to one tablespoon of prepared dressing for a large salad. Better yet, chase a few dashes of olive oil with lemon juice, vinegar, and freshly ground black pepper. To add more flavor and nutrients, toss in herbs, raisins, and fresh garlic.

PRIME BEEF

Though red meat contains immune-boosting nutrients such as iron, zinc, and B-complex vitamins, many cuts—those marked "prime" in particular—are loaded with saturated fat, the fat thought to raise the risk of colorectal and other cancers. By contrast, some cuts of lean beef (look for loin or round in the name) can be lower in total fat than a skinless chicken thigh if you trim visible fat before cooking.

COFFEE

While caffeinated coffee has its health benefits—it may even help block some of the cellular damage caused by free radicals—it is also a natural diuretic, which means it can make you lose certain nutrients through excessive urination. Too much coffee will leave you thirsty and fatigued, so you're apt to reach for yet another cup of coffee, only adding to the problem. The calories and saturated fat from sugar and cream are also troublesome. Try to limit yourself to no more than two cups a day.

FROZEN YOGURT

Frozen yogurt is sometimes touted as a healthy alternative to ice cream—but watch out! The icy stuff often bears little resemblance to its creamier counterpart. For one thing, frozen yogurt is heavy on sugar and sometimes fat. And it may contain far less, if any, living bacteria than regular yogurt does, especially if it is made with ice milk. Even yogurts labeled as containing "live active cultures" may not have enough of the beneficial bacteria to make a difference.

Why Weight Matters

You may already know that being overweight has been linked with a wide variety of health problems, including diabetes, heart disease, and certain cancers. But did you know that it can also impair your immune system?

Consistently consuming too many calories has been shown to increase the incidence and severity of specific types of infectious diseases, indicating that the immune system isn't functioning as well as it should. What's more, burn patients who are overweight run a higher risk of infection than their slimmer counterparts. The body's defenses seem to suffer the most in people who are very overweight. For example, being obese—defined as 20 percent above your ideal weight—is a risk factor for poor wound healing, especially after surgery. And obese people don't respond as well to the hepatitis B vaccine.

Why does weight matter to the immune system? For one thing, every extra kilogram translates to 200 extra grams of tissue that the immune cells must constantly patrol and defend. A kilogram here or there won't have much impact, but once those kilograms start adding up, the bulk can alter your levels of certain stress hormones while sapping your stamina and your psychological well-being—all variables that take a toll on the immune response. Finally, being overweight is sometimes associated with protein and micronutrient deficiencies, even if you are eating too much food.

There has been little research into exactly how excess body weight directly affects the immune system. But studies do link obesity to reduced NK cell activity. NK cells have many functions, but they are especially important in controlling cancer cells and battling acute infection. That's why their activity is an excellent barometer of the overall health of your immune system.

WEIGHING IN is not the best way to track weight, since kilograms fluctuate naturally. For a more accurate reading, take regular measurements, too.

Interesting!

Both children and adults who watch four or more hours of television a day have more body fat and a greater body mass index than those who watch less than two hours.

What's the Right Weight for You?

Do you need to lose weight? If so, how much? For the most accurate answer, calculate your Body Mass Index (BMI). Divide your weight (in kilograms) by your height (in meters squared). For example, a 74-kg (164-pound), 1.73-meter (5-foot 8-inch) man would calculate his BMI this way:

Step 1. $1.73 \times 1.73 = 3$
Step 2. $74 \div 3 = 25$ BMI

According to the latest guidelines, a healthy BMI is between 18.5 and 24.5. The range is wide because there is great individual variation in bone and muscle mass among healthy people. Women tend to have less muscle and bone than men do, so a healthy BMI for a woman will usually fall toward the bottom of the range. A BMI between 25 and 29.9 is considered overweight. A BMI of 30 or higher is considered obese. A very low BMI is not necessarily good. Those below 19 may be at risk for problems such as osteoporosis.

No need to go too low.

Remember, however, that contrary to today's fashion-model ideal, you really can be too thin. Being super-skinny may compromise your immune system in two ways. First, when you severely restrict your intake of fat or calories, you're almost certainly not eating enough to get sufficient amounts of important nutrients that your immune system needs, especially protein, zinc, and antioxidants. Two, if you're reed-thin, you may not be nourished well enough to produce certain immune agents called complement proteins. These proteins spring to action when faced with foreign or disease-carrying cells, piling up on top of the invaders until they are destroyed. Inhibiting these proteins flings open the door to disease.

Besides suppressing your immune system, being underweight carries its own health risks. For instance, it adversely affects fertility in both men and women. Women with a BMI under 18 may have trouble metabolizing estrogen and progesterone, hormones

Start-Up Strategies

Rather than deny yourself your favorite foods, reduce portion sizes, choosing, say, 15 chips instead of the whole bag. Three other small but essential steps for long-lasting success:

1 Make it a point to eat some fat. Fit in about 30 grams a day to avoid a "rebound" effect. A study at Boston's Tufts University study found that five hours after volunteers ate a low-fat meal, they consumed 81 percent more calories than did those who dined on a high-fat meal.

2 Watch portion size. Weight gain results from eating too many calories, no matter where they come from. Cut your typical portions of everything except fruits and vegetables by at least 25 percent. Eat less in restaurants, where portions tend to be very big. Keep serving bowls off the table.

3 Move more. Take a brisk one-kilometer walk each day. Even small, fidgety moves, such as chewing gum or drumming your fingers, can burn about 11 calories an hour, according to the Mayo Clinic and the *New England Journal of Medicine*.

that can affect sex drive, menstruation, the ability to conceive, and the ability to carry a pregnancy to term.

Truth be told, you do not have to get down to a "normal" weight to cut down on your immune system's workload and reduce many major health risks. By dropping as little as 5 to 10 percent of your body weight—that's 4 to 9 kilograms for a 90-kilogram person—you can boost your immune function and get your cholesterol, blood-pressure, and blood-sugar levels under control. Greater rewards are in store if you lose weight *and* become more active. And of course, getting more exercise is one of the best ways to shed excess kilograms.

You'll also slim down faster and stay that way longer if you don't dine out often. Not only is it harder to resist the appealing variety on restaurant menus, but meals tend to be higher in calories, lower in fruits and vegetables, and far larger than typical home-cooked fare. Another tip for shedding kilograms without going hungry: Eat several small meals and snacks at regular intervals throughout the day. "Grazing" helps keep your blood sugar steady, keeps your energy level high, and prevents overeating.

The Best Way to Drop Kilograms

No question: If you eat only small portions of tuna fish, cottage cheese, and lettuce, you'll slim down quickly. But, as you've probably heard before, most people who choose that kind of self-denial route eventually gain back what they've lost—and then some. The problem? Being too rigid inevitably makes you feel deprived, which sooner or later backfires, making "forbidden" foods completely irresistible.

Still tempted to starve yourself? Keep reading. A Louisiana State University study found that restricting food choices and keeping a close watch on calories actually triggered overeating, especially when study subjects were alone. Another small study performed at the Uniformed Services University in Bethesda, Maryland, found that overweight women who ate 1,800 calories a day and allowed themselves to give in to cravings in moderation shed weight more slowly but ended up losing almost twice as much after a year as a comparable group on a strict 1,200-calorie-a-day low-fat diet. The lesson: There is no sorcery or shortcut to weight loss. Eating sensibly while making small changes to your diet and lifestyle makes it much more probable that you will get down to a healthy size—and stay there.

Keep your eyes on the right prize. Rather than trying to lose weight for the sake of appearance alone, focus on getting the biggest nutritional payback possible from every meal. You'll reduce your calorie total automatically because you'll be filling up on fruits, vegetables, and grains. More important,

HEALTH HINT

Scent-sational

The aromas of banana, green apple, and spearmint may help you feel less hungry, according to research in the *Journal of Advancement in Medicine*. Scents that might make you eat more: peppermint, cinnamon, and whiffs of fresh-baked bread.

you'll have the satisfaction of working hard toward the goal that matters most: better health. And remember: It's a *long-term* goal. Don't think you've lost the battle if you cave into a craving for ice cream; you haven't. Remember, too, that calories don't turn to kilograms as rapidly as you might think. To gain a kilogram, you have to take in 8,000 more calories than you expend. That takes a few days to happen, so today's fried shrimp dinner isn't likely to become tomorrow's lumpy thigh.

Low-calorie cooking pointers. There is no one way to prepare low-fat, nutrient-rich foods to fit every lifestyle, every taste preference, or even every kitchen. Clearly, though, some cooking methods are better for you than others.

For starters, turn to your microwave. Because prolonged exposure to heat destroys some nutrients, many foods benefit from the microwave's quick-cooking action. A Cornell University study concluded that broccoli, brussels sprouts, cauliflower, cabbage, and asparagus retain 75 percent more vitamin C when cooked in a microwave than when boiled.

Like microwaving, steaming softens the cellulose of vegetable cells—making the nutrients more readily available to the body—without soaking the food in water, which leaches out valuable nutrients. Steaming or microwaving also seals in a food's flavor without the need for added fat during preparation. Remember, though, to use a small amount of fat when cooking foods rich in such fat-soluble compounds as lycopene. The body needs a little fat to absorb the lycopene from tomatoes and other foods, such as carrots.

{ "The body is not set in stone; it is plastic and moldable, repairable and educable—you can always do something." }

—MIRKA KNASTER, PH.D., L.M.T. / MASSAGE THERAPIST

WHAT'S A SERVING?

This chart, based on Health Canada guidelines, makes clear just how easy it is to fit healthy foods into your diet, gain control of portion sizes, and keep track of what you eat—simple steps that, together, make better health and weight loss easier. Five servings of vegetables, for instance, doesn't mean five huge salads a day, but one-eighth of a head of lettuce and 120 ml each of broccoli, diced tomatoes, and carrot sticks, chased with 180–250 ml of juice.

FOOD GROUP	THUMBS-UP CHOICES	SERVING SIZE	COMPARISON
CARBOHYDRATES	Brown rice, multigrain cereals, oatmeal	120 ml	One muffin cup
FRUITS	Apples, cantaloupe, grapefruits, nectarines, oranges, papaya, peaches, tomatoes, watermelon	1 medium piece	Baseball
VEGETABLES	Asparagus, broccoli, cabbage, carrots, cauliflower, leeks, mushrooms, onions, zucchini	120 ml	Large ice-cream scoop
DAIRY	Fermented milk products with live active cultures, including yogurt and kefir; nonfat milk	250 ml	China teacup (not a mug)
PROTEINS	Cooked lean fish, meat, or poultry; tofu	60-85 grams	Computer mouse
	Cooked dried beans	250–350 ml	Your fist
FATS	Almonds, cashews, walnuts, pecans	30 grams	Golf ball
	Olive or canola oils	1 teaspoon	A quarter
	Salad dressings, peanut butter	2 tablespoons	Two tea bags

30 Ways to Cut 100 Calories

Want to lose weight? Do the arithmetic. More than half of Canadian adults have a BMI of 25 or higher—but need to lose only 10 kilograms or less to be back in the normal range. (To calculate your BMI, use the equation on page 56.) At 8,000 calories per kilogram, 10 kilograms of extra weight is the equivalent of a whopping 80,000 calories—but spread over a year, that works out to a mere 200 calories per day.

In other words, if you shave 200 calories a day from your diet—and/or burn off those calories with physical activity—you'll have lost 10 kilograms in 365 days. You don't even have to resort to such tedious diet strategies as counting calories. Just make two of the delightfully easy and quick changes below. Each will save or burn about 100 calories. Simply choose the ones that work best for you, or use them as inspiration to come up with your own.

1. Do you crave bacon? Substitute two thin slices of turkey bacon (135 CALORIES) for two thick slices of pork bacon (224 CALORIES).

2. Poach two large eggs (150 CALORIES) instead of frying them in one tablespoon butter (250 CALORIES).

3. Pour four tablespoons of whole milk (60 CALORIES) in your coffee, rather than four tablespoons of light cream (232 CALORIES).

4. Instead of one 85-gram corn muffin (258 CALORIES), have one 60-gram buttermilk waffle with one teaspoon of pure maple syrup and one tablespoon of whipped cream from a can (185 CALORIES).

5. Lunch on 85 grams of ham (133 CALORIES), not one plain hamburger (274 CALORIES).

6. Switch from a 30-ml cola (150 CALORIES) to a 30-ml glass of water (0 CALORIES).

7. Stretch 250 ml of deli coleslaw by mixing it with two 225-gram packs of shredded carrots. Have 250 ml of this mixture (100 CALORIES) in place of 250 ml of regular coleslaw (200 CALORIES).

8. Pass on 250 ml of orange sherbet (270 CALORIES). Feast instead on two large, chilled navel oranges (130 CALORIES).

9. Eat one-tenth of a blueberry pie (300 CALORIES) instead of one-tenth of a pecan pie (400 CALORIES).

10. When stir-frying, use one tablespoon of oil (120 CALORIES) in a nonstick wok rather than two tablespoons of oil (240 CALORIES) in a plain steel wok.

11. Trim the visible fat from a 100-gram steak (100 CALORIES).

12. Really hungry? Grill or broil a 170-gram slab of salmon (310 CALORIES) in place of a 170-gram slab of prime beef tenderloin (406 CALORIES).

13. Get an order of fries (210 CALORIES) instead of "super-sizing" (540 CALORIES), or eat a baked sweet potato (136 CALORIES).

14. Rather than eating 500 ml of rice pilaf (400 CALORIES), mix 120 ml of pilaf with 500 ml of chopped vegetables (LESS THAN 200 CALORIES).

15. Add protein to a salad with one sliced hard-boiled egg (78 CALORIES) instead of 55 grams of shredded cheese (200 CALORIES).

16. Dine on 120 ml of beef stew (110 CALORIES) instead of one knockwurst link (209 CALORIES).

CALORIE SHAVERS: Munch 355 ml of light popcorn (100 calories) instead a 60 ml of mixed nuts (210 calories). Or vacuum twice a week for 30 minutes (200 calories) instead of only once!

17. Top a 100-gram serving of spaghetti with 120 ml of tomato sauce (125 CALORIES) instead of meat sauce (242 CALORIES).

18. Indulge yourself with two tablespoons of whipped cream from a can (14 CALORIES) atop 250 ml of strawberries (110 CALORIES) instead of one strawberry ice cream sundae (267 CALORIES).

19. Sip two 120-ml glasses of red wine (160 CALORIES) instead of one 120-ml extra-dry martini (254 CALORIES).

20. Eat a large banana (114 CALORIES) instead of 45-grams chocolate-covered peanuts (240 CALORIES).

21. Forgo four caramels (120 CALORIES) for one lollipop (22 CALORIES).

22. Eat five vanilla wafers (190 CALORIES) instead of 10 (380 CALORIES).

Activity Options

CALCULATIONS BASED ON A 64-KILOGRAM ADULT

23. Treat yourself to a 20-minute shopping spree (112 CALORIES).

24. Drive 156 golf balls at the range (100 CALORIES AT SIX SWINGS A MINUTE).

25. Slow-dance to seven songs for a total of about 26 minutes (100 CALORIES).

26. Spend five minutes walking up several flights of stairs (101 CALORIES).

27. Participate for just 10 minutes in a low-impact aerobics class (104 CALORIES).

28. Push yourself to run a high-energy kilometer in six minutes (70 CALORIES).

29. Play tag—you're it!—with your children for 15 minutes (116 CALORIES).

30. Take a brisk 13-minute walk (100 CALORIES).

On the horizon...new diet aids

For now, diet and exercise are the keys to shedding pounds and keeping them off—but there may be more help in the future. Here's the scoop on some current research that scientists hope may one day yield novel approaches for fighting flab.

ANTIOBESITY VACCINES

Research in the *International Journal of Obesity* suggests that, in some cases, a virus may contribute to obesity. First documented in chickens, virus-induced obesity interferes with how the body absorbs and stores food energy, triggering the gain of substantial amounts of body fat. The research is the first to suggest that one day an antiobesity vaccine could become a reality, bringing an end to counting calories for some.

AROMATHERAPY SKIN PATCHES

A study out of St. George's Hospital in London, England, found that vanilla-scented skin patches spurred weight loss by lessening cravings for sugary foods. When 200 overweight volunteers were randomly given either the vanilla patch, a lemon-scented patch, or no patch, those who wore the vanilla patch for four weeks lost both their appetite for sweets and about two kilograms. People in the other groups lost almost nothing.

GENE THERAPY

A British study points to a day when injections may offer a safe route to slimness if obesity is caused by a lack of the hormone leptin. Normally, fat cells use leptin to signal the brain when the body has enough fat stores. But some people don't secrete enough leptin, so hunger never abates. Proof of the potential: When injections of leptin were given to one obese girl whose body didn't make the hormone naturally, her weight began a steady descent, and she was able to keep the kilograms off.

APPETITE-CONTROL PILLS

Recently, while testing an experimental cancer-fighting compound called C75, scientists accidentally discovered that it blocks an enzyme that turns food into fat. What's more, the compound also seems to halt production of neuropeptide Y, the brain chemical that stimulates appetite. In tests, mice lost interest in food within 20 minutes of being dosed with C75 and went on to lose even more weight than fasting mice that were untreated. Development of a C75 antiobesity drug is under way.

Menus for a New Way of Eating

Bursting with flavor and immune-boosting phytochemicals, the eating plan that follows reveals how deliciously easy it is to load up on fruits, vegetables, yogurt, and other nutritional powerhouses to give your immune system the raw materials it needs to stay strong.

EAT THESE EVERY DAY: garlic or onions, broccoli or cabbage, dark green or yellow vegetables, berries or citrus fruits, and beans or nuts.

Enjoy every bite. From crunchy vegetables to juicy chunks of pork, from carrot juice to red wine, from sweet fresh fruits to . . . marshmallows. *Pork? Red wine? Marshmallows?* Is this a fairy tale from the Land of Good-for-You-Make-Believe? No, because this is not a diet. There's no deprivation involved. Although developed by a registered dietitian to put as many immune-boosting foods on your plate as possible, the plan was also designed to keep your taste buds happy.

The menus are not set in stone. Mix and match within categories of foods (fruits, vegetables, meats, and so on) to suit your preferences. Cancer experts recommend choosing at least one serving of a carotene-rich fruit or vegetable daily, such as apricots, cantaloupe, carrots, kale, mangoes, romaine lettuce, pumpkin, spinach, or sweet potatoes; at least one serving of a vitamin C-rich food, such as broccoli, brussels sprouts, tomatoes, cabbage, kiwis, cherries, or oranges; at least one serving of a high-fiber fruit or vegetable, such as apples, blueberries, carrots, cooked beans, or strawberries; and several servings of cruciferous vegetables each week—broccoli, brussels sprouts, cabbage, or cauliflower.

For peak immunity, adapt those guidelines and the following plan to fit your lifestyle—being sure to avoid excessive fat, sugar, and sodium. You'll be eating well now and in the future.

Feel full and satisfied. Although this is not a weight-loss plan—each day's meals average 1,700 calories and 46 grams of fat—it incorporates many of the edibles found by investigators at the University of Sydney, Australia, to have the most power to fill you up and curb your cravings. These include fish, oranges, beans, and lentils. So eat up, and stay satisfied!

DAY 1

Breakfast

◆ **Phyto-Cocktail:** Place in a blender 500 ml frozen blueberries, 250 ml silken tofu, 250 ml soy milk, 1 tablespoon honey, 1 tablespoon ground flaxseed, and ¼ teaspoon grated lemon zest. Puree.

FABULOUS FLAXSEED

Flaxseed contains alpha-linolenic acid, an omega-3 fat that may help treat autoimmune diseases. Grind the seeds to break the hull and unleash the beneficial compounds. Store in the refrigerator.

Lunch

◆ **Broccoli-Stuffed Baked Potato:** In a small nonstick skillet, heat 1 teaspoon olive oil. Add ⅛ teaspoon red pepper flakes. Cook for 1 minute. Add 350 ml broccoli and 120 ml chicken broth. Cover. Simmer until crisp-tender. Cut 1 baked potato in half lengthwise. Scoop out pulp, leaving skins intact. Mash and combine with broccoli mixture, 60 ml plain nonfat yogurt, and 2 teaspoons grated Parmesan. Refill skins. Bake 30 minutes at 175°C.

◆ **Crunchy Salad:** In a medium bowl, combine 250 ml cauliflower florets, 60 ml grape tomatoes, 2 tablespoons diced red bell pepper, 1 tablespoon finely chopped cilantro, and 1 scallion. Add 1 tablespoon lemon juice mixed with 2 teaspoons olive oil. Salt to taste.

◆ 250 ml vegetable juice

Snacks

◆ 1 orange
◆ 30 grams dark chocolate

Dinner

◆ **Fish in Wine Sauce:** Place a 140-gram mackerel or tuna fillet on a 30-cm piece of foil. Top with 1 tomato, chopped; 1 red pepper, sliced; 1 tablespoon white wine; and 2 teaspoons fresh tarragon, chopped. Season with salt and pepper. Top with a lemon slice. Fold the foil into a pouch to enclose the fish. Bake at 250°C for 10 minutes or until fish flakes easily.

Dessert

◆ **Strawberry Shortcake:** Top 1 piece angel food cake with 120 ml nonfat vanilla yogurt and 120 ml sliced strawberries.

◆ 250 ml nonfat milk

DAY 2

Breakfast

◆ **French Toast:** In a blender, puree 60 ml silken tofu and combine with 60 ml calcium-enriched vanilla soy milk. Add ⅛ teaspoon ground cinnamon and ⅛ teaspoon ginger. Heat a nonstick skillet coated with cooking spray over medium-high heat. Dip 2 pieces whole-grain bread in mixture, soaking both sides. Cook in skillet until browned on both sides, about 5 minutes. Drizzle with honey.

◆ 250 ml orange juice

HOORAY FOR HONEY

Studies show that eating 1 tablespoon of locally harvested honey per day may curb hay fever symptoms. It contains pollens that help desensitize the immune system to the plant particles that cause sneezing.

Lunch

◆ **Tuna-Tofu Caesar Salad:** Make dressing by pureeing 60 ml silken tofu, 2 teaspoons red wine vinegar, 1 teaspoon olive oil, 1 tablespoon water, ¼ teaspoon Worcestershire sauce, ¼ teaspoon Dijon mustard, and ¼ teaspoon anchovy paste. Toss with salad consisting of 500 ml torn romaine lettuce leaves and 110 grams canned, water-packed tuna, drained; 1 tomato, sliced; 60 ml red onion, thinly sliced; 60 ml cucumber, sliced; and 60 ml croutons.

Snacks

◆ 500 ml cubed watermelon
◆ 30 grams cashew nuts

Dinner

◆ **Shiitake Chicken:** In a medium nonstick skillet coated with cooking spray, brown 110 grams of boneless chicken breast, cut in 2.5-cm-thick strips and seasoned with salt and pepper. Add 250 ml sliced fresh shiitake mushrooms, ¼ teaspoon dried thyme, 2 teaspoons olive oil, and a pinch of salt. Stir, browning for 5 minutes. Add 2 tablespoons red wine to skillet. Simmer 2–3 minutes.

◆ ½ steamed acorn squash sprinkled with ⅛ teaspoon ground cinnamon

Dessert

◆ 250 ml nonfat yogurt with 30 grams raisins

Menus for a New Way of Eating

DAY 3

Breakfast

- 250 ml tomato juice
- 1 whole-wheat bagel, toasted, drizzled with 1/2 teaspoon olive oil and topped with tomato slices
- 120 ml nonfat yogurt with 1 tablespoon walnuts and 60 ml diced papaya

DON'T SKIP BREAKFAST

People who bypass breakfast tend to have weight problems and less resistance to disease. Replace coffee, devoid of phytonutrients, with phytonutrient-rich green tea.

Lunch

- **Gazpacho:** In a food processor or blender, finely chop 1 scallion, 1/2 red bell pepper, 1/4 cucumber, 1 teaspoon minced basil, and 1 teaspoon snipped dill. Mix with 500 ml spicy vegetable juice, 1 teaspoon olive oil, and 1 tablespoon red-wine vinegar.
- 1 piece crusty whole-grain bread topped with 1 tablespoon goat cheese

Snacks

- **Cherries Jubilee:** In a blender, puree 250 ml frozen cherries, 250 ml calcium-enriched vanilla soy milk, 1 tablespoon honey, and 1/8 teaspoon cinnamon. Blend until smooth.
- 1 pink grapefruit
- 250 ml green tea

Dinner

- **Lemon-Garlic Grilled Salmon:** Combine 1 tablespoon soy sauce, 1 tablespoon olive oil, 2 teaspoons fresh minced ginger, 1 teaspoon chopped garlic, and 1/2 teaspoon grated lemon zest. Marinate a 140-gram salmon fillet in this mixture for 30 minutes. Grill until fish flakes easily.

Dessert

- **Sweet Potato Delight:** Cut 1 baked sweet potato in half lengthwise. Top with 2 tablespoons walnuts, 2 tablespoons mini-marshmallows, and 1 tablespoon semi-sweet chocolate chips. Broil 15 cm from heat, until marshmallows are golden brown.

DAY 4

Breakfast

- Top 250 ml nonfat yogurt with 120 ml sliced strawberries, 60 ml diced kiwi, and 2 tablespoons bran.
- 250 ml green tea

Lunch

- **Sardine Sandwich:** Combine 2 tablespoons nonfat sour cream, 1 tablespoon Dijon mustard, 1 teaspoon snipped dill, and 1/4 teaspoon grated lemon zest. Spread mixture on 2 pieces pumpernickel bread and top with 2 tomato slices, 2 slices red onion, and 4 cucumber slices. Top each half with 3 canned sardines.
- **Watercress Salad:** Combine 2 teaspoons olive oil, 2 teaspoons orange juice, 1 teaspoon mustard, and 1/2 teaspoon honey. Toss with 500 ml watercress.

A SALUTE TO SARDINES

These soft-boned fish are full of omega-3 fatty acids. Half of a 100-ml tin also provides 50 percent of the RDA for vitamin B_{12} and 12 percent of your calcium needs (from the edible bones), plus potassium, vitamin D, and protein.

Snacks

- 30 grams dark chocolate
- 250 ml green tea

Dinner

- **Tuna with Corn Salsa:** Combine 120 ml frozen corn kernels, thawed; 120 ml canned black beans, drained; and 60 ml roasted red peppers, chopped. Add 1 teaspoon orange juice, 1 teaspoon olive oil, and 1 teaspoon chopped cilantro. Season 140 grams of fresh tuna with salt and pepper. Grill or broil 10 cm from heat for 6–8 minutes. Top with corn salsa.
- **Spinach Salad:** Combine 2 teaspoons chopped onion, 1 tablespoon olive oil, 2 teaspoons balsamic vinegar, 1/8 teaspoon poppy seeds. Toss with 500 ml torn spinach leaves.

Dessert

- **Old-Fashioned Baked Apple:** Place 1 Granny Smith apple, cored, in a small baking dish. Fill hole with 2 tablespoons raisins, 1 tablespoon chopped walnuts, and 1/8 teaspoon cinnamon. Pour 1 tablespoon orange juice in bottom of baking dish. Cover. Bake at 175°C until tender. Top with nonfat vanilla yogurt.

DAY 5

Breakfast

◆ 350 ml wheat bran flakes topped with 60 ml raisins and 250 ml nonfat milk or calcium-enriched soy milk

◆ 250 ml cubed cantaloupe

> **Say Yes to Yellow-Orange**
> A European study found that regularly eating cantaloupe, pumpkin, and other yellow-orange foods helps shield the skin from sun damage.

Lunch

◆ **Shrimp Salad Pita:** Combine 140 grams cooked shrimp, chopped, with 1 tablespoon mayonnaise, 2 tablespoons diced celery, ½ teaspoon snipped dill, ¼ teaspoon grated lemon zest, and ⅛ teaspoon chopped garlic. Fill 1 whole-wheat pita with shrimp salad mixture and 250 ml watercress.

Snacks

◆ 350 ml frozen red grapes
◆ 250 ml green tea

Dinner

◆ **Pork with Caramelized Onions:** In a nonstick skillet coated lightly with olive oil, brown 110 grams boneless pork loin (2.5 cm thick) seasoned with salt and pepper, then remove. In same skillet, cook 2 medium onions, sliced, and ½ teaspoon thyme in 2 teaspoons olive oil over medium-low heat until golden brown, about 20 minutes. Increase heat to medium; add pork, 2 tablespoons balsamic vinegar, and 2 tablespoons chicken broth. Cover. Cook 8–10 minutes.

◆ **Savory Pumpkin Puree:** In a small saucepan, mix 120 ml canned pumpkin puree, 1 tablespoon chicken broth, 2 teaspoons sugar, ⅛ teaspoon cinnamon, and ⅛ teaspoon grated fresh ginger. Cook, stirring, 5 minutes.

◆ **Cheesy Cauliflower:** Steam 500 ml cauliflower florets until tender. In a medium bowl, toss cauliflower with 1 tablespoon grated Parmesan cheese, 1 teaspoon olive oil, ¼ teaspoon grated lemon zest, a pinch of salt, and a pinch of cayenne.

Dessert

◆ **Peanut Butter and Honey Crunch:** Stir 2 tablespoons of peanut butter in 250 ml nonfat yogurt. Sprinkle with sunflower seeds. Drizzle with honey.

THE ULTIMATE STIR-FRY

Eat 500 ml of this tantalizing stir-fry, and you'll be getting four of your daily five to nine vegetable servings. Substitute for any dinner on the plan.

250 ml chicken broth
2 tablespoons low-sodium soy sauce
1 tablespoon cornstarch
1 tablespoon mirin (Japanese cooking wine)
1 teaspoon sugar
230 grams large shrimp, peeled and deveined
1 teaspoon plus 1 tablespoon olive oil, divided
230 grams extra-firm tofu, cut in 1.5-cm cubes
3 cloves garlic, minced
2 carrots, sliced into rounds
1 onion, chopped
1 tablespoon chopped fresh ginger
1 head (0.5 kilogram) broccoli, cut in florets
1 red bell pepper, sliced
110 grams shiitake mushrooms, sliced
250 ml snow pea pods, trimmed
3 scallions, sliced
1 tablespoon chopped fresh cilantro
Steamed rice (optional)

Combine broth, soy sauce, cornstarch, mirin, and sugar in a small bowl. Set aside. Coat a wok lightly with olive oil and place over medium heat. Add shrimp and cook 2 minutes or until opaque. Remove. In same wok, heat 1 teaspoon oil over medium heat. Add tofu and cook 4 minutes, stirring frequently, or until golden. Remove. Heat 1 tablespoon oil over high heat. Add garlic, carrots, onion, and ginger. Cook, stirring, 2–3 minutes. Add broccoli and bell pepper. Cook 4–5 minutes, stirring frequently. Add mushrooms, pea pods, and scallions, and cook, stirring frequently, 5–8 minutes. Return shrimp and tofu to pan. Add reserved broth mixture. Reduce to a simmer; cook 1 minute. Sprinkle with cilantro. Serve over rice (optional). Makes 2 liters.

PER 500-ML SERVING: Calories 259, fats 9g, cholesterol 86mg, sodium 561mg, carbohydrates 26g, dietary fiber 6g, protein 22g

Menus for a New Way of Eating

DAY 6

Breakfast

- **Honey Raisin Oatmeal:**
  Cook 250 ml oatmeal in
  500 ml nonfat milk or
  calcium-enriched vanilla
  soy milk. Mix in ¼ tea-
  spoon cinnamon and
  2 tablespoons raisins.
- 250 ml green tea

Lunch

- **Salmon-Chickpea Salad:**
  Crumble 110 grams cooked
  salmon over 350 ml
  baby greens and 120 ml
  cooked chickpeas. Toss
  with ½ tomato, diced;
  ¼ red onion, diced; and
  ½ teaspoon chopped fresh
  mint. Toss again with
  1 teaspoon olive oil and
  1 teaspoon cider vinegar.

Snacks

- 250 ml baby carrots dipped
  in 2 tablespoons low-fat
  blue cheese dressing
- 1 apple

Dinner

- **Garlicky Pesto Pasta:**
  In a blender, finely grind
  1 teaspoon pine nuts and
  a pinch of

salt. Add 60 ml packed
basil leaves, 60 ml packed
parsley leaves, and 1 clove
garlic, peeled. Blend well.
Add 1 tablespoon olive oil
and process until smooth.
Add 2 teaspoons grated
Parmesan. Blend well.
Toss with 350 ml cooked,
warm bow tie pasta.

> **SIZE MATTERS**
> Enriched pasta—in proper
> portions—won't make you
> fat. And it's a good source
> of B vitamins and iron.

- **Pepper-Tomato Salsa:** In a
  large bowl, combine
  250 ml diced red, yellow,
  or orange bell peppers;
  ½ tomato, seeded and
  diced; ½ tablespoon
  lemon juice, ½ tablespoon
  chopped green chilies,
  ½ tablespoon minced
  cilantro, 1 teaspoon
  minced onion, and ½
  tablespoon balsamic vinegar. Let stand one hour.
- 250 red wine or
  sparkling grape juice

Dessert

- **Tropical Sundae:** Top
  250 ml diced mango with
  a dollop of nonfat vanilla
  yogurt. Sprinkle with
  2 teaspoons mini-chocolate
  chips and 2 teaspoons
  crushed walnuts.

DAY 7

Breakfast

- Top 1 whole-grain frozen
  waffle with 60 ml
  blueberries and 60 ml
  sliced strawberries.
  Sprinkle with cinnamon.
- 250 ml unsweetened
  grapefruit juice

Lunch

- **Pepper-Garlic Pizza:**
  Drizzle one 13-cm whole-
  grain prepared pizza crust
  with ½ teaspoon olive oil.
  Spread 120 ml prepared
  tomato sauce over crust.
  Top with 120 ml sliced
  red or yellow bell pepper,
  2 tablespoons chopped
  onion, ¼ teaspoon minced
  garlic, ⅛ teaspoon dried
  basil, ⅛ teaspoon dried
  oregano, and 60 ml shredded part-skim mozzarella
  cheese. Bake in 175°C
  oven until cheese bubbles.
- 250 ml calcium-enriched
  orange juice

Snack

- **Banana S'More:** In a
  microwave-safe bowl,
  cover 2 graham crackers
  with 1 sliced banana.
  Top with 2 tablespoons
  mini-marshmallows and
  microwave on high for
  30-second intervals until
  marshmallows begin to

melt. Drizzle with 1 tablespoon chocolate sauce.
- 250 ml nonfat milk or
  calcium-enriched soy milk

Dinner

- **Lentils with Couscous:**
  In a medium saucepan
  over medium-high heat,
  combine 250 ml cooked
  red lentils with ½ tea-
  spoon olive oil, ½ tea-
  spoon minced fresh garlic,
  ⅛ teaspoon turmeric,
  ¼ teaspoon grated lemon
  zest, 1 tablespoon chopped
  onion, and 1 tablespoon
  chopped celery. Heat
  through and toss with
  350 ml cooked couscous.
- 250 ml chopped broccoli,
  steamed with 1 teaspoon
  lemon zest and 1 clove
  garlic, peeled and sliced

Dessert

- **Fruit and Yogurt Parfait:**
  In small glass, alternate
  120 ml nonfat vanilla
  yogurt with 60 ml sliced
  kiwi and 60 ml diced pears.
  Top with a dollop of nonfat
  yogurt and 1 tablespoon
  slivered almonds.

> **BRING ALONG BANANAS**
> A satisfying substitute for
> processed sweets, the
> perfectly portable banana
> is loaded with potassium
> and magnesium.

WHY SO MUCH SOY?

If you choose soy milk instead of regular milk in this menu plan, you'll get up to seven servings of soy a week. Why so much? Studies suggest that phytochemicals in soy help lower cholesterol, inhibit the growth of cancer cells, and reduce the risk of osteoporosis. But because some substances in soy have still-unexplained hormonal effects, limit your intake to no more than 55 to 110 grams a day.

NAME	WHAT IT IS	HOW IT IS SOLD
TOFU	A cheese-like food (BELOW, LEFT) made by combining dried and rehydrated soybeans with a thickener, such as calcium salts. Use cubed in stir-fries or mashed in place of eggs in salads.	In cakes of soft, firm, and extra-firm textures, either water packed in a plastic container or loose in tubs
SILKEN TOFU	Custardy, very soft version of tofu. Blend into soups, sauces, smoothies, and salad dressings.	Water or vacuum packed in 335- to 550-gram cakes
SEASONED, PRESSED TOFU	Small cakes of extra-firm tofu marinated in soy sauce and spices. Dense and chewy, it tastes a bit like an aromatic cooked chicken. Use in salads, add to stir-fries, or grill with barbecue sauce.	Usually three 110-gram cakes packaged in a plastic pouch
TEMPEH	Whole soybeans, sometimes mixed with another grain such as rice or millet, fermented into a rich cake with a smoky or nutty flavor. Marinate and grill or add to soups, casseroles, or chili.	Usually one flat rectangular cake in a plastic pouch
EDAMAME	Soybeans (BELOW, CENTER) harvested when green. Serve as a snack or vegetable dish after boiling in salted water for 15 minutes.	Frozen or fresh, shelled or in the pod, in Asian and natural food stores
SOY MILK	Liquid (BELOW, RIGHT) pressed from soaked, cooked, and ground whole soybeans. Use in place of cream in soups, whirl in smoothies, or add to recipes for baked goods in place of milk.	Regular, low-fat, or non-fat; plain or flavored with vanilla, chocolate, or carob; in glass, paper, or plastic containers
SOY POWDER	Soy protein concentrates extracted from defatted soy flakes and formulated to contain 92 percent soy protein—more protein than any other soy product. Stir into drinks and casseroles.	Packaged, in natural-food stores

Immune Power in a Glass

When you're not sticking to the preceding menu plan, it may seem hard to fit in five or more servings of fruits and vegetables daily. The easy solution: Try drinking your produce by the glass rather than chewing it by the kilogram.

Smoothie Savvy

1 Use fully ripe fruits. They typically have better flavor and, sometimes, higher nutritional value. Too sweet? Add a squeeze of fresh lemon or lime juice. Too tart? Add honey, maple syrup, or unsweetened applesauce.

2 Frozen fruit makes a thicker drink. Spread diced fruit on a cookie sheet and freeze for two to four hours. Transfer the pieces to a resealable bag when hard. Most supermarkets also carry frozen unsweetened strawberries, blueberries, raspberries, and melon.

3 The smaller the ice cubes, the better your blender can handle them. Fill trays only halfway or set the automatic icemaker to the smallest setting.

4 Experiment. Try unsweetened fruit nectars, such as mango, guava, or apricot, instead of juices; silken tofu instead of yogurt; or buttermilk instead of nonfat milk. Flavor with vanilla extract, orangeflower water, grated ginger, or chopped fresh mint.

When American scientists concocted a shake made of either pureed strawberries or spinach and gave it to study participants, the volunteers' blood levels of antioxidants rose by approximately 15 percent within two and a half hours—equivalent to the effect of ingesting 1,250 mg of vitamin C. Although the drinks used in the study aren't available commercially, you can get the same effect from a blender drink made with approximately 500 ml of strawberries or one 280-gram package of spinach.

More juicy details. Need more reasons to indulge in these cool drinks? Unlike fruit juices—in which the liquid is extracted and the pulp is left behind—smoothies deliver a slew of good-for-you fiber. Nearly any soft fruit can be sliced and added directly to the blender: apples, avocados (yes, they are fruits!), bananas, berries, papayas, and more. Smoothies also make it simple to fit more soy into your diet. Thirty grams of soy (in the form of silken tofu, soy milk, or soy protein powder) will thicken your smoothie and add 20 grams of protein, less than 1 gram of fat, and 100 calories to your daily nutrient intake.

Drinking smoothies may provide a side benefit by crowding out high-fat ice creams and highly refined desserts you might otherwise reach for to satisfy your sweet tooth. Convinced by these tidbits? Then it's time to get creative.

Quick Tip

The name "smoothie" covers a multitude of concoctions, including some made with fruit syrups and high-calorie add-ins, such as ice cream, peanut butter, or protein powders. To keep your smoothie hovering around the 300-calorie level, make it at home or have it made with ice or nonfat yogurt instead of ice cream or frozen yogurt.

BASIC IMMUNE POWER SMOOTHIE

If you have a blender and two minutes to spare, you can whip up a perfect smoothie. Start with this basic recipe.

250 ml plain nonfat yogurt
180 ml carrot, orange, or red grape juice
30 grams silken tofu
1 medium apple, peeled, cored, and diced
250 ml frozen berries
60 ml chopped ice

Combine yogurt, juice, and tofu in a blender. Add fruit and ice and blend until smooth. Garnish with a sprig of mint. Makes 500–750 ml.

PER 250-ML SERVING: Calories 206, fats 1g, cholesterol 2mg, sodium 135mg, carbohydrates 42g, dietary fiber 5g, protein 10g

Tasty variations. Here are four ideas for more immune-boosting "power punches." Each is a great hunger satisfier that's loaded with flavor and nutrients. For maximum enjoyment, serve smoothies in frosted glasses: Dip glasses in cool water, then place them in the freezer for five minutes. Use immediately.

Craving Crusher Combine 60 ml nonfat vanilla soy milk, 250 ml diced kiwi, and ½ banana in a blender. Add 120 ml frozen green grapes, 6 ice cubes, 1 teaspoon lime juice, 2 teaspoons honey (optional), and 1 teaspoon chopped fresh mint. Blend until smooth. Makes 500–750 ml.

PER 250-ML SERVING. Calories 235, fats 3g, cholesterol 0mg, sodium 73mg, carbohydrates 48g, dietary fiber 4g, protein 6g

Beta Blaster Combine 250 ml frozen cantaloupe, 120 ml orange or carrot juice, and 120 ml apricot nectar in a blender. Add 120 ml frozen mango slices and 80 ml chopped red bell pepper. Blend until smooth. Makes 500–750 ml.

PER 250-ML SERVING. Calories 122, fats 1g, cholesterol 0mg, sodium 11mg, carbohydrates 30g, dietary fiber 2g, protein 2g

Berry Berry Good Combine 250 ml nonfat raspberry yogurt and 60 ml cranberry juice in a blender. Add 250 ml frozen unsweetened strawberries and 180 ml frozen unsweetened blueberries. Blend until smooth. Makes 500–750 ml.

PER 250-ML SERVING. Calories 199, fats 2g, cholesterol 5mg, sodium 74mg, carbohydrates 42g, dietary fiber 3g, protein 6g

Soy Fast Combine 250 ml nonfat soy milk, 250 ml frozen pineapple chunks, 120 ml frozen peach chunks, 55 grams silken tofu, and 2 teaspoons honey in a blender. Blend until smooth. Makes 500–750 ml.

PER 250-ML SERVING. Calories 133, fats 1g, cholesterol 0mg, sodium 54mg, carbohydrates 29g, dietary fiber 2g, protein 40g

Water: The Forgotten Ingredient

The jury may still be out on some of the popular nutrition advice that gets bandied about, but one thing is certain: Drinking plenty of fluids, especially good old-fashioned water, will truly benefit your health.

Unfortunately, those who heed this advice are in the minority. The average Canadian drinks about four 250-ml glasses of water each day, while taking in roughly the same amount of dehydrating fluids, such as coffee and cola. That's bad news, since every system in the body, including the immune system, depends on water for such vital tasks as regulating temperature and carrying nutrients around the body.

Since the body loses water each day due to perspiration, secretion, and elimination, it needs a consistent intake or it cannot function at its best. Even mild dehydration—a state you're already in when thirst first hits—can result in fatigue. It may also pose a threat to your urinary tract: A Harvard University School of Public Health study of 48,000 men found that those who drank at least six 250-ml glasses of water a day were only half as likely to get bladder cancer as men who drank just one glass.

How much is enough? Exactly how much fluid you need each day is an individual matter—it's not necessary to adhere to the eight-glasses-a-day edict. No one, in fact, is sure where that advice originated. Instead, your best bet is to monitor your urine color and frequency. Pale yellow urine is a good sign that you're getting plenty of fluids. (But don't judge urine color within a few hours after taking vitamin supplements, since the unused vitamins, particularly the B vitamin riboflavin, turn your urine a bright yellow.) Frequent urination is another good sign, although it may also be caused by a medication you're taking or by a medical condition.

Spread your fluid intake over the day to keep your body's water levels steady, and drink past the feeling of thirst, since that sensation shuts off quickly once you begin drinking, well before you've replenished lost fluids. You can rehydrate with any fluid—water, milk, juice, a smoothie, an herbal infusion, or even a lightly carbonated soft drink.

Sports drinks, which supply electrolytes (sodium and other minerals that are lost through sweat), are proven to be effective in keeping you hydrated during rigorous exercise, such as high-altitude hiking or bike racing in 32°C (90°F) heat.

BOTTLED, FILTERED, or straight from the tap, drink any kind of water you like. The important thing is to drink enough.

What's Inside the Bottle?

Bottled water is often labeled with such terms as "artesian," "mineral," or "spring." To create a single standard for all water bottlers to follow, Health Canada has designated specific definitions for each of these terms. Here are the current meanings:

1 Artesian water is pumped to the ground surface from an underground source or spring through a layer of water, rock, or sand below the ground—a natural filter known as a confined aquifer.

2 Mineral water is obtained from a geological and physically protected underground water source—not public community water. It must contain no less than 500 mg/l of total dissolved solids.

3 Purified water is produced by distillation, deionization, or other processes, and contains not more than 10 mg/l of total dissolved solids. Purified water that is vaporized and condensed may be labeled "distilled."

4 Natural mineral water is mineral water that maintains its bacteriological purity, is bottled in close proximity to the source, is not subjected to treatment that will modify its fundamental mineral content, and is not shipped in bulk.

5 Spring water comes from an underground source that contains less than 500 mg/l total dissolved solids. Spring water may be treated, but can not be labeled "natural."

Hazardous to your health? As necessary as water is, it can sometimes pose a danger. Everywhere you look, there's another scary news story about one of the many things that can go wrong: Underground fuel tanks or factory waste-holding chambers may spring leaks, for example, and contaminate well water. Herbicides and animal waste can run off from farms and taint reservoirs. Fortunately, these problems rarely occur because there are effective safeguards to protect public water supplies.

Still, experts agree that one particular water danger is unusually worrisome—the hazard from waterborne microscopic parasites and viruses. No one knows the extent of these threats because the symptoms of infection (nausea, stomach cramps, and fatigue) are the same as those of stomach viruses and food poisoning. What's known is that ingesting a single one of these microorganisms—*Giardia lamblia, Cryptosporidium,* or virulent strains of *E. coli*—can cause serious or even fatal illness, especially in the very young and people with weakened immune systems. According to Environment Canada, as many as 34,000 die worldwide every day from water-related illness.

The best protection. Even though treated water is essential to prevent a variety of illnesses, some Canadian communities do not have water treatment of any kind. Provincial, territorial, and municipal governments establish and enforce their own standards and objectives, generally based on Health Canada's *Guidelines for Canadian Drinking Water Quality.* For those concerned about their community's water supply, a private tester can be hired to evaluate how water is treated, what contaminants it contains and at what levels, what the health effects of those contaminants can be, and what levels are considered unhealthy.

HEALTH HINT

Eat Your H$_2$O

Health Canada recommends Canadians consume two liters of water daily. Eating plenty of fruits and vegetables, especially watermelon (which is 98 percent water), cucumbers (96 percent), and lettuce (94 percent), as well as soups, cooked pasta, and gelatin desserts, can contribute up to one liter of water to your diet per day.

Stocking Your Kitchen For Health

Variety is the spice of life—and the key to enjoyable, healthy eating. So fill your kitchen with a wide array of good-for-you foods, and follow the shopping, cooking, and storing tips in this section to make the most of every immune-boosting bite.

Relish the Flavors

Too often, unless we're adhering to a carefully designed eating plan, we shy away from healthy foods because, let's face it, they sound boring. But nothing could be further from the truth. Ask any chef: Fruits, vegetables, legumes, whole grains, and other foods rich in phytochemicals can also be among the most flavorful foods of all. Just use these ideas to bring out their zing.

◆ **Replace fat with flavor.** Add palate-pleasing seasonings to ensure that you won't miss the fat. Cover a Cobb salad with a nonfat yogurt dressing flavored with Tabasco, vinegar, honey, garlic, and onions, and you'll never miss the blue cheese.

◆ **Light a fire.** Grilling brings out maximum flavor in vegetables. Instead of having hamburgers, sausage, or steak at your next cookout, grill fish and a medley of veggies, such as squash, eggplant, and onions. Sprinkle a light coating of oil on both the vegetables and the fish before grilling so they won't stick.

◆ **Give plain-Jane salads a buzz.** Chop fresh carrots, scallions, celery, and red or yellow peppers. Add to store-bought salsa and mix in lemon, lime, cumin, or garlic for a chunky, tangy dressing. Serve over your usual green salad.

◆ **Remember, opposites attract.** Surprising combinations, such as diced fruits and berries in green salads, scallops with rosemary, or peaches with peppers, tickle the taste buds.

◆ **Be cool.** Add mint or cilantro to foods for a refreshing edge.

◆ **Use an artist's eye.** Let your plate be your canvas. Choose foods for their color, arrange them artfully, use garnishes for extra visual appeal, and pile the plate high—food should look satisfying, not skimpy.

THE NUTRIENTS in fruits and vegetables are fragile, so take home fresh, locally grown produce when it is available.

Shopping List

Keep these staples on hand and you'll never have trouble making creative, immune-tuning meals.

• Canned chick peas and black beans. Heat with garlic and turmeric and serve with brown rice and salsa for a fast, fiber-filled, nutrient-dense meal.

• Marinara sauce. Heat and mix with sauteed onions and garlic for added antioxidants.

• Frozen vegetables. Use as side dishes or to add quick color, flavor, and nutrients to soups, pilafs, stir-fries, and pasta dishes.

• Frozen fruits. Snack on unsweetened blueberries by the handful. Use anything that appeals in smoothies and on yogurt or cereal.

• Canned soups. Stock up on fiber-filled lentil, vegetable, minestrone, split pea, and black bean varieties. Research shows that eating soup before meals can reduce calorie intake by one-third.

• Frozen veggie burgers. They are low in fat and perfect topped with a dollop of ketchup for its flavonoids and lycopene (and, of course, its taste!).

• Canned seafood. Use albacore tuna, salmon, clams, sardines, and oysters in salads, soups, casseroles, and omelets for a dose of omega-3s and minerals.

• 100 percent whole-wheat pita pockets. Keep in the freezer, then thaw, toast, and stuff for sandwiches. Or cut into triangles to replace high-fat crackers.

• Quinoa. Although classified as a grain, this yummy nutty-flavored food is really the dried, protein-filled seed of a leafy plant. Use in place of rice.

• Canned nonfat chicken broth. Perfect for whipping up nourishing vegetable soups (add frozen veggies) or as a flavoring base for pilafs.

• Jerusalem artichoke pasta. Sold in many supermarkets, this "pasta" is made from flour ground from Jerusalem artichokes (tubers that taste like artichokes). It's a source of inulin, a carbohydrate thought to stimulate the immune system.

• Bottled condiments. Use liberal amounts of salsa, capers, olives, anchovies, crushed garlic, and roasted red peppers—they're inherently nutrient-rich.

Pamper Your Produce

For maximum retention of nutrients, produce should be labeled "handle with care." It's best to buy locally grown fruits and vegetables, which retain far more phytochemicals than anything that must travel a long distance to reach you. Opt for organic produce if you can; it is often grown in better soil, so it has a higher mineral content. Wash fruits and vegetables only when you're ready to use them. That way, the protective oils and other barriers that lock in freshness will stay intact. Proper storage is important, too. Many nutrients lie in or just beneath the skin, where light and heat can break them down. Here's a rundown of storage areas in the kitchen and which produce items keep best in each, plus shopping tips.

The Refrigerator

In crisper drawers. These compartments provide the perfect humid atmosphere for the following.

Apples. Buy tight-skinned fruits and refrigerate in an open plastic or paper bag to stop ripening and prevent mushiness. Keep for up to three weeks.

Asparagus. Kept at room temperature, asparagus would lose about half of its vitamin C content within two days. Choose small, fresh stalks that are uniform in size so that they cook consistently.

Carrots. Store in a loosely sealed plastic or paper bag for up to a week.

Green beans. Select unblemished, unwrinkled beans. Store for up to four days in a zip-top plastic bag.

Lettuce. Keep lettuce away from all fruits. Apples, for example, give off ethylene gas, which can cause brown spots on lettuce.

On open shelves. Refrigerator shelves are the place for any items, like the ones below, that need cool, circulating air to retain their nutrients.

Berries. Loosely cover with plastic or place in a paper bag. Use as soon as possible.

Corn. Wrap unhusked ears in a damp cloth and use within a day or two.

Cucumbers. Place on the top shelf, which is the warmest part of the refrigerator, so that ice crystals don't form around the seeds.

Green, red, and yellow peppers. Keep in a loosely sealed plastic or paper bag. Use within four days.

Herbs. Wrap them in a damp paper towel, place in a plastic bag, and refrigerate for up to five days.

Mushrooms. If you buy them in a cardboard container, remove the outer layer of plastic and wrap the container with paper towels. If you buy them loose, store them in a brown paper bag. Clean mushrooms by wiping them with a damp cloth or rinsing them quickly just before you use them.

The Countertop

Avocados, lemons, limes, mangoes, oranges, grapefruits, melons, nectarines, papayas, peaches, and plums. Keep in the coolest countertop area of the kitchen. Refrigerate only if fully ripened.

Tomatoes. Never refrigerate. Cold temperatures destroy the flavor and texture of the pulp. Instead, place stem-side down away from direct sunlight.

A Cool, Dark Place

Garlic. Store in a dry and ventilated area for up to 10 weeks. If garlic sprouts, it loses much of its pungency, but it's still edible.

Onions, potatoes, and root vegetables. Circulating air keeps them fresh, so put them in open baskets.

Who Says Fresh Is Best?

Surveys show that almost all North Americans (92 percent) think that the fresh vegetables sold in the supermarket contain far more vitamins and minerals than frozen. Wrong! A University of Illinois-Urbana study found that most "fresh" produce—after sitting for up to a week in a refrigerated truck or railroad car, then spending several more days in a store's cold case—contains significantly lower levels

FROZEN VEGETABLES are a fast source of fiber, nutrients, and antioxidants.

of vitamins A, C, and E than its frozen or canned counterpart, even without the canning liquid. This is because produce loses 10 to 50 percent of some nutrients between the time it is picked in the field and the moment it is served. But nutrient loss is halted as soon as vegetables are frozen or canned, which usually happens within hours of picking. With proper storage, the nutritional value is retained even after a year in the deep freeze. Texture, of course, is altered, but frozen vegetables make fine additions to soups, stews, and casseroles—especially when "garden" fresh is not available.

Antioxidant experts also tout dried fruit as a healthy option. Although some nutrients, especially vitamin C, are lost during drying, the fruit retains a wealth of health-promoting substances, including iron and fiber. It also doesn't spoil easily, isn't messy, and can help satisfy a craving for sweets.

Feast on Prime-Time Fish

Good fish is certainly good for you, but eating bad fish can really make you sick. Although safety standards exist, you still must be a wise consumer. How? First, buy from sources you trust. A fish market or seafood department in a food store should be clean, with the fish laid out not just on ice, but in a refrigerated display case.

If it's practical for you, select a whole fresh fish; you can judge its freshness more accurately. Whole fish should have a sheen—no slime and no discolorations. If the skin is leathery or has wrinkles, or if the tail is dried out, the fish has lost enough moisture to be past its prime. Look for clear, protruding eyes and bright pink or red gills. It's also important to take a whiff: The gills should smell like a fresh ocean breeze, not "fishy." Smoked fish should have a sheen and a fresh smoky aroma.

It's harder to recognize a truly fresh fillet. The flesh should be moist with no gaps between the flakes. Also, look along the bone line. The color there should be red, not brown. Opt for fillets or steaks that are freshly cut and on ice. Plastic wrapping can trap bacteria and make fish spoil more quickly.

◆ **How to store.** Pick up your fish at the end of your shopping trip to reduce the time it's unrefrigerated. Unpack, pat dry, cover loosely with plastic wrap, and store on a plate at the back of the bottom refrigerator shelf, where it's coldest. Wrapped in two layers of freezer paper, fish can be frozen for up to three months. Cook it immediately after thawing. Refreezing destroys the flavor and texture.

Build Up Your Frozen Assets

To make sure you always have healthful foods on hand, cook and freeze a few meals on the weekend. For the tastiest, most nutritious outcome, use only the best ingredients, and follow these tips:

1 Set your freezer temperature at zero. Food lasts longer when it's stored at colder temperatures.

2 Cook, puree, and freeze any kind of vegetable or fruit and use it, thawed, to enrich casseroles, soups, or stews. Also try blanching whole or cut-up vegetables. Experiments have shown that more nutrients are retained if vegetables are blanched, or plunged in boiling water for about three to four minutes before freezing. Blanching kills any bacteria and inactivates enzymes so that they cannot cause discoloration and disagreeable flavors. Fruits need not be blanched.

3 Undercook dishes you're preparing for the freezer. Subtract about five minutes from the usual cooking time for rice and noodles in particular. On their own, these starches freeze poorly, but they're fine in casseroles.

4 Pack freezables in airtight containers or heavy-duty zip-top plastic bags. Label each batch with the date, name of contents, and number of servings using a permanent ink marker.

5 Use your freezer to store and preserve herbs. First, dry them thoroughly (in the sun is easiest) or they will be mushy and discolored when thawed. De-stem and pack them loosely in freezer bags. They can be used either directly from the freezer or thawed.

6 Cool foods to room temperature before freezing. This helps prevent large ice crystals from forming during freezing and giving an "off" taste later when they melt.

7 Thaw meals by placing them in the refrigerator for 24 hours before reheating. Defrost with the wrapping on so that condensation forms outside of the wrap, not on the food. Cook as soon as defrosted, while the food is still cold.

Supplemental Insurance

Imagine how great it would be if you could take a pill to ensure that every cell within your body would perform at peak capacity—a state we call "perfect health." Impossible? Not necessarily.

Over the past decade, more than 10,000 scientific articles from every part of the world have imparted the same general message about the health effects of vitamins and minerals. Whether the experiment involves people, animals, or cells in test tubes, higher levels of vitamins and minerals are almost always associated with good cell performance, while lower levels are almost always associated with impaired cell performance. The reason is obvious: Vitamins and minerals are essential for initiating and promoting all of the biochemical processes that the body performs to maintain normal health. There's even some evidence that many vitamins positively influence the behavior of genes.

Food first. Scientists emphasize that food is the greatest source of these powerful "medicines." When you bite into an apple or chew on a carrot, you're getting a highly specific "combination package" of phytochemicals, vitamins, minerals, and other health-promoting substances.

Strong evidence supporting the benefits of fresh, unprocessed foods to the immune system first emerged almost 60 years ago, when Weston A. Price, an adventurous dentist from Cleveland, observed that the isolated populations he encountered in his worldwide travels were surprisingly unburdened by the diseases of industrialized nations. Price observed cultures free from tuberculosis (one of the most prevalent infections in his time), dental disease, cancer, and arthritis, in such far-flung places as Africa, the Andes Mountains, and New Zealand. These disease-resistant peoples ate foods they grew themselves or gathered from the wild. They were also physically active. When individuals from such cultures moved to the developed world, they fell prey to infectious and degenerative diseases. On returning to their native villages, Price's subjects often got well.

Although some of Price's theories were outlandish, his central observation still stands: The immune system functions best when the diet consists

PURITY AND POTENCY can vary from one brand to another, so ask your pharmacist to recommend a quality supplement.

mainly of plant foods complemented occasionally by small amounts of animal protein.

The Case for Supplements

How do nutrient deficiencies affect the immune system? Scientists have repeatedly observed that they reduce the vigor of T-cells. Furthermore, when a nutrient deficiency is treated and corrected, immune response improves. These findings show a direct and specific relationship between nutrition and immune-system functioning.

Unless you are careful about tracking and analyzing your diet, it's hard to be sure that you are taking in the nutrients you need in the appropriate amounts. Besides, eating something doesn't guarantee that you're absorbing its nutrients. Your habits (being on a very low-fat diet, for example), genes, or biochemistry can decrease your nutrient absorption, as can stress, illness, or intense physical exertion.

Researchers estimate that 35 to 40 percent of older people have suboptimal blood levels of more than one nutrient. Finding out which ones you may be lacking is impractical and expensive; you'd have to have both your dietary intake and blood levels of more than 52 different nutrients measured, something no reputable health professional would suggest. Therefore, the best bet for most people is to take a daily multivitamin-multimineral supplement. An all-in-one supplement is an especially good idea since some nutrients work best when combined with others. For peak immunity, choose a pill that contains all the following essential vitamins and minerals.

Vitamin C

Vitamin C, or ascorbic acid, works on several levels to support immune function. Besides enhancing the activity of immune cells, it is needed in the production of collagen, the principal protein found in all connective tissue. By helping maintain this tissue, vitamin C slows the spread of infections through the body.

◆ **The proof.** At least one study has shown that levels of vitamin C do not have to be very low to cause a decline in immune function. A three-month study done by U.S. researchers found that when otherwise healthy men aged 25 to 43 took in 20 mg or less of vitamin C a day, they showed a delayed reaction to a skin test designed to provoke an immune response. Another study has shown that vitamin C may prevent reblockage of arteries after angioplasty.

◆ **The dose.** The recommended daily allowance (RDA) of vitamin C is 90 mg a day for men and 75 mg a day for women. (Many RDAs are different for men and women due to the average woman's smaller body mass.) However, another recent study suggested that a higher dose—225 mg—is optimal for preventing disease.

Just because the RDA is on the low side, some people jump to the illogical conclusion that the more vitamin C you get, the better off you are. But taking more than 2,000 mg daily may cause headaches, increased urination, severe indigestion, or abnormal facial flushing. High doses may also affect the results of certain medical tests.

HEALTH HINT

Give It Time

If you're taking a specific supplement to treat a condition, wait a month or two before deciding if it's helpful. The effects are subtle. In fact, the real payoff may be that you'll avoid some illnesses you could get down the line rather than feeling remarkably better right now. In some ways, taking vitamins is like maintaining your car—act today instead of waiting until something breaks down.

Quick Tip

Once opened, vitamins are good for about a year, or until they pass their expiration date, whichever comes first. Heat, light, and exposure to air will make them degrade faster, so store them in a cool, dark place, like a cupboard.

Vitamin E

The story on vitamin E and immunity is long and positive. Vitamin E is present in higher concentrations in immune cells than in any other cells of the body. Vitamin E also prevents oxidative damage in cells—the type of damage linked to lowered immune response. Additionally, vitamin E "thins" the blood, allowing immune cells to navigate through the body more efficiently.

B-COMPLEX VITAMINS aren't the subjects of rave reviews as often as vitamins C and E, but they're just as important.

A caution to note: People taking medicine to prevent blood clots (Coumadin, aspirin, or garlic capsules) should talk to their doctor before taking vitamin E supplements, since the combined effects can pose a risk of excessive bleeding.

◆ **The proof.** Researchers at Boston's Tufts University studied 88 people aged 65 and older who took 60 mg, 200 mg, or 800 mg of vitamin E or a placebo daily for nearly eight months. The findings, reported in the *Journal of the American Medical Association:* Immune function rose in all three treatment groups. But those who took 200-mg doses of vitamin E showed the best response—a 65 percent improvement in an important measure of immune function known as the delayed-type hypersensitivity skin response. That group also had a much stronger antibody response to both the hepatitis B and tetanus vaccines. The fact that the 800-mg group didn't show a better response than the 200-mg group suggests that more isn't necessarily better.

◆ **The dose.** The RDA is 13 international units (IU) for men and 10 IU for women. Those numbers are based on a minimum requirement. Many experts recommend closer to 400 IU as an optimal dose. What does seem clear from current research is that too much—about 1,500 IU or more—has the opposite effect: It suppresses immunity.

GOOD QUESTION!
Is natural vitamin E better than synthetic?

Whether a vitamin is natural or not usually makes no difference. But E is an exception: Studies show that the natural variety (d-alpha-tocopherol) is more easily absorbed and retained by the body. That's because synthetic E (dl-alpha-tocopherol) is based on just one of several components in its natural counterpart. Natural E is more expensive, however, and makers of synthetic E usually add extra E to offset the difference.

B-Complex

Studies show that vitamins B_6 and B_{12} are particularly vital to the health of elderly people. Yet many older Canadians apparently are unable to absorb these vitamins well, resulting in a deficiency that is rarely diagnosed.

◆ **The proof.** A Tufts University study found that when healthy elderly people had vitamin B_6 almost completely taken out of their diets, their immune response went down. Even more telling was this finding: The amount of B_6 needed to restore strength to their immune systems was higher than the estimated average requirement of 2 mg. Most interesting of all: When participants were given

50 mg of B$_6$ daily, their immunity was boosted above the level it started at. Similarly, the *Annals of Internal Medicine* reported that low B$_{12}$ blood levels are linked with a poor immune response. Patients over 65 who had a subtle B$_{12}$ deficiency (half the group) mounted less of an immune response to a pneumonia vaccine.

◆ **The dose.** The RDAs for vitamin B$_1$ are 1.1 mg for women and 1.2 mg for men; for B$_2$: 1.1 mg (women) and 1.3 mg (men); for niacin: 14 mg (women) and 16 mg (men); for choline: 425 mg (women) and 550 mg (men). Men and women have the same RDAs for pantothenic acid: 5 mg; B$_6$: 1.3 mg; B$_{12}$: 2.4 mcg; folate: 400 mcg; and biotin: 30 mcg.

Iron

Iron's main function is to help red blood cells carry oxygen to all parts of the body. It does this by attaching itself to a protein called hemoglobin in red blood cells. Most people, especially premenopausal women, need dietary iron from sources such as red meat to avoid iron-deficiency anemia, a condition that leaves tissues starved for oxygen and more vulnerable to infection. Any loss of blood can lead to anemia. In fact, an estimated one in five menstruating women has anemia because of heavy menstrual periods.

◆ **The proof.** A double-blind, placebo-controlled trial of 42 non-anemic women with slightly low iron reserves found that iron supplements significantly increased the benefits they gained from exercise. And one study of 296 men with HIV infection linked high intake of iron to a decreased risk of developing AIDS six years later.

◆ **The dose.** The RDA for adults is 10 to 15 mg. Don't take iron supplements unless you need them. Iron overload is just as unhealthy as anemia.

WOMEN who eat iron-rich foods, such as red meat, chicken, and leafy greens, are unlikely to become iron deficient.

Magnesium

The importance of this mineral, especially in relation to immunity, is often overlooked. Magnesium is crucial for the growth of white blood cells and for their maturation into aggressive disease fighters. Low levels of magnesium in tissues are associated with lower levels of immunoglobulins and antibody-forming cells. Magnesium deficiency (which can be triggered by stress, among other things) also encourages the production of cell-damaging free radicals.

◆ **The proof.** Several studies show that various types of cancer, including lymphoma and leukemia, are more common in areas where there are low magnesium levels in the soil and, consequently, low levels in locally grown food. The association between high rates of lymphoma (cancer of immune-system cells) and low levels of magnesium strongly suggests a link between magnesium deficiencies and impaired immunity.

◆ **The dose.** The RDA for magnesium is 250 mg for men and 210 mg for women. Good food sources include tofu, almonds, cashews, and Brazil nuts.

Selenium

Selenium is an antioxidant that protects cells from free-radical damage. It is also a precursor to glutathione peroxidase, another important antioxidant, which is made chemically available to the body only with the help of selenium.

◆ **The proof.** A study tested selenium as a possible skin-cancer preventer in more than 1,300 patients. Participants received a placebo or 200 mcg of selenium a day for four and a half years and then were followed for another six

years. While the results did not show any reduction in skin cancer risk, the selenium group had a 37 percent reduction in overall cancer incidence and a 50 percent reduction in death from cancer. The effects appeared strongest for certain types of cancer: prostate (63 percent lower risk), colorectal (58 percent lower risk), and lung (53 percent lower risk).

Studies of geographical variation in cancer rates suggest that high levels of selenium in the soil are associated with reduced cancer risk. In addition, research on blood samples from large groups of people also shows that cancer is more common in people who have low blood levels of selenium and glutathione peroxidase.

◆ **The dose.** Although there is no RDA for selenium in Canada, experts agree a minimum of 100 mcg is required daily. To fit more in, eat Brazil nuts. One nut contains 120 mcg of selenium. Other good food sources include broccoli, seafood, poultry, and garlic, as well as grains such as oats and brown rice.

Many experts also recommend taking supplements of up to 400 mcg selenium a day. That's the safe upper limit, though; take a lower dose if you ordinarily eat

Easy-to-Swallow Advice

Supplements—whether vitamins, minerals, herbs, or micronutrients—can help you make up for what you miss in your diet and for any special needs caused by individual quirks of your biochemistry. These factors may be influenced by your overall health, your age, your genetic makeup, and your lifestyle. Keep in mind:

1 There are no magic bullets. **Good as they can be, supplements are just supplements. When it comes to strengthening your immune system, they're never a replacement for a healthy diet, exercise, stress-reducing routines, and good sleep habits.**

2 Consult a doctor who is supplement savvy. **If you are looking for a doctor who is up-to-date on current research, you may have to shop around. Make sure you take the advice of one who truly understands the value of supplements.**

3 It doesn't pay to take pills you don't need. **If you're taking supplements for a specific reason and you don't see an improvement after a month or two, or if your symptoms have worsened, consult your doctor before continuing to use it.**

some selenium-rich foods. At higher levels, selenium may cause a toxic reaction called selenosis, which is marked by loss of hair and damage to fingernails and toenails.

Zinc

Zinc is important in the maintenance of all body tissues. Inconclusive but widely reported research suggests that it may stave off infections by raising the quantity and quality of T-cells while helping to inhibit the replication of cold-causing viruses. Zinc is also needed to synthesize DNA, an essential part of growth and healing.

◆ **The proof.** In one study, lozenges containing 13.3 mg of elemental zinc were tested against a placebo in a group of 100 patients with cold symptoms. Both sets of patients took one lozenge every two hours while awake. The zinc group had significantly less coughing, nasal congestion, and other symptoms than the control group.

◆ **The dose.** Strict vegetarians are more prone to zinc deficiencies because they shun zinc-rich meats and seafood. Regular supplements of about 25 mg of zinc a day appear best for general immune tuning, but you need a higher dose (one 25-mg lozenge every two hours while you're awake) to battle a cold. Why lozenges only? Scientists think that the dissolving lozenge releases zinc to fight the cold virus at the exact site of infection—the mucous membranes in the mouth and throat.

More Immune-Tuning Compounds

In addition to the so-called "essential" vitamins—A, B, C, D, E, and K—cells need a number of other compounds to function properly. These enzymes, antioxidants, and protein-building blocks are vital to

VITALITY STEMS FROM getting enough of all the essential vitamins as well as some lesser known nutrients.

the immune system, but chances are you've never heard of them because they have not been studied as thoroughly as vitamins have. Consequently, researchers don't know all of their functions, let alone their possible medical applications. But some preliminary findings are nothing short of dramatic, making clear that our knowledge about how foods and nutrients can enhance health and healing is still very rudimentary. The following guide gives an overview of some of the unsung but readily available compounds that contribute to a strong immune system.

Alpha-Lipoic Acid

Alpha-lipoic acid (ALA) boosts levels of adenosine triphosphate, a chemical used in virtually every cell function. It's also a unique, broad-spectrum antioxidant capable of scavenging and destroying free radicals in both water and fat, which means it can affect cell membranes as well as cell interiors. ALA also allows the body to reuse several antioxidants that would ordinarily be eliminated after disabling unstable free radicals. For these reasons, ALA has been called "the universal antioxidant."

◆ **The proof.** Research in humans is limited, but results from animal studies are dramatic. In one experiment, almost all mice on a diet severely deficient in vitamin E

GRAPE SEED EXTRACT strengthens blood vessels, making it easier for immune cells to circulate around the body.

lost weight and became very sick. The exception: Mice that were fed the vitamin E–deficient diet—and given ALA—remained in perfect health. Other evidence indicates that ALA may be useful in the treatment of such conditions as diabetes, heavy-metal poisoning, and radiation damage, and there has been some very preliminary research suggesting that it suppresses replication of HIV and boosts immune function in AIDS patients. In Germany, ALA is a prescription drug used to treat nerve damage in diabetics.

◆ **The dose.** The body creates enough ALA to take care of basic metabolic needs, but ALA acts as an antioxidant only when it is present in excess. Since few foods (only yeast and liver) contain more than tiny amounts of ALA, the only way to create a surplus in the body is through supplements. For general immune support, doses of 50 to 150 mg are typical. Note: ALA is sometimes labeled "thioctic acid."

◆ **Safety considerations.** Though ALA appears to be safe (except for a few reports of allergic reactions), the long-term side effects of taking large supplemental doses are not known.

Coenzyme Q$_{10}$

Called CoQ for short, this remarkable coenzyme—a substance that's needed in order for other enzymes to carry out their jobs—is found in every cell of the body. It's required for several steps in the production of energy. Since being identified in 1957, CoQ has shown itself to be so important for normal body functioning that some researchers have taken to calling it "Vitamin Q." Animal studies suggest that it's a powerful immune stimulant, one that boosts antibody response and increases the numbers of granulocytes, specialized immune cells that contain toxic granules released mainly to fight parasitic infections.

In addition, CoQ may help suppress inflammation and also scavenge free radicals, helping protect our DNA from the kind of damage that, over time, causes cancer. As an antioxidant, CoQ also reduces your susceptibility to diabetes, chronic fatigue syndrome, heart disease, and a host of other ills.

◆ **The proof.** Although it's too soon to call CoQ a proven cancer fighter, a small Danish study of breast cancer patients found that those who took 390 mg of CoQ daily for several months had an improved immune-system response. Some patients experienced remission of their disease; one woman even became cancer-free. Further studies are needed to see if these results can be replicated. When CoQ was prescribed to open-heart surgery patients—100 mg was given daily for 14 days before and 30 days after the procedure—it led to faster recovery than a placebo. Preliminary data from studies of AIDS patients suggest that maintaining high levels of CoQ may slow the course of that disease.

◆ **The dose.** CoQ is present in small amounts in a wide variety of foods, but it is particularly high in organ meats such as heart, liver, and kidney, as well as in beef, soy oil, sardines, mackerel, and peanuts. The compound is fat-soluble, meaning the body needs fat to absorb it. Absorption is not typically a problem, though, since foods that contain CoQ are themselves high in fat. If you use supplements, look for a brand with an oil base. The general dosage is 30 to 60 mg taken twice a day with meals.

◆ **Safety considerations.** Side effects are rare, but some people notice a rapid heartbeat or upset stomach. CoQ may also intensify the effect of heart stimulants, so check with your doctor before using it if you're taking prescription heart medication.

Grape Seed Extract

Made from the tiny seeds of red grapes, this extract contains high concentrations of procyanidolic oligomers (PCOs), compounds that have antioxidant properties many times more powerful than those of vitamin C and vitamin E. PCOs are believed to exert a powerful, positive influence on even the tiniest blood vessels, increasing blood flow to the extremities and helping immune system cells travel quickly to their destinations. It may also help correct tumor-inducing damage to DNA. Its anti-inflammatory effect may help allergy sufferers.

◆ **The proof.** At least one test-tube study at the Creighton University School of Pharmacy and Allied Health Professions in Omaha, Nebraska, demonstrated that grape seed extract in high concentrations reduced the activity of breast cancer and lung cancer cells by as much as 47 percent.

◆ **The dose.** For antioxidant protection, the general dosage is 100 mg daily. Choose supplements standardized to contain 92 to 98 percent PCOs. Pine bark extracts, such as Pygnogenol (a brand of extract derived from the bark of maritime pines), contain the same active ingredient but are more expensive.

◆ **Safety considerations.** None known.

L-Carnitine

Originally isolated in ground beef, this amino acid derivative plays a critical role in the body's use of its fat stores and in keeping cells healthy, especially when they are under acute stress from chronic diseases such as diabetes and heart disease. Research suggests that it plays an important role in overall cardiovascular health. L-carnitine also appears to increase oxygen intake, especially in highly trained athletes, although not all research confirms this. Like CoQ and so many other compounds discussed in this chapter, L-carnitine also has the ability to act as an antioxidant.

◆ **The proof.** Low levels of L-carnitine are often seen in patients with HIV infection. A pilot study, published in the journal *Blood,* found that treating HIV-infected people with six g a day of L-carnitine for six months significantly strengthened their white blood cell response.

◆ **The dose.** L-carnitine is not an essential amino acid because the body can synthesize it from other amino acids, but sometimes our production of it is slow (especially when we are sick). Meat and dairy foods tend to be rich sources of L-carnitine. In general, the redder the meat, the higher the L-carnitine content. Grains, fruits, and vegetables contain little or no L-carnitine, so strict vegetarians should consider taking up to 100 mg a day in supplement form. Purchase it in individual supplements or together with other amino acids. Blood levels are lower in pregnant women, apparently because of increased demand from the fetus, so pregnant women may want to ask their doctors about taking an L-carnitine supplement.

◆ **Safety considerations.** Occasionally, at very high doses, L-carnitine reportedly causes nausea, diarrhea, and upset stomach.

{ "It is the body that is the hero, not science, not antibiotics, not machines or new devices." }

—RONALD J. GLASSER, M.D. / PEDIATRIC NEPHROLOGIST

The Healthy Pleasure of Food

Such self-control! That's a compliment nearly everyone trying to stick to a healthy diet loves to hear. But when it comes to food, an attitude of rigid self-denial won't get you very far. Why not? Because eating should be enjoyable. If it isn't, you'll be back to your old habits in no time flat.

Dieting, the way most people do it, simply doesn't work. It's stressful, time-consuming, and inevitably unsuccessful. Sooner or later you fall off the wagon, and when you do, your apparent failure of will can make you feel like a quitter. And there's nothing healthy about that.

Truth be told, incorporating healthier foods in your diet doesn't require any heroic acts of will-power. It takes only minor adjustments in your everyday eating—small changes that add up to last-ing results. With a bit of planning and a belief in the pleasure principle—that is, the idea that it's your right to enjoy great-tasting food every day—it's actually easy to eat for better health. The more satis-fying your meals, the less likely you are to stray.

A Different Way of Thinking

From now on, throw out the idea of trying to achieve a 100 percent perfect diet. It isn't realistic. Commit instead to being conscious of and excited about eat-ing nutritious foods, then delight in the experience. Your goal starting today is to make sure that what you eat is not just good for you, but good tasting, too. Also take time to savor every forkful of flavor, lingering over meals and snacks. To enhance your pleasure and put success within reach:

◆ **Focus on variety.** We all have a natural instinct to eat a variety of foods to stimulate our taste buds and improve the nutritional quality of our diet. But too often we satisfy that drive the wrong way— by sampling many types of sweets, say, rather than many types of vegetables. Instead of doing that, try, over the course of a day, to get your carbohydrates and proteins from varied sources—whole grains or starchy vegetables and nuts or tofu. Eat frequent mini-meals—they'll make it easier to find variety and help you avoid excessive hunger. In restaurants, opt for two appetizers rather than a main course to sample a wider assortment of foods and enjoy even more taste sensations.

◆ **Use flavor boosters to make foods come alive.** Slather tangy, grainy mustard on vegetable sandwiches to make them downright delicious. Sprinkle Worcestershire or soy sauce on steamed broccoli to add savory richness, and add a little fresh, grated ginger to give it a sweet, spicy bite. Pump up low-calorie salad dressings with the aroma of cumin and cinnamon.

◆ **Give in to cravings sometimes.** Once in a while, indulge in your favorite "forbidden" foods. That way, you won't feel deprived, so healthy eating will be easier in the long run. If you want a serving of ice cream, for example, balance it out by cutting back on calories from other dairy and fat sources.

UNCOMMON KNOWLEDGE
Brave New Vegetables

No question about it: Eating the right foods decreases your risk for deadly diseases. But coming soon are superfoods that won't just decrease risk—they'll all but guarantee that you won't get certain illnesses. Already, animal studies have shown that genetically modified cherry tomatoes can increase antibody production against respiratory syncytial virus, a potentially serious infection in young children and the elderly. And researchers at New York state's Cornell University report preliminary success with giving human volunteers potatoes laced with an edible vaccine against the Norwalk virus, a common cause of food poisoning.

{ "Food is a psychologically satisfying, enjoyable part of life. It should stay that way, even when you're trying to eat healthfully." }

—JANET WALBERG RANKIN, PH.D. / PROFESSOR OF HUMAN NUTRITION, VIRGINIA TECH UNIVERSITY

Nature's Pharmacy

Thousands of years ago—long before anyone knew anything about bacteria and viruses—healers were using herbal tonics to strengthen the body's "shield" against disease. Now, modern scientists are finding that many of those ancient remedies really do rev up the immune response.

Herbal Immune Boosters

Herbal medicines are Nature's gift of health. Derived from plants or plant products, they are loaded with properties that have the power to heal. But herbal remedies can also be toxic.

The same ingredients that exert a desired effect in the body may also, under certain circumstances, cause unexpected problems—problems that aren't always reported in headline-grabbing stories about an herb's healing powers. It can be tough to separate fact from fiction, since hype still reigns in media reports. It's often not clear that much of the research cited is based on test-tube or animal studies and not on studies in humans. Closer examination of how these "amazing natural cures" affect people is needed to know if their potential benefits extend to us.

To help you cut though the confusion, this chapter presents a straightforward guide to herbs considered to have immune-enhancing effects. Time has shown that, in general, these herbs are safe—if you follow the label instructions and keep these important dos and don'ts in mind.

Get a diagnosis. Never use herbs to treat symptoms without being certain what is causing those symptoms. Check with your doctor before using herbs if you have a chronic health condition or are pregnant or nursing. Consult a pediatrician or other expert before giving herbal products to children, especially those under five.

Stay skeptical. If you consult an herbalist, ask about his or her training and experience in treating people with your condition. Avoid anyone who wants you to discontinue standard medical care or who refuses to communicate with your doctor.

Do what the label says. Herbs may vary in potency from manufacturer to manufacturer, so follow the dosage instructions on the label, even if they are different from advice you might read elsewhere.

ECHINACEA, applied as a poultice to cuts and burns, may stimulate tissue repair and healing.

ASTRAGALUS ROOT, sliced and dried, helps fight infections. It can be boiled with other herbs to produce a medicinal soup.

Don't double up.
Never take herbs and drugs that have the same effect, such as the antidepressant herb St. John's wort and the drug Prozac.

Ask your pharmacist. Some herbs interact with drugs, especially blood thinners, sedatives, and antidepressants. (See page 99 for more information.) Many pharmacists have computer programs that alert them to any dangerous interactions among medications you are taking.

Listen to your body. Even if you have no known allergies, you might develop an allergic reaction to an herb. If you notice unusual symptoms, stop taking the herb and consult a doctor or an allergist. If you have trouble breathing after taking an herb, dial 911.

Champion Immune Enhancers

Advocates of both natural and conventional medicine have been impressed by these two herbal remedies' ability to stimulate the immune response.

Astragalus

Astragalus membranaceus
Long the tonic of choice among traditional Asian herbalists for treating people prone to infections, astragalus heightens the effect of interferon, the body's natural antiviral agent. It is also thought to increase T-cell activity.

◆ **Discoveries.** The best evidence to date for its immune-stimulating effects comes from the University of Texas Medical Center in Houston. Test-tube studies there found that the polysaccharides (a type of carbohydrate) in astragalus restored function to cancer patients' damaged immune cells.

VITAL STATISTICS: HERBAL REMEDIES

70 percent
Percentage of Canadian supplement and herb manufacturers who import ingredients

43 percent
Percentage of Canadian health product and ingredient imports from the United States

95–98 percent
Projected percentage increase in Canadian sales over the next five years

41 percent
Percentage of Canadian natural health stores in Ontario

90 percent
Percentage of retail stores that are Canadian owned

◆ **Put astragalus to work.** Simmer three tablespoons of dried, shredded root in three cups of water or broth for 30 minutes; drink one cup three times a day. For supplements, follow label directions.

◆ **Safety considerations.** Astragalus is not recommended for people with autoimmune disorders, such as multiple sclerosis. It also may interfere with immunosuppressive drugs.

Echinacea

Echinacea angustifolia, E. pallida, E. purpurea
These three North American plants were the most widely used medicines of the Plains Indians. Today, people around the globe use them to promote resistance to colds and flu by boosting certain immune defenses, including interferon, T-cells, and natural killer (NK) cells. Echinacea's polysaccharides (carbohydrate molecules) also help tissues regenerate, making the herb useful for healing wounds.

◆ **Discoveries.** German research has uncovered a host of infection-fighting properties in these remarkable plants. In one trial, 108 people prone to upper-respiratory infections took either a placebo or 4 ml of fresh-pressed juice of *E. purpurea* leaves twice a day for eight weeks as a preventive measure. Those taking echinacea enjoyed almost twice as many

BORAGE blossoms have a cucumber-like taste. Try freezing them in ice cubes and add them to punch.

infection-free days as the others. When they did get sick, their symptoms were less severe and shorter lived.

Echinacea's best proven use, however, is as a treatment for colds and flu. Three placebo-controlled studies provide the proof. In one, 199 volunteers who considered themselves especially susceptible to colds were randomly assigned a daily dose of 240 mg of *E. purpurea* extract or a placebo to be taken at the first sign of a cold. The echinacea was given in two tablets daily for eight days. Doctors considered the echinacea effective in 68 percent of cases; the placebo was effective in only 40 percent of cases.

Echinacea may have other benefits, too. Studies of *E. purpurea* extract published in the journal *Immunopharmacology* showed it may enhance immune response in patients with chronic fatigue syndrome and AIDS, as measured by NK cell function. However, there is much debate about the safety of echinacea in patients with AIDS.

◆ **Put echinacea to work.** Take one to two teaspoons of standardized extract of *E. purpurea* three times daily at the very first sign of illness and continue for eight to ten days. As a general immune system stimulant, herbalists often advise taking echinacea in cycles: 300 mg daily for ten days; none for one

week; repeat. The reason is that the herb is thought to lose its effectiveness if taken continuously.

◆ **Safety considerations.** Don't take echinacea if you have a systemic disease, such as tuberculosis or an autoimmune disorder, or if you take immuno-suppressive drugs. Echinacea has little effect in people with allergies, whose immune systems already are working at capacity most of the time.

More Plants for Your Medicine Chest

The herbs listed below are used by alternative practitioners—and some doctors—to enhance the immune response directly or indirectly (for instance, by promoting better sleep).

A garden of health...

Many herbs can be grown in home gardens, but only certain plant parts have medicinal effects.

HERB/ MEDICINAL PART

Borage: leaves, flowers

Calendula: flowers

Echinacea: flowers, seeds, leaves, stems, roots

Elder: berries, flowers

Lemon balm: leaves

St. John's wort: flowers, leaves

Yarrow: flowers, stems

Berberine Herbs

Berberis vulgaris (Barberry),
B. aquifolium, also known as
  Mahonia aquifolium (Oregon grape)
  Historically, these herbs have been used to treat skin problems and cleanse the blood by removing toxins. Both contain berberine, an antimicrobial compound shown to work against some bacteria, yeast, fungi, and protozoa, especially those that cause cholera.

◆ **Discoveries.** Test-tube research suggests berberine may slow abnormal cell growth and reduce inflammation, making it useful as a psoriasis treatment. When 443 people with psoriasis used an Oregon grape ointment topically for 12 weeks, 74 percent of the group reportedly improved.

◆ **Put berberine to work.** For throat, urinary, gastrointestinal, or respiratory inflammation or infection, steep

2 to 4 g dried root for 10 minutes; drink daily for five to seven days. For skin problems, use a topical cream or ointment containing 10 percent berberine extract; in general, these should be applied three times daily to affected areas.

◆ **Safety considerations.** Do not take internally during pregnancy; berberine may trigger contractions.

Borage

Borago officinalis
Researchers recently determined that borage seeds are an excellent source of gamma linolenic acid (GLA), a fatty acid that is used by the body to produce prostaglandin E1, one of several natural chemicals that reduce inflammation. GLA also may inhibit the spread of tumors by restricting blood vessel growth.

◆ **Discoveries.** A small British study of women with breast cancer showed that taking a cocktail of GLA (which also is found in evening primrose oil) and the anticancer drug tamoxifen significantly sped up the women's response to the medication. High doses of GLA may help treat rheumatoid arthritis, especially when combined with conventional treatments.

◆ **Put borage to work.** Borage seed oil is sold in capsules; follow directions.

◆ **Safety considerations.** Only the seeds are used. Borage leaves contain alkaloids that can damage the liver.

Buying Herbal Supplements

1. Note the form of the herb listed on the package. When possible, select a standardized extract. Standardization ensures that each dosage contains the same percentage of active compounds. (Even plants of the same species can vary greatly in the quantity and strength of these compounds. Only with standardization can you be sure you're getting the right amount.) Otherwise, choose a product labeled "whole herb." These contain all of the herb's distinct compounds in the ratio nature provided.

2. Check the expiration or best-if-used-by date. Discard the product if the date has passed.

3. Read any health warnings, cautions, and contraindications to be certain that the herb is appropriate for you.

Don't expect to find any specific therapeutic benefits listed on the label. Because herbs are classified as dietary supplements, not medications, manufacturers are prohibited by law from claiming that their products help prevent or treat specific health conditions.

Elder

Sambucus nigra
Antioxidants seem to give this herb its antiviral properties. Elder is used to soothe sore throats and promote fever in cold and flu patients—a sign that the immune response has been activated.

◆ **Discoveries.** In test tube studies, a standardized elderberry extract was shown to inhibit a variety of flu viruses. Also, when researchers gave 27 people who had just come down with the flu either a placebo or an elderberry extract, 93 percent of the elderberry group improved after two days, compared to 25 percent of the placebo group.

◆ **Put elder to work.** If using a syrup, follow label directions. Or simmer two teaspoons of dried flowers in one cup of water for 10 minutes; drink several times daily. Elder flowers, soaked in hot water, are used as a remedy against acne.

◆ **Safety considerations.** All products made from elder leaves or bark are for external use only.

ELDERBERRIES are entirely edible and may be used to make wine or jam.

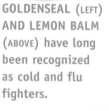

GOLDENSEAL (LEFT) **AND LEMON BALM** (ABOVE) **have long been recognized as cold and flu fighters.**

in Denmark showed that ginseng can stimulate white blood cells to clear bacterial infections (in this case, a type of chronic pneumonia) more effectively, as well as reduce damage to affected cells. Other data suggest that ginseng may cut the risk of cancer, particularly of the stomach.

◆ **Put ginseng to work.** To use as a general health tonic, steep one teaspoon of finely chopped dried root in hot water for 10 to 15 minutes. Or choose capsules containing 100 to 200 mg of extract standardized to contain 4 to 7 percent ginsenosides and take twice a day. Take for up to three months, followed by a two-week hiatus.

◆ **Safety considerations.** The leading herbal authority, Germany's Commission E, reports no side effects.

Ginseng

Panax ginseng

Ginseng is renowned as an adaptagen, so called because it helps the body adapt to stresses of all sorts. It also purportedly has the power to help the body recover from illness, increase physical and mental stamina, and stave off fatigue. Its chief active ingredients, ginsenosides, are credited with the ability to switch from stimulating to sedating effects, based on the body's needs. A related species, American ginseng *(P. quinquefolius)*, has a similar chemical makeup, but its use is not as well-researched.

◆ **Discoveries.** The most convincing investigation was a 1996 double-blind study (neither the researchers nor the subjects knew who took ginseng versus a placebo) of 501 volunteers. It found a significant improvement in quality of life (rated on such issues as depression, personal satisfaction, energy level, sex life, and sleep) in people who took 40 mg of ginseng extract and a multivitamin daily, compared to those who only took a multivitamin. Animal experiments at University Hospital of Copenhagen

Goldenseal

Hydrastis canadensis

A native to North America and one of the best-selling herbal remedies in Canada, goldenseal root is used to treat colds, urinary tract infections, gum inflammation, and wounds.

◆ **Discoveries.** Goldenseal is known to combat microbes, although it is not clear how potent this effect is when the herb is taken internally. It also has been credited with curing warts, which are caused by viruses. Applied externally, it soothes hemorrhoids.

◆ **Put goldenseal to work.** At the first signs of a cold or the flu, take 250 to 500 mg three times a day, or take 10 to 15 drops of tincture three or four times daily for five days. Dab tincture directly on warts.

◆ **Safety considerations.** Avoid if you have heart disease or high blood pressure.

> "Herbs and plants are medical jewels gracing the woods, fields, and lanes, which few eyes see and few minds understand."
>
> —CAROLUS LINNAEUS / NATURALIST (1707–1778)

Lemon balm

Melissa officinalis

Since the days of ancient Rome, lemon balm—named for its delicate lemony perfume—has been a favorite remedy for insomnia, colds, and circulatory problems. Its chemical constituents have been shown to inactivate viruses, reduce inflammation, and ease gastrointestinal complaints.

◆ **Discoveries.** Research has documented that lemon balm's active components inhibit the herpes virus (both simplex type 1, which causes cold sores, and simplex type 2, or genital herpes). Studies have shown that, applied topically, lemon balm speeds the healing of herpes lesions and lengthens the time between recurrences.

◆ **Put lemon balm to work.** To ease insomnia, pour one cup of hot water over one to three teaspoons of lemon balm leaf, steep for 10 minutes, strain, and drink one cup three times a day. Treat herpes flare-ups by applying lemon balm cream in a 70:1 standardized concentration four times daily until blisters heal.

◆ **Safety considerations.** The herb may cause excessive fatigue, especially if taken with a sedating drug. Don't take it internally if you have a thyroid disorder.

HEALTH HINT

One to Shun

Some books about herbs advise using comfrey roots and leaves to heal external wounds and stomach ulcers. Those benefits are not well-documented, but the dangers of comfrey are. Many varieties contain alkaloids that can cause liver damage and may promote cancer if taken internally or applied to broken skin.

Licorice

Glycyrrhiza glabra

Glycyrrhizin, an active component in licorice, raises interferon levels, inhibits some viruses, reduces inflammation, and helps to suppress coughs.

◆ **Discoveries.** Glycyrrhizin may block the formation of "giant cells," which, in HIV-positive people, signal that the infection is moving to active AIDS. It also may stop the flu; mice injected with normally lethal amounts of flu virus lived when treated with glycyrrhizin.

◆ **Put licorice to work.** Simmer two teaspoons of powdered root in one cup of water, strain, and drink three times daily. Use real licorice root; most licorice candy sold in the United States has no active ingredient.

◆ **Safety considerations.** Anyone with kidney, liver, or blood-pressure problems should not use licorice.

MILK THISTLE enhances the liver's function, which, in turn, helps decrease the risk of many ills.

Milk Thistle

Silybum marianum

The seeds of the milk thistle plant have been used for centuries to protect the liver. Their major active component, silymarin, reportedly helps counteract the effects of alcohol, heavy metals, drugs, solvents, pesticides, and other toxins by stabilizing the

On the horizon...medicinal mushrooms

Touted for centuries in Asia as immune-system boosters, a variety of mushrooms are being studied by scientists to verify those powers. Although their benefits now exist in theory, early findings suggest that some mushrooms may truly be medicinal.

CORDYCEPS *(Cordyceps sinensis)*

An adaptagen like ginseng, cordyceps extracts have been shown to kill human leukemia cells in test tubes. Other research indicates that cordyceps enhances immune-cell activity in patients on dialysis. One theory why these and other mushrooms have such potent antimicrobial properties: To survive in moist, dark places, they needed to develop chemical weapons to prevent attacks by viruses and bacteria.

MAITAKE *(Grifola frondosa)*

Japanese clinicians have long used maitake to improve immune function and treat some cancers. Studies have focused on its tumor-fighting constituent, D-fraction—also called grifolan, a beta-glucan polysaccharide, or chain of sugar molecules. Some scientists think it may help stabilize blood glucose levels, possibly preventing or lessening the effects of diabetes, including hypertension and high cholesterol.

REISHI *(Ganoderma lucidum)*

Test-tube and human studies have shown that reishi is rich in a long list of complex phytochemicals that appear to provide antiallergic, anti-inflammatory, antiviral, antibacterial, and antioxidant benefits. Cancer patients report less pain and better appetites after taking it. Additionally, a protein isolated from reishi—Ling Zhi-8—appears to reduce the risk of transplant rejection, possibly a sign that reishi acts directly on the immune system. Reishi also is reputed to elevate mood.

CORIOLUS *(Coriolus versicolor)*

Research indicates that PSK, an extract of this mushroom, contains natural cancer-fighting substances. Japanese studies have shown that it enhances immune recovery in sick mice. In one trial, half of a group of people undergoing radiation treatment for lung, colon, and breast cancers took PSK, while the other half took a placebo. Survival rates were about 20 percent higher among those given PSK. Study subjects took about three g of the dried extract daily, divided into five doses.

outer membrane of liver cells. In Europe, emergency-room doctors use a drug derived from milk thistle to save the lives of people who accidentally ingest the deathcap mushroom.

◆ **Discoveries.** Clinical trials have shown that silymarin revs up the immune response. It also protects the liver from harmful by-products of the detoxification process and helps liver cells regenerate after they've been injured.

◆ **Put milk thistle to work.** A protective dosage for healthy people is 200 mg of extract standardized to contain 70 to 80 percent silymarin.

◆ **Safety considerations.** On occasion, milk thistle may have a mild laxative effect.

St. John's Wort

Hypericum perforatum
Used medicinally for thousands of years and once thought to have magic powers, today this herb is prescribed by German doctors about 20 times more often than Prozac as an antidepressant. Because

St. John's wort has antimicrobial effects, physicians in Germany also recommend it for external use on superficial wounds and bruises. Its antiseptic properties are attributed to two of its active components, hypericin and pseudo-hypericin.

◆ **Discoveries.** Its antidepressant qualities are well documented in Canada and use as a prescription antidepressant is gaining popularity in the medical field. Research is more sparse on its germ-fighting abilities, although one report claimed first-, second-, and third-degree burns treated with a St. John's wort ointment healed three times faster than similar burns did when treated with conventional methods—with less scarring.

◆ **Put St. John's wort to work.** Three times a day, take 300 mg of a standardized extract that contains 0.3 percent hypericin or 5 percent hyperforin.

◆ **Safety considerations.** St. John's wort may interact with several medications (see page 99). It also may cause photosensitivity in fair-skinned people; be cautious about sun exposure, including protection of the eyes, while taking this herb.

QUIZ: ARE YOU HERB SAVVY?

1 St. John's wort can be used to help heal wounds. ○ TRUE ○ FALSE

2 Licorice root (LEFT) is an immune-system booster. ○ TRUE ○ FALSE

3 If a book or an article lists a different dosage than the product's label, follow the label. ○ TRUE ○ FALSE

4 Many herbal remedies are as potent as drugs. ○ TRUE ○ FALSE

5 In sensitive people, natural herbal medicines may have adverse effects even in low doses. ○ TRUE ○ FALSE

6 Standardized extracts help ensure proper dosing. ○ TRUE ○ FALSE

All are true. Count the number of times you answered correctly.
FOUR OR MORE Great! You have a good basic understanding of the recognized benefits and safe use of herbs, yet are properly cautious and skeptical.
THREE OR LESS Your herbal wisdom needs bolstering. For some well-researched information, see the Canadian Health Network's web site at www.canadian-health-network.ca/1alternative_health.html.

Yarrow

Achillea millefolium

Traditionally, yarrow is used to stop bleeding and promote wound healing, hence its many nicknames including "nosebleed" and "wound wort." It also reportedly helps alleviate colds and sore throats.

◆ **Discoveries.** Healing chemicals identified in yarrow include two potent anti-inflammatories. Another chemical obtained from yarrow, achilletin, has been shown to stop bleeding in animals. Japanese investigators recently isolated three antitumor compounds from yarrow. Animal tests suggest that these compounds may lead to new chemotherapy drugs for leukemia.

◆ **Put yarrow to work.** Prepare an infusion by steeping one to two teaspoons of dried yarrow in one cup boiling water for 10 minutes; drink up to three cups daily. The infusion also may be applied to cuts, scratches, rashes, bruises, and chapped skin.

◆ **Safety considerations.** Do not use to treat large, deep, or infected wounds. Extended use may make the skin more sensitive to sunlight. Yarrow also may cause reactions in people who are allergic to ragweed or other members of the daisy family.

CAT'S CLAW'S anti-inflammatory compounds may help people with arthritis.

Cat's Claw

Uncaria tomentosa, U. guianensis

A story passed down by Peruvian Indians tells of a hungry hunter who, about 2,000 years ago, came upon a jaguar clawing at a vine and drinking the water seeping from it. Right after the animal finished drinking, it made a successful kill. The hunter decided to drink from the vine, too. The next day, he woke up full of newfound strength that led him to a successful kill as well.

Ever since, the Indians have relied on the vine to improve vigor and stamina, treat inflammation and infection, and help the body recover from illness. But it wasn't widely known until the late 1960s, when a European teacher, Arturo Brell, and a U.S. professor, Eugene Whitworth, came across and studied cat's claw samples. Although they found many active components, they didn't market their discovery, but others did. Today, it is widely used as an immune-tuning wonder herb. Despite its name, no cats are used in making cat's claw products!

◆ **Discoveries.** Animal studies at Albany Medical College in New York found that cat's claw prevented the stomach irritation associated with such anti-inflammatory medications as ibuprofen—damage that can make the stomach susceptible to infection. When the same researchers exposed human cells to peroxynitrite, an oxidant that causes cell death, cells that also were exposed to cat's claw were unharmed.

◆ **Put cat's claw to work.** Boil two tablespoons of bark in one pint of water for 10 minutes; steep five minutes, strain and drink throughout the day. Or take a 20 to 60 mg capsule of standardized extract with 4 percent alkaloids once daily.

◆ **Safety considerations.** None known.

YARROW flowers and leaves reportedly contain more than 100 biologically active compounds.

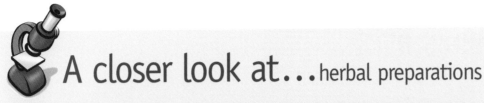

A closer look at...herbal preparations

Although the fresh leaves and roots of medicinal plants are sometimes tossed in salads or served as vegetables, for healing purposes they traditionally are transformed and taken in other ways. In addition to tablets and capsules, common preparations include:

INFUSIONS AND DECOCTIONS

Infusions are made by covering the fresh or dried leaves, flowers, or stems of a single herb or blend of herbs with boiling water and steeping in a covered container for up to 10 minutes. The usual ratio is one ounce of dried herb to one pint of water. Decoctions are made by placing the plant parts in cold water, bringing the mixture to a boil, and then simmering for 10 to 20 minutes to produce a more potent brew.

TINCTURES

These liquids are made by soaking dried or fresh herbs for several weeks to extract and intensify their active components. The herbs are usually soaked in alcohol (such as vodka) because it acts as a preservative as well as extracting the plant's active components, but nonalcoholic versions can be made using vinegar or glycerin. Because tinctures generally are much stronger, volume for volume, than infusions or decoctions, doses are smaller.

SYRUPS

Often herbs don't taste very good, especially to children. To disguise their flavor and make them more palatable, herbal tinctures, decoctions, or infusions are sometimes mixed with fruit extracts, molasses, cane sugar, or honey. (Caution: Never give honey to children under two years of age because it may cause botulism.) Syrups also make soothing remedies for coughs and sore throats because they coat irritated tissues.

OINTMENTS

An ointment is a salve that does not penetrate the skin like a cream but protects it and delivers active herbal ingredients to sore or swollen areas. Ointments may be made in a double boiler by melting two ounces of beeswax, petroleum jelly, or vegetable lanolin. Once this base is liquid, add some finely chopped fresh herbs, an essential oil, or a tincture. (You may add up to two ounces of fresh herbs or 80–120 drops of oil or tincture.) Simmer the mixture for up to 20 minutes, strain, pour into a glass container, and allow to harden.

Why Herbs Work

You saw it on the news or took the recommendation of a friend and now you are... delighted? Disappointed? **The difference, sometimes, is whether or not you believe the herb will work.**

Start talking about herbal medicine in most circles and you're bound to encounter a committed skeptic, someone who sneeringly attributes every and any health benefit linked to herbal medicine to the "placebo effect"—the idea that if we really believe something will help us get better, it will. Guess what: That's true, at least some of the time. But that's not a reason to automatically deny herbs a place in the modern treatment mix. If it were, you'd have to throw out 80 percent of conventional medicines, too. According to a study by the U.S. Office of Technology Assessment, "only 20 percent of modern medical remedies in common use have been scientifically proven to be effective .... It is not that these treatments do not offer benefits: Most of them do. But the benefits may come from the placebo effect, in which the very act of undergoing treatment helps the patient recover."

bearing on the remedy's effectiveness. Similarly, doctors say that if there are several treatment options, patients usually will do better when they make the choice themselves, after the doctor outlines the possible side effects and outcomes.

Is it surprising that our beliefs and our physical health are so intertwined? Not to scientists and doctors who know that the immune system and the brain are intimately connected. Without a doubt, what occurs in the brain, including thoughts, can produce changes in the immune response through various routes, including specialized nerve pathways and chemical messengers. The result may be to impair or enhance aspects of immune function, something that Chapter 6, "Immunity and the Mind," will explore in greater detail. Does this mean you should dismiss the possibility that the complex compounds in plants might have a "real" effect on your body?

DOCTORS don't routinely discuss herbal remedies; bring up the subject yourself.

> ## HEALTH HINT
>
> ### *Yackety-Yak*
>
> Approach any recommended plant-derived or "natural" remedy with an inquiring mind. Ask questions. Seek answers from qualified experts rather than relying on advice from a clerk in a health-food store, who may not have special training or knowledge.

Placebo Power

Researchers say that the placebo effect is enhanced when patients take the time to search out something that might improve their health. Although the psychological and physiological mechanisms underlying the effect are complex and poorly understood, it seems that going out, finding, and taking a remedy (even an over-the-counter cough syrup) gives us a sense of control over our health, which has a

SOME DON'T MIX

Medicinal herbs contain powerful, pharmacologically active compounds. Because of this, you should always tell your doctor if you are using herbal medicines, particularly if he or she is plans to prescribe medication for you or if you already are taking any prescription or nonprescription drugs.

HERB	PHARMACEUTICALS	POTENTIAL INTERACTIONS
ASTRAGALUS, ECHINACEA	Immunosuppressive drugs	These herbs are known to stimulate the immune system, so taking them may counter the effects of drugs prescribed to tone down the immune response, including some treatments for allergies and autoimmune disorders.
GARLIC	Lipid-lowering agents (such as Lipitor, Lopid, or Zocor); hypoglycemic agents, including insulin; aspirin or blood-thinning medications; blood-pressure lowering drugs	May enhance the action of these medications. For example, one small study showed that blood clotting time doubled for patients taking Warfarin and garlic. May increase the risk of unusual bleeding after surgery; discontinue garlic supplements several weeks before invasive medical procedures.
LEMON BALM	Thyroid medications, sedatives	May alter or boost the action of these drugs.
LICORICE	Blood-pressure lowering drugs; hormone therapies; cortico-steroids; some cardiac drugs	May decrease effectiveness of some of these medications and increase the effectiveness of others.
ST. JOHN'S WORT	Antibiotics; decongestants; oral contraceptives; antidepressants; protease inhibitors; and cardiac or blood-thinning drugs	May alter the effectiveness of these and many other medications by as much as 50 percent. Also may dangerously elevate blood pressure if taken with MAO-inhibitors (a type of antidepressant) or trigger drowsiness, restlessness, sweating, or other symptoms when taken with other antidepressants, including Paxil, Prozac, or Zoloft.

The studies cited earlier in this chapter show that such blanket rejection would be foolish. Herbal medicine is complicated. While some herbs may do no more than exert a placebo effect, others clearly contain pharmacologically active chemicals. You should experiment—safely.

Until recently, it was almost impossible to find scientifically reliable studies on the safety and effectiveness of herbs. Reports often were anecdotal—based on the unconfirmed testimonials of anonymous patients—or they relied on data from the manufacturers' own labs, published in obscure journals and never confirmed independently.

Today, the situation is improving. Validated research findings have been appearing in major medical journals in recent years, and more are on the way. In 1997, the federal government reacted to the increased public interest in natural health products when it asked the Standing Committee on Health to establish guidelines to ensure consumers a balance between choice and medical safety. As a result, Health Canada created the Natural Health Products Directorate (www.hc-sc.gc.ca/hpb/onhp).

Although more information on herbal medicine is available today, always use appropriate caution when experimenting with herbal remedies. Use them only with ailments that you're certain aren't serious—the kinds that almost always clear up on their own with time, such as colds. Otherwise, use herbs only with your doctor's knowledge, especially if you have a serious or chronic medical condition. A University of California at San Francisco study found that asthma sufferers who used alternative therapies were hospitalized more often than those who stuck to conventional treatment; using the wrong herb or another ineffective therapy delayed a proper diagnosis and effective medical care from allergists and lung specialists.

Tea: A Sip in the Right Direction

According to legend, the Chinese Emperor Shen Nung—known as the great "divine healer"—believed that drinking boiled water promoted health. As the emperor was boiling his water one day in 2737 B.C., a gust of wind sent a few stray leaves from a nearby *Camellia sinensis* plant into the pot. The emperor sipped the brew and declared that it gave one "vigor of body, contentment of mind, and determination of purpose."

Today, approximately 3,000 varieties of tea are made from this single plant, at least 300 in China alone. In the West, Great Britain may rank number one in tea consumption, but an Angus Reid survey indicates that 9 out of 10 Canadians are tea drinkers.

And, yes, the emperor was right. There now is ample proof that tea in its many forms possesses an astounding number of health benefits, from supporting the immune system to reducing the risk of cancer to helping prevent tooth decay.

What makes it such a wellness powerhouse? The star compounds are called catechins. These are related to the antioxidants in wine, and, like other antioxidants, help prevent cell damage by harmful molecules called free radicals. Indeed, researchers at the University of Kansas have shown that tea's antioxidants are more powerful than those in even the most antioxidant-rich vegetables.

The task of extracting, purifying, and identifying the various compounds in tea is a long and difficult process. However, it seems that the more scientists know about what is in tea, the more they are convinced of its benefits. The fact that tea contains no calories further enhances its reputation as a healthy beverage.

Green, black, and oolong. All "real" tea—versus herbal tea—is made from the leaves of the same evergreen bush that Emperor Shen Nung encountered. How those leaves are processed determines the type of tea. Green tea is made by steaming or barely heating the leaves immediately after plucking. Black tea is fermented—a drying process in which enzymes within the tea leaves cause oxidation (the same process that turns a sliced apple brown), darkening the leaves and degrading some of the tea's beneficial chemicals. Oolong tea is partially fermented to a point between black and green.

HEALTH HINT
Great Green Tea

Bring fresh, cold water to a boil, remove from heat and let cool for two minutes. Use one tea bag per cup (one level teaspoon if loose tea) and brew for four minutes. Serve immediately in a china cup. (It does make a difference!) Do not drink while scalding hot. Downing too-hot beverages appears to increase the risk of esophageal cancer. Do not serve with milk, as the calcium in milk may bind to the tea's phytochemicals and reduce their health-promoting properties.

GOOD QUESTION!
Can drinking tea interfere with iron absortion?

It can when you drink it with vegetables, particularly iron-rich vegetables such as spinach. Tea contains tannins, natural substances that inhibit the body's absorption of non-heme iron, the form of iron in vegetables. You can counter this effect by adding a vitamin C source to your meal; just squeezing a lemon into your tea will do. Otherwise, drink all the tea you want, with meals and between them. It won't affect your absorption of heme, the iron in meat.

Reading the Benefits of Tea Leaves

Fermentation destroys the catechins in tea, so green tea offers the strongest healing powers because it is not fermented. It contains up to 40 percent catechins, compared to between 8 and 20 percent in oolong and about 4 percent in black tea. Researchers also have discovered that green tea, unlike other teas, contains a potent antioxidant compound called epigallocatechin gallate (EGCG), which appears to inhibit an enzyme that helps tumors spread.

Numerous reports have found that EGCG kills cultures of human cancer cells. Mayo Clinic researchers are testing whether EGCG can reduce the rate of cancer in a special strain of mice bred to develop prostate tumors. Human trials could follow if preliminary results are promising.

Black tea doesn't contain EGCG; the compound probably breaks down during fermentation. But since it does contain catechins, it is still an effective disease fighter. One study looked at the tea-drinking habits of 35,369 postmenopausal women in Iowa. It found that those who drank two or more cups of black tea a day had significantly fewer cases of cancer of the digestive and urinary tracts than did women who favored other beverages. No wonder tea is now the subject of inquiry in research labs worldwide.

GREEN TEA has greater disease-fighting power than either black or oolong tea.

More anticancer benefits.

Thanks to Oregon State University studies, we now know that tea's antioxidant properties alone do not explain its remarkable cancer-prevention potential. It also may stop the development of some cancers once it has begun. In one experiment, animals were given high doses of carcinogens called heterocyclic amines (HCAs, the same cancer-causing chemicals produced when meat is charred), accompanied by regular-strength black tea administered beforehand or afterward. The results: The animals given tea showed significantly more resistance to the kinds of cellular changes that signal the beginnings of cancer, no matter when the tea was administered.

Other recent research has identified ways that the chemicals in tea can inhibit the spread of cancer. For example, a series of Case Western Reserve University studies revealed that the polyphenols in both green and black tea can prevent skin cancer when given to mice topically (rubbed onto the skin). Similar results were achieved in Rutgers University labs, where mice given green or black tea were significantly less likely

Quick Tip

To keep teas fresh-tasting and potent, store in airtight, opaque containers in a cool, dry place (not inside the refrigerator). Many teas come packed in metal tins that close tightly for optimal storage. Clear glass canisters are okay if they are placed in a closed cupboard away from light.

to develop skin cancer lesions following exposure to ultraviolet-B radiation, the major risk factor for skin cancer in humans. Moreover, studies carried out jointly by the U.S. National Cancer Institute and the Shanghai Cancer Institute indicate that drinking at least one cup of green tea a day for six months or longer lowers the risk of esophageal cancer by 50 percent overall in women and by 60 percent in men and women who do not smoke.

Today's tea research even offers some hope for people who already have cancer. A survey of 472 Japanese women with breast cancer found that those who drank the most green tea before their diagnoses were least likely to have lymph node involvement or to suffer cancer recurrences.

VARIETIES OF GREEN TEA

Genmaicha
Green tea blended with toasted rice. Because of its unusual taste, it is sometimes called "popcorn tea."

Gunpowder
Chinese tea that is rolled into pellets, which open like flowers in hot water. It has an earthy flavor.

Gyokuro
The most highly valued Japanese tea. Also known as "Pearl Dew," it makes a surprisingly rich, herbal-tasting brew.

Maccha
The powdered tea used in the famed Japanese tea ceremony. The leaves it is made from are called *tencha* before powering.

Tooth Decay

Green tea is tooth-friendly because it is packed with polyphenols that fight off the bacteria that cause tooth decay. In addition, the fluoride in tea provides a helpful boost to tooth enamel. One small-scale Japanese study found that when volunteers used a special mouth rinse of tea polyphenols after each meal and before bedtime, they significantly reduced the development of plaque, even though none of them was brushing or flossing!

Weight Loss

Promising evidence suggests that tea compounds may aid weight loss. Investigators at the University of Geneva in Switzerland discovered that healthy young men who took two capsules of green tea extract containing 50 mg of caffeine and 90 mg of EGCG daily burned about 80 more calories each day than those taking capsules containing just 50 mg of caffeine or a placebo. The men, who ranged from slim to overweight, all followed the same diet and

FOUR CUPS of green tea a day will steep you in compounds that delay disease.

exercise routines. Researchers speculate that EGCG may trigger fat oxidation and thermogenesis, the process by which the body burns fat to produce heat.

Additional Benefits

A study of 3,454 people who were free of heart disease found that sipping about two cups of black tea daily lowered the risk of severe atherosclerosis (narrowing of the coronary arteries) by 46 percent. Drinking four cups a day cut the risk by 69 percent. In other studies, green tea was shown to lower total cholesterol levels and raise HDL (good cholesterol). It also prevents the oxidation of LDL, or "bad" cholesterol, even in animals fed high-fat diets. (The oxidation of LDL makes it more likely to stick to artery walls, clogging the arteries.) Other British research involving postmenopausal women indicated that women who drank tea had significantly greater bone-mineral density than those who did not. That's not all: A study in the *Proceedings of the National Academy of Sciences* suggests that drinking green tea may lessen rheumatoid arthritis symptoms.

Drink to Your Health

How much tea should you drink? There still is no definitive answer. However, researchers estimate that drinking four or more cups of green tea per day would offer significant protection. That approximately matches the per capita consumption in Japan, which has lower rates of many cancers than western countries, a difference that may or may not be related to the population's fondness for green tea. Black tea drinkers need to fit in a few more cups a day to reap as much benefit as green tea seems to confer. Bear in mind, herbal "teas" are actually infusions. They do not contain the same compounds as regular tea; therefore, they do not deliver the same benefits.

Concerned about tea's caffeine content? Green tea contains only about 25 mg per cup. Black tea yields about 35 mg; brewed coffee, 105 mg. Whether decaffeinated tea has the same health benefits as caffeinated tea is unclear because studies have focused on caffeinated tea. What is clear is that the amount of active compounds retained in decaffeinated tea depends on the method used to remove the caffeine. One process employs a solvent called ethyl acetate; the other uses carbon dioxide and water. The first process yields tea that retains about 30 percent of its catechins; the second, about 95 percent. (This tea, however, is often more expensive.)

If you don't like the taste of tea, there's another option: green tea supplements. A dose of 300 mg standardized to contain 80 percent total polyphenols and 55 percent EGCG is equal to drinking about four cups.

WHETHER PREPARED from tea bags or in the traditional manner from powder, green tea is a very healthy brew.

Easy over Ice

Today, Canadians spend $250 million on tea and consume 7 billion cups each year, 10 percent of which is served over ice. But in order for that frosty glass of tea to bolster your body's disease-fighting abilities, it must be brewed at home. A U.S. study of bottled teas sold in grocery stores found that none contained catechins, which apparently are lost in processing. Another negative: Most ready-to-drink teas have hefty calorie counts—145 calories per 350-ml glass on average, compared to 64 calories for homemade tea with four teaspoons of sugar.

Tips on brewing. Use one teaspoon of quality loose-leaf tea for every six-ounce glass of tea desired. Let it steep for at least three minutes but not more than five. Set on the countertop until tepid to prevent clouding, then refrigerate. Keep covered during brewing and cooling to lock in the aroma, natural color, and health benefits by avoiding oxidation, which occurs if tea is left open to the air. Serve over ice, with lemon wedges and mint sprigs. Sweeten to taste. For variety, add one large piece of sliced, peeled fresh ginger root to the water before boiling and steeping. Leave the ginger in for two hours and remove. Another option: Mix three parts green tea to one part mint infusion. Stir in an equal amount of cold fruit juice and serve over ice.

HEALTH HINT

Sun Tea: Unsafe

It may sound healthful to let tea steep in warm sunlight for several hours to draw out it benefits before drinking it on ice. In actuality, those conditions encourage bacteria to multiply.

Immune-Boosting Scents

The ancient Greeks, Romans, Egyptians, and Chinese all relied on essences pressed from the aromatic peel, bark, seeds, roots, leaves, and flowers of plants to prevent and treat illness.

When smoothed on the skin, added to a bath, or inhaled in the form of steam, these aromatic "essential oils" were believed to ease tensions, heal wounds, and revitalize the body. Today, this practice, called aromatherapy, is gaining some acceptance among Western doctors as a way to use the senses to benefit health. There even is a smattering of evidence to support the value of using aromatic oils to help the immune system fight a variety of ailments. For example, tea tree oil—an antiseptic discovered by aboriginal Australians—was found to make white blood cells more active. And inhaling lavender oil was shown to be more effective than a placebo for insomnia.

For safety's sake.

Aromatic oils generally are safe to use provided you never take them internally or use them undiluted on the skin unless directed otherwise by a physician or herbalist. The exception: Tea tree oil may be used full strength on pimples, insect bites, or minor burns.

HEALTH HINT

How to Use Oils

To use the scented oils in the chart, unless otherwise indicated mix about ten drops with a half ounce of an unscented carrier oil (almond or olive), then use as a massage oil. For a compress, add 2–8 drops of scented oil to a bowl of hot water and immerse a clean cloth. Squeeze the cloth out and place it on the skin. For inhalation, add six drops of scented oil to a bowl of steaming water. Drape your head with a towel, close your eyes, lean over the bowl, and inhale. Avoid steam if you have asthma.

AT-A-GLANCE GUIDE

THE PLANT OIL

BERGAMOT *Citrus bergamia*
Derived from the rind of an orange-like fruit, this oil has a tangy scent.

CEDARWOOD *Cedrus atlantica, Juniperus virginiana,* or *J. mexicana*
Most "cedarwood" oil comes from juniper!

CHAMOMILE (ROMAN) *Anthemis nobilis* (FAR RIGHT)
Pressed from daisy-like flowers, it has a fruity aroma.

CLARY SAGE *Salvia sclarea*
Not to be confused with the common sage, *Salvia officinalis.*

CYPRESS *Cupressus sempervirens*
Distilled from the cones of the cypress tree.

EUCALYPTUS *Eucalyptus globulus*
(LEFT) Its head-clearing aroma is a key ingredient in Vicks VapoRub.

GINGER *Zingiber officinale*
A staple of Asian cuisine, ginger is used in Indian medicine to combat arthritis.

LAVENDER *Lavandula officinalis* (RIGHT)
The oil is taken from the fresh, blue flower spikes.

PEPPERMINT *Mentha piperita*
Now wild throughout the United States, this plant is native to Europe and Asia.

TEA TREE *Melaleuca alternifolia*
Products made with this plant have a menthol-citrus scent.

THE CLAIM	FOR BEST RESULTS
Fights skin infections and may relieve the pain of shingles and chicken pox.	Massage mixed with a carrier oil into the skin, inhale, or add five drops to running bathwater. May increase sensitivity to the sun, resulting in severe burning or uneven skin pigmentation. Choosing an oil labeled bergaptene-free will reduce photosensitivity problems.
North American Indians used this scent to treat respiratory infections, and today it is believed to ease coughing and other cold and flu symptoms. It's also an effective insect repellent.	Inhale or use as a compress. Causes skin irritation in some people. May increase menstrual flow. Avoid if pregnant.
Known for its calming effects, it is thought to reduce inflammation and fight skin infections.	Use topically or add 6–10 drops to running bathwater. Low toxicity makes it particularly safe, even for children.
Its antiseptic and astringent qualities help relieve skin inflammation, including acne. It also is used to ease tension headaches.	Mix up to five drops in about 10 ml of water and use in an aromatic oil burner. Do not use if drinking alcoholic beverages. Avoid if operating machinery or driving. Do not use while pregnant.
This aroma is said to build emotional and mental resolve. Inhaling it may help relieve the symptoms of throat and respiratory infections.	Place a few drops on a radiator or in a saucer of water and leave in a warm part of the house. May cause allergic reactions. Avoid if you suffer from high blood pressure.
A powerful antiseptic and healing agent, it also is renowned as a treatment for respiratory complaints.	Massage mixed with a carrier oil onto the chest, or add three drops to the dust bag of your vacuum cleaner to repel dust mites and freshen the air throughout your home. Nontoxic externally, but internally it is very toxic—3.5 ml is usually fatal.
Noted for its warming and decongestant properties, ginger also helps fight off colds and flu and reduces fever by inducing perspiration.	Massage mixed with a carrier oil onto the chest, inhale, or add six drops to running bathwater. May irritate the skin if applied undiluted.
Alleviates stress and depression, induces relaxation and sleep, and promotes circulation.	Use topically or add 10 drops to bathwater. Sheets washed in water containing lavender oil may promote sleep. Nontoxic, but the scent may trigger nausea if too much is used.
Relieves pain when applied externally to sore muscles. Also fights fever and helps to ease headaches and respiratory infections.	Only a small amount of peppermint is required, whether used topically or in bathwater. Keep eyes closed when inhaling its scent and wash hands thoroughly after use. Keep away from the faces of small children; may cause wheezing or an involuntary gagging response.
Widely recognized as a powerful tool against a variety of harmful bacteria, viruses, fungi, molds, and parasites.	To ease skin infections and inflammation, add three to five drops to bath water. For relief of respiratory ailments, add two drops to a bowl of steaming water and inhale the vapor for five minutes.

Sources: Alan Hirsch, M.D., Neurological Director, Smell and Taste Treatment and Research Foundation; consultant John Steele, Lifetree Aromatix.

Natural Ways to Beat the Blues

What about using herbs to treat the blues, which we all get occasionally? It can be a wise, immune-strengthening idea. Why? When sad feelings hang around too long, relationships and job performance aren't the only things that suffer. Research shows that being down a lot can have a profound effect on your immune response.

In any given year, many Canadians turn to an anti-depressant medication like Prozac, Paxil, or Zoloft to normalize their moods. The good news is that these medications have brought great relief to millions. The bad news: Not everyone responds to the drugs, and some others experience such inconvenient side effects—fatigue, weight gain, lagging libido, and more—that the negatives may outweigh the benefits.

It's not surprising. Depression, according to the *Archives of General Psychiatry,* is one of the most common ailments for which people turn to complementary medicine—treatments such as herbal remedies that are meant to enhance conventional medical care, not replace it. But depression is very different from the blues. It is a serious condition that should be treated by a qualified health professional. Some signs are easy to recognize—persistent sadness, feelings of hopelessness, or thoughts of suicide or death, which require immediate treatment. But there are subtler signs as well that an expert can usually detect better than a layperson. These signs can include:

◆ Poor appetite or overeating;
◆ Sleeping too little or too much;
◆ Low self-esteem;
◆ Difficulty concentrating or making decisions;
◆ Irritability, agitation;
◆ Pessimism;
◆ Worry, anxiety, excessive crying;
◆ Loss of interest or joy in once pleasurable things;
◆ Unexplained aches or pains.

See a health care professional if you have any of these symptoms to a degree that interferes with your

NATURAL MOOD BOOSTERS

THE REMEDY

ST. JOHN'S WORT
Unlike some herbal fads, dozens of studies have established that St. John's wort is better than a placebo—and almost as good as some prescription medications—at relieving symptoms of mild to moderate depression if taken several weeks.

SAM-e
Pronounced "sammy," it's S-adenosylmethionine, a naturally occurring molecule found in almost every cell of the body.

KAVA (LEFT)
The ground roots of the kava-kava tree seem to relieve some symptoms of clinical anxiety and some of the stress of ordinary living.

LIGHT
For many people, the shorter amount of daylight in fall and winter triggers a type of blues or depression known as seasonal affective disorder or SAD.

EXERCISE
Numerous studies have shown that exercise of all kinds can be inexpensive, effective therapy for anxiety, mild-to-moderate depression, and low self-esteem.

VOLUNTEER WORK
Helping others reduces isolation and gives a person a sense of accomplishment and purpose, feelings that many depressed people lack.

work or family life. Relieving depression can have a positive effect on your immune system, potentially increasing the number of white blood cells and their response to health threats. The sadder you feel, the more you stand to benefit. For those who are feeling just plain blah, the chart below offers a look at some safe and popular self-care steps that will help you stabilize your mood.

THE PROOF	HOW TO USE IT
A review of 23 clinical trials found that St. John's wort lifted mild-to-moderate depression more effectively than placebos. But the studies were short—no more than eight weeks—so long-term research is needed.	For mild depression, search out products with 0.3 percent hypericin or 3–5 percent hyperforin. Take one 300 mg capsule, three times a day with food. Do not combine with prescription antidepressants. Consult a pharmacist before using with other drugs of any kind.
Several small-scale studies indicate that oral SAM-e supplements may ease depression, most likely by raising levels of serotonin and dopamine, two neurotransmitters that help regulate mood.	For mild depression, take 400 mg each day for two weeks on an empty stomach. If you're still blue, raise the dosage to 600 mg a day. If you aren't better within two weeks, see a doctor. Do not take with prescription antidepressants or if you have been diagnosed with bipolar depression.
European investigations involving several hundred people with clinical anxiety found that those who took kava felt much better than those who took a placebo.	The studies used 300–400 mg daily doses of kava extracts. Health Canada currently advises Canadians against kava consumption, until studies can rule it out as the source of some cases of liver toxicity.
Studies have found that decreased daylight leads to a drop in the secretion of serotonin and an increase in melatonin levels, causing seasonal depressive symptoms to surface in some individuals.	Spend more time outdoors, sit in front of a south-facing window several times a day, or invest in a light box: Exposure to 5,000–10,000 lux (a measure of the light's intensity) for 20–30 minutes per day at a distance of 30 cm to 1 meter from the box will keep most people upbeat through even the darkest days of winter.
Although the mechanism of the benefit is not clear, some experts theorize that aerobic exercise may encourage the release of endorphins, the brain's so-called "feel-good" chemicals. One study found that depressed patients who jogged or walked briskly for 30 minutes three times a week improved their moods as much as those who took antidepressant medications.	Try to get on the move for 20–60 minutes, three times a week—outdoors, when you can, to take advantage of sunlight.
Researchers who analyzed 37 studies on volunteering found that older people who offered their time to others were happier over-all, had a better sense of well-being, and were less likely to feel sad and anxious.	You don't need to join an organized volunteer group to experience a mood lift. A University of Michigan study showed that informally offering help to a friend, family member, or neighbor who needs it is just as effective.

Can Homeopathy Help?

Homeopathy is a system of healing that attempts to stimulate the body to cure itself. It is based on a theory called the Law of Similars: Like heals like. Symptoms of disease, such as fever or inflammation, are seen as signs of what the body needs to heal itself. Studying those signs helps a homeopath determine what course of action might best lend the body a helping hand.

Instead of trying to suppress the symptoms, as a conventional doctor most likely would, a homeopath may use remedies designed to heighten them. Suppose you have a cold, and your eyes and nose are running. Rather than giving an antihistamine to dry those secretions up, a homeopath might prescribe allium cepa, a remedy made from onions to encourage more tearing and nasal discharge.

Less is more. Remedies are prepared from highly diluted plant, mineral, or animal substances. If you look at a homeopathic preparation in a health food store or pharmacy, you will notice a number after the name, commonly 6, as well as other numbers rising in a scale: 30, 200, 1M (1,000). Sometimes a "C"—standing for centesimal (one-hundredth)—is written after the number. These represent the potency, or the number of times that the remedy has been diluted. In many cases, the doses are so diluted that no detectable trace of the source material remains.

Between each dilution, the remedy is vigorously shaken and banged, a process called succussion, which supposedly ensures the release and transfer of what homeopaths call "energy" from the original substance to the remedy. Practitioners believe that the greater the number of dilutions and successions, the greater the power of the remedy. You may wonder how homeopathy can possibly work if the original compounds are so diluted. Practitioners reply that theirs is an "energy" medicine that transfers healing power to the patient much like the jump start from the battery of one car to another. This unorthodox explanation makes many scientists and conventional medical practitioners doubt that homeopathy has any direct effect on health. After all, how can nothing cure something?

Yet research suggests that homeopathic remedies can ease the symptoms of some illnesses, including migraines and seasonal allergies. A combined analysis of 89 studies in *The Lancet* concluded that the response to homeopathic treatment could not be explained by the placebo effect. On average, patients were nearly twice as likely to benefit when given homeopathic remedies as when given placebos.

HOMEOPATHIC REMEDIES often are formed into tiny pellets, which are generally placed under the tongue and left to dissolve.

Friends, Not Foes?

The biggest danger from homeopathy comes from using its remedies to treat serious illnesses—infections or cancer, for example—that require the guidance of a conventional physician. But the very weakness of the dilutions required to make homeopathic remedies means that in most cases those remedies can safely be used during or after treatment with traditional medications, including antibiotics.

Although you might imagine that all homeopathic remedies are extracted from gentle flowers, in reality many remedies, including top choices for helping the immune system—what

homeopaths refer to as the "vital force"—derive from some of Mother Nature's nastiest creations. These include:

1 Belladonna. Extracted from deadly nightshade (LEFT), this homeopathic medicine is regarded as a premier fever reducer. It also is given for a range of inflammatory conditions, such as sore throat, sinus infections, or flu.

2 Arsenicum. Prepared from arsenic (CENTER), which is a notorious poison, dilutions make its use as a homeopathic remedy extremely safe. It is a common remedy for indigestion and for diarrhea associated with food poisoning.

3 Apis. Obtained from crushed honeybees (BELOW, LEFT), this remedy is relied on to calm restlessness and irritability and to treat inflammatory conditions, such as hives, insect bites, and conjunctivitis, when accompanied by stinging pain or swelling.

4 Mercurius. This remedy is made from the heavy metal mercury (BELOW), best known as a feared environmental pollutant. It is used for colds, flu, sinusitis, earaches, and gum abscesses, especially when the symptoms include swollen lymph nodes, night sweats, offensive breath, intense thirst, sensitivity to change in

temperature, drooling during sleep, or excessive mucous discharge.

5 Lachesis. Poison from the fangs of bushmaster snake (BELOW) is said to give this remedy its punch. Homeopaths recommend it for patients with a range of symptoms including sore throats, throbbing headaches, menstrual problems, and hot flashes.

The Latest News

Results of another trial reported in the *British Medical Journal* again suggest that homeopathic remedies are more effective than inactive placebos for treating certain ills. Researchers in Glasgow, Scotland, randomly divided 51 chronic hay fever sufferers into two groups: 24 of the study subjects received daily homeopathy and 27 received a daily placebo over four weeks. In addition, all of the subjects kept a diary in which they recorded their nasal air flow measurements and symptoms such as sneezing, runny nose, and eye or chest discomfort. Neither the investigators nor the patients knew who was in which group.

HEALTH HINT

Doctors Who Do

In Canada today, homeopathy is not regulated in any province. However, several provinces are lobbying for regulation of the homeopathic profession. Provinces are working in affiliation with the Homeopathic Medical Council of Canada. The HMCC is a national association that keeps a register of homeopathic doctors. For more information contact the HMCC at 416-638-4622 or visit their web site at www.hmcc.ca.

The results: Those who received homeopathy had a 28 percent improvement in their symptoms compared to a 3 percent improvement in the placebo group.

Feel worse before you feel better. Because homeopathic remedies are given in such minute dilutions, there is little chance of any harm arising from taking them. A child could swallow a whole bottle and not be harmed. As a result, it's generally safe to try to treat minor problems at home with a commercial homeopathic first-aid kit, sold in many pharmacies. Finding precisely the right remedy can be difficult, though, because not all people are treated with the same remedy for the same ailment. A cough in one person, for example, often is attacked with a different remedy than it would be in another individual, depending on the cough's characteristics and what else is going on in that person's life.

Typically, on your first visit to a homeopath, you will be asked detailed questions about your symptoms, as well as about your moods, interests, food preferences, urination, and energy level to gather the "total" picture needed to tie together the mind and body. You may have a physical exam, too, especially if you are seeing a homeopath who also is a physician. Remember, once you are given a remedy, you may feel worse before you feel better. The idea is to stimulate rather than suppress symptoms as a way to heighten the immune system response. Doubters say this caveat allows just enough time for the remedy to get the credit for healing that the the body does all on its own.

A HEALING BALM

Calendula, a sweet-smelling balm made from the petals of an ornamental marigold-like flower, *Calendula officinalis*. Long prized by herbalists and homeopaths as a gentle antiseptic that speeds skin healing, it is the leading natural first-aid remedy for rashes, abrasions, cuts, and burns. It is applied mostly as a cream, sometimes combined with St. John's wort to further speed healing.

Are there any dangers? Clearly, the microdoses used cannot by themselves cause harm. Homeopathic remedies are, by design, so watered down as to render the "active" ingredients inactive. Homeopathic belladonna, for instance, probably contains no real belladonna at all. Yet patients may be misled into risky self-medication when they take vaguely labeled remedies for very real symptoms, such as earaches, exhaustion, or pain. Homeopathic treatments also can be expensive and are rarely covered by medical insurance. Still, the Canadian Medical Association neither accepts nor rejects homeopathy, viewing it instead as an alternative therapy that some doctors may use when and where appropriate.

Maximizing the Healing Potential

Homeopathic remedies are reportedly quite sensitive to environmental conditions. They can be neutralized, even spoiled, by various culprits, including:

◆ **Strong odors.** The aromas of coffee, camphor, perfumes, spices, and even cooking foods are said to disarm homeopathic remedies.

◆ **Light.** Bright sunlight and fluorescent or halogen light can disrupt a remedy's subtle energy. To avoid this, many remedies are sold in opaque containers.

◆ **Heat.** Extreme heat, such as the temperature inside of a closed car on a summer day, supposedly neutralizes remedies. Cold, even freezing, temperatures are OK.

◆ **Energy fields.** Computers, metal detectors, electric blankets, and clock radios can generate magnetic or low-volt energy fields that reportedly neutralize a remedy if exposure is prolonged.

> ## Interesting!
>
> Although no one knows how it works, a recent analysis of seven studies of oscillococcinum, the homeopathic remedy used most frequently to treat the flu, found that it does shorten the duration of flu symptoms (by about six hours), but can't prevent infection. Its principal ingredient comes from the heart and liver of a duck.

> ### GOOD QUESTION!
> #### What's the most reliable way to learn more about alternative medical practices?
>
> The Canadian Health Network web site offers excellent information on a wide range of alternative therapies, www.canadian-health-network.ca/1alternative_health. html. Or check the online databases on the web site of the Natural Health Products Directorate, a division of Health Canada created to better inform Canadians, www.hc-sc.gc.ca/hpb/onhp/welcome_e.html.

More Flower Power

Like homeopathy, the Bach Flower Remedies, developed early in the twentieth century by British physician Edward Bach, aim to treat the person, not the disease or its symptoms. Each of the 38 remedies created by Bach is directed at a particular characteristic or emotional state, such as "procrastination" and "failure to learn from mistakes." They are made from the blossoms of plants set out in the sun in a bowl of purified water, then diluted and preserved with brandy. The process is said to preserve energy from the flowers, which then can transform the negative attitudes that cause illness into positive ones that stimulate healing. Less studied than homeopathy and treated by the medical profession with considerable skepticism, Bach's form of healing nonetheless is wildly popular today.

Vials of the most famous potion designed on Bach's principles—Rescue Remedy, "for use in emergencies of all kinds"—sell by the millions worldwide each year. The tincture can be taken undiluted, a few drops at a time, or three to four drops can be stirred into water, then sipped throughout the day.

Broaden Your Health Horizons

Enthusiasm for herbal therapies has been growing at a phenomenal rate in recent years, with no sign of slowing. Bookstore and library shelves are crowded with hundreds of volumes devoted to these complex, often amazing plants that have been used as folk medicine for thousands of years. It's hard to imagine that there's anything left to be known.

There is. Even though research has demonstrated the beneficial effects of many herbs, many doctors will tell you that there's no value to using them. The truth is more complicated. Many modern medicines were created from herbs. In fact, some 25 percent of U.S. prescriptions are filled with plant-derived drugs. But the benefits of many widely used herbal remedies that haven't been tested rigorously are not as well documented. Until they are, conventional doctors will continue to be cautious about their use, and many will outright disparage them.

Proven cures. What they won't mention is that the all-time, best-selling pain reliever, aspirin, is an herbal remedy. In the fifth century B.C., the Greek physician Hippocrates first prepared it from willow bark and prescribed it for the pain of childbirth. The antibiotic erythromycin was developed from a tropical fungus. And vincristine, one of the most common chemotherapy drugs, comes from a flower, the Madagascar periwinkle.

Impressive? Yes. Yet when it comes to strengthening your immune system, don't expect herbs to work like miraculous magic bullets and deliver astonishing benefits while making no demands on you other than to remember to swallow them. Magic bullets don't exist. No herb is a substitute for a healthy diet and other good habits, but adding one or more to an already immune-boosting lifestyle may bolster your protection against disease.

A new vision. A major attraction of medicinal plants and other alternative therapies is that they invite you to take an active role in managing your own health. Of course, you should not take this role to the extreme of refusing or stopping effective conventional treatment. Instead, make herbs and other healing techniques part of an amalgam of approaches that will be far more potent than any one method you can use in your quest for better health.

This chapter is not meant to be a complete course in herbal medicine and the immune system. It is a guide. If you have specific questions, consult an herbalist, pharmacist, naturopathic physician, or medical doctor knowledgeable in herbal medicine.

UNCOMMON KNOWLEDGE
Don't Get Ripped Off

Although Health Canada's Natural Health Products Directorate (www.hc-sc.gc.ca/hpb/onhp/) tests the contents of some herbs and nutritional supplements, there is no guarantee you're getting what's listed on all labels. What to do? Check out Consumer Lab (www.consumerlab.com), which privately tests supplements to determine if the contents are pure and match the label claims. Those that hold up to Consumer Lab's standards are listed on the site and can display the trademarked CL seal. Products already reviewed include various brands of SAM-e, ginseng, and vitamin C. The findings are provocative: Many tested supplements lacked key components or did not contain advertised percentages of active ingredients. In the case of ginseng, some products were found to contain pesticides and heavy metals.

{ "Your lab is your body; experiments going on there constantly allow you to find out what suits you and what doesn't." }

—RUDOLPH BALLENTINE, M.D. / PSYCHIATRIST, HOMEOPATH, AND HERBALIST

CHAPTER 4

Charge Up with Exercise

Cars, computers, TV remotes, escalators—it's hard not to be sedentary these days. Yet experts say that one of the simplest and most profitable investments you can make toward a stronger immune system is to get up and get moving. Invest just a little time, and the return will be greater than you can imagine.

A Giant Step toward Wellness

Everyone knows that the eyes are windows to the soul. Likewise, the body's appearance and vitality reflect the health of the immune system. And nothing is more likely to improve your body's functioning and make you feel good living in it than getting up and moving.

It's no accident that fitness enthusiasts tend to take far fewer sick days than their sedentary peers. There's plenty of evidence that when you enjoy being active and can do so easily, your resistance to disease is at its best. To understand why, think of your immune cells as cops. When they're hanging out at the station instead of patrolling the streets, the crooks are more active. But when they're on the beat, the crime rate drops. Exercise gets your immune "cops" circulating. For example, numerous studies have shown that working out increases the activity of natural killer (NK) cells—immune system cells that attack developing tumor cells and help ward off infection.

Take a moment to check in with your body right now. How does it feel? Are you sitting comfortably with good posture, or slouching and forcing your muscles and organs into awkward positions? Is your body telling you, "I feel nurtured, relaxed, and fit"? Or is it saying, "I ache," "My muscles are tense," or "I'm pushed to the limit"? If your body is full of vigor, congratulations; this chapter will point you toward new approaches to exercise that will further enhance your body's infection-fighting abilities. If your body is saying it's uncomfortable, don't be daunted. Research has verified time and again that it's never too late to start boosting your health with exercise.

EXERCISE has an immediate effect on your body. Circulation improves and calorie burning accelerates.

A kick to the immune system. The fastest way to feel energized is to exercise, and the effects will be immediate. A simple 10-minute walk will decrease tension, banish fatigue, and boost mental alertness for hours afterward. Make it a daily routine, and pretty soon, you'll be toning muscles, strengthening your heart, and improving the functioning of most organs and systems in your body. Exercise immediately lightens the workload of the immune system, speeding the elimination of germs and other threats by:

◆ **Stimulating circulation.** Immune cells travel more quickly through the body, attacking and destroying invaders before they can do harm.

◆ **Making you breathe deeply.** When you breathe forcefully, you often expel more waste, notably carbon dioxide, through your lungs.

◆ **Accelerating perspiration.** As a result, metabolic by-products are eliminated faster through the skin.

◆ **Increasing muscle activity.** This helps move dead white blood cells and debris through and out of the lymphatic vessels.

◆ **Improving self-confidence and self-esteem.** This helps minimize the negative effects of stress.

Jump to it. Three or four brief sessions of strength training (such as lifting weights) and moderate aerobic exercise per week are all you need to supply your immune system with a greater number of NK cells, according to a review of 629 studies by the International Society of Exercise and Immunology. Although the number of NK cells drops back

---

VITAL STATISTICS: EXERCISE

5

Times per week you should walk for 30 minutes at a rate of 6.5 km/h to cut your risk of colon cancer

95 percent

Percentage of Canadians dieters who regain the weight they've lost

28 percent

Percentage of overweight Canadians who do not exercise regularly

39 percent

Percentage of Canadians who exercise less than twice a week

Interesting!

Dieting can be bad for your health. A number of studies show that some diets may lack foods with important nutrients necessary for good health. For example, some individuals may develop osteoporosis if on a long-term low-calcium diet. Dieting can also be tough on the wallet. North Americans spend nearly $40 billion on diets and diet aids every year— an average of $133 per person.

---

down to pre-exercise levels within hours, each workout pays off with a small but cumulative benefit that reduces the risk of infection and disease over the long term. Exercise physiologist David Neiman, Ph.D., of Appalachia State University in Boone, North Carolina, tested the immune cell activity of a dozen women over the age of 65 (he focused on this age because older people are most prone to infections). This group, on average, had been exercising 90 minutes a day for 12 years. Then he compared their immune cell functioning to that of a group of sedentary and overweight people over age 65. The fit women's immune defenses were about 55 percent stronger than those of the sedentary group.

Add years to your life.

Moderately active people, even those who smoke or suffer from hypertension, have a lower mortality rate than couch potatoes. Here's the proof: For an ongoing project known as the College Alumni Health Study, which has been underway since 1960, researchers have tracked the physical activity levels, other lifestyle habits, and personal characteristics of 71,044 Harvard College and University of Pennsylvania graduates. Analyzing data from periodic questionnaires sent to participants, the scientists have repeatedly observed a significant protective effect from exercise. For example, they found that postmenopausal women who burned more than 1,000 calories a week in activities ranging from tennis to gardening cut their breast cancer risk in half compared to women who burned less than 500 calories a week. And men aged 45 to 84 who burned more than 1,500 calories a week lived almost two years longer than those with less active lifestyles.

It's never too late. One of the most important fitness discoveries in the past decade has been that even very old people who are housebound or living in nursing homes can get stronger—and stay stronger—through exercise. In fact, research shows that the right kind of exercise can make people who are 65 and older the strongest they've ever been, while also stimulating their circulation, filling their lungs with more oxygen, revving up calorie burning, and improving their well-being.

One study showed that after people in their seventies completed a 26-week program of three endurance training sessions a week, their aerobic capacity increased by 22 percent. Another study, from the Jean Mayer USDA Human Nutrition Research Center on Aging at Tufts University in Boston, found that when nursing-home residents joined a weight-training program, every participant more than

How we stay fit...

In 1942, 41 percent of all workers in a Gallup survey said they walked to work. Today, few of us commute that way, but 41 percent still walk to stay fit. Here are the most popular ways to work out:

ACTIVITY/ PARTICIPATION

Walking 41 percent

Weight training 29 percent

Cardio machines 28 percent

Jogging 20 percent

Competitive sports 15 percent

Fitness classes 11 percent

Swimming 3 percent

Source: Maritz Poll

doubled his or her strength. In 10 short weeks, several subjects developed such well-toned muscles that they were able to toss aside their walkers in favor of canes.

The right equation. Which type of exercise is best? Doctors have compared the effectiveness of moderate aerobic exercise in building lean muscle mass and improving health with that of resistance training—any kind of training that involves lifting weights (even the weight of your body). They concluded that you're best off doing both types of exercise.

But what is considered moderate aerobic exercise? The generally accepted definition is any activity done at a comfortable pace that's intense enough to raise your heart rate but mild enough to let you carry on a conversation and keep talking comfortably for up to 60 minutes. Another way to gauge intensity is to note how tired you feel during the hour after you finish the activity. If you're exhausted, you're probably pushing a little past the moderate mark.

For a more precise calculation, you'll need to determine your maximum heart rate by subtracting your age from 220. If you're 50, for example, your maximum heart rate is 170. When you exercise, aim for a heart rate of 55 percent to 80 percent of your maximum. To calculate the

{ "The sovereign invigorator of the body is exercise, and of all the exercises, walking is the best." }

—THOMAS JEFFERSON / THIRD PRESIDENT OF THE UNITED STATES (1743-1826)

EXERCISE IN A BOTTLE?

When it comes to getting fit, we all know that nothing takes the place of getting up and getting moving. But that never stopped anyone from dreaming about finding a magic pill that would build muscle and pare pounds effortlessly. Sorry! There's no substitute for the real thing—despite the plethora of potions that claim otherwise. Here's the lowdown on what those "slim-down" miracles *really* do.

THE PILL	THE CLAIM	THE FACTS
CALCIUM PYRUVATE A mineral made in the body and found naturally in food.	Subtracts fat, adds muscle.	In studies of obese people on very-low-fat diets, daily doses of up to 75 g improved weight loss—slightly. But that amount is much greater than can easily be taken in over-the-counter supplements.
CHITOSAN An insoluble fiber made from the shells of crab and shrimp.	Absorbs fat to prevent weight gain.	Researchers found it has no more positive impact on health than a phony look-alike pill. On the negative side, it may block the absorption of fat-soluble nutrients, such as vitamins D and E, and fat-soluble drugs.
CHROMIUM PICOLINATE An essential nutrient that most Canadians get too little of because they eat too many refined foods.	Blocks the absorption of fat and helps burn calories effortlessly— even during sleep.	A carefully controlled study found that taking 400 mg daily had no effect on body fat, weight, or muscle mass. High doses may cause mood changes and sleep disturbances. To add more chromium to your diet naturally, eat corn, peas, and prunes.
CONJUGATED LINOLEIC ACID A mixture of different chemical forms of an essential fatty acid.	Burns fat and boosts muscle gain.	Preliminary studies show that taking it resulted in no increased fat loss in humans, but it did in some animals.
EPHEDRA (MA HUANG) A plant that contains stimulating compounds called ephedrine alkaloids, which are extracted and sold as dietary supplements.	Controls appetite and helps burn fat.	Taken with caffeine, it may fight flab. But there have been reports of heart attacks—and deaths—associated with ephedra. Health Canada issued a voluntary recall, stating those suffering from high blood pressure and diabetes are at increased risk.
GARCINIA CAMBOGIA (Hydroxycitric acid) Extracts from an Indian fruit that competes with an enzyme needed during digestion.	Prevents carbohydrates from turning into fat and whisks away extra kilograms.	A study in the *Journal of the American Medical Association* and other published research report it has no effect on burning fat or calories in humans.

Source: Tedd Mitchell, M.D., Cooper Clinic

percentages, multiply your maximum heart rate by .55 and .80. For a 50-year-old, the target heart rate, then, is between 93 and 136 beats per minute. Determine your own exercise heart rate by pausing about 10 minutes into your workout, locating your pulse on the side of your neck, and counting the beats for 10 seconds. Multiply that number by six for your one-minute heart rate.

Also, track your resting heart rate each day as soon as you wake up. If it's usually 70 beats per minute but it's 10 beats faster one morning, you may be overdoing your exercise. Take a day off to recuperate.

To reap the most health benefits from exercise, you need to expend about 300 calories beyond what you normally do in a day. How long will that take? It varies. Someone who weighs 70 kilograms can do it in a mere 26 minutes by jumping rope. By contrast, the same person would have to shoot pool for almost two hours to expend 300 calories.

Sweat: It's Good for What Ails You

Need more incentive before you put on your sneakers and dust off your stationary bike? There's plenty of proof that an active lifestyle is one of the most effective prevention and treatment strategies you can employ against a wide variety of diseases.

In fact, many health experts now advise *everyone* to be active at least 30 minutes every day, from light activities, such as walking, to more intensive workouts, such as aerobics. The next few pages list some common ailments for which exercise is good medicine. If you have one of these conditions, even the thought of exercise may be daunting. But give it a try—you won't regret it.

Arthritis

If you're one of the 4 million Canadians (about two-thirds of them women) who have arthritis, exercise can help reduce the pain and inflammation and preserve or restore range of motion and flexibility in each affected joint. Low-impact aerobic exercises like swimming, walking, and bicycling are ideal for arthritis patients.

Depression

If you're suffering from the blues, don't be surprised if your doctor scribbles out a prescription that reads, "Take an exercise class." Research done at Duke University Medical Center in Durham, North Carolina, shows that regular exercise can have longer-lasting benefits than antidepressant medication. The study involved 156 people ages 50 and older who had been diagnosed with depression. Each was randomly assigned to one of three treatments: the antidepressant sertraline (Zoloft), exercise classes, or a combination of the two. At the end of four months, all showed lower rates of depression. But when researchers checked in six months later, they

PHYSICAL ACTIVITY performed most days of the week reduces the risk of developing or dying from heart disease, stroke, diabetes, and some types of cancer.

QUIZ: HOW FIT ARE YOUR EXERCISE FACTS?

1	The older you are, the less exercise you need.	○ TRUE ○ FALSE
2	Working out cranks up your appetite.	○ TRUE ○ FALSE
3	Not exercising turns muscle into fat.	○ TRUE ○ FALSE
4	Sweat loss equals weight loss.	○ TRUE ○ FALSE
5	Exercise needs to be continuous to provide real benefits.	○ TRUE ○ FALSE

All are false. Count the number of times you answered correctly.

FOUR OR MORE You know the difference between exercise fact and fiction.

THREE OR LESS Your belief in fitness myths may be holding you back from getting all the benefits exercise has to offer. The facts: Exercise gets more important as you age; regular workouts blunt your appetite; unused muscle just declines, it doesn't turn into fat; when you sweat, you lose fluids—you can't lose weight without burning calories; and several short bursts of activity (three sessions of 10 minutes each, for example) are as good as 30 minutes of continuous exercise.

found that the people who exercised were much less likely to have suffered a depression relapse than those in the medication group or the medication-plus-exercise group.

Diabetes

The 2 million Canadians who suffer from type 2 diabetes, the most common form of the disease, all share the same problem: Their muscles have difficulty absorbing glucose—a sugar that provides energy—from their bloodstream. Exercise can help. Why? According to researchers at Brigham Young University, exercise activates a gene that tells the body to make more of a protein that carries glucose to muscles. What sparks the process is an enzyme released when muscles contract.

This explains why diabetics who exercise regularly are sometimes able to reduce their need for medication and maintain a normal immune system, and why diabetics whose disease is not properly controlled are more vulnerable to infections. Exercise also helps delay or stop cardiovascular disease, which is the leading killer of people with diabetes. And exercise plus other healthy lifestyle habits can help control weight.

Achieving and maintaining a healthy weight is a major challenge for many diabetics.

Heart Disease

Physical activity protects against heart disease more powerfully than just about anything else. Part of its preventive mechanism stems from its effect on the immune system.

When you exercise, your body is better able to process the stress hormones that can increase heart rate and blood pressure. (Elevations in either of these measures are risk factors for heart disease.) But that isn't the end of the story. Working out can protect the heart by raising the level of the brain chemical serotonin, best known for its ability to affect mood and personality but also shown to influence heart disease risk. When people with low serotonin levels experience stress, it seems to prompt the immune system to behave as if there were an injury in need of repair. This raises levels of two immune system chemicals, or cytokines: interleukin 1 alpha and tumor necrosis factor alpha. Unfortunately, these cytokines contribute to atherosclerosis, a buildup of fat in the arteries that can lead to a heart attack.

GOOD QUESTION!
Is it safe to exercise while you are sick?

Let your body be your guide. If you have a cold with no fever, you're probably safe doing moderate exercise, such as walking. It may even provide temporary relief from nasal congestion. However, if you have signs of the flu (fever, fatigue, muscle aches, or swollen lymph glands), rest is a must for your immune system to do its best work. Once you're better, build up to your prior exercise levels gradually. If you have a chronic illness, ask your doctor before resuming your regimen.

Impotence

New findings confirm that even minimal exercise can help men enjoy a healthy sex life as they age. Scientists at the New England Research Institutes in Watertown, Massachusetts, spent nine years studying the habits of 593 men aged 40 to 70. Periodically, the men filled out questionnaires about their sex lives and other lifestyle issues, including their level of physical activity.

At the beginning of the study, none of the men reported erectile dysfunction. But at the end, 17 percent did. A review of the questionnaires showed that men who burned at least 200 calories a day through exercise—the equivalent of a brisk two-mile walk—were far less likely to develop impotence than inactive men. The more exercise they did, the lower the risk became.

Even inactive men who began exercising during the course of the study showed a lower risk of impotence. The probable reason is that physical activity improves the elasticity and flexibility of blood vessels, allowing blood to flow freely to the penis. An added bonus: Studies show that sexual activity helps strengthen the immune system.

Obesity

You don't need to be told that one of the first laws of leanness is that you must exercise. But did you know that with exercise alone you may be able to lose just as much weight as with strict dieting? One study showed that obese men who exercised for an hour a day without changing their usual eating habits lost as much weight in three months (7 kilograms) as men who cut 700 calories out of their regular daily diet. Even better, those who exercised improved their cardiovascular fitness by 16 percent, while the dieters' fitness levels did not change. The exercisers also lost more than one kilogram more total body fat.

Ulcers

Experts used to blame ulcers on stress. But now it's clear that about 80 percent of the holes or breaks in the protective mucous lining of the stomach or duodenum (the upper part of the small intestine) are caused by a bacterium, *Helicobacter pylori*.

ULCERS (ABOVE) are less common in people who exercise.

Surprisingly, exercising seems to protect against at least some ulcers. An analysis of 20 years of health records from 11,000 people showed that those who walked or ran at least 16 kilometers a week were 62 percent less likely than inactive subjects to develop a duodenal ulcer.

> "The vision must be followed by the venture. It is not enough to stare up the steps—we must step up the stairs."
>
> —REVEREND VANCE HAVNER / BAPTIST PREACHER (1901–1986)

What About Cancer?

Experts have long emphasized that a healthy diet has the potential to stave off certain cancers. Now they're saying the same thing about exercise. One reason for that conclusion: Research indicates that breast-cancer risk may be directly related to a woman's exercise habits, possibly because physical activity helps lower the amount of estrogen bombarding breast tissue.

In one major study, women under 40 who exercised at least 3.8 hours a week were found to have reduced their breast cancer risk by approximately 60 percent. More frequent exercise was shown to be more protective. Another large study found that highly active women appear to be at a much lower risk of ovarian cancer, regardless of their age.

Other intriguing findings: A look at the health of men revealed a direct link between their activity levels and their colon cancer risk. Men who did physical work had about half the lifetime risk of men with desk jobs who spent most of their days seated. And Harvard Medical School researchers found that people who walked about 16 kilometers a week (equal to a brisk 30-minute walk, five times a week) were half as likely to develop colon cancer as more sedentary subjects.

How does exercise ward off cancer?

Several explanations have been offered. First, exercise leads to higher levels of NK cells, the frontline defense against the emergence of tumors that might produce cancer. Second, being seriously overweight is statistically related to the development of certain types of cancer—breast cancer in particular. It seems logical, then, that people who exercise regularly would be less likely to be obese and therefore more likely to avoid the types of cancer that are influenced by body size. Exercise also speeds the passage of food through the body, leading to faster elimination of potentially cancer-producing compounds in food. This might explain, in part, an exercise-related decrease in colon cancer.

Exercise and Chronic Illness

If you have a long-term health problem, don't automatically assume you should not exercise. Physical activity can increase energy, strength, balance, and coordination, as well as ease pain. But be sure to ask your doctor for guidelines, especially if you have any of these ailments:

1 Heart conditions
- Angina (chest pain)
- Atherosclerosis
- Coronary artery disease
- Heart valve disease
- High cholesterol
- Hypertension (high blood pressure)
- Low blood pressure
- Past heart attack or past bypass surgery
- Heart rhythm disorder

2 Lung conditions
- Asthma
- Chronic bronchitis
- Emphysema
- History of collapsed lung

3 Bone or joint disorders
- Arthritis
- Lower back pain
- Osteoporosis

4 Other health issues
- Autoimmune disorders
- Blood disorders
- Neurological problems, such as a history of stroke, a seizure disorder, or Parkinson's disease.
- Pregnancy
- Vision or hearing impairments

How to Get Started

The first step is always the hardest, especially when you're making a change. Fear of aches, pains, and injuries keeps many would-be exercisers from lacing up their sneakers and heading out.

The solution is simply to be realistic about your fitness goals. Push yourself too hard and you'll wind up sore and discouraged. Exercise sensibly and you'll gradually build strength and endurance without getting hurt. Also:

◆ **Have a complete physical examination.** It should include a stress test—also called a treadmill test or stress ECG—which measures how the heart responds to exertion. It usually involves walking on a treadmill or pedaling a stationary bike at increasing levels of difficulty while a technician monitors your heart rate and blood pressure.

It's also wise to ask your doctor which types of exercises would be best for you, especially if you're over 40, if you're overweight, or if you have a history of smoking or heart disease.

START TO GET IN SHAPE before taking up a new sport.

◆ **Don't take up a sport to get into shape;** get into shape to take up a sport. Someone who is 15 kilograms overweight and has arthritic knees should focus on strengthening the thigh and leg muscles so they can withstand the stress of the sport before taking up tennis or jogging.

◆ **Start with one day of working out followed by one day of rest.** Your eventual aim should be to exercise five (or more!) days a week, alternating harder workouts (vigorous aerobic exercise) with easier ones (stretching, light weight lifting).

◆ **Always warm up and cool down.** Warming up gets your muscles ready and your heart pumping so that you can exercise without straining anything or depriving your muscles of oxygen. Stretch all of your muscles (see pages 132 and 133) and do some deep breathing. Your cooldown should include the same things—stretching to get the muscles back to their resting length and deep breathing to slow your heart rate and keep the oxygen flowing to all your organs.

◆ **Wear the right clothing.** Keep in mind that your sensations of cold and heat will change as you work out. Exercise, which produces heat, increases both sweating and blood flow to the skin. If the humidity is low, your body can lose a lot of heat when sweat evaporates. Don extra clothing layers in cold weather to keep from losing body heat. Wear silk or another nonabsorbent fabric next to your skin. On a cold day, a sweat-drenched T-shirt will chill you through and through. Layered clothing will also keep you comfortable on cool spring and fall days; just shed a garment when you start to feel warm. Stay indoors when the heat index, a measure of both temperature and humidity, rises above 90.

◆ **Drink up.** Sip water before, during, and after exercise. (Don't wait until you get thirsty.) Otherwise, you may become dehydrated, which makes your body less effective at cooling itself. Dehydration also "thickens" the blood, increasing the workload on a heart already working overtime to keep you moving at a faster-than-normal pace.

CHECK YOUR MEDICINE CABINET

Your medications—prescription or not—may change the way your body responds to exercise, sometimes in ways that can be dangerous. If you take any medication regularly, check with your pharmacist to see if it can cause problems. A few to watch out for:

THE PILL	ITS PURPOSE	POINTS TO REMEMBER
ANTIBIOTICS (CIPROFLOXACIN, SPARFLOXACIN, LEVOFLOXACIN, and others)	To kill disease-causing bacteria in the body	A class of antibiotics called fluoroquinolones (often prescribed for bronchitis, urinary tract infections, and intestinal infections) may increase your risk of tendinitis or a tendon rupture. If the antibiotic you're taking belongs to this class, ask if a substitute could work as well for you.
ANTIHISTAMINES (DIPHENHYDRAMINE, CYPROHEPTADINE, and others)	To diminish allergy symptoms	Antihistamines reduce your ability to sweat, so they leave you vulnerable to overheating during a workout. Some also cause drowsiness or slowed reflexes. Wait at least half a day after taking such drugs to do activities that require physical or mental coordination or fast response time, such as using gym machines.
DIURETICS (FUROSEMIDE, METOLAZONE, and others)	To control high blood pressure	These drugs flush water from your body, so they increase the risk of dehydration during exercise. Combining diuretics with exercise can be especially dangerous for older people with heart disease.
IBUPROFEN (generic; sold under several brand names)	To reduce pain and inflammation	This type of painkiller accelerates dehydration by reducing blood flow to the kidneys. Acetaminophen (Tylenol and others) does not have this effect. Aspirin and naproxen do, but to a lesser degree.
FAT-ABSORPTION BLOCKER (ORLISTAT)	To aid weight loss by blocking absorption of up to 30 percent of dietary fat	Patients who eat fatty food while taking this medication are likely to have unpleasant side effects including flatulence and diarrhea, which may be more likely to occur during exercise.

Tougher Isn't Smarter

Given all the benefits of exercise, you may be ready to run out and train for a triathlon. If a moderate workout is good, more must be better, right? Wrong. In fact, heavy exercise may weaken the immune system and leave you vulnerable to illness. Toronto researchers compared two groups of sedentary but healthy young men. All performed 40 minutes of aerobic activity, but one group exercised three days a week, and the other, five days a week. Blood tests determined that heavier exercise actually decreased the level of cells that produce antibodies. While both the light and heavier programs increased some immune activity, the lighter program was better for helping to strengthen the immune system.

Dangers of the fast lane. Not too long ago, exercise experts held to the punishing credo of "No pain, no gain." If you didn't push yourself to the wall, your efforts were deemed pretty much a waste time. Today, that attitude has bitten the dust, thanks partly to studies showing that marathon runners were five times more likely to be sick with an infection one week after a big race than runners who trained for the event but did not compete. And that's not all: Running three hours at a marathon pace is known to depress an athlete's immune system—as measured by levels of NK cells—by up to 65 percent for several hours. If a marathoner who has just finished a three-hour run encounters someone with a cold, the runner's body will be less capable of fending off the cold virus before symptoms develop.

Pay Attention to Pain

If you feel good after you exercise, you're probably doing things right. Pain is never appropriate. In fact, fitness researchers say, the exact opposite is true. If something hurts, stop what you're doing and assess the situation to prevent further damage.

◆ **Look for signs of injury.** Swelling, redness, tenderness, or pain that persists whether you're moving or not mean you may have damaged a muscle or joint. So are immobility, weakness, and popping or snapping sounds in joints.

◆ **Immediately try "RICE"—Rest-Ice-Compression-Elevation.** If you fall, twist an ankle, or jam a finger, cool the injured area with ice or a cold pack, wrap an elastic bandage around it, and elevate it above the level of the heart. Application of cold is generally the first step in treating exercise-related injuries. By constricting the blood vessels and inhibiting blood flow to the injured area, it decreases swelling. Reduced swelling means

LIFTING WEIGHTS can help you turn fat to muscle, improve your balance, gain strength, and build bone mass.

inflammation is under control, so healing will be more rapid. But leave off the ice or cold packs if you have arterio-sclerosis (hardening of the arteries) or poor blood circulation.

◆ **Consider consulting a physician after beginning RICE.** If you have severe pain that seems to originate in a joint or bone or pain of any intensity that persists for more than two weeks, see a doctor. Also get medical care for any wound that shows signs of being infected—oozing, pus, red streaks, swollen lymph nodes, or fever.

◆ **Avoid heat if there is swelling.** A hot bath may feel good, but it is not a good idea. The heat will relax the walls of your blood vessels, increasing the flow of blood and fluid to the injured area, thereby making the inflammation worse.

◆ **Use aspirin, ibuprofen, or naproxen to reduce inflammation and pain.** Aspirin, ibuprofen, and naproxen (nonsteroidal anti-inflammatory drugs) are generally the best bets for managing sports injuries. But use them sparingly, following package instructions to the letter unless your doctor tells you to do otherwise. Aspirin and similar drugs inhibit the body's release of chemicals called prostaglandins. About 25 years ago, scientists discovered that blocking prostaglandins relieved pain caused by injuries, arthritis, and—in particular—menstrual cramps. Now it seems that prostaglandins aren't all bad; they may, in fact, be responsible for some of the early steps in injury repair. Some studies indicate that blocking these chemicals too aggressively may inhibit healing.

Risks of intense workouts. Working out too heavily can do more than dampen the immune response—it can make even highly dedicated, extremely fit people ill. The reasons:

◆ **Increased exposure to germs.** If you travel to compete in a race or participate in a bike-a-thon, you'll encounter lots of people who may harbor viruses with which your immune system is unfamiliar. If one of these viruses winds up in your body, you stand a good chance of getting sick.

◆ **Nutrient deficiencies.** People who exercise religiously sometimes try unproven diets to increase their strength and/or endurance. Such diets can lead to deficiencies of important nutrients, such as essential fatty acids or vitamin E. It is well recognized that these deficiencies can cause impaired immune function.

◆ **Muscle damage.** Repeatedly tearing muscle tissue during exercise can trigger acute immune reactions in injured areas and throughout the body. In the short term, this immune activation serves to repair damaged tissue. However, repeatedly deploying immune cells to damaged muscle fibers may decrease resistance to infection, since it directs much of the body's defensive force to one task rather than keeping it at the ready.

◆ **Environmental drains.** Running, biking, or even walking long distances in extremely hot or cold weather places extra strain on the immune system. If your route goes through a city and you're committed to covering a set number of miles in a certain number of days, you're adding more stresses—namely, gulping polluted air and, if you fall behind schedule, going without enough sleep.

What you can do. It may sound overly simple, but serious athletes should be especially keen on careful hand washing, especially before meals. Hand contact is a major route for transmitting respiratory viruses, which are responsible for most of

RUBBER SANDALS worn in the locker room protect against infections like warts and athlete's foot.

the illnesses that pass from person to person. Since immunosuppression seems to be linked to harsh exertion, don't overtrain. Other pointers:

◆ **Eat a varied diet** to ensure a good balance of nutrients.

◆ **Avoid unnecessary germs.** If possible, stay away from crowds.

◆ **Consider antioxidant supplements.** There's no conclusive proof that supplements help you perform better or stay well, but some specialists tell athletes to take 1,000 mg of vitamin C and 400 IU of vitamin E each day.

◆ **Keep vaccinations current.** Get a flu shot each year and consider extra inoculations against the viruses that may be encountered during travel.

Exercise Gym Germs

As more people realize the importance of health and fitness and head to gyms to work out, we face increased chances of being exposed to colds, flu, strep, and other germs as we sweat and strive to get healthy. From the rest rooms to the showers to the equipment, the gym is full of warm, moist areas

SMART SHOPPING
Choosing a Health Club

A health club membership can be a good motivator to exercise. It will put you in a setting with other patrons whose goals are similar to yours. Although there is much competition between health clubs for your membership dollars, picking one that is right for you does not have to be difficult. Visit the club at a time of day when you would be likely to work out. Check for crowdedness (are there lineups for equipment use?) and the availability of classes. Tour all the club's facilities to ensure all equipment functions properly. Check for cleanliness, good ventilation, and lighting in the gym and locker room.

where bacteria and viruses can thrive—and where you can easily come in contact with them. Rather than running to hide, fight those nasty germs on their own turf. Here's how:

◆ **Shower, shower, shower.** Wash thoroughly before and after a swim, steam, sauna, or whirlpool. Use liquid dispenser soap in the locker rooms. Bar soap can host many different types of germs.

◆ **Be selfish.** Don't share towels or clothes. Unhygienic fabrics can spread diseases such as pinkeye, skin rashes, or fungus infections.

◆ **Wipe it off.** Use a small towel to wipe off equipment, including free weights, machines, and mats, before and after you use them (although the salt in sweat inhibits the growth of bacteria).

◆ **Dry your body first.** The same fungus that tries to take up residence between your toes can create a rash in the groin area or under the breasts.

◆ **Close your mouth.** Public pools may contain small amounts of cryptosporidium, chlorine-resistant protozoa spread when young children accidentally soil their swimsuits.

◆ **Check the hot tub.** It can harbor a number of microbes, including pseudomonas, which causes skin infection. The water should

EXERCISE—unlike dieting, which deprives you of the pleasure of food— rewards you with the thrill of newfound energy and vitality.

have between one and five parts chlorine per million parts water and a pH level of around 7.5.

◆ **Don't overworry.** If you're wondering about particularly serious viruses such as hepatitis B and HIV, be assured they can't be transmitted through sweat or by using the pool, hot tub, or sauna.

Fit at Any Weight

Quick. Create a mental picture of someone who's fit. What do you see? Rock-hard biceps? A flat stomach? A lean, mean muscle machine? How about someone a bit chunky? Or someone whose weight is off the chart? Even with extra kilograms you can be fit!

Heavy and still healthy. How is it possible to be fat and fit? Some fitness-fatness gurus like University of Virginia exercise physiologist Glenn Gaesser, Ph.D., are convinced that many overweight people's health problems lie in a couch-potato lifestyle. The real problem isn't being overweight; it's being inactive. The chronic ills associated with excess weight—diabetes and high blood pressure in particular—ease in a matter of weeks when hefty people start an exercise program and eat more fruits and vegetables.

The most persuasive support for this controversial theory so far comes from a study of about

25,000 men and 7,000 women done at the Cooper Institute for Aerobic Research in Dallas. The study, known as the Aerobics Center Longitudinal Study, found that people who were unfit and thin had a significantly higher death rate from all causes than people who were fit (defined as being able to walk on a treadmill longer than 60 percent of the population) and fat.

The most striking finding from the Aerobics Center Longitudinal Study was that being fit reduced mortality rates even in people with other risk factors for heart disease, including high blood pressure. Remarkably, even significantly overweight smokers and former smokers who were physically fit had lower death rates than thin but unfit people.

The larger picture. On the other hand, there are hundreds more studies to support the traditional view that obesity by itself increases your chance of developing a host of health problems. The bottom line: If you're genuinely obese, you're best off losing weight if you want to achieve optimal health. Still, if you are fit and fat, there's a strong likelihood that you're healthier, overall, than someone who is normal weight but never gets any exercise.

Whether you carry extra kilograms or not, exercise will increase your muscle mass and provide many other health benefits, including pumping up the

Interesting!

Instead of paying attention to kilograms, check your waist circumference to see if you're carrying excess abdominal fat, which is an independent risk factor for disease. A waist measurement over 100 cm in men and 90 cm in women signifies increased health risks in people whose body mass index (BMI, see page 56) is above 25.

Tips for Overweight Exercisers

1. One step at a time. **Exercising regularly will give you the energy to be active. But overdoing it will make you quit. So exert yourself only enough to feel slightly taxed, not exhausted.**

2. Dress comfortably. **There's no reason to feel self-conscious. Anything goes, as long as it provides freedom of movement. In general, wear lighter clothing than the outdoor temperature would warrant for normal activity.**

3. Search out a low-impact aerobic exercise program. **It will give you a real workout without putting excess stress on the joints, something that overweight exercisers are more prone to do. Ask friends to join you—it makes staying motivated much easier.**

4. Be active with your children or grandchildren. **Have fun together in the park instead of watching television or sitting at the computer.**

rate at which you burn calories. In fact, beginning exercisers may burn calories five to seven times faster during exercise than they do while resting. Furthermore, once you stop exercising, your metabolism does not immediately slow down. It will continue to burn calories at a slightly higher-than-normal rate for hours, possibly because your body works harder after exercise to repair tissue damage and rebuild your energy stores.

Moving toward Immune Power

Enjoyment is the key to sticking with your resolution to fit in more physical activity. Increase your odds of getting hooked by picking a sport or type of exercise that you already like doing. Then become better at it by reading up on it, watching videotapes, or joining a gym and taking classes.

Other factors to consider: What's a good match for your current physical condition and your lifestyle? What time of day can you exercise? Do you know someone who would like to work out with you? Do you love gadgets? Maybe the answer is to buy an exercise machine. Whatever type of exercise you choose,

remember: Start slowly and gradually build up to 20 minutes per session for general health maintenance, or 45 minutes for weight loss. Health Canada's *Physical Activity Guide* suggests focusing on three key areas:

Flexibility. You develop loose, easy-moving joints through such activities as yoga, stretching, gymnastics, or swimming. To maintain flexibility and protect against injuries, you also need to warm up and cool down all major muscle groups, including those of the arms, chest, back, stomach, hips, and legs, before and after other types of exercise. Experts suggest that to increase flexibility, you should hold a mild stretch for 30 seconds and repeat it three times while breathing normally.

Endurance. We develop the ability to exercise without exhaustion through aerobic activity. This includes any activity that uses large muscle groups in a continuous, rhythmic fashion for sustained periods of time. Something as simple as a brisk, 20-minute walk counts as aerobic exercise and has the added bonus of being a weight-bearing activity that helps strengthen your bones. Other exercises that combine aerobic and weight-bearing benefits include dancing, stair climbing, and rope skipping. Non–weight-bearing aerobic exercises include bicycling, stationary cycling, swimming, and rowing.

Three to four days of aerobic activity is fine for general health maintenance. But if you're trying to lose weight, aim for four or more days a week, and rest at least one day a week.

Strength. Also referred to as muscular conditioning, strength training improves posture, reduces the risk of back injury, and helps

THE SOLE NECESSITY

If you've tried to buy sneakers recently, you know that the canvas high-tops of the past have been replaced by high-tech athletic gear—and thank goodness! Wearing shoes designed for the exercise of your choice can prevent the "pain" that otherwise might precede the "gain" of a more fit physique. Select shoes with sufficient cushioning and shock absorption, a foam arch support (unless your arches are flat), and a one-centimeter space between the big toe and the shoe tip.

maintain flexibility. A University of Florida study also found that having strong muscles is linked to higher levels of enzymes that combat the unstable molecules known as free radicals. Over time, free radicals—which are released when the body uses oxygen— damage cells and may contribute to the development of many chronic diseases. In the Florida study, older people who lifted weights three times a week for six months showed less oxidative cell damage than those who did not lift weights.

Use free weights or machines, and be sure to exercise every major muscle group, including the muscles of the arms, chest, back, stomach, hips, and legs. Start with a weight that's comfortable to handle and lift eight times in a row. Gradually add more repetitions until you can complete 12. For greater strength conditioning, add more weight and/or more repetitions, in sets of 8 to 12, when the exercise becomes easy.

Working Out Safely

Before you jump into any workout, here are four points to keep in mind.

◆ **Focus on form.** Always use controlled movements. When stretching, hold each stretch for at least a count of 10, with the goal of working up to a count of 30, and never jerk or bounce.

◆ **Breathe right.** If you are like most exercisers, you need to fight two tendencies: not paying attention to your breathing, and holding your breath. This is especially important for people with heart or circulatory problems or high blood

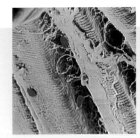

How Muscles Enlarge

Toning, body shaping, body sculpting, weight lifting, strength training—all are names for exercises that increase the size of your muscles by increasing the number of myofibrils, thread-like strands (ABOVE) that form each muscle fiber. Whatever it's called, this type of workout not only beefs up your muscle size, it delivers a weight-control bonus: Since muscle burns calories at a higher rate than fat even when you are not working out, you can eat more good food without worrying about weight gain or you can lose weight more easily.

pressure, since blood pressure rises temporarily when you hold your breath. Instead, inhale when exerting—while actually lifting weights, for example. Exhale as you perform the easier motions, such as lowering weights.

◆ **Add in aerobic conditioning.** It's an essential element of any total conditioning workout. Aim to do vigorous walking, swimming, or other exercises that speed your heart rate two or three times a week. These activities work your heart and lungs and burn fat.

EXERCISE blunts the thirst mechanism, so remind yourself to drink up.

◆ **Lean on friends.** It's easier, safer, and a lot more fun to work out with others. Exercise classes offer built-in companionship, often bringing together people who are at roughly similar fitness levels. Your community might also have a walking club you can join.

{ "Patience, persistence, and perspiration make an unbeatable combination for success." }

—NAPOLEON HILL / SELF-IMPROVEMENT AUTHOR (1883-1970)

Total Body Tune-Up

The following exercises, designed to improve flexibility and strength, will help you prepare your whole body for more strenuous activity. At first, just move through the routine at a comfortable pace. When that gets easy, try picking up the pace.

Before long, you'll be running through these basic moves to warm up before you really get down to business, then repeating them to cool down at the end.

Why are warm-ups so important before exercise? Like an engine on a cold morning, your muscles need to be coaxed in and out of action. When they aren't ready to meet the increased demands of exercise, you'll get tired faster and take longer to recover.

Surprisingly, the common notion that stretching before you exercise helps prevent injuries was recently debunked by Australian researchers. Stretchers and non-stretchers were found to have the same injury rate. But stretching was still deemed important for loosening tight muscles that might restrict your normal range of movement.

After you stretch, it's time to warm up—a different activity altogether. Stretching helps your muscles prepare to go a greater distance, literally lengthening them beyond their usual span. Warm-ups raise your heart rate and prime your muscles for action. All it takes is about five minutes of jogging in place, doing jumping jacks, or skipping a rope.

If you're planning to walk, run, bicycle, or swim, your warm-up can consist of starting your activity slowly and picking up the pace gradually until you are into a full workout.

TOTAL BODY WORKOUT

Achieve full-body fitness in a jiffy with this at-home routine. You'll work your heart, tone your muscles, and burn a few hundred calories.

Workout Time
20 minutes

Frequency
2–3 nonconsecutive days per week

Intensity
Monitor your pre- and post-workout heart rate (see page 118) to be sure you are exercising at a moderate intensity. If the workout seems too easy, add more sets or repetitions. If it seems too difficult, scale back.

Ultimate Goal
Eventually, you want to do this workout five days a week, along with an aerobic activity, such as biking, walking, or jogging, for 20 minutes.

HAMSTRING STRETCH

◆ Stand with your feet shoulder-width apart and pointed straight ahead.

◆ Bend slowly forward, arms stretched in front of you, with your back flat and abdominal muscles tight.

◆ Bend knees slightly, stretching gently and steadily.

◆ Hold 20 seconds.

USE THESE MUSCLES
Out of the gym:
Rowing or kayaking
In the gym:
Straight leg raises or elliptical training machine

THIGH STRETCH

◆ Hold your left foot in your
  right hand. Slowly pull the heel
  of your left foot toward the
  middle of your buttock.
  (Don't pull toward the side.)
◆ Use your other hand to keep
  your balance. Stretch gently
  and steadily, without bouncing.
◆ Hold for 20 seconds and then
  switch legs.

USE THESE MUSCLES
Out of the gym:
Taking the stairs or
bicycling
In the gym:
Stair machine or treadmill
(on an incline)

CALF STRETCH

◆ Face a wall, standing about two feet away. Lean
  forward and rest your forearms on the wall with
  your forehead on the back of your hands.
◆ Bend one leg and move it toward the
  wall. Keep your back leg straight, with
  the foot flat and pointed forward.
◆ Push your leg forward until you
  feel the stretch in your calf and
  hamstring. Stretch gently
  and steadily. Do not bounce.
◆ Hold for 20 seconds and
  then switch legs.

USE THESE MUSCLES
Out of the gym:
Taking the stairs,
hiking on hills, or
bicycling
In the gym:
Stair machine or treadmill
(on an incline)

SIDE AND ARM STRETCH

◆ Stand with your knees slightly bent.
◆ With your right hand, gently pull
  your left elbow behind your head as
  you bend to the right side.
◆ Hold for 20 seconds and then
  switch sides.

USE THESE MUSCLES
Out of the gym:
Swimming laps, playing
tennis, shoveling snow, or
cross-country skiing
In the gym:
Lateral pull-downs, seated
rowing machine, or ellip-
tical training machine

SHOULDER STRETCH

◆ Clasp your hands together behind your
  back. Keeping your arms straight,
  raise them gently.
◆ Hold for 20 seconds while
  stretching steadily.

USE THESE MUSCLES
Out of the gym:
Golf, rock climbing,
swimming laps, or
playing racquet sports,
such as tennis
In the gym:
Seated rowing machine
or shoulder press

Total Body Tune-Up

JUMPING JACKS

Good for a full-body warm-up

◆ Stand with your arms hanging loosely at your sides and feet slightly apart.

◆ Snap your feet farther apart (a little more than shoulder width) while raising your straight arms above your head until your hands clap together.

◆ Immediately reverse direction, sweeping your arms back down to your sides and snapping your feet back into the starting position. Repeat in a steady rhythm.

Your ultimate goal:

At least five full minutes of this warm-up

MORE WARM-UPS
Out of the gym:
Brisk walking or bicycling
In the gym:
Stair machine or treadmill

MODIFIED PUSH-UPS

Good for chest, shoulders, and triceps

◆ Lie facedown on the floor and place your hands directly underneath your shoulders with your fingers facing forward. Keep your head in line with your spine—don't look up! Your back should be straight, with the abdominal muscles pulled in.

◆ Balancing on bent knees (you can use a cushion), lift your upper body by pushing up with your arms until they are straight. Your palms should be pressed into the floor; elbows should point back rather than out at the sides; the head, neck, back, and hips should be in line.

◆ When your arms are almost fully extended, pause for two seconds, then move down and up again slowly, without touching the floor.

MORE CHEST BUILDERS
Out of the gym:
Rowing, pushing a stroller or baby carriage, or mowing the lawn
In the gym:
Chest presses or boxing

Your ultimate goal:

Two sets of 20 repetitions

SUMO SQUAT

Good for quadriceps, hamstrings, and gluteals (buttocks)

◆ From a standing position, place your feet shoulder-width apart, toes slightly turned out, knees relaxed (not locked).

◆ Slowly lower your hips down as if you're trying to sit in a chair. Keep your abdominals tight and your knees aligned with your big toes. Stop before your knees extend beyond your toes.

◆ Reverse, keeping knees slightly bent.

Your ultimate goal:

Two sets of 16 repetitions

MORE REAR RESHAPERS
Out of the gym:
Skating, hiking on hilly terrain, or swimming laps
In the gym:
Stair climber

HAMSTRING CURLS

Good for back of thighs

◆ Stand near a wall or other support with your feet parallel, about six inches apart, toes pointing forward.

◆ Shift the left foot back a few inches from the right, extending your arms in front of you for balance.

◆ Bend the left leg at a 90-degree angle and flex the foot to squeeze the hamstring.

◆ Extend the bent leg backward until you feel a strong contraction in your hamstring and buttock. Keep your abdominal muscles pulled in to support your lower back. Hold this position for a count of two. If you have trouble balancing for this exercise, use a straight-backed chair for support.

Your ultimate goal:

Two sets of 16 repetitions with each leg

MORE LEG TONERS
Out of the gym:
Biking, hiking on hilly terrain, speed walking, or jogging in place
In the gym:
Seated or pronated leg-curl machine

Total Body Tune-Up

TWISTING CRUNCHES

Good for sides of the stomach

◆ Lie on your back with your fingers laced behind your head. Hold your elbows slightly out to the sides and keep your chin pointing upward. Bend your knees and rest your feet flat on the floor.

◆ Squeeze your abdominals while lifting your left knee. As you raise your knee, twist your right shoulder toward it, exhaling as you rise. Be sure to reach with your shoulder, not with your elbow. Tense your abdominals for 2–4 seconds, then slowly lower your body to the starting position and repeat on the other side.

Your ultimate goal:

One set of 30 repetitions on each side

MORE TUMMY TRIMMERS
Out of the gym:
Golfing, martial arts, Irish dancing, tennis, or racquetball
In the gym:
Kickboxing or yoga

LEG–ARM EXTENSIONS

Good for the entire back

◆ Lie facedown, resting your forehead on your left hand. Extend your right arm forward, out over your head, with the palm facing down.

◆ Take a deep breath and lift your right hand and left leg off the floor, keeping both straight. Exhale.

◆ Hold for two seconds before lowering to the floor, then switch arms and legs.

Your ultimate goal:

Two sets of eight extensions on each side

MORE BACK BUILDERS
Out of the gym:
Swimming, rock climbing, tennis or another racquet sport, shoveling or hoeing in the garden
In the gym:
Yoga, water aerobics, or lateral pull-downs (never behind the head)

A closer look at...fitting in more fitness

Stumped for creative ways to sneak fitness into your daily routine? When it comes to working out, consistency is what gets results. Still, sometimes there's really no way to make time for your workout. On those days, try these fitness fixes while you are...

TALKING ON THE PHONE

Instead of sitting, pace or stand and pull in your lower abdominal muscles so they feel as if they're flattened against your hipbones. Keep your chest up and your shoulders relaxed. BENEFIT: a whittled middle. On your cell phone? Stand with your toes on the edge of a step or curb, heels slightly lower. Lift your heels as high as you can, then sink them as low as they can go. BENEFIT: shapelier calves.

CLIMBING STAIRS

Skip the elevator. To get more from step climbing, use this technique. Begin by pushing off the inside of your left foot, then plant your entire right foot on the next step, pushing down into your heel to lift all your weight on your right leg. That way you're using your weight for resistance and muscle strengthening. BENEFIT: aerobic conditioning, stronger inner thighs, buttocks, and hamstrings.

STOPPED IN TRAFFIC

Make the most of the drive to work or to the mall. When sitting at a stoplight, pull your navel back toward your spine, allowing your pelvis to tilt. Contract and hold for a count of five seconds, then release. Repeat as many times as you can. BENEFIT: a trim waist and strong back. Or put your arms out to your sides and stretch your fingers, palms, and forearms. (You'll need to open the window for this one.) Hold for five seconds, then relax. BENEFIT: stretches your arm and back muscles.

PREPARING DINNER

Keep a filled 1½-liter water bottle on your kitchen counter. Hold it in your palm and bend your arm, bringing the bottle up to your shoulder for a biceps curl. Pause at the top, tense the front of your arm, then release. Repeat 10 times with each arm. BENEFIT: shapely, sculpted arms. Store cans on low shelves. When you squat to reach for the items, keep your back straight and stomach in. Standing up, squeeze your bottom and abdominals. Repeat 10 times. BENEFIT: a more defined rear end.

Take Up the Walking Habit

Eager for another easy way to get a total body workout, increase your heart rate—and send your calorie burn sky high? Lace up your walking shoes and head out the door. It's okay to start at a snail's pace. You'll soon be adding greater challenges as your stamina—and dedication—grow.

Why walk? Studies show that four out of five women who start walking for exercise keep walking. In contrast, 50 percent of women who take up other activities, including swimming, stair climbing, and running, call it quits within the first few weeks. What gives walking its staying power? It's one of the easiest activities to fit into a busy day, especially if you divide it up into three 10-minute increments. Besides the physical benefits, studies show that walking fights insomnia and depression. It's also a bargain: You need only a good pair of shoes—properly fitted at an athletic-shoe store—to get your foot out the door.

Take your first step. Anyone who has been sedentary for a long time should start by going only as far as it takes to begin feeling out of breath; stop if you feel joint pain. Reasonably fit people should begin by walking 10 minutes a day, then increase their workout time by 10 percent each week. In other words, this week walk for 10 minutes, next week for 11 minutes. In the beginning, focus on increasing the amount of time that you walk, not the intensity of your pace. Eventually, you can toss in some stints of jogging to call more muscles into motion without too much stress. Or simply add power intervals by pushing your pace up to around 10 km/h for three minutes at a time.

Try out a treadmill. It can't compare to walking outside and communing with nature, but indoor treadmill walking offers its own benefits. For one, people tend to walk slightly faster on a treadmill, and they don't pause, so they burn more calories.

Many treadmills are also cushioned so they absorb as much as 40 percent of the impact that would otherwise fall on your joints. Some treadmills have a visual display to monitor your heart rate and the distance you walk. And most important, the weather can't mess up your workout plans.

PEDOMETERS PAY OFF

You've heard the pitch: Take the stairs instead of the elevator, and walk, don't drive, to the corner store. You'll be more motivated to comply if you wear a pedometer—a tiny monitor clipped to your waistband that counts the number of steps you take. A Johns Hopkins University research shows that people who wear one walk an average of 40 minutes a day—about 11 minutes more than those who don't. Pedometers are sold at sporting goods stores.

Confidence is synonymous with correct walking posture: Stand tall with your **chin** up and lean forward slightly.

Keep your **shoulders** back and relaxed, away from the ears. The chest should be lifted, not slumped.

Let your **arms** swing naturally at a 90-degree angle, in rhythm with the rest of your body. If your arms dangle at your sides, you'll burn 5–10 percent fewer calories. Loosely cup your hands, but never clench them. Holding them in fists can raise your blood pressure. If moving your arms tires you out at first, do it for 10 minutes at a time. Rest them for the next 10 minutes, then move them again.

Your **back** should be straight and your **hips** should swivel forward and back instead of swaying side to side.

Abdominal muscles should be pulled in. Tuck your **pelvis** slightly under your hips.

Gently extend your **forward leg** as you place the foot on the ground heel first. Keep your knees soft, not locked.

Walk briskly, about 6 km/h, leaning forward at the **ankle** ever so slightly. After your **heel** strikes the ground, roll onto the ball of your foot. Don't let your feet point inward or outward, and don't slap the ground. Avoid blisters by dabbing petroleum jelly on your heels before heading out the door. Don't wear cotton socks for fitness walking. They bunch up when wet, leading to painful blisters. Instead, wear synthetic or synthetic-cotton blends, preferably ones designed for walkers, with extra padding in the heel.

Exercise Your Options

You say you hate formal exercise? No problem. Even if you never go near an aerobics class, you can still rack up 30 minutes of physical activity a day— and have more fun than you ever imagined you could doing it.

Anything that gets you moving counts, even a few short spurts of activity (10 minutes here, 15 minutes there), according to Health Canada's *Physical Activity Guide*. And the more enjoyment you get from the activity, the longer you're likely to do it.

Need some ideas? Here's a guide to just a few of the activities that can get you moving without counting repetitions or looking at your watch every five minutes. Among the main listings, chances are there's at least one you're already doing or could easily begin tomorrow—if not today. The options that appear in boxes are for the somewhat more adventurous, but they're well worth exploring if you're so inclined. Finally, yoga—an ancient discipline with many modern variations— has something to offer anyone seeking flexibility, toning, pain relief, relaxation, and peace of mind. Practiced by itself or as a complement to other fitness activities, yoga is a staple of healthy living.

Dancing: Swing into Action

Dance! It's fun, it requires no special equipment, and it burns just as many calories as jogging. Besides all that, you can cut a rug just about anywhere. Stuck at home on your own? Pop in your favorite CDs and bop around to your heart's content. If you don't fancy going it alone, take up dancing at your local community center or dance school. That way, you'll get the benefits of socializing while you exercise.

Dancing has other proven physical benefits as well. It increases bone density, for one. A recent Austrian study found that when post-menopausal women with osteoporosis spent about three hours a week dancing, their spines became more dense.

DANCING cuts stress and increases energy, improving strength, muscle tone, and coordination.

Tempted to hit the dance floor? For starters, just move to the music. If you want to add fancier steps, you can always take lessons later. Try different forms of dance, each of which offers distinctly different health benefits. The elegant moves of ballet, for instance, build strength. High-energy salsa, tap, and swing are great for aerobic conditioning, and belly dancing trims your waist.

To avoid injury, keep your weight centered over your feet, especially when you're turning: shoulders over hips, hips over knees, knees over ankles. For added safety, wear snug-fitting (not tight) shoes that will provide a stable base for all your dance moves. In other words, no spike heels.

Reasons to try dance:

◆ **It helps tone your muscles.** That, in turn, gives you greater endurance for all kinds of activities.
◆ **It improves coordination and balance.** The result: a lower risk of falls.
◆ **It makes you feel energized.** And it's a terrific stress reducer.

CROSS-COUNTRY SKIING: NOT JUST FOR KICKS

There is no better exercise than cross-country skiing. This endurance sport (also called Nordic skiing) originated about 5,000 years ago, when people living in the area known today as Scandinavia strapped the bones of large animals to shoes with leather thongs.

Technically, it's not much more complicated today than it was back then, although the equipment has become more sophisticated. Cross-country skiers now use runners made of fiberglass, wood, or plastic. It's just a matter of gliding through fresh powder or of scooting over icy patches or through slush.

Cross-country skiing is one of the few activities that requires you to use all of the major muscle groups in both the upper and lower body at the same time. This results in a sizable aerobic benefit as well as a great caloric expenditure.

Also, unlike downhill skiing, it places little stress on the joints, so it's suitable for people of all ages and most fitness levels.

Finally, the gliding motion stretches your muscles, especially those in your calves, hamstrings, and lower back. As if all that weren't enough, cross-country skiing immerses you in the beauty of wintertime nature and lets you enjoy it at a relaxed pace afforded by few other sports.

Reasons to try cross-country skiing:

◆ **It's a comprehensive, total-body workout.** Yet because it's low impact, the injury rate is lower than that of similar sports.
◆ **It can strengthen your cardiovascular system.** Plus, it promotes weight loss and reduces stress, freeing the immune system to fight illness.
◆ **It burns 550 calories per hour.** That's if you weigh 70 kilograms. If you're heavier, you'll burn even more.

Gardening: A Growth Sport

Puttering around the garden with a sun hat and trowel may not sound much like exercise, but research has shown that gardening can enhance health at any age. In fact, depending on how you go about it, tending a garden can be as tough a workout as kayaking, rowing, or lifting weights. A team of researchers led by exercise physiologist Barbara Ainsworth, Ph.D., of the University of Minnesota, found that such gardening tasks as digging and trimming hedges require as much energy expenditure as table tennis and skateboarding. More heavy-duty tasks—mowing the lawn with a hand mower or turning over soil with a shovel, for example—require about as much energy as using a stair machine. In addition, gardening makes you stretch a whole assortment of muscles, so it helps increase your flexibility.

In fact, gardening may well be the perfect whole-body exercise: It strengthens the heart, improves circulation, and provides ample stress

HIKING: EXERCISE WITH A VIEW

We all know that walking is terrific exercise, but the equally simple option of hiking offers all the same benefits, squared.

When you take your walks off-road, you get to enjoy the beauty of the great outdoors while giving your lower body a great low-impact and physiologically diverse workout. Because of the irregular surfaces of most hiking trails, you generally get the equivalent of a good, long workout on a stair machine or a treadmill. A good hike challenges both the serious athlete and the person who's just seeking better health. You don't need any sophisticated gear, but if you use a walking stick (as most experts recommend), you'll exercise your upper body as well as your legs, while reducing the risk of injury from missteps.

Comfortable, sturdy, broken-in shoes are a must—if not hiking boots, then good cross-training sneakers. The right shoes will protect you from blisters and falls. Wear layers of loose-fitting clothes, preferably of materials such as nylon or polypropylene that will wick moisture away from your body. And always bring extra water and snacks along.

Reasons to try hiking:

◆ **It never gets boring.** There's new scenery around every turn in the trail.

◆ **It is a great way to lose a few excess kilograms, thereby improving your immune response.** For starters, you can walk off 300 to 400 calories an hour on a moderately challenging trail. That could add up to 2,000 calories—a full week's worth of calorie burn—in a half-day hike. You can burn more calories by increasing speed.

◆ **It will make you feel better while clearing and sharpening your mind.** The result? You'll want to hike again!

relief. Gardening is also a particularly good activity for novice or older exercisers, since you can always garden at your own pace. It even can save you money and improve your diet!

Tantalized? Remember, gardening does qualify as exercise and will probably use muscles that you don't otherwise notice. Be sure to warm up by walking briskly around the yard, and do some arm, back, neck, and leg stretches prior to starting your chores. Take regular stretch breaks throughout your time in the garden.

When you reach down to pull weeds, don't bend from the waist. Instead, squat or kneel, using a pillow or pad to cushion your knees. Be sure to lift properly as well: Bend at the knees, keep your back straight, and don't twist your upper body.

As your level of fitness improves, add more strenuous tasks to your routine—shovel mulch or turn compost.

Reasons to try gardening:

◆ **It can help you heal, both physically and emotionally.** Quietly tending your garden is a real stress buster, giving you a break from the general rush of life. The serenity of the outdoors is a proven immune booster. (See Chapter 6, "Immunity and the Mind.")

◆ **It's a real workout.** Gardening is especially appealing to people who don't like to exercise just to burn calories.

◆ **It lets you enjoy the fruits of your labor— fresh, unprocessed foods.** Not surprisingly, gardeners consume most kinds of vegetables more often than non-gardeners do. When you plant your garden, fill it with varieties of immune-boosting foods. (See Chapter 2, "The Miracle of Food.")

WEEDING burns about 105 calories an hour, while mowing a lawn with a push mower expends about 195 calories.

Golf: Not Just Putting Around

The Royal Canadian Golf Association estimates 5.2 million Canadians play golf—a number that is rising. Many golfers figure that 18 holes is enough exercise to stay in shape. But is it?

The answer: It depends. Although you'll swing a club at least 70 times as you make your way through 18 holes, the real benefits of golf come from walking the course. If you ride a motorized cart from hole to hole, you're missing out on

GOLF AND SWIMMING can help you lose weight, especially if you use proper technique. Have your swing or your stroke checked by a pro.

treadmill, or jogging track.

Just beware: Even though it is not a strenuous sport, golf is not without risk. The golf swing is a forceful, repetitive movement that involves everything from your ankles to your wrists, so it can lead to overuse injuries in several parts of the body.

The most common injuries involve the lower back, shoulders, and elbows (similar to tennis elbow). The single easiest way to prevent a golf-related injury is to stretch and warm up for at least 10 minutes before hitting the links (see page 132). It's also a good idea to have your swing assessed by a professional. To prevent sunburn and skin cancer, always wear a hat and use sunblock.

Reasons to try golf:
◆ **It burns an average of 1,360 calories per game for a 70-kilogram person.** That's 1,088 calories more than if you just sat around watching TV for four hours.
◆ **It's a pleasant way to stride far.** The average course requires five miles of walking per 18 holes.
◆ **It improves balance.** It also helps build up your trunk muscles and tone your calves, hamstrings, buttocks, and quadriceps.

Swimming: Get in the Groove

Swimming is ideal for people with arthritis and other joint problems. Unlike many other sports, it places absolutely no stress on joints and ligaments. That's why it's also a good exercise for people who are overweight. People with asthma, too, can swim laps comfortably. The warm, moist air around pools prevents exercise-induced asthma attacks.

much of what golf has to offer. After all, how much physical exertion does it take to turn a steering wheel?

Skip the cart, however, and one of the fastest growing sports in Canada can count as a great workout. According to a study reported in the *American Journal of Medicine,* golf confers many health benefits. Researchers in Finland assigned 55 sedentary but healthy men to play golf two or three times a week for 20 weeks, then compared them with a control group of 55 men who remained inactive. Golfers surpassed the control group in treadmill endurance, and they also enjoyed decreased weight, trimmer waistlines, and healthier cholesterol levels—all from simply walking around the golf course and lugging their own bags.

While golf is not aerobic—the miles of walking are interrupted too often by stops—the uneven terrain of the course exercises a wider range of muscles than the consistent surface of a sidewalk,

MARTIAL ARTS: MORE THAN SELF-DEFENSE

If aerobics classes fail to provide the kick you're looking for, a better option may be the latest trend in fitness classes: martial-arts–inspired workouts like Tae-Bo and kickboxing. After all, nothing delivers cardiovascular conditioning like an hour of energy-packed flying kicks.

If you're the more traditional type, look to the ancient martial arts, such as judo, aikido, jujitsu, karate, or kung fu. All provide an aerobic workout that engages the whole body and emphasizes balance and coordination.

Although these techniques have been around for centuries, there has been relatively little scientific research on martial arts. The one martial art that has been studied with any thoroughness is Tai chi chuan, or tai chi, a conditioning exercise of graceful, controlled movements that can be done even by people unable to perform more vigorous activities because of age, illness, or disabilities. In one study that demonstrated tai chi's benefits, men and women aged 58 to 70 did an hour of the exercises four or five times a week. Over time, the men's cardiovascular fitness increased by 16 percent and the women's by 21 percent. Thanks to tai chi, they could climb stairs and walk briskly without getting breathless.

Reasons to try martial arts:
◆ **It develops discipline.** This commitment will help you make other changes in your life. All martial arts practices start with a goal, then teach you the steps you must take to accomplish it.
◆ **It is a great way to keep your body strong and your mind sharp as you age.** Good martial arts training improves coordination and flexibility.
◆ **It builds confidence and poise.** It also lets you release anger, anxiety, and other health-damaging emotions.

In fact, almost anyone can benefit from swimming, since it forces you to utilize virtually every muscle group in your body. The water provides complete cushioning, so there's practically no risk of injury. Evidence is emerging that swimming also has unique psychological benefits almost like meditation. While you glide through the water, you take time out from the rest of the world and get completely lost in your own thoughts. (If you'd like more social interactions, try water polo or synchronized swimming.)

To get more out of swimming, vary your strokes. You'll engage a range of muscle groups if you alternate styles. Try one lap of crawl, one lap of breaststroke, one lap of backstroke, and so on.

Reasons to try swimming:
◆ **It's the ultimate no-impact aerobic sport.** It gets your heart pumping, increasing circulation of blood and lymph, while leaving your joints completely stress-free. Water exercises benefit seniors, pregnant women, arthritis sufferers, or anyone with an injury.
◆ **It provides a full-body workout.** Just be sure to alternate among a few different strokes.
◆ **It's a great calorie burner.** Even at a leisurely pace, a 70-kilogram swimmer will burn nearly 300 calories in half an hour. You'll get exercise even if you simply stay in one place: Five minutes of treading water at a relaxed pace will burn nearly 60 calories—or even more if you weigh more.

Yoga: Uplifting Moves

Exercise trends come and go. One week it's step aerobics, the next, Tae-Bo, the next, spinning. In time, last week's craze is always replaced by a new one. But one type of exercise has endured through the ages: yoga.

Developed five centuries ago by Hindu swamis of India as a way to unite the body with the mind, it's been handed down from teacher to student ever since. Now, conventional medical research is finding that the regular practice of these ancient poses and stretches, which are done in conjunction with deep breathing, can help prevent and treat a range of ailments. Yoga poses, called asanas, can make your body stronger and more flexible, improve your sense of balance, and increase your energy.

Flexibility in focus. Yoga is not a cure-all. But by increasing your joint flexibility, it can have far-reaching benefits.

First, the slow-

SALUTATION TO THE SUN is a series of yoga poses often performed at the start of the day.

motion movements of yoga ease you into exercise without causing strain or pain. Even if you are only able to move an inch and hold a position for five seconds, you are already enhancing your body's flexibility and increasing your physical performance. A flexible joint can move through a greater range of motion than a stiff, unused one. Over time, increased flexibility makes exercise more pleasurable.

Moreover, recent studies show that the static stretching you do in yoga poses—a gradual and controlled elongation of the muscles held for 15 to 30 seconds—helps reduce muscle soreness after exercise. This relieves the immune system of having to mount an inflammatory response, which is one of its normal functions. When tissues are injured during exercise (or by bacteria, toxins, or heat), they release chemicals that attract the immune system's white blood cells to "eat" dead or damaged cells. This process, called phagocytosis, causes thousands of white blood cells to die.

Another key benefit is that yoga, done properly, reduces the risk of lower back pain. The stretching poses increase tissue temperature, which in turn promotes muscle relaxation and reduces stress to the lower back.

Stretching also speeds the transport of blood and nutrients directly to muscles, resulting, some experts say, in a reduction in accumulated toxins. Another little-known benefit is increased neuro-muscular coordination. Studies show that nerve-impulse velocity (the time it takes a signal to travel to the brain and back) is improved with stretching. This helps opposing muscle groups work in a more synergistic, coordinated fashion.

Even more benefits. Increased flexibility also means enhanced enjoyment of physical activity. Unlike more frenetic exercises that improve flexibility, yoga helps relax both mind and body, thereby heightening your sense of well-being. It also helps control blood pressure and teaches the body how to rest deeply and release stress. This, in turn, can reduce the adrenal glands' production of cortisol, a powerful hormone secreted at times of high stress and fear. Over time, excess cortisol can impair immune function and contribute to the development of chronic diseases.

The best type for you. There are several different branches of yoga, known as "paths," each with its own methodology and emphasis. Most but not all forms practiced in Canada are based on Hatha yoga, which emphasizes gentle stretching and strengthening poses. If you are a beginner, sample several different classes and teachers before deciding which is best for you.

◆ **Ananda yoga.** Since ananda means "state of bliss," this branch of yoga fittingly focuses on the gentlest poses, accompanied by whispered affirmations of serenity. The scents of aromather-apy oils and the music of cymbals, bells, and ancient horns contribute to the enchantment.

◆ **Bikram yoga.** Named after practitioner Bikram Choudhury, this style of yoga is con-ducted at room temperatures between 32°C and 40°C, which Choudhury believes prepares muscles for intense stretching. An extremely demanding technique, Bikram yoga is generally

Before You Hit the Floor

If you're curious about this more than 2,000-year-old exercise tradition, here are some tips to help your first foray into yoga go smoothly.

1 Talk to your doctor. Certain medical condi-tions may rule out specific poses. If you have high blood pressure, glaucoma, a history of retinal detach-ment, or heart disease, for instance, your doctor may advise you not to do hand, head, or shoulder stands. Because they tend to increase blood flow to the head, such positions could aggravate any of those conditions.

2 Fit the class to your abilities. Talk to the teacher before signing up to alert him or her to your newcomer status and make sure you'll be comfortable with the level.

3 Wear comfortable clothes. Good choices are tights, bike shorts, or stretchy leggings and a T-shirt. You want to move easily and be able to see your body. Leave off the shoes and socks.

4 Don't overdo it. Push yourself, but don't be talked into anything that feels overly difficult. A good yoga teacher will guide—rather than force—your body into correct form.

5 Stay at home, if you prefer. Rent a few beginner videotapes or spring for some one-on-one sessions with a private teacher.

6 Eat early. Try not to have a meal within two hours of class.

inappropriate for beginners, except those who are in very good shape.

◆ **Iyengar yoga.** Founded roughly 60 years ago, Iyengar is a modern take on classical poses with emphasis on precise body alignment. Special emphasis is placed on holding certain postures for several minutes.

◆ **Kripala yoga.** This very gentle, introspective practice is distinguished by the length of time practitioners hold each posture. Most other approaches call for more frequent posture changes. A blend of techniques, Kripala is taught in three stages: postures, breath, and body awareness.

◆ **Kundalini yoga.** An ancient form of Hatha yoga, the focus here is on stationary postures said to awaken the "kundalini" or "coiled serpent spirit" within each person. Intense breath work, chanting, and meditation are also used to tap into that energy. Kundalini is related to Tantra yoga, which employs special exercises to develop, balance, and control the sexual response. The pop musician Sting made headlines several years ago when he revealed that he used tantric techniques to prolong sex for up to five hours.

◆ **Power yoga.** This path involves a fast-paced sequence of standing and floor postures done as a vigorous workout to purify and strengthen the body. An offshoot encourages the use of props such as straps, blocks, blankets, and sandbags to help you get into poses.

AN ANYWHERE, ANYTIME ACTIVITY, yoga can be done with little or no equipment.

A word to the wise. Almost anyone can benefit from yoga, including the elderly, children, and people with chronic health problems. Still, it's risky to try yoga without consulting your doctor if you are pregnant or if you have problems with your heart, circulation, neck, or spine. Medical precautions are also warranted if you suffer from multiple sclerosis, chronic fatigue syndrome, or recently broken bones. If you've been injured or had surgery, be sure you've healed completely before practicing yoga.

Yoga students who have no serious physical problems should tell their teachers if they have any back, neck, or knee pain, so that they can avoid added stress in these areas.

THE PLOW, a yoga pose that only advanced students should try, is said to improve circulation, thyroid function, and immune system function.

On the horizon...the ultimate workout

Already, some exercise bikes let riders tie into the World Wide Web and set off on virtual races against other cyclists in cyberspace. Coming soon: More innovations that will make exercise safer, more personalized, and more exciting.

FOREVER-FRESH GYM WEAR

A U.S. chemist has developed a way to stop stench in workout wear. Fabric is laced with chlorine atoms that get "charged" when washed with bleach, then kill any bacteria and other microorganisms they encounter, including those that thrive on sweat and cause body odor. The concept could yield new germ-killing clothing for workers in food plants and other settings where cleanliness is crucial.

GREATER ATHLETIC PROWESS

The Australian government is using computers to compare youngsters' physical attributes—such as height and arm span—with a database of attributes found in elite athletes in particular sports. The hope is to identify children with specific talents so they can start training early. The same technology could be used to encourage everyone to be more active by matching them to activities they can excel at and, therefore, enjoy.

HOME-GROWN SPARE PARTS

No matter how careful you are, you may sustain an injury one day. The joints are especially vulnerable—and hard to repair. In 50 more years, though, getting hurt should be less of a worry, thanks to ongoing research that may make it possible to grow new knees, bones, and other tissues in a lab. How? By inserting your DNA into donated human stem cells—immature cells that haven't yet become specialized and so may be coaxed into becoming whichever type of cell your body needs.

THOUGHTFUL WORKOUT EQUIPMENT

Treadmills that read your needs and adjust accordingly are already here, but the next step is nearing: Exercise machines with sensors that decode your medical and fitness records off a chip, then automatically adjust your workout to your body size and needs, even setting resistance levels based on your last workout. The computer programs that will run these custom workout machines will be based on the wisdom of the world's best coaches, trainers, and exercise physiologists.

More Alternate Routes to Fitness

No doubt by now you're convinced that an active lifestyle really can yield enormous benefits. But you may still be wondering how, with the hectic schedules, lengthy commutes, and other pressures most of us face, anyone can find the time to make exercise a priority.

Only the committed few can, it turns out, which is partly why 80 percent of us don't get enough exercise to improve our health appreciably. It's not for lack of trying. Just about everyone has, at one time or another, started to exercise diligently with every intention of continuing for life.

Unfortunately, though, research shows that up to 72 percent of people who begin a fitness

program abandon it within six months. When you change jobs, start a relationship, or do anything else that eats up time, exercise is often left by the wayside. In addition, plain old boredom drives many a would-be exercise enthusiast back to the easy chair.

To keep your fitness plan interesting—and your motivation high:

◆ **Think activity, not exercise.** You don't have to spend a fortune on a gym membership, fancy equipment, or a workout wardrobe to be fit. As you saw on the previous pages, plenty of recreational activities qualify as exercise, with no requirement that you go anywhere near a gym. Any physical activity—even doing something as simple as borrowing an overworked friend's dog to take for a long walk—will do you good.

◆ **Mix it up.** Varying your activities will keep you far more stimulated than spending 20 minutes every other day on the same stationary bike. Can't face another session on the stair climber at the gym? Try the rowing machine. Is the sky gray and dismal? Take a walk around your local mall or borrow an exercise video from the library. Feeling cranky? Check out that boxing class.

◆ **Get some company.** Instead of going solo, join up with a friend or family member who will encourage and support you. Knowing that someone is waiting for you at the gym, you'll be more inclined to go when you start entertaining second thoughts.

◆ **Combine fitness with pleasure.** With all the electronic devices at our fingertips today, it's easy to combine a workout with entertainment. Borrow an audio book from the library and listen to it on your evening walk. Tape your favorite television show and watch it while stretching. Caution: Distractions work best for aerobic activities. Strength-training exercises, specifically weight lifting, require your full attention.

VARY YOUR FITNESS regimen, biking one day, walking another, going for a swim when it suits you.

Should You Hire a Personal Trainer?

Personal trainers can charge anywhere from $25 to $200 an hour, so you can rack up a big bill in a matter of months, even weeks. Now, why would that be worth it? If you're the kind of person who needs someone to strong-arm you into working out, a personal trainer can definitely pay off if you can afford one. Alternatively, if you've never worked out before, he or she can get you off to a good start. You don't have to sign up long term. Two or three sessions should be enough to help you design a program based on your strength, flexibility, balance, age, and equipment options.

A professional trainer will devise a program that includes cardiovascular, strength, and flexibility training. To find the right trainer, look for:

1 Someone certified by one of the major national groups: the Canadian Alliance of Professional Fitness Trainers, the Canadian Personal Trainers Network, the Canadian Association of Fitness Professionals, the Canadian Aerobic Instructors' Association, or the

National Fitness Leadership Advisory Committee. Another good sign is a college or university degree in physical education, exercise physiology, kinesiology (the science of muscle movement), anatomy, or sports psychology.

2 Someone who asks a lot of questions about your health. He or she should want to know all about your needs and limitations in order to design an appropriate workout. If you are under medical care, be sure the trainer

is willing to discuss your exercise plan with your doctor. People with chronic illness or other special needs should seek trainers with experience addressing those needs. Ask your prospective trainer for references. Reputable professionals are always happy to provide the names of other clients with health concerns similar to your own.

3 Someone who has liability insurance and clearly written business policies. A reputable personal trainer also should make sure you understand his or her cancellation and billing procedures. The best way to avoid confusion is to have such rules in writing.

4 Someone who is up-front about fees. Rates vary widely. Some trainers will work with up to four people at a time to cut costs.

5 Someone you like. You want a trainer who not only can help you strengthen and tone your body, but who can also inspire you and give you positive feedback that will bolster your confidence to take on new challenges.

Activity as a Way of Life

Become active at least three to five days a week, and right away both your brain and your body will begin to feel renewed. Within six to eight weeks, you'll have far more energy and much less stress. Easy, right?

Here's the catch: You must be consistent or your gains will start to slip as quickly as they accrued. Within three weeks, you could be back to square one. Luckily, moderate daily activity is all you need and it's within almost everyone's reach. The secret of success lies in better thinking.

Wipe the Slate Clean

If you've made and broken repeated promises to exercise, don't get wrapped up in the past now. This time will be different if you believe it will. In one study, Oregon State University researchers put people who saw themselves as couch potatoes on a 14-week workout program designed to change their "exercise identity." By the end, they saw themselves as exercisers. Not only did they want to keep working out, but they stuck with it despite time constraints and other obstacles that might have caused less devoted people to drop out. Want to get similar results?

◆ **Be positive.** If you tell yourself you'll enjoy exercising, the chances are much better that you will.

◆ **Pick a date.** Research shows that anytime you take on a big

life change, the likelihood of making a smooth transition is much greater if you plan ahead. Most people who want to switch from a sedentary to a more active lifestyle do best if they make a written commitment. Remind yourself in writing of why you want to exercise, jot down when and how much you will do, then pick a definite start date within the next few weeks.

◆ **Think small.** Great expectations lead to great disappointments. On the other hand, if you set and achieve smaller goals ("I will manage to walk five minutes a day"), you'll increase your confidence and your stamina quickly.

◆ **Don't push too hard.** Remember, it takes only 30 minutes of extra activity to cut your risk of developing a range of diseases. Of course, no one's saying that you should stop at that point—it's just the minimum practical goal. Expending up to 2,000 calories a week in exercise (the equivalent of walking 30 kilometers) maximizes health benefits. Beyond that, the returns level off.

◆ **Daydream.** Think of how different you'll look and feel one year from now. Envision a new you—feeling more energetic, wearing great new clothes—and describe that vision in writing, too. Imagining the future will make it easier to move forward. It will also help you realize that if you miss your walk one day, there's no need to berate yourself or promise that you'll do twice as much tomorrow. You're in it for the long haul. If you couldn't do it today, you will do it tomorrow.

◆ **Reward yourself.** Take a day off work, call an old friend, do anything that makes you feel good. It can work wonders, particularly during the first few weeks, before the intangible rewards—feelings of satisfaction, pride, and self-confidence—kick in.

◆ **Plan wisely.** Schedule workouts on your calendar as you would any other appointment. Program an electronic watch to beep when it is time for your walk or swim.

◆ **Be a big mouth.** Let everyone know about your new exercise program. Ask friends and family to support and encourage the endeavor.

HEALTH HINT

Keep a Record

Keep your goals in focus by keeping track of when and how much you exercise. Record your progress right after each workout. Otherwise, you may forget and lose out on the satisfaction of seeing written proof of your steady improvement. Once your success is down in black and white, you'll have little trouble following through.

"Everyone is an athlete. The only difference is that some of us are in training and some are not."

—GEORGE SHEEHAN, M.D. / CARDIOLOGIST (1918-1993)

CHAPTER 5

The Power of Sleep

It's only natural in today's 24-hour society to want to sleep less and do more. But slow down. Eye-opening research makes clear that if you miss even a few hours of shut-eye tonight, you're more likely to get sick tomorrow.

Your Body's Secret Weapon

Each of us spends about a third of our lives—24 years, on average—asleep or attempting to sleep. Anything that consumes so much time must be important—and, as it happens, sleep truly is essential, particularly for a healthy immune system.

The Greek philosopher Aristotle thought warm vapors arose from the stomach to induce sleep. Modern anthropologists theorize that our prehistoric ancestors survived because nocturnal predators like saber-toothed tigers could not find them in the silence of their sleep.

Today, scientists have proof that chemical changes throughout the body bring on sleep. But the mechanism through which sleep restores us is as much a mystery today as it was eons ago.

One thing is certain. We can't do without sleep, as research has dramatically demonstrated. In one of the earliest sleep experiments, mice kept awake for two weeks ate more but still lost weight. Their body temperatures fluctuated wildly. Then, after two more weeks of sleeplessness, all of the animals dropped dead. Blood samples showed that a massive infection had killed them. Common bacteria their immune systems should have been able to control multiplied rapidly and overwhelmed every organ. Day after day of wakefulness caused the animals' immune systems to "crash."

Fatal familial insomnia, a rare genetic disease, is an extreme example of the danger of sleep deprivation in humans. Initially, its victims have trouble falling asleep. In time, they are completely unable to sleep, and they die within about three years. Partial sleep loss is clearly less of a threat, but it still impairs immunity. Even when young, healthy people sleep only three or four hours a night, their bodies are less efficient at processing carbohydrates, managing stress, keeping hormones in balance, and fighting infections.

Brain drain. Sleep is not only vital to proper immune function, it also seems essential for giving the brain a chance to store information and perform maintenance when it's not relaying messages to and from the outside world. That explains why losing just two to three hours of sleep a night for a week seriously undermines mood, memory, and alertness in the typical adult.

VITAL STATISTICS: SLEEP

20
Number of years the average 60-year-old has slept

85
Number of Canadian sleep clinics in 2001

8–9
Hours of sleep most adults need each night

33 percent
Percentage of adults who average 6.5 hours or less of sleep each night

4 million
Number of Canadians with a sleep disorder

2 billion
Estimated dollar cost to Canadian companies in lost productivity due to fatigue

---

{ "Sleep debt is potentially as detrimental to health as poor nutrition or a sedentary lifestyle. It may be as bad as smoking." }

—EVE VAN CAUTER, PH.D. / ENDOCRINOLOGIST, UNIVERSITY OF CHICAGO

ONE PURPOSE OF SLEEP is to give the body and mind time for essential maintenance and repair.

The Link to Immunity

As anyone who has had a bad cold or the flu knows, infectious diseases tend to make us feel sleepy. Why? Cytokines, immune system hormones that flood the body during an infection, also act as powerful sleep inducers, forcing the body to conserve energy and other resources that the immune system needs to mount an attack against infectious organisms.

When we are well, sleep allows our immune systems to take care of business by squelching cold germs, healing cuts, repairing tiny tears in muscles, and nipping cancer in the bud. Getting a good night's sleep may be one of the most important things we can do to stay healthy and live long. We can eat well, take our vitamins, and get lots of exercise. But if we don't sleep, none of that will matter. An immune system without sleep is like a car without gasoline. Eventually, it will just stop running.

Lack of sleep causes a decline in several facets of immune function. For one thing, it amplifies the negative effects of stress. (See Chapter 6, "Immunity and the Mind.") In one study, recently bereaved widows and widowers who were having trouble sleeping were found to have fewer natural killer (NK) cells—white blood cells that destroy viruses, bacteria, and cancer cells—and therefore weaker immune responses than other grieving people who were able to sleep normally.

Our mounting sleep debt. If Aristotle missed the mark with his theories about digestion and slumber, it probably wasn't for lack of shut-eye. Before the advent of electric lights, bedtime

SLEEP DEPRIVATION means fewer natural killer cells (PINK) are available to attack and destroy cancer cells (ORANGE).

was determined largely by circadian rhythms, the body's inner timetable of sleeping and waking regulated in part by light and darkness. These cycles are also known as our biological clock. Long ago, people slept when darkness fell; when the sun rose, they rose with it.

Lights: a health hazard?

These days, we pretty much ignore the schedule that Mother Nature so carefully mapped out. The average Canadian today gets only about seven hours of sleep a night—two hours less than at the beginning of the century and at least four hours less than in Aristotle's time. We don't need sleep any less than he did. We've just decided, as a society, that sleep isn't that essential.

Blame it on Thomas Edison, who invented the lightbulb so that he could stay awake all but three hours a night. Edison was a true believer in widespread use of lightbulbs to give everyone a chance to work more hours and tap into their own genius as he had done.

Think Edison was right? Not a chance. A recent U.S. survey of 1,154 adults aged 18 and older paints a far gloomier picture. Consider this:

◆ **51 percent** of those surveyed reported that sleepiness interferes with how much work they get done.

◆ **68 percent** said sleepiness impedes their concentration.

◆ **66 percent** complained that being tired made it harder to handle stress.

Overall, respondents estimated that the quality and quantity of their work declined about 30 percent when they were sleepy, yet 45 percent admitted that they often sleep less so they can accomplish more.

Interesting!

People who are under anesthesia or in a coma are often said to be asleep, but they're not. Comatose or anesthetized people cannot be awakened and do not produce the complex, active brain wave patterns (measurable ups and downs in electrical activity) seen in normal sleep. Instead, their brain waves are very slow and weak, so that even the most primitive responses, such as reacting to pain, are shut down.

How much is enough? We typically think of eight hours as being the ideal good night's sleep, but individual needs vary greatly. Each of us has several "clock" genes that influence our natural sleep/wake cycles. Most people are programmed to go to sleep at around 10:00 P.M. and get up at 6:00 A.M.; others (though far fewer) are set to slumber at 9:00 P.M. and get up at 4:00 A.M.; and some do best going to sleep at 3:00 A.M. and rising at 11:00 A.M. When you sleep is less important than how long you sleep; the optimal amount leaves you feeling awake and alert for the next 16 hours. But since sleep is a low priority in today's fast-paced

---

QUIZ: ARE YOU GETTING ENOUGH SLEEP?

1	I'm grumpy and distracted for no clear reason.	○ TRUE	○ FALSE
2	I often zone out while watching TV at night.	○ TRUE	○ FALSE
3	I'm in dreamland as soon as my head hits the pillow.	○ TRUE	○ FALSE
4	I like to stay up late during the week, then catch some extra Zzzs on weekends.	○ TRUE	○ FALSE
5	I need an alarm clock (or two!) to wake up.	○ TRUE	○ FALSE
6	I need a cup of coffee first thing in the morning.	○ TRUE	○ FALSE

Count the number of times you answered true.

NONE You seem to be getting plenty of sleep and your immune system appreciates it.

ONE OR MORE You're sleep deprived. Certain habits may be interfering with the quantity and quality of your sleep. Consider discussing these results with your physician or other health-care provider to rule out a hidden sleep disorder.

The Stages of Sleep

There are five distinct stages of sleep—four stages of deep or non-rapid eye movement sleep (non-REM) and one of rapid eye movement (REM) sleep. Non-REM and REM sleep are as different from each other as they are from wakefulness.

Every night, we go through four to six sleep cycles during which we alternate between the two states.

Non-REM sleep consists of these stages:

Stage 1. During this stage, the eyes barely move, muscle activity slows, and you drift in and out of slumber. Someone in stage 1 sleep can be awakened easily and will remember fragmented images from a pre-dream state.

Stage 2. Eye movements stop and brain waves become slower. There are occasional bursts of rapid brain waves called sleep spindles. You really must be prodded to wake up during this stage.

Stage 3. This transitional stage ushers in the deepest sleep of the night, marked by the appearance of extremely slow brain waves called delta waves, which are mixed with smaller, faster brain waves. It is

exceedingly difficult to wake someone during stages 3 and 4, which together are referred to as deep sleep.

Stage 4. Now there is no eye movement, the muscles are relaxed, the blood pressure is at its lowest, and the heart and breathing rates are at their slowest. The brain produces delta waves almost exclusively. This is when the

body repairs itself with the help of a hormone called somatostatin, which helps maintain the health of muscles and other soft tissue.

REM sleep. When we switch into REM sleep (which usually happens about 70 to 90 minutes after we fall asleep and recurs throughout the night), our breathing becomes more rapid, irregular, and shallow. Heart rate increases and blood pressure rises. The synchronized brain waves characteristic of deep sleep break up and begin to look like those of wakefulness.

The hyperactivity in the brain is coupled with almost total lack of movement—earning the REM stage its nickname, "paradoxical sleep." People awakened during REM sleep often describe odd dreams.

world (indeed, some go-getters pride themselves on needing just a few hours a night), many of us don't know how it feels to be adequately rested.

To find out, suggests sleep expert James Maas, Ph.D., try for a week to go to bed a full eight hours before you need to get up. If you rise rested and feel that way throughout the day, you've slept enough. If not, add about 15 minutes to your sleep time each day for a week. Soon, you will hit on the right formula. Your alarm clock will be superfluous—you'll just wake up when it's time to.

How much is too little? You're likely to have a "sleep debt," similar to being overdrawn at the bank, if:

◆ **It's hard for you to get out of bed in the morning.** Sleeping extra hours on weekend mornings is a sign of sleep deprivation, too.

◆ **You feel drowsy during the day.** Even dozing in a boring meeting is a sleep-debt indicator.

◆ **You often fall asleep within five minutes of lying down.** You probably need at least one more hour of sleep than you get each night.

Better Sleep Equals Longer Life

Sleep is, perhaps, the only genuine fountain of youth. There is plenty of compelling evidence that how well you slumber is the most important predictor of how long you'll live, exerting a stronger influence than other characteristics of good health, such as being physically fit and not smoking.

Sleep matters

Based on studies started in the early 1970s, researchers at the California Human Population Laboratory have identified getting regular sleep as the number one habit linked to longer life. This research placed sleep ahead of exercising (which is known to promote sleep), eating breakfast, and refraining from snacking, notes sleep expert Allan Hobson, M.D.

Controlling weight, not smoking, and moderating alcohol intake also predicted good health, but they, too, trailed sleep. So just how critical is good sleep? Does it actively lengthen people's lives? Does it measurably boost their immune function? The original data didn't say. Scientists had to wait years for confirmation to be sure that sleep indeed does all that—and more.

TO BE FULLY ALERT, you need to spend a third of your life sleeping.

Uncovering the mystery. It took more than a decade of animal research by James Krueger of the University of Tennessee before the evidence emerged. Krueger found that when animals are not allowed to sleep, proteins produced by bacteria accumulate in their spinal fluid. Since levels of these proteins are low in well-rested animals, it seems logical to assume that sleep deprivation encourages the growth of at least some kinds of bacteria in the body.

Even more fascinating was the discovery that these proteins enhance deep sleep, cause fever (which induces sleepiness), and make the brain and immune system release interleukin-1, a powerful substance that helps destroy bacteria, viruses, and tumor cells—and makes you drowsy.

Put another way, lack of sleep sets the immune system up for a big fall. At first, immune cells mobilize, sending interleukin-1 and other chemicals to the rescue (and, in the process, making the body want to sleep). But if sleep isn't forthcoming, bacteria and their proteins build up relentlessly and eventually prevail. As Hobson put it, "Sleep enhances the immune system and the immune system enhances sleep."

Similarly, scientists at the Scripps Research Institute noticed a buildup of a certain chemical called a fatty acid primary amide in the spinal fluid of sleep-deprived cats. When they injected the same chemical into rats, the rats immediately fell asleep.

What happens in humans?

It turns out that chronically sleep-deprived humans also exhibit immune changes— changes that decrease their resistance to

A Mystery: Why Do We Yawn?

One of the first things you're likely to notice, if you are sleep-deprived, is a drastic increase in the frequency of your yawns. Experts say that in this situation, yawning is brought on by a decrease in the amount of oxygen that reaches the brain. People who don't get enough sleep tend not to take very deep breaths. Opening your mouth wide brings more oxygen into your body. Another trigger for yawning is boredom. Scientists compared yawning in teenagers who watched music videos and teenagers who watched a dull color test bar pattern. As you might expect, those who watched the test bar pattern yawned more (5.78 yawns in 30 minutes) than those who watched the videos (3.41 yawns in 30 minutes). More facts about yawning:

1. The average yawn lasts about six seconds. A natural way to induce sleep is to force yourself to yawn (and keep yawning). By the sixth yawn or so, you should feel drowsy.

2. Scientists have seen fetuses yawn in the womb as early as 11 weeks after conception. Yet before birth we don't take oxygen in through our lungs.

3. Many animals yawn, including fish, snakes, and crocodiles. Some male animals, men included, yawn in connection with penile erections.

4. Frequent yawning can indicate an underlying medical problem. Causes range from motion sickness to encephalitis to brain tumors.

5. Yawns become contagious to people between the first and second years of life. After that, seeing a person yawn often triggers yawns. Reading about yawning causes yawns. Are you yawning right now?

infection. Michael Irwin, M.D., a professor of psychiatry at the San Diego Veteran's Medical Center in California, recently discovered that limiting a person's sleep time to three to four hours nightly (about half of their normal rest) reduces the number of NK-cells and decreases the activity of T-cells. Both reductions mean the immune system is flagging. By contrast, Irwin found, people who are allowed to sleep nine hours instead of their usual seven hours each night usually have greater-than-normal NK-cell activity.

Lose a little, lose a lot. It's pretty much accepted now that when people go without sleep for a long time, their immune systems are weakened. But what about when they stay up extra late just one night but get up at their normal time in the morning? To answer that question, Irwin's team kept 42 healthy people awake between 10:00 P.M. and 3:00 A.M., then drew their blood and checked their levels of various white blood cells. The result: Even after one night of sleep deprivation, the subjects had far fewer NK-cells in their bloodstream.

BLOOD PRESSURE hits a 24-hour low at about 4:00 A.M. If you're up, you might feel faint.

What Do You Get When You Give Up Sleep?

If you cut your sleeping time short on a regular basis, you may be adding hours to your day, but you could also be subtracting time from your life. That's what researchers in Chicago reported recently in the medical journal *The Lancet*. They found that young adults who don't get enough sleep may be increasing their risk for conditions that usually come with older age, such as type 2 diabetes, high blood pressure, and memory loss.

The researchers studied a group of healthy adults over a 16-day period when they first were deprived of sleep and then were allowed to recover. Throughout this time, the subjects' blood-sugar

{ "I think we dream so we don't have to be apart so long. If we're in each other's dreams, we can play together all night." }

—BILL WATTERSON / CARTOONIST, CALVIN & HOBBES

and hormone levels were monitored. The study found that when the subjects were deprived of sleep, their bodies showed signs of insulin resistance, an early stage in the development of diabetes. Their levels of hormones that control the production of insulin and thyroid hormone were closer to those seen in older people. After the subjects were allowed to sleep, these levels returned to normal. Yet doctors suspect that when people are chronically deprived of sleep, these irregular levels may persist and lead to health problems.

Sleep in brain disorders. Sleep problems are common features of many neurologic disorders, including Alzheimer's disease, stroke, and head injury. The disruptions that occur in these conditions may be caused by changes in the parts of the brain that control sleep. Altered levels of neurotransmitters (brain-cell messenger chemicals) may also be involved. The powerful drugs used to treat serious neurologic diseases and injuries probably contribute to sleep problems as well.

Sleep plays an important role in seizure disorders as well. For example, researchers have found that REM sleep keeps epileptic seizures confined to the area of the brain where they originate. (Some types of seizures tend to spread from one part of the brain to another.) Going without sleep, therefore, may accelerate seizures in some people.

Interesting!

Sleeping too much is not good either. A 23-year British study that followed over 1,500 elderly people found that those who spent 12 or more hours in bed a day were twice as likely to die as people who spent less than nine hours a day in bed. The difference persisted even after figures were adjusted to reflect the fact that people with serious illnesses spend more time in bed.

Better Health by the Clock

Chances are, you wake up most mornings to the sound of your alarm clock ringing. But if there's one clock you should pay more attention to, it's your body clock, genetically programmed into your cells, tissues, and organs.

Scientists who study the body's clock (chronobiologists) have found that very little of what the body does is random. Instead, your physical responses to your environment are governed by patterns that repeat themselves continuously, whether it's every few minutes, every day, every month, or every year. These patterns are orchestrated by this internal timekeeper, also known as the circadian rhythm. Following or veering from these cycles in your daily habits can affect the severity of disease symptoms, the accuracy of medical tests, and your body's response to medications.

What makes us tick. Our master clock is really just a tiny cluster of nerve cells about the size of this "v." Called the suprachiasmatic nucleus (SCN), it lies deep within the brain in an area called the hypothalamus, which controls such basic functions as food intake and body temperature.

Although the SCN has no direct contact with the outside world, it is influenced by light. How is that

A Wake-Up Call

Not just in health, but in all aspects of life, when you cut back on sleep, you run into trouble. Leading researchers have found that lack of sleep has these effects:

 You're less likely to be happy. A comparison of dozens of published studies on sleep deprivation by Bradley University psychologists June Pilcher, Ph.D., and Allen Huffcutt, Ph.D., found that people asked to rate their mood on a scale of 1 to 100 typically choose a number less than 10 when they are sleep deprived. Well-rested people, by comparison, score an average of 50.

 It's harder to learn something new. A study from Trent University in Canada concluded that inadequate, irregular sleep severely impairs the learning process, cutting the amount of new information that your brain can process by as much as 50 percent.

3 Coping becomes more difficult. At Rush Presbyterian-St. Luke's Medical Center in Chicago, studies of people going through separation or divorce found that poor sleep and mood disorders persisted for an entire year after the emotional trauma. Researchers concluded that the study subjects remained depressed because their fitful sleep kept them from dreaming normally. Dreaming may be a mood-regulating process that helps us work through anger and other emotions, notes researcher Rosalind Cartwright, Ph.D.

 Sex becomes a snore. All 30 respondents to a Bethesda National Naval Medical Center survey of patients with sleep apnea (see page 181) scored below normal on every measure of sexual functioning. After being treated for apnea, though, they all improved dramatically, especially in two areas: the intensity of their sexual drive and their ability to achieve orgasm.

5 You may be misdiagnosed. People who are sleepy are often misdiagnosed as being depressed because the symptoms of sleep deprivation—irritability, difficulty concentrating, and reduced energy—are so similar to those of depression. But shut-eye, not an antidepressant, is what they need. In these cases, better sleep quells depression without drugs like Prozac.

BODY TEMPERATURE RHYTHMS

Although the average body temperature for humans is about 37°C, it fluctuates in a set pattern on a daily basis. Triggered by your internal body clock, it hits its low (about 35.5°C) between 3:00 A.M. and 6:00 A.M., then climbs sharply during the morning hours. It dips again, briefly, around 3:00 P.M. (setting the stage for a good nap), then climbs again to its peak around 7:00 P.M., before falling—sending the physiological signal that it's time for sleep—as the night begins.

24-HOUR TIME CLOCK

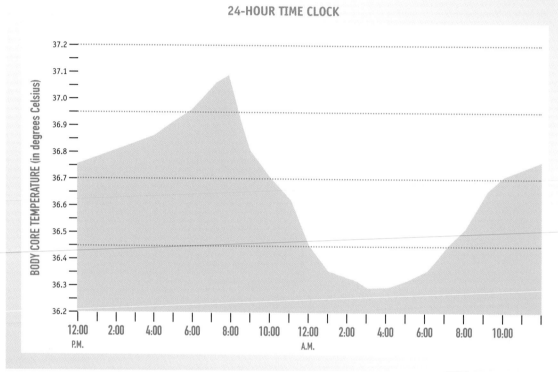

SOURCE: Helen Burgess, M.D., Biological Rhythms Research Lab, Rush-Presbyterian-St. Luke's Medical Center.

possible? Light receptors in the back of the eyeball send messages along nerve fibers to the SCN. The SCN takes the information, interprets it, and passes it on to another tiny structure in the brain, the pineal gland. This gland secretes the so-called time-keeping hormone melatonin, levels of which increase at night. The SCN also sends information about time to the pituitary gland, which triggers the secretion of more hormones that profoundly influence the immune system.

It is increasingly clear that adhering to this natural body clock and scheduling your activities by it can help keep you energized and healthy in curious ways that are now coming to light. Here are some time-wise tips based on these findings.

Morning is the best time to...

◆ **Become pregnant.** About 50 percent of hopeful couples—most of whom are perfectly healthy and fertile—don't conceive in the first three months of having unprotected sex. Trying in the morning might help. Cornell University Medical College research shows that men tend to produce more sperm around 6:00 A.M. than at other times.

◆ **Eat to lose weight.** A University of Minnesota study suggests that the body burns calories better early in the day. People who ate only one 2,000-calorie meal a day for a week lost weight if they ate their meal in the morning—yet they gained weight if they ate the same meal at night!

Eating once a day is unrealistic for most people, and even unhealthy for some (diabetics, for example), but the study suggests that merely consuming more of your calories earlier in the day rather than later is better for weight control.

◆ **Get an injection.** Shots given between noon and 3:00 P.M. are up to four times more likely to cause soreness than shots given earlier in the day.

◆ **Elucidate like Einstein.** Concentrating on complex tasks is easier in the mid-morning. Levels of cortisol, a stress hormone that also boosts mental alertness, start building about two hours before you wake up and typically peak at about 10:00 A.M.

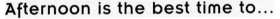

Afternoon is the best time to...

◆ **Nap.** The human body is naturally inclined to rest in the middle of the afternoon.

◆ **Be tested for allergies.** As explained by chronobiologist Michael Smolensky, Ph.D., of the University of Texas at Houston School of Public Health, sensitivity to skin tests can be three times greater in the morning than later in the day. One small, unpublished study, he says, found that 20 percent of allergen skin tests were negative when performed in the morning but positive later in the day.

◆ **Exercise.** Muscles are relaxed, and joints move more easily when body temperature is higher.

◆ **Apply a soothing salve.** Topical medications (those applied to the skin) are more effective and work up to twice as long, because body temperature is higher, which increases absorption of the salve.

Evening is the best time to...

◆ **Cure an ulcer.** Peptic ulcer medications are best taken around 6:00 P.M., with dinner. That way they can better block the normal late-night peak in secretion of stomach acid.

◆ **Visit a sick friend.** After about 9:00 P.M., your number of white blood cells is at its natural high, providing you with stronger protection against any germs you might encounter.

◆ **Treat high blood pressure.** Time-delayed drugs for blood pressure are now on the market. Taken before bedtime, the drugs kick in shortly before morning, when blood pressure rises most quickly.

◆ **Take cholesterol-lowering medications.** Your liver produces most of the cholesterol you need at night. This release, combined with dinner (typically a large meal) means that cholesterol is at a high at night. As a result, cholesterol-lowering statin drugs, such as lovastatin and pravastatin, are more effective when taken in the evening.

◆ **Make love.** Don't wait until the late-night news is over. Testosterone levels peak about 10:30 P.M. in both men and women—and the higher the testosterone, the more one's thoughts turn to romance.

GOOD QUESTION!
How can I get my body clock back into rhythm?

The best way to keep your body rhythms in line is to get up at about the same time each morning, regardless of how much sleep you got the night before. Having a reasonably regular bedtime helps, too. A difference of an hour or so from day to day probably isn't too important, but it's wise to avoid major differences, say, on weekends. It also helps to take daily walks in the sunlight and eat meals at regular intervals.

The Virtues of Napping

Many people in Latin American and Mediterranean countries wouldn't do without their afternoon siesta, typically a three-hour break during which workers go home, eat, sleep, and relax.

But in Canada, one of the world's most work-driven nations, pausing to refresh has decidedly negative connotations. Real adults work all day—they don't slack off. So, although legions of people would love to succumb to a quick, restorative nap—and would probably benefit from it—they resist because they fear being seen as lazy. Not that they always succeed in abstaining: Polls show that 60 percent of adults slip in a nap at least once a week. They nap at their desks, on the subway, or while watching TV.

Why it's natural to nap. The reason is simple: We all have a built-in, physiological desire for a nap in the afternoon. How do we know this? When researchers had volunteers spend time in an underground room with no clocks or clues as to day or night and told them to sleep whenever they wanted, the subjects slept in two cycles: a longer session at night and a shorter period—a nap—during the day.

"CLAPPERS" are closet nappers who try to hide their healthy habit from others.

Fortunately, the myth that napping is wasted time may be changing, thanks to well-documented studies showing that short snoozes can improve mood, performance, and health. For example, nap-loving Latin Americans and Europeans usually score better on tests that measure stress than North Americans.

What's more, studies at the University of California at San Diego show that the sooner you can recover from modest sleep losses, the faster you restore your immune response to normal.

Quick Tip

Can't bring yourself to nap? Push your coffee cup aside at break time and head outdoors instead. You might expect physical activity to have the opposite effect of a nap, but many people find that the fresh dose of oxygen from a brisk walk boosts energy in much the same way.

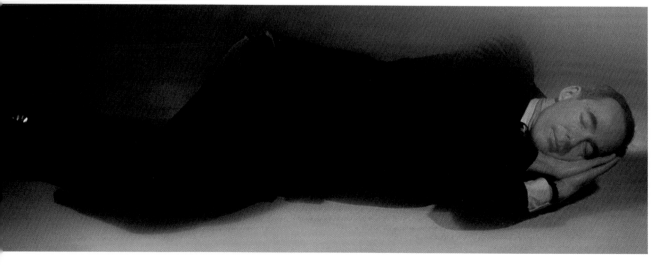

And what quicker way is there to make up for a night of little sleep than with a nap the next day?

Corporate Canada wakes up.

Several studies have found that short naps increase concentration and counteract stress, another immune-system depressor. That may explain why people who nap are not only more productive at work, they are absent less often. No wonder the Metropolitan Transit Authority, which runs the New York City subway system and two suburban railroads, is considering 10- to 20-minute "power naps" for its train operators and bus drivers. And ever since scientist Mark Rosekind, Ph.D., completed studies showing that pilots who take 40-minute sleep breaks on long flights fare better on vigilance, alertness, and decision-making tests, several European airlines now require their pilots to take time out for a midflight snooze.

Naps also can improve health and most other aspects of life for the 2 million Canadians whose work schedules require them to be awake for night shifts or rotating shifts. Due to a preset morning waking mechanism in the body's internal clock, many shift workers find it hard to sleep past noon even after an overnight shift.

A 20-MINUTE NAP is long enough to improve alertness.

What's Your Napping Style?

While some people have trouble napping, most of us succumb to the need for a nap at one time or another, depending on our typical sleep patterns.

1 Replacement sleepers nap to get a much-needed energy boost because they don't sleep enough at night.

2 Split sleepers regularly divide their total sleeping time into two groups—midday and night. Not surprisingly, this is common among night or split-shift workers.

3 Long sleepers simply enjoy more than a "full" night's sleep. A famous example: Winston Churchill napped every day, even at the height of his wartime responsibilities. "Nature had not intended man to work from eight in the morning until midnight, without the refreshment of blessed oblivion, which, even if it lasts only 20 minutes, is sufficient to renew all vital forces," he wrote.

4 Prophylactic sleepers nap to store up for a planned deficit because of travel, work obligations, or a night on the town.

By supplementing their morning sleep with a 15- to 20-minute nap before leaving for work, they can minimize their level of sleep deprivation.

Productive ways of napping.

To maximize the benefits of this quick, no-cost route to physical and emotional health, try following these napping strategies.

◆ **Be consistent.** As much as possible, hold to the same time frame so that you don't disrupt your biological clock and nocturnal sleep pattern. A 20-minute nap is ideal for most people. It provides enough restorative down-time without lulling you into the deeper, harder-to-snap-out-of stages of sleep.

◆ **Time it right.** The ideal window for napping is about 12 hours after the middle of your night's rest, or around 3:00 P.M. for most people. Remember, however, that each of us has our own internal clock, so no specific time is off-limits unless it interferes with your nighttime sleep.

◆ **Avoid night napping.** It will delay your falling-asleep time, making it harder to get up in the morning. If you're sleepy, turn the television off and go to bed.

◆ **Cue your body.** If you follow a similar pre-nap routine every day—closing the door, doing a few simple stretches, turning on some soft music, turning off the light, loosening your collar, clutching a teddy bear—in time those actions will always get you ready to sleep.

◆ **Don't fret if you don't fall asleep.** A classic Ohio State University study indicated that merely lying down and resting may be as beneficial as actually snoozing. In the study, 20 habitual nappers were monitored during a one-hour nap in the laboratory, as were 20 non-nappers who rested in bed without falling asleep. The subjects then were given a series of performance tests and asked to describe their moods before and after the experiment. The nappers slept 61 percent of the time, while the others did not get any sleep at all. And although both groups improved significantly in mood and performance, neither outdid the other.

◆ **Lie down if you can.** Reclining helps you feel as if you slept much longer than you actually did.

◆ **Monitor the effects of your naps.** If you nap easily but have a hard time falling asleep at your regular bedtime, you may need to shorten or cut out daytime naps.

Do Not Disturb

> PROTECT YOUR NAP TIME: Take a few minutes to turn off the lights and unplug the phone.

Other Energizers

Can't nap? If you or your employer are resistant to napping, there are other ways to fight your natural midday slump. To perk up:

◆ **Be cool.** Open the window, head outdoors, take a cool shower, or turn the air conditioning on full blast. Just as a warm, humid environment makes you feel lethargic and fatigued, a cool one can reverse that effect.

◆ **Move and shake.** Being active makes you more energetic—an effect that can last for hours. But timing is important. To boost your energy, exercise in the morning or early afternoon. Wait too long (later than 7:00 P.M., for example) and you might be a little too perky to fall asleep easily when bedtime rolls around. In general, try not to exercise within three hours before you go to bed.

◆ **Drink enough liquids.** Dehydration can make you sleepy, so always keep water close by.

◆ **Get excited.** If you're frequently lethargic, you may be suffering from a common problem that can not only make you sleepy but also raise your risk of illnesses such as heart attack and, possibly, cancer. It's boredom, a frequent sign of depression. To get out of your rut, move on to a new challenge. At work, mix up what you're doing—swap responsibilities with a coworker or ask for a new project. If you're home and doing your ironing, turn up some music and try to synchronize your task to the beat. Better yet, take a break and call an old friend for all the latest gossip. Look, too, for long-term solutions to boredom, such as joining a club that sparks your interest.

UNCOMMON KNOWLEDGE
None Better Than Some?

Grabbing just a few hours of sleep may tax your mind and body more than staying awake all night long. When researchers compared the mental and physical performance of volunteers who were kept awake for 48 hours straight to that of people who were awakened every few hours, they were surprised to find that people who went without sleep altogether did much better than the ones who slept intermittently. Their conclusion: Being forced to stay awake for hours on end may push the body into a crisis mode that lets it adjust, temporarily, to its sleepless state. In contrast, repeatedly interrupting sleep may disrupt the biological clock, creating a more noticeable sleep deficit.

CAFFEINE COUNTDOWN

One of the best ways to make sure your nighttime hours are spent sleeping instead of tossing and turning is to avoid caffeine. Caffeine's stimulant effect stems from the fact that it is similar in structure to adenosine, a chemical that helps induce slumber. Since the two chemicals compete for the same receptors throughout the body and the brain, the more caffeine you drink, the less adenosine is available for making you drowsy. That's why caffeine temporarily heightens concentration—and delays the onset of sleep. To complicate the problem, a surprising number of common foods and beverages contain caffeine. Here are some examples.

PRODUCT	SERVING SIZE	CAFFEINE (MG)
COFFEE, BREWED, MAXWELL HOUSE	150 ml	60–120
COFFEE, INSTANT	240 ml	88
BEN & JERRY'S NO-FAT COFFEE FUDGE ICE CREAM	250 ml	85
EXCEDRIN	500 mg	65
RC COLA, REGULAR OR DIET	355 ml	48
COCA-COLA	355 ml	46
DIET COKE	355 ml	46
SNAPPLE ICED TEA, ALL VARIETIES	473 ml	42
DR PEPPER, REGULAR OR DIET	355 ml	40
PEPSI	355 ml	38
DIET PEPSI	355 ml	36
BLACK TEA, LEAF OR BAG	150 ml	35
LIPTON TEA	250 ml	35
ANACIN	400 mg	32
HERSHEY'S MILK CHOCOLATE BAR	1 bar	31

PRODUCT	SERVING SIZE	CAFFEINE (MG)
HÄAGEN-DAZS LOW-FAT COFFEE FUDGE ICE CREAM	250 ml	30
ARIZONA ICED TEA	500 ml	30
GREEN TEA	250 ml	25
BARQ'S ROOT BEER	355 ml	22
CHOCOLATE MILK	250 ml	5
COFFEE, DECAFFEINATED	250 ml	5
YOPLAIT CAFÉ AU LAIT YOGURT	175 ml	5
COCOA OR HOT CHOCOLATE	180 ml	5
MOUNTAIN DEW	355 ml	0
LIPTON SOOTHING MOMENTS PEPPERMINT TEA	250 ml	0
MINUTE MAID ORANGE SODA	355 ml	0
7-UP, REGULAR OR DIET	355 ml	0
CELESTIAL SEASONINGS, ALL VARIETIES	240 ml	0
BARQ'S DIET ROOT BEER	355 ml	0
SPRITE, REGULAR OR DIET	355 ml	0

When Sleep Eludes You

Most people have trouble sleeping now and then. Some, however, regularly lie awake for long periods after going to bed; others wake in the wee hours, unable to fall asleep again. Although very few people actually stay alert for whole nights, those who sleep only a few hours often feel as if they never closed their eyes.

In all of these situations, the diagnosis is the same: insomnia, the most common sleep disorder. About 1 in 10 people has moderate insomnia, and approximately 1 in 100 is affected severely.

Is it insomnia? Any time you experience a big change in your daily routine—for example, traveling, starting a new job, going into the hospital, or moving into a new home—there's a chance it will trigger insomnia. Arguing with a family member or watching an action-packed program on television late at night can also cause a night or two of restless sleep. This type of insomnia usually doesn't last for more than a few days before going away on its own.

Sleep problems that continue for more than a few days may signal chronic insomnia, a condition that often requires professional help or a change in behavior to get under control. Sometimes an underlying medical problem, such as arthritis, leg cramps, lower back pain, or frequent urination, is to blame.

More often, insomnia is the result of habits that interfere with sleep. For instance, some people gulp coffee to prop open their eyes all day, then mellow out with alcohol at night. This pattern inevitably ruins their sleep.

A learned disorder. Although insomnia can have many causes, most people who suffer from it have what researchers call conditioned or learned insomnia. Nagging worries of any kind will naturally make it hard for you to fall asleep. Trudging to bed and trying to force yourself to sleep make matters worse, since your body fights back by staying wide awake. Even after your worries clear up, this learned response persists.

Luckily, patients with this type of insomnia can unlearn their conditioned wakefulness, usually without medication. The first step is to get control of your worries, which have a way of descending at bedtime. To keep this from happening, designate a specific time in the evening—maybe a few minutes after supper—to jot down your concerns and compose a to-do list for the next day. This simple step really can promote the calm and relaxation that aids sleep. Praying or meditating can help reduce overall worry levels as well. (See Chapter 6, "Immunity and the Mind.")

Quick Tip

If an emotional crisis is disrupting your sleep, talk to your doctor. Sleeping pills such as Ambien (zolpidem) and Sonata (zaleplon) are fine for short-term treatment of this kind of insomnia. They can help a lot if lack of sleep is making a hard time even worse.

GOOD QUESTION!
Can hormonal changes related to menopause alter normal sleep patterns?

Yes. A major poll found that about 36 percent of menopausal and postmenopausal women experience hot flashes that interfere with sleep about five days a month. What's more, half of all menstruating women experience hormone-related sleep disturbances. In fact, a woman's sleep is disrupted an average of two and a half days each menstrual cycle.

No Counting Sheep Required

Did you know that one of the best ways to relax before sleep is to tense up? So says Virginia State University sports psychologist Serena Reese, Ph.D. She advises her patients who have trouble drifting off to practice progressive muscle relaxation—deliberately tensing your muscles, then releasing the tension and letting stress ebb away. Here is a shortened version of the technique for you to try.

1 Get into bed and turn off the lights. Lie flat on your back in a comfortable position. Close your eyes and breathe deeply in and out four or five times.

2 Start with your toes. Take note of the sensations associated with them—the feel of the bed sheet against them, how cold or warm they are. Then inhale and scrunch your toes down toward the soles of your feet, squeezing as hard as you can. Hold for 5–8 seconds.

Beginners usually make the mistake of allowing muscles other than the intended group to tense as well. In this step, for example, don't tighten up your calves and legs, just your feet and toes.

3 Quickly let go and exhale. Feel all of the tightness flow out of your muscles. Stay still and relaxed for about 10 seconds.

4 Next, go through the same process of tensing and relaxing every major muscle group in your body from your feet to your head in this sequence: feet, legs and feet, hands, hands and arms, buttocks, abdomen, shoulders,

and head. When you reach your shoulders, roll your head slowly from side to side.

5 After that, lift your shoulders up to your ears, hold them there for 10 seconds, then drop them. Inhale slowly. Curl your shoulders in, lifting them up off the bed. Hold for 5 seconds, exhale, and release. Repeat.

6 Close your eyes as tight as possible. (Make sure you've taken out your contacts.) Squeezing your eyes shut, wrinkle your forehead, pull a frown, clench your teeth, and purse your lips. Hold for 4–8 seconds.

7 Open your eyes and feel your face relax. Smile as broadly as you can. Hold, release, and relax. Breathe in deeply and stretch.

Next, spend less time in bed. If you usually lie there for eight hours—two of which find you anxiously waiting for sleep—get into bed two hours later. You'll get nearly the same amount of sleep with less of the insomnia-related frustration that can trigger even more sleeplessness.

Getting better sleep, even if it's slightly less than the full night's sleep you need, means that you'll carry less sleep debt into the next day—and sleep more soundly that night. Soon your sleep should be back in rhythm with your body, and you'll be getting eight or so luxuriant hours regularly.

Other approaches

Sleeping pills, in general, are approved by Health Canada only for treating insomnia that lasts two weeks or less, the type that typically occurs as a result of an upheaval in your life. If your doctor prescribes a sleeping pill for you, use it only as directed.

If you take sleeping pills too long, it may become hard to sleep without them. Another reason to limit their use comes from a recent *Journal of Gerontology* study showing that, although people who take sleeping pills do fall asleep, they don't have normal sleep cycles.

A chemical darkness. Books and magazines may trumpet melatonin—the so-called "chemical expression of darkness"—as the wonder drug of the decade. But is it? Hardly. It's not really a drug at all, but a hormone produced by the pineal gland, which is nestled between the two hemispheres of the brain. Furthermore, melatonin promoters'

SYNTHETIC MELATONIN may be safer than its "natural" counterpart, which is extracted from the pineal glands of sheep.

claims that it miraculously cures a wide range of complaints besides insomnia have never been proven.

It's true that melatonin in the body controls the circadian rhythm so we sleep at night and stay alert during the day. The amount of light that reaches the eyes controls the amount of melatonin the pineal gland produces. Light slows production of the hormone, which is one of the reasons why we are alert and filled with energy on bright, sunny days and fuzzy-headed and lethargic on dull, cloudy days. Toward evening, as the light dims, the pineal gland starts gradually secreting melatonin in increasing amounts, bringing on a more relaxed, drowsy state, and, eventually, sleep. With the sun's rise, melatonin levels drop, and we begin awakening.

Still, the results of studies on melatonin's use for insomnia are inconsistent. Researchers at Brigham and Women's Hospital in Boston recently found that melatonin levels do not decline with age, indicating that the hormone has nothing to do with sleep disorders in older adults, as previously believed. And while health experts don't dispute melatonin's effect on sleep, there's no consensus on how it's best used or even if it is safe. There have been reports of unpleasant side effects, including depression, disturbing dreams, and next-day grogginess.

Is it for you? If a doctor has ruled out medical conditions that may be causing your insomnia and if daytime sleepiness is affecting your work, you could give melatonin a try. Remember

UNCOMMON KNOWLEDGE

In Search of the Sandman

"If only I could get a good night's sleep" is a common lament, particularly among older Canadians, but why is a matter of dispute. Intriguing new research by Ohio State University sleep expert Charles Pollak, M.D., suggests that older people simply don't need as much sleep as younger people do. Other possibilities: As we get older, our sleep patterns shift, often without our realizing it. Physiologically, we start getting sleepy earlier than we used to, so we go to bed earlier. But then we wake up before we expect to—and assume we didn't get a full night's rest. Insomnia in the elderly can also be associated with living alone, having limited activity, and using certain drugs.

that although melatonin is sold without a prescription, it is still experimental. Until there's a better understanding of its effects, take it under medical supervision.

The optimal dose. Massachusetts Institute of Technology research suggests that a melatonin dose of a fraction of a milligram (about 0.5 mg) at bedtime may be large enough to induce sleep and shift the sleep cycle. Anything more should be avoided because of the chance that raising the amount of melatonin in the body might disrupt the body's own production of the hormone or the production of other hormones. For example, many researchers are concerned that high doses of melatonin could suppress steroid hormone production, particularly in women, resulting in suppressed ovulation and increased risk of bone loss and heart disease.

Do not use melatonin if you are trying to get pregnant, are already pregnant, or have an immune-system disorder. If you decide to use melatonin, take it at the same time every night. Because Health Canada doesn't consider melatonin a drug, it isn't regulated, so different brands may vary considerably in their strength and purity. Synthetic melatonin, which is manufactured under laboratory control, may be safer than the natural hormone, which is extracted from the pineal glands of sheep.

What Else Can Cause Fatigue?

Fatigue is physical or psychological weariness that does not go away even with rest. When you're physically fatigued, your muscles feel weak and ineffective. You might notice this when you climb stairs or carry bags of groceries. Psychological fatigue may make it difficult to concentrate for as long as you'd like. In severe cases, you might not feel like getting out of bed in the morning and doing your regular activities.

DRUGS THAT CAN DISTURB SLEEP

Antidepressants
Prozac, Paxil, and other serotonin-reuptake inhibitors sometimes disturb normal sleep patterns.

Asthma Medications
Some inhaled and oral treatments, such as steroids and theophylline, can act as stimulants.

Beta-Blockers
They can cause insomnia, nighttime awakenings, daytime sleepiness, and vivid dreams.

Decongestants
The common one, phenylpropanolamine, can act as a stimulant.

Diuretics
"Water pills" may disrupt sleep by causing frequent urination.

Painkillers
Aspirin, ibuprofen, and naproxen can decrease melatonin synthesis. Some aspirin-based nonprescription painkillers contain caffeine.

Fatigue is one of two main ways the body warns you about a problem. The other way is pain. Most of us pay attention to pain and stop doing whatever causes it. Fatigue often gets short shrift; it tends to build so slowly that we somehow manage to ignore it. Over time, though, fatigue can weaken the immune system. Studies show that people who report constant fatigue and have HIV or another immune disorder tend to get sicker faster than people who aren't always tired.

See your doctor if you're always feeling tired. For the most accurate diagnosis, you'll need to answer these questions:
◆ **How long have you been feeling tired?** Did it happen gradually or suddenly?
◆ **How has your physical activity changed** in the past three to six months?
◆ **When are you tired?** Is it after certain activities, like climbing stairs? Do you wake up tired?
◆ **How do you feel when you're tired?** Sad? Achy? Chilled? Short of breath? Fine but exhausted?

14 Keys to a Good Night's Zzzs

Did you sleep well last night? Or did you wake up feeling fatigued and sluggish, perhaps wondering if you really slept at all? Although you may think it's a simple matter of throwing back the bedcovers and falling in, restful slumber requires preparation.

Whether you're a confirmed night owl or an early-to-bed, early-to-rise type, you will doze off more easily if you follow these steps.

1. Stick to a schedule. Try to wake up at the same time every morning no matter when you fell asleep or how well you slept. Making up for lost sleep by sleeping in on weekends makes it harder to get up on Monday. Also try to keep the same bedtime every night.

2. Seek the sun. Research suggests that we all need at least two hours of sunlight each day to keep our biological clock on track. But studies show that most healthy older people and even many young people don't meet their quota. Men average 90 minutes of sunlight per day, women, 45 minutes—and elderly patients in nursing homes get an average of a paltry 2 minutes of sun most days.

SEEING THE SUN is essential for regulating your sleep cycle.

3. Exercise. Although a workout within three hours of bedtime may interfere with sleep, physical activity earlier in the day helps induce bedtime drowsiness. One study found that people who ran or walked for 40 minutes three days a week had longer periods of deep sleep than people in a more lethargic control group. An analysis of 12 studies on the subject found that exercise is most likely to improve sleep in women and older people.

4. Eat early. Finish your evening meal by 6:30 P.M. so your body's digestive processes will be at rest when you go to bed. This will help you avoid stomach acid reflux, which causes heartburn, a painful problem that can disrupt sleep.

A HOT NIGHTTIME BATH is a proven ticket to dreamland.

5. Hop in the tub. Soaking in a hot bath an hour and a half before bedtime will raise your body's core temperature, then cause it to cool—a biological signal that it's time to snooze. Researchers at McLean Hospital in Belmont, Massachusetts, studied female insomniacs in their 60s and 70s and found that those who bathed in water temperatures of about 40.5°C spent more time in deep, slow-brain-wave sleep, the type you need to recover from fatigue.

6. Develop a bedtime ritual. Following a routine every night before bed will slide you into sleep. Play the same piece of music, write in a diary, read a good book, and, of course, brush and floss your teeth.

7. Turn in on time. Your body was designed to stay in sync with the cycles of nature, including daylight and darkness. That means we're programmed to sleep between 10:00 P.M. and 6:00 A.M. In the habit of staying up much later? Try getting up progressively earlier by a few minutes each morning, over several days. You'll soon fall asleep earlier at night.

FOR SOUND SLEEP, listen to soft, soothing music.

8. Drink fewer liquids. Cutting back during the two-hour period prior to bedtime will minimize the need for nighttime trips to the bathroom.

9. Nix nicotine. Tobacco is harmful in many ways, but nicotine's stimulant effect is what makes it contribute to insomnia. If you can't quit smoking, avoid cigarettes for at least two hours before turning in.

10. Put on socks and mittens. Wearing socks and mittens to bed will widen blood vessels in the hands and feet, a vital step to opening the gates of sleep, according to Swiss research. The study found that when the body prepares for sleep, blood vessels in the extremities dilate. As it flows through these wide-open channels near the surface of the skin, the blood itself cools down. Then, when cooler blood returns to the internal organs, body temperature falls and sleep automatically follows.

11. Stay cool. On a cold night, it's natural to want to curl up under a toasty electric blanket, but don't. It could interfere with deep sleep by halting the necessary drop in your body's temperature. It's best to use just enough covers to keep you from being cold. Turn on the electric blanket to take the chill off the sheets if you like, but switch it off before getting in bed.

12. Don't toss and turn. Research shows that the longer you lie awake in bed, the more fragmented sleep becomes. If you aren't asleep 20 minutes after you turn in, get up and read a dull book, sew, or listen to classical or New Age music with a slow beat and no lyrics. A small study in the *Journal of Holistic Nursing* found that soft, instrumental music helped 96 percent of elderly subjects fall asleep faster and stay asleep longer.

13. Take some valerian. This ancient herb (no relation to Valium) is shown to reduce the time needed to fall asleep and to improve sleep quality over time. Use a standardized extract (0.8 percent valeric acid, the active ingredient) and follow the label directions, taking it about 30 to 45 minutes before bedtime. Do not use valerian with sleep-enhancing or mood-regulating medications, such as diazepam (Valium) or amitriptyline (Elavil). In rare cases, valerian has a stimulating rather than sedating effect and may cause nervousness.

14. Focus on staying awake. It's a time-tested technique called "paradoxical intention." When you'd normally be tossing, turning, staring at the clock, and generally struggling to sleep, concentrate instead on staying awake with your eyes open. Before long, your eyelids will droop and you'll slide gently into dreamland.

The 15th Key: Create a Sleep Sanctuary

Chances are you've heard this advice before: Save your bed and bedroom for sleep and lovemaking only. That way you avoid associating it with reading, TV, and other activities that can set the mind whirring.

That's a good starting point—but it doesn't begin to touch on the many ways you can make your bedroom more conducive to sleep, so that you'll drop off and wake up smiling.

SIMPLE CHANGES in your bedroom environment may help you fall asleep faster when you go to bed.

Start with the mattress. After all, we spend more time on it than on any other piece of furniture in our homes. Given all of the evidence that good sleep is an important determinant of good health, it makes sense that the right mattress might help you live a longer, happier, more productive life.

Logical, yes. Unfortunately, a good mattress is the most overlooked sleep essential of all. One reason: There's no scientific evidence showing a correlation between the quality of a mattress and the quality of sleep; the issue hasn't really been studied. Still, through trial and error, experts have come up with plenty of tips that can help you select the best mattress. Following these suggestions should give you a better foundation for a good night's sleep.

◆ **Don't think too hard.** A too-firm mattress can't preserve your spine's alignment as you shift your position throughout the night. It lacks the give to cup your body at points like the neck and the curve in the lower back. On the other hand, a mattress that's too soft will let your spine sag and leave you with a backache. What you want in a mattress is similar to what you want in a comfortable desk chair—something that gently supports your body and keeps your spine softly curved, as it is when you're standing up straight. If you can't find a happy medium, try placing a back board about a half-inch thick under your mattress.

◆ **Take the palm test.** When you consider buying a new mattress, don't just lie flat on it for a few seconds. Instead, try a variety of sleeping positions and test more than one mattress. When you find one you like, lie flat on top of it and slide your hand, palm down, between the small of your back and the mattress. If you can get the whole hand through and there's still a gap, it's too hard. And if, when you recline, the base of your spine is lower than your heels, it's too soft.

Pillow Talk

Pillows are as important as mattresses for keeping your neck and spine in good alignment so you can sink into restful sleep. Without the right pillow, even the most comfortable mattress won't deliver deep, divine slumber.

Which pillow is best? The answer depends mainly on personal preference. Some people feel cozy when they sink into a big, fluffy pillow; others feel as if they're smothering.

Your pillow should be soft enough to conform to the contours of your head and neck, yet thick enough to support them in a neutral position with no upward or downward tilt. Sounds simple—but because of technological advances and fads, pillows today come in a far more diverse array than they used to. Here's some inside information on different pillow shapes and fillings.

1. **Down.** This soft, breathable, and natural filling easily molds to your head and body. Contrary to popular belief, down does not aggravate allergies, but it is expensive.

2. **Synthetic down.** This hypoallergenic, man-made fiber is reputed to be just as comfortable as down, but it's sold at about two-thirds the price.

3. **Feathers.** A firmer, less expensive filling than down, feathers also have quills that can poke through all but the most tightly woven pillow covers.

4. **Polyester.** It's washable, synthetic, and generally not expensive, but polyester fill may form clumps over time.

5. **Cotton.** This firmer filling is preferred primarily by people who want an all-natural, animal-free product.

6. **Smart foam.** These pillows are made of heat-sensitive foam that conforms to the shape of your head and neck.

7. **Buckwheat hulls.** In Japan, the crunchy outside parts of buckwheat groats are a traditional filling for beanbag-like pillows. In Canada, such pillows are touted as giving uniform support to the neck and head area, as well as being airy and breathable so that they stay cool in the summer. Some sleepers, however, complain that the pillows are too noisy.

8. **Neck rolls.** Cylinder-shaped to hold the neck in a neutral position, these pillows are ideal for people who have neck pain and stiffness, as well as those who often wake up with a sore neck.

9. **Mediflow water-base pillow.** This polyester-filled pillow is stuffed with an insulated water bag that you fill to your desired firmness. The fluid makes the pillow respond to head motion during sleep, which eases neck pain and improves sleep—a claim supported by a 1994 Johns Hopkins University School of Medicine study.

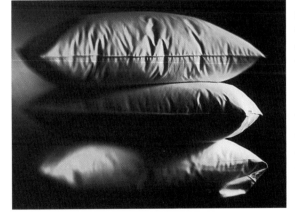

◆ **Watch out for hype.** Luxury mattresses are selling faster than just about any other products in the very lucrative mattress industry. But the features that make for luxury—such extras as silk coverings, gold-plated metal fittings, and individually encased, hand-tied coils—won't have any effect on the quality of your sleep.

◆ **Go with your gut.** The ultimate test is personal preference. Be aware, though, that your first impression may not be enough to base your purchase on. It pays to ask about the store's return policy. You want to be able to give a new mattress a trial at home. Also, check the warranty. Most premium mattresses come with a 10-year warranty.

◆ **Watch for wear.** The average mattress lasts no more than 10 years before its springs stop supporting you properly. Don't wait until the sags are as deep as potholes before replacing it.

SNOOZE FOODS

One way to ensure a restful night's sleep is to calm your brain. Protein foods that contain the amino acid tryptophan, which the body converts to sleep-inducing chemicals, can help. The best bedtime snack mixes protein (like eggs), complex carbohydrates (to displace amino acids other than tryptophan), and calcium (to help the brain use the tryptophan). One such treat: an oatmeal cookie and a glass of milk.

More Steps to Bedroom Bliss

◆ **Paint your bedroom pink.** Once you have selected your bedding, it's time to take advantage of the powerful psychological effects of colors. Some generalizations to keep in mind before covering your walls: Pink reportedly exerts a tranquilizing effect within minutes. It suppresses hostile and anxious behavior. Earth tones, such as off-white, beige, and cool greens and blues, are also soothing. Avoid primary colors, especially red, which is highly stimulating.

◆ **Keep it dark and cool.** Darkness and a drop in body temperature tell the brain it's time to sleep, so hang blackout shades or heavy drapes and set the bedroom thermostat around 18°C. Consider installing a ceiling fan.

◆ **Nix the noise.** If you live near a busy street, airport, or other noise generator, place your bedroom as far away from the racket as possible. Use wall-to-wall carpeting and hanging tapestries to absorb sound and dull the noise-reflecting qualities of hardwood floors and plaster walls. If necessary, use earplugs to block intrusive sounds. You can also turn on a low-level fan or play recordings of environmental sounds—surf or waterfalls—to block the noise and lull you to sleep.

◆ **Eliminate distractions.** Some bedrooms are anything but restful places, with blaring televisions, jangling phones, computers, exercise equipment, and piles of clutter—all of which are symbols of activity, sources of anxiety, and serious distractions from dreamland. Move all of your electronics to another room. If they absolutely must stay in your bedroom, put them in an armoire and keep the door shut at night.

◆ **Cover your clock face.** If you're having trouble sleeping, it's best not to focus your attention on the time. Looking at a clock every five minutes while you're in bed can actually make insomnia become entrenched. Mute audible tick-tocks by covering your clock face with a towel, and turn the clock face away from view.

◆ **Be a sentimentalist.** Decorate the bedroom with objects, photos, and souvenirs that help you recall pleasant times in your life.

◆ **Cultivate companionship.** Sleeping alone after years with a partner can cause sleep disturbances. Consider getting a cat or dog to cuddle, or use an extra pillow.

◆ **Get a night-light.** Even brief exposure to bright light in the middle of the night will trigger a drop in levels of the sleep hormone melatonin, signaling your body that it's time to rise and shine and disrupting your normal sleep cycle. Instead, stick to a night-light.

◆ **Try another room.** If you still find it difficult to sleep, try moving to another room to get your rest. Sometimes you associate insomnia so closely with your bedroom that you expect *not* to sleep there. Switch your environment, expect to sleep, and chances are you will.

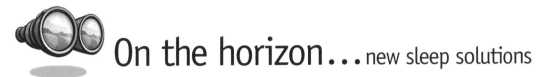

On the horizon... new sleep solutions

Feeling tired? In the future, you can expect preventive measures and cures for sleep disturbances to be far more sophisticated (and in some cases more fun) than most of today's options. Here's a sampling of what researchers currently are looking into.

GENE THERAPY

Drowsy dogs and ravenous rodents (sleepiness and hunger have similar brain regulators) have helped biologists find the genes responsible for narcolepsy, a disorder that causes its human victims to fall asleep any time, without warning (see page 181). Researchers think human narcolepsy sufferers have a similar defective gene. The finding could eventually lead to cures for several sleep problems.

GROUP THERAPY

Thanks to research published in the *Journal of the American Medical Association,* weekly group therapy sessions for insomniacs may soon be in vogue. The study found that troubled sleepers who talked with peers and were taught behaviors that promote shut-eye had far more success than another group who took a sleeping pill, a third group who received both the therapy and pills, and a fourth group who got no treatment at all.

LIGHT RELIEF

Cornell University research found that shining a bright light on the back of the knees helps adjust the body's internal clock. Using the light just before a person's temperature hits its lowest point, at about 5:30 A.M., delays the body clock by three hours the following night. Conversely, shining it just after that low temperature point advances the clock by three hours. These odd and as yet unexplained findings might one day help travelers keep their body clocks in sync when crossing time zones.

NAP ROOMS

Research shows that sleep deprivation diminishes work productivity by impairing short-term memory, dulling perception, slowing reaction time, and weakening the immune system (which sets workers up for colds, flu, and absenteeism). That's why some cutting-edge companies have set up nap rooms where employees can sack out for 15 minutes or so during their breaks. Those enlightened employers include Nike, the athletic-wear company, and *MacWorld* magazine.

When to Call the Sleep Doctor

Do you get eight hours of sleep and still spend the day dragging? You may not be sleeping as well as you should. If you have a sleep disorder, it's actually possible to sleep without getting any rest. If so, you're not alone.

About 15 percent of the population has a chronic sleep disorder. Some disorders, like insomnia—the inability to sleep (see pages 170–173)—are easy to recognize, although medical tests and careful monitoring of your sleep habits may be necessary to find the underlying cause. Others have more subtle effects. People with sleep disorders may not recognize that sleep is the problem. They complain of constant fatigue but insist that they're sleeping just fine. Alternatively, they may be fully aware of their restlessness and frequent waking, but they don't know what's triggering these problems or how to address them.

If you are unaccountably tired, the first thing to do is visit your doctor. It may turn out that heartburn, arthritis, depression, or almost any common ailment is either disrupting your sleep or depleting your energy. (See page 183 for a list of possible causes of fatigue.) Once illness is ruled out, an expert—often a neurologist specializing in sleep disorders—can do a thorough workup that includes monitoring your brain and body functions overnight. A growing number of large medical centers have special clinics devoted to studying sleep and treating sleep disorders.

The Leading Sleep Disorders

More than 80 different sleep disorders, many of which can be treated effectively, have been identified so far. The most common ones, in descending order of prevalence, are described on the next two pages.

ENHANCE YOUR SLEEPING HOURS and your waking ones will improve, too.

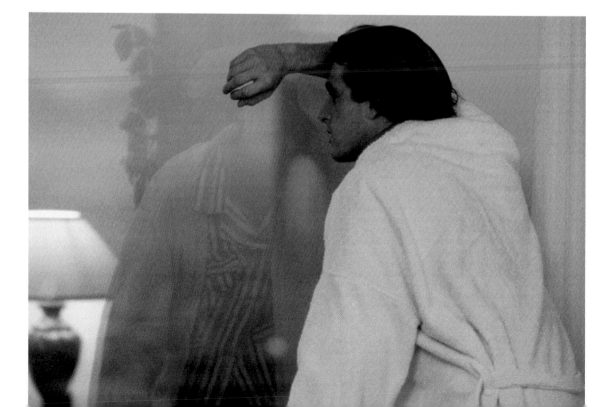

Sleep Apnea

Irregular breathing during sleep, a condition known as sleep apnea, can be life threatening. One type, obstructive sleep apnea (OSA), is the most common medical cause of excessive daytime sleepiness. It is generally marked by loud snoring, which occurs when the upper airway is blocked by the tongue or soft palate during sleep.

A person with obstructive sleep apnea can stop breathing for up to 90 seconds at a time as many as 200 times each night. When breathing is stopped, oxygen levels in the blood can drop dangerously low, triggering a brief awakening that lasts only a few seconds, until breathing resumes. As oxygen levels fall, carbon dioxide levels rise. The combination of oxygen deprivation and carbon dioxide buildup puts a severe strain on the body, sharply increasing the risk of high blood pressure, heart attack, and stroke.

Additional symptoms include gasping or snorting during sleep, drowsiness while driving, accidents, and personality changes or memory loss. Other types of sleep apnea share some features of OSA. They include:

◆ **Central apnea.** This condition also causes breathing to cease during sleep, but the cause is thought to be neurological; no physical obstruction is involved.

◆ **Mixed apnea.** A condition with features of both OSA and central sleep apnea, mixed apnea involves both an obstruction in the airway and a neurological dysfunction.

The chance of having sleep apnea increases with age. In middle age, 9 percent of men and 4 percent of women have it. Among the elderly, the rates are 27 percent of men and 19 percent of women.

◆ **Possible treatment.** For patients with mild sleep apnea, losing weight and avoiding alcohol, tranquilizers, sleeping pills, and antihistamines before bedtime often helps. If the apnea is very mild, you might consider asking your dentist about a dental appliance—a small plastic device that fits in the mouth—to help control snoring. You wear the appliance while you're asleep to prevent the jaw and tongue from obstructing the air passages.

One of the most effective treatments for OSA is continuous positive airway pressure, in which air is pumped through a mask worn over the nose to keep the nasal passages open during sleep. Antidepressants also may be used to treat central sleep apnea.

Narcolepsy

Extreme daytime sleepiness, even after a normal night's rest, is the main symptom of narcolepsy. People with this condition may abruptly fall asleep in the middle of tasks or conversations. The sleepiness is accompanied by sudden episodes of muscle weakness in response to strong feelings,

Interesting!

It is called injection snoreplasty and if you snore, or sleep next to someone who does, this treatment—a quick shot in the soft palate at the back of the mouth—may put an end to sleepless nights. Researchers at an army medical center claim a 92 percent success rate in stopping snoring with the chemical sodium tetradecyl sulfate, which stiffens the palate and keeps it from fluttering during sleep.

> "A night of sleep is as much preparation for the subsequent day's activities as recovery from that of the previous day."
> —ALLAN HOBSON, M.D. / NEUROBIOLOGIST, HARVARD MEDICAL SCHOOL

such as anger, surprise, or amusement. Sometimes narcoleptics have terrifying dreams or hallucinations just as they are falling asleep.

Narcolepsy often becomes apparent in young adulthood, and it lasts for life. A definitive diagnosis requires testing and evaluation by a sleep specialist.

◆ **Possible treatment.** Narcolepsy is treated using scheduled naps and medications that stimulate the central nervous system and help alleviate the sudden muscle weakness.

Restless Leg Syndrome

One in 10 Canadians gets uncomfortable sensations of creeping, twitching, and tingling in their legs when they lie down at night. The sensations, known as restless leg syndrome (RLS), force them to move constantly, making sleep difficult. People with RLS often have periodic limb movement disorder (PLMD)—a repetitive jerking in their arms and legs. These movements can occur every 20 to 40 seconds and cause repeated awakening. In one study, RLS and PLMD accounted for an estimated 33 percent of the insomnia seen in people older than age 60.

◆ **Possible treatment.** In mild cases of restless leg syndrome, patients sometimes can relieve their symptoms by massaging their legs, exercising, and

---

GOOD QUESTION!
Is chronic fatigue syndrome a sleep disorder?

No. A sleep disorder involves difficulty staying awake or falling asleep, which is different from feeling so fatigued for so long that you can barely move. In fact, a diagnosis of chronic fatigue syndrome is made only after other possible medical causes, including sleep disorders and psychological problems, have been ruled out. As yet, the cause is not known.

---

giving up alcohol and caffeinated beverages. Persistent cases are often treated with medications, such as carbidopa-levodopa (Sinemet).

Other Sleep Robbers

Many things other than sleep disorders or medical conditions can disturb your sleep. These include:

Frequent flying. Whether you go for business or pleasure, traveling across time zones can throw your biological rhythms out of whack. The resulting fatigue and sleep disruption are particularly severe for people who cross time zones several times a month. Some studies indicate that taking melatonin (see page 172) can help.

Stress. Considered by most experts to be the number one cause of short-term sleeping problems, stress is often triggered by job pressures, family problems, and bereavement. (See Chapter 6, "Immunity and the Mind.")

Painful erections. Nocturnal erections are part of the normal physiologic rhythm for men. On occasion, however, sleep-related erections are painful, so they cause waking. Doctors sometimes prescribe drugs that suppress REM sleep (such as some antidepressants) to men who are often jarred from sleep by painful erections.

Vivid dreaming. Scientists do not know much about how or why we dream, but they do know that the intensity of dreams varies from person to person. In fact, some people experience such vivid and exciting dream imagery that it prevents deep sleep. Adults also can have nightmares, although those types of anxiety-provoking dreams tend to be more common among children, whose dreams are more easily influenced by television viewing or scary real-life events. Severe cases of vivid dreaming may require treatment with behavior modification techniques or medication.

A closer look at…hidden causes of fatigue

Maybe your exhaustion isn't due to a lack of sleep. Other common culprits behind "TATT"—the shorthand doctors give to the widespread problem of being "Tired All The Time"—include depression (see pages 106 and 218) and the following energy sappers.

ACTIVE INFECTIONS

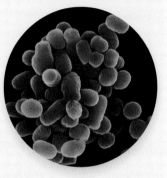

Even if you don't have obvious symptoms, an undetected infection may be making you tired. Early- or late-stage Lyme disease may manifest itself as fatigue you just can't shake, as may brucellosis, which is caused by *Brucella abortus* bacteria (RIGHT, magnified 8,666 times), which humans can catch by coming into contact with infected sheep, goats, or cows or drinking milk from these infected animals.

ALLERGIES

Histamine and other chemicals released during the allergic response tend to cause sleepiness. Paradoxically, allergy attacks caused by triggers such as ragweed or dandelions (LEFT) can keep you up all night wheezing and sniffling, as can airway irritation caused by dust mites. Furthermore, many medications used to treat allergies, such as over-the-counter antihistamines, can exacerbate the fatigue. See an allergist to discuss options for controlling symptoms.

ANEMIA

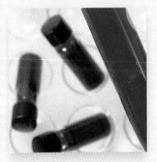

The main job of red blood cells is to carry oxygen from the lungs to the rest of the body. If you don't have enough red blood cells, or if they aren't carrying enough oxygen, the result may be anemia accompanied by fatigue severe enough to keep you from performing even routine tasks. A simple blood test can detect anemia. If the test is positive, your doctor will look for the underlying cause (a bleeding ulcer or poor diet, for example) and prescribe the appropriate treatment.

LOW HORMONE LEVELS

In men, low levels of the hormone testosterone can cause exhaustion, weight loss, and a lack of interest in sex and other normal activities. In women, low levels of estrogen can cause similar problems. Too little or too much of other important hormones, such as thyroid hormone or thyroid-stimulating hormone, can also result in fatigue. Luckily, hormone levels can easily be checked with blood tests. If needed, pills, patches, creams, or injections will restore normal levels.

Awake and Recharged

Everyone should know exactly how much sleep he or she requires to feel wide awake, dynamic, and energetic all day long," declares Cornell University sleep expert James B. Maas, Ph.D.

But knowing you should get more sleep doesn't necessarily mean you will. One-third of all Canadians—almost 10 million people—sleep no more than 6.5 hours a night. The pressure to keep going, they say, is simply too great to resist.

No time to sleep? Some high-powered people are proud of their modest sleep needs. As James Gleick observed in his 1999 book *Faster,* "Overwork equals importance." But is it really work that's eating into our sleep time?

No, say many time-use experts. Instead of sleeping, we're watching TV.

Studies have found that North Americans overestimate their weekly work hours and underestimate their free time by about 10 and 20 hours respectively. Hour for hour, the extra time people think they spend working matches the time they spend glued to the tube. The message for tired-out TV addicts: Forgo some of those shows and you'll have the time to sleep.

The tube isn't the the only sleep thief in modern life. These days, there's just more stuff to do—surf the web, shop after dinner, go to concerts, movies, and plays. If all this activity is making you get to bed late, take charge. Resolve to make your bedtime sacrosanct, then let nothing short of a natural disaster interfere with it. To find more time for serious sleep:

◆ **Keep an activity log.** A planned behavior change should always start out with observation. For five to seven days before changing or enforcing your bedtime, make hourly notes of what you are doing all day long. When you stop one activity and start another, jot down the time so you'll know how many minutes you spend on each task. Review your log to figure out where your time goes and how to free it up for more sleep.

◆ **Program your VCR.** Choose the shows you most want to see, pop a tape into the machine, and enter the time and date codes for automatic recording. (If you're flummoxed, ask a teenager for help.) Watch your shows while you're doing mind-numbing tasks such as ironing or folding laundry, and fast-forward through commercial breaks to save time. You can also combine viewing with working out on a treadmill or exercise bicycle.

◆ **Unplug the phone.** Calls from friends and family members a few time zones to the west can keep you up an extra hour or more. Turn off the ringer at night and give a few select people a back-up number (a cell phone, beeper, or unlisted line) for emergencies.

◆ **Figure out your priorities.** In the morning, make a quick list of things to do before bedtime. Assign every item a rank from most to least important, and tackle them in that order. If anything's left on your list after dinner, bump it over to the next day's roster.

Who snoozes the most...

Just like people, animals have a daily pattern of rest and activity, with most larger animals needing less sleep than smaller ones. Here's the rundown of their average slumber.

SPECIES/HOURS	
Brown Bat	19.9
Lion	13.5
Cat	12.1
Rabbit	11.4
Dog	10.6
Bottlenose Dolphin	10.4
Chimpanzee	9.7
Pig	7.8
Seal	6.2
Elephant	3.6
Horse	2.9
Giraffe	1.9

185

{ "Sleep resettles us emotionally, cognitively, immunologically.
It's just good."
—DAVID DINGES, PH.D. / CHRONOBIOLOGIST, UNIVERSITY OF PENNSYLVANIA SCHOOL OF MEDICINE }

CHAPTER 6

Immunity and the Mind

Even the most skeptical doctors now agree that stress can make us sick. But recent research reveals that the best solution isn't only working less and relaxing more. Loving yourself and others, speaking your mind, and cultivating optimism are also essential for achieving true mental and physical health.

The Perils of Stress

Your heart pounds, your pulse races, your breath quickens, and your muscles tense. In an instant, your mouth goes dry and butterflies rustle in your stomach. It feels as if you're about to engage in a life-or-death struggle.

In reality, though, your pride is the only thing at stake. Your boss has moved your deadline from 2:00 P.M. tomorrow to 5:00 P.M. today so he can start his vacation early. You're just about to scream—but all you can do is stew.

The situation has evoked your stress response, also known as the fight-or-flight reaction, a set of physical changes triggered by the mind's perception of a threat. When the alarm sounds, the brain tells the body to gear up and prepare to meet some extraordinary demands. Scientists think this response is left over from our prehistoric ancestors, who lived in constant danger and needed to be able to shift into physical high gear in an instant. Without the stress response, our species wouldn't have gotten past the Ice Age.

In modern life, though, fight or flight is something of an anachronism. We rarely need to fend off predators, but our bodies still respond to all kinds of adversity—from daily hassles like traffic jams to major upheavals like the death of a spouse—as if strength and speed were the qualities we needed.

What is stress? Stanford University biologist Robert M. Sapolsky, Ph.D., defines stress as anything that upsets the body's natural means of self-regulation. Moment by moment, the body

Interesting!

Think there's too much on your plate? Consider the alternative—boredom, which experts say is closely akin to stress. Why? Because being in a rut, just like being overtaxed, is linked to harmful behaviors, such as overeating, smoking, or drinking.

NEW TECHNOLOGY has created new pressures—we try to do more work in less time.

adjusts its blood pressure, temperature, heart rate, hormone levels, and a host of other variables. These are all controlled by the brain, which tells the endocrine system (hormone-secreting glands and organs) what delicate adjustments to make under ever-changing circumstances, including such physical disruptions as injury, illness, and prolonged exposure to temperature extremes.

The stress response originates in the hypothalamus, a pea-sized organ deep inside the brain. The hypothalamus is also where emotions and memories are processed and basic feelings and urges—hunger, thirst, desire, rage, panic, and pain—are controlled. Perhaps because the hypothalamus processes both emotional reactions and physical sensations, events that threaten your sense of security, self-esteem, or social standing—your child's bad report card, for example, or your spouse's job loss—can throw your body into the same state of high alert as a broken bone or the sound of squealing brakes. And over time, the physical response to mental stress can take a heavy toll on the immune system, the heart, and possibly the brain. Paradoxically, the stress response can have positive short-term effects on the immune system as well.

What causes stress? Anything that provokes intense feelings, whether the feelings are painful (anger, sadness, or fear) or pleasurable (joy or excitement), can trigger a stress reaction. That's why positive events like the birth of a child or a sudden financial windfall are often classified as stressors. The common denominator, experts say, is change. When the circumstances and routines of your life are altered, whether for better or for worse, you have to adjust, and the effort and unpredictability involved make for stress.

MENTAL STRESS triggers a burst of physical energy appropriate for fueling battle or escape, but not for dealing with personal conflicts.

In 1967, University of Washington psychiatrists Thomas Holmes and Robert Rahe reported on the connections between 43 major life events or changes and stress-related illness. Besides proving that risk of illness increased in the year following any of these events, the researchers were able to rank each item from most to least stressful.

Researchers from the University of Florida and Auburn University recently reevaluated the stress questionnaire developed from this study, known as the Social Readjustment Rating Scale (SRRS). One goal of the new research was to determine whether the same stressful events are still correlated with illness. The findings: The link between high stress and poor health is as strong as ever, but the

VITAL STATISTICS: MOOD

10 percent
Percentage of Canadians who suffer from mood disorders

12,000
Number of road rage incidents reported by the Canadian media between 1998 and 2000

124
Number of books related to optimism listed on Amazon.com

4,899
Number of books related to stress listed on Amazon.com

200 billion
The cost in dollars of stress and stress-related disorders in North America each year

ranking of stressors has changed. Although death of a spouse and divorce were the top 2 stressors in both years, experiencing sex difficulties climbed from number 13 in 1967 to number 10 in 1997. The chart on the right compares the top 10 stressors for both years.

A more complete picture. Each person, of course, has a unique response to stress. Some people, for reasons no one can explain, are able to roll with the punches that would knock many others to their knees. And although going through several major changes such as the ones in the SRRS is correlated with becoming ill, a high score on the scale translates to only about a 30 percent increase in risk. Clearly, other factors are involved. Here are some of the possibilities.

◆ **Control.** Stressors such as death and financial hardship due to a general economic downturn can't be controlled. In contrast, changing from a job that has become routine to a more stressful but also more challenging job is entirely within your control. Many studies suggest that major life changes you decide to make on your own trigger weaker stress responses than those you're forced to make.

◆ **Desirability.** Getting married, having a baby, or getting a job promotion can be stressful because all of them involve change. But many experts believe that desirable changes have less potential to affect health than undesirable ones.

◆ **Hardiness.** The term "hardiness" refers to a set of traits that seems to protect some people from the ravages of stress. Hardy individuals are highly committed; they stick things out instead of second-guessing. They have a strong sense of personal control—if not over events themselves, then over the way in which events affect them. Finally, they also view adversity as a challenge to be overcome; they don't see themselves as victims of unfair circumstances.

◆ **Coping.** Poor coping, reflected in disrupted eating and sleeping habits under stress, is related to weakened immunity. In one trial, researchers inoculated more than 100 people with a flu vaccine, then measured their production of antibodies—a reliable index of the strength of their immune response. The investigators found that people who tended to be overly anxious under stress had weaker responses to the vaccine than people who stayed on an even keel.

◆ **Lifestyle.** People with poor eating, sleep, and exercise habits tend to have stronger physical responses to mental stress than people with a healthy lifestyle. Harmful habits like smoking, drug abuse, and heavy drinking magnify the detrimental effects of stress. In a catch-22, people are more likely to turn to these habits in difficult times.

THE MOST STRESSFUL EVENTS

1967	1997
1. Death of spouse	1. Death of spouse
2. Divorce	2. Divorce
3. Marital separation	3. Personal injury or illness
4. Jail term	4. Marital separation
5. Death of close family member	5. Jail term
6. Personal injury or illness	6. Getting married
7. Getting married	7. Change in health of family member
8. Fired at work	8. Death of close family member
9. Marital reconciliation	9. Change in financial state
10. Retirement	10. Sex difficulties

Source: Scully JA, Tosi H, Banning K. "Life event checklists: revisiting the social readjustment rating scale after 30 years," *Educational and Psychological Measurement* 60:864–876. (2000)

{ "It's not the amount of stresses in life that affects health and well-being, but one's response to the stressful situations." }

—PAMELA SMITH, R.D. / SPORTS NUTRITIONIST AND WELLNESS COACH

"Last straws" and ongoing stress.

Although the best-known stress research focuses on the impact of major life events, some psychologists think another type of stress is just as damaging to people already overburdened. It's the stress of inconveniences and squabbles that drain your energy, take up your time, and make you angry and frustrated. Your bus is running late. Your office mate makes too much noise. Your insurance won't authorize payment for a prescription until 30 days after your last refill—which contained only a 21-day supply.

Added up, these little problems, which stress researchers call daily hassles, take their greatest toll if there's also a major ongoing stress in your life. One such ongoing stress is the responsibility of caring for someone with a chronic disease, particularly if the disease causes inevitable, progressive deterioration, as Alzheimer's disease does. A recent study found that people taking care of a relative with Alzheimer's disease had fewer circulating T-cells and less control over latent herpes viruses (which remain in the body in a dormant state and can recur when the immune system is weakened) than a control group not burdened with caregiving.

The caregivers also experienced more illnesses (especially colds) and psychological distress. The more isolated they felt, the poorer their immune response was. Other studies have shown that caring for an Alzheimer's patient doubles and may even triple the risk of depression. One of the most thoroughly documented physical effects of depression is compromise of the immune system.

A Stress–Cancer Connection?

It seems plausible that stress could contribute to the development of cancer. Some people whose statistical risk of the disease is low develop aggressive, untreatable tumors. And a few people whose risks are quite high—heavy smokers, for example— live into their 90s and die in their sleep. Could an unhealthy response to stress be the factor that tips the scales against the first group?

The idea is not new. Galen, a Greek physician in the second century A.D., observed that perpetually sad women were particularly prone to cancer. Since then, many physicians have noted that a disproportionate number of cancer patients have histories of shouldering emotional burdens.

Essential Coping Skills

We all cope with stress in different ways—some of us far more effectively than others. To shed some light on which coping skills blunted the health effects of stress most reliably, University of Chicago researchers followed a group of business executives for eight years as they faced the ups and downs of running a company. Those who stayed healthiest shared these traits:

1 They didn't distort problems. They viewed the curve balls in life as challenges and opportunities rather than threats to be feared.

2 They reached out to others. Each set aside time for projects they felt were meaningful—for instance, ones involving community.

3 They felt in control. They set realistic goals and, if needed, readjusted those goals to make them more attainable.

But is the connection a matter of conventional wisdom (which is often wrong) or scientific fact? In animals, at least, the links are real. Studies involving animals—mostly rats—have slowly built the case for the link between stress and the progression of cancerous tumors. In one such study, rats exposed to tumor-promoting substances developed cancer at a much faster rate when subjected to the stress of random electrical shocks than rats that were spared the shock or given the means to control it.

If you already have cancer, reducing your stress levels may help you recover. Researchers at Pittsburgh Cancer Center found that breast cancer patients who felt they were getting less than ideal support from friends and family had less NK-cell activity and were more likely to have lymph-node involvement than similar patients whose friends and families were helpful and caring. And scientists investigating the effects of stress on immune function in women infected with both HIV and human papilloma virus (a sexually transmitted disease linked to cervical cancer) have seen connections among stressful events, a decline in NK cells, and a greater likelihood of precancerous cervical cells making the transition to malignancy. They also have preliminary evidence that reducing stress can lower cancer risk.

Slowing the course. Stress is probably not a direct cause of cancer, but it seems to promote the spread of the disease by weakening the body's defenses. Support groups, which help allay stress, have been found to prolong survival in melanoma, breast cancer, and lymphoma patients. Caring for the mind, then, may help the immune system keep cancers in check.

Quick Tip

Even if you think you manage stress well, your body may be screaming for help. Insomnia, back pain, heartburn, headaches, loss of appetite, and lowered sex drive are just a few of the physical symptoms of chronic stress.

DO YOU RECOGNIZE THESE SYMPTOMS OF STRESS?

Behavioral

Drinking too much, eating too much or too little, fidgeting, fist clenching, talking too fast or too loud

Emotional

Anger, defensiveness, depression, irrationality, listlessness, mood swings, worry

Mental

Confusion, memory problems, poor concentration, racing thoughts, vivid dreams

Physical

Cold hands and feet, grinding teeth, headache, heart palpitations, increased sweating, indigestion, itching, loss of libido, sore neck, rapid breathing, tense muscles, weight loss or gain

The Two Faces of Stress

A lawyer comes down with the flu the day after an important court appearance. A couple takes off for a much-needed vacation—and both get sick. Someone trapped in an unhappy marriage suffers one acute infection after another. Coincidence? Increasingly, researchers think not.

As studies of the links between major life events, everyday hassles, and illness have shown, being under emotional pressure increases the risk of getting sick. Evidence from a new field of science called psychoneuroimmunology (the study of brain-immune system interactions) further indicates that immune function and state of mind are intimately intertwined. One study, for example, found a link between mood and day-to-day fluctuations in the amount of immunoglobulin A (IgA) in saliva; IgA levels were higher on days when the people in the study were upbeat and lower on days when they felt less cheerful. IgA, an antibody produced by the immune system, is our first-line defense against the entry of infectious organisms through the respiratory tract.

Benefits of stress? As anyone who has ever faced a deadline knows, the main benefit of the stress response is that it brings you to a peak of function. When the stress hormones are coursing through your bloodstream, you think faster and with greater clarity. Your awareness sharpens, your reaction time quickens, and your pain receptors are dampened by a "fix" of feel-good hormones. In a crisis, you may even be capable of superhuman physical feats like lifting a two-ton car to free an injured child.

Recent research also suggests that stress does more than just enhance your short-term physical and mental performance. Occasional stress may actually help the immune system defend the body against infection.

How can stress boost immunity? Through the actions of cortisol and other steroids, hormones produced by the adrenal glands in response to stress. It turns out that during the initial stages of the stress response, cortisol and several related hormones perform a kind of rescue mission, yanking lymphocytes (the immune system cells that perform roaming surveillance, looking for invaders) out of circula-tion and rushing them to wherever the body is actively fighting off an infection. This helps explain why we stay well in the thick of stress but start aching, coughing, and sniffling a day or so after stress begins to ease off and our immune systems resume their regular pace and activities.

The down side. The discovery that occasional stress may temporarily jack up your immune system doesn't change the basic fact that sustained stress is harmful. A whole body of research shows how stress hormones damage the cardiovascular system, the digestive system, and other body systems above and beyond the immune system. Some evidence suggests that at persistently high levels, stress hormones may even damage the brain, causing memory lapses, anxiety, and an inability to control emotional outbursts.

Stress hormones also have direct effects on the organs of the immune system—the thymus, lymph nodes, bone marrow, and spleen. The thymus, which each day pumps out millions of infection-fighting lymphocytes (white blood cells), is a prime target of stress hormones. In fact, one of the earliest discoveries linking immune function to the stress

BRIEF BURSTS OF STRESS can actually enhance immune function.

GOOD STRESS/BAD STRESS

Yes, we often feel frenzied, confirm numerous psychological surveys. But it's possible to enjoy life and thrive with a hectic lifestyle—if it's loaded with good stress, the kind that's energizing and motivating. How can you tell it apart from bad stress—the kind that can rob you of your health and happiness?

STRESS THAT'S GOOD	STRESS THAT'S BAD
Facing something with enough excitement to override any fears.	Facing something with a mixture of dread, worry, and anxiety.
A filled-to-the-brim schedule that still contains several activities you find satisfying and look forward to doing.	An overloaded schedule stuffed with obligations that you don't enjoy and wouldn't fulfill if you had a choice.
More commitments—wife, mother, PTA president, and valued employee—than you might like, but none that you would want to give up completely.	Feeling that what you do is unimportant, unfulfilling, and not worth the effort.
Working toward a valued goal and knowing that life will slow down once you achieve it.	Feeling out of control and overwhelmed with no end in sight and no help on the horizon.
Feeling challenged, alert, and energetic—primed to tackle the task at hand, whatever it may be.	Wanting to crawl under the covers and stay there rather than take a stab at getting through the day.
Tired enough to get restful, deep sleep.	Restless sleep, ulcers, back pain, or recurrent minor ills.

response was the observation that after being bombarded with the stress hormone cortisol, the thymus shrank and produced fewer T-cells, a group of lymphocytes that orchestrates the actions of other immune cells.

Cortisol also reduces the activity, number, and lifespan of other lymphocytes. Too much cortisol robs some lymphocytes of their disease-fighting power, pulls others out of circulation, and eventually kills some outright. It also suppresses an immune-system chemical called interleukin 2, which alerts lymphocytes to the presence of germs.

Natural killer (NK) cells—lymphocytes that locate and destroy abnormal or virus-infected cells—are the immune cells most affected by stress. Researchers have found that both short- and long-term stressors decrease the numbers and activity of NK-cells.

Finally, stress seems to lessen the body's ability to heal wounds, so if you're planning elective surgery, try to schedule it for a time when you're unlikely to be under lots of pressure. It might also be helpful to start practicing relaxation techniques such as meditation several weeks before you have your operation.

Drawing conclusions. Researchers are reluctant to say that stress, by itself, is enough to make us sick. The immune system is so complex and capable of such ingenious tactics to thwart its enemies that a stress-related change in one part of the system might not hurt the system as a whole.

"Just because your immune function goes down during a stressful period doesn't mean you are going to get sick," says Janet Kiecolt-Glaser, Ph.D., who, in collaboration with her husband, Ronald

{ "Doctors don't know everything really. They understand matter, not spirit. And you and I live in spirit." }

—WILLIAM SAROYAN / WRITER AND PLAYWRIGHT (1908-1981)

Glaser, Ph.D., has conducted numerous studies of stress-related changes in immune function. "Where stress seems to have the greatest impact on health is on individuals who already have poor immune function due to age or diseases that impair the immune system, or on individuals who have already been chronically stressed for reasons other than health."

This doesn't mean you should stop worrying about stress unless you're already sick. There is unassailable evidence that stress is one of the factors that predispose people to illness. As researchers learn more about the stress response, they may be able to come up with new ways to help people stay well despite unmitigated stress.

For now, the best bet is to learn how to cope. Start by allowing yourself some pleasure and getting involved with others (see pages 204 and 205). Stress-management techniques (see pages 198–203) can also help.

The lessons of grief.

It's tempting to make broad generalizations about how the mind affects the body, but blanket statements never do justice to the subject. In simplistic terms, the death of your spouse or life partner will probably damage your own health—at least in the short run.

But a recent study of 40 HIV-positive men who had lost their partners to AIDS shows that emotional pain can lead to

spiritual growth, which is linked to better health. After their partners' deaths, one-third of the men had, in the process of grieving, committed themselves to living meaningfully, with an awareness that each day is a gift.

The researchers analyzed the medical records of all the bereaved men for the first 4 to 10 years after their partners died and found some interesting connections between health and renewed dedication to life after grieving. The men who mourned their losses and gained a new respect for life through their experiences had slower declines in immune function than men who were bitter or merely accepting.

In addition, 13 out of the 25 study participants who survived for several more years had learned positive lessons from their grief. By contrast, among the 15 men who concluded that their partner's death symbolized the futility and meaninglessness of life, only 3 became long-term survivors.

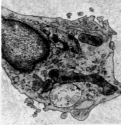

UNCOMMON KNOWLEDGE
The Brain's Immune System

Mounting evidence shows that the brain has an extensive defense network that functions like a private immune system. The key soldiers are microglias (ABOVE), cells activated only when brain cells are harmed or threatened. Once aroused, microglias secrete some of the same deadly chemicals that immune-system cells use to destroy invaders—chemicals so potent that they also destroy nearby healthy cells. This has aroused suspicion that zealous microglias may contribute to certain brain disorders, such as Alzheimer's and Parkinson's disease. If so, figuring out how to control microglia activity might one day yield new cures.

Close-Up: Fight or Flight

Prepare yourself: It's either fight or flight. That's what the brain tells the body when it perceives a threat, whether it's a pouncing tiger in your path or an angry driver you accidentally cut off.

The instant the brain senses a crisis, it sends danger signals in the form of chemical messengers that alert the body to prepare for action. The hypothalamus, a small regulatory organ located deep within the brain, sets the stress response in motion with a direct command to the adrenal glands: "Release adrenaline!" This powerful hormone increases your blood pressure and heart rate, triggering a rush of heart-pounding excitement. The adrenal glands also release cortisol, a hormone that helps move glucose (the sugar the body uses for fuel) out of storage and into circulation.

Although some of the body's systems are put on red alert during times of stress, the immune system is powered down to conserve energy. After all, there's no reason to make antibodies to attack potential cancers unless you know that you'll survive the current crisis. Latent viruses, such as herpes, have an easier time resurging, since the body cannot defend itself as well. The relatively few white blood cells on hand are deployed to the body's front line—the skin— where injury or infection is most likely.

In the absence of real physical demands, the burst of nervous energy from a stress response dissipates slowly. The heart rate stays fast, the blood pressure remains elevated, and blood sugar stays high. In the long term, these effects can damage your health, increasing your risk of hypertension, diabetes, and heart disease. That's why it's important to tackle stress head-on.

STRESS AND SEX DRIVE

In times of stress, production of sex hormones in the gonads—testicles (BELOW) in men, ovaries in women—screeches to a halt and sexual energy is redirected toward survival. This can trigger diminished desire, erectile dysfunction, or an inability to achieve orgasm. Since most couples are not aware that a blunted sex drive can be a physical result of stress, they may blame each other or assume that the relationship is flawed, which can only make matters worse.

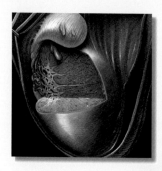

The **bone marrow** increases production of blood cells to carry extra oxygen and help fight infection.

The **thyroid gland** secretes hormones to speed metabolism, providing an energy boost. Prolonged stimulation can lead to insomnia and increased appetite.

The **lungs** expand to deliver more oxygen to the muscles and heart. Breathing becomes rapid. Nostrils flare. Air passages widen.

The **heart** beats harder. If it's already having trouble keeping up with routine demands, the added strain could be the last straw, resulting in a stroke or heart attack.

The **pancreas** secretes extra insulin, a hormone that ferries glucose into all your cells, for a burst of energy. Blood sugar soars and may stay high for some time. Eventually the body may become less responsive to insulin, setting the stage for diabetes.

The **liver** pumps out additional cholesterol to provide slow-burning fuel that can take over where blood sugar leaves off. If stress is chronic, the extra cholesterol could lead to hardening of the arteries.

Activity in the **stomach** and **intestines** shuts down to conserve energy. Stomach acid levels rise, which may cause "butterflies," nausea, or vomiting.

Sweat glands go into overdrive to cool heated muscles, and the **skin** "crawls" as tiny blood vessels near the surface contract and hairs stand on end—a reaction that made our ancestors seem larger to enemies.

Learning to Relax

Fortunately, everyone can learn to exert some control over stress. With the help of these proven stress-management techniques, you can improve your health, attitude, productivity, relationships, and longevity.

In choosing which strategies to try, keep these points in mind. First, no single method is uniformly successful: A combination of methods is generally most effective. Second, what works for one person does not necessarily work for someone else. Third, the more strategies you explore, the more likely you are to find one you like.

Give yourself time to practice the technique you choose. It may seem difficult, but the more you practice it, the easier and more effective it will be.

Break the vicious cycle. The fight-or-flight response itself can make the idea of relaxation seem threatening. Constant stress from family or financial problems, for instance, may keep you in a heightened state of alertness. Over time, perpetual vigilance can create feelings of hopelessness and powerlessness, major symptoms of depression. That means your immune system will be weakened by two forces—the continuous barrage of stress hormones generated by the fight-or-flight response and the slowing of all body processes that goes along with depression.

The following techniques will help reduce your baseline stress level so you can feel more in control and start to change the circumstances that made you feel so stressed.

MEDITATION offers a gentle way to slow yourself down during a hectic day.

Meditation: Speedy Serenity

The most studied and simplest technique for coping with stress is meditation. Even if you just can't see yourself sitting cross-legged and saying "om," you can still learn to achieve focus and relaxation, the real essence of meditating. To calm your mind and ease your body into a deeply relaxed state, all you have to do is concentrate on your breath and ignore intrusive thoughts. Physiologically, a meditative state is the polar opposite of the fight-or-flight response.

There's ample evidence that meditation, practiced regularly, reduces work-related stress and anxiety and helps control high blood pressure. For example, several researchers have found that transcendental meditation (TM), in which you repeat a word or phrase to achieve mental focus, reduced blood-vessel constriction, keeping blood pressure in check. In one experiment, a group of

> **Quick Tip**
>
> Busy people often drown themselves in clutter. Such chaos can amplify stress, especially if important things keep vanishing. Spend some time each day getting rid of superfluous stuff. As a rule, if you haven't used it in a year, you don't need it.

people who regularly practiced TM was compared to a group who did not. The first group meditated for several minutes, during which the other group simply relaxed. Immediately afterward, the meditation group had lower blood pressure than the relaxation group, although the two groups had similar heart rates. This difference suggests that meditating made the blood vessels relax.

Findings from a Harvard Medical School study show that the effects of regular meditation last longer than previously believed. Study participants who meditated for 10 to 20 minutes a day maintained low levels of stress hormones for several hours after each session was over.

◆ **What to do.** Sit comfortably in a place where you will not be disturbed. Close your eyes or keep them open and softly focused on something in front of you. Pay attention to your breathing. Notice how your stomach expands and contracts as you inhale and exhale. If troubling thoughts enter your mind, simply return your focus to your breathing. Practice this exercise for about 20 minutes every day.

The readings are presented to you as sounds or video images. The goal is two-fold: one, to make you more adept at recognizing how you feel when, for example, your blood pressure is rising or you're gearing up for an asthma attack, and two, to teach you how to adjust those physical responses so you can avoid episodes of illness. With repeated biofeedback sessions, you learn to short-circuit the cycle of stress-related symptoms.

Research has shown that biofeedback can reduce blood pressure by up to 16 points. Also, a study published in *Diabetes Care* found that biofeedback training contributed to a 22 percent increase in circulation in a group of patients with diabetes-related blood vessel damage.

◆ **What to do.** Many psychologists and nurses offer biofeedback training. It costs at least $50 per session and usually requires 5 to 20 sessions. A less expensive alternative, heart-rate monitoring, is based on similar technology. Heart-rate monitors, sold in sporting-goods stores for about $125, are lightweight chest bands to which heartbeat sensors are attached. The sensor transmits your heart rate to a digital display worn

Biofeedback: Wired for Health

Since the 1970s, biofeedback has been widely used to teach people how to alter involuntary physical reactions in which emotional tension plays a role. Migraine sufferers, for example, can use biofeedback to prevent headache-triggering spasms in the arteries leading to the brain.

At the start of a biofeedback session, a technician hooks you up to a computer that monitors one or more of the following: heart rate, pulse, brain-wave patterns, muscle activity, skin temperature, and perspiration.

UNCOMMON KNOWLEDGE
What About Guided Imagery?

Guided imagery, sometimes called visualization, is a popular self-help technique for people with a wide range of medical conditions. To practice it, you vividly imagine your body engaged in fighting your disease. Proponents believe that if we visualize desirable changes frequently and intensely enough, we can make them occur. In one type of guided imagery, the Simonton Method, cancer patients supplement traditional treatment by creating mental pictures of chemotherapy agents and white blood cells systematically killing cancer cells. While such techniques may focus the mind the same way meditation does, there's no evidence that they do anything else. But many rational people use visualization. As long as you acknowledge its limitations, guided imagery may have calming effects that can only do you good.

{ "A merry heart doeth good like a medicine, but a broken spirit drieth the bones." }

—PROVERBS 17:22

on your wrist like a watch. For stress reduction, wear the monitor for 10 minutes while you sit quietly, breathing in and out. Periodically check the monitor; your heart rate should start to slow down after a few sessions.

Laughter: Mirthful Medicine

People love to laugh, so much so that the average adult chuckles 17 times a day and the average six-year-old laughs 300 times. We also instinctively turn to humor for help in coping with the difficulties that beset us every day. Laughter feels good, comes naturally, and boosts our spirits.

SOME LIKE IT FUNNY

The idea of laughter as medicine gained great popularity in 1979, after Norman Cousins's landmark book, *Anatomy of an Illness*, appeared. In the book, Cousins described how a steady diet of *Candid Camera* reruns and Marx Brothers movies helped him recover from an illness diagnosed as fatal. Tap into the same power by renting any of these titles, listed by the American Film Institute as the funniest movies ever: *Some Like It Hot, Tootsie, Dr. Strangelove, Annie Hall, Duck Soup, Blazing Saddles, M*A*S*H,* and *It Happened One Night.*

While there's little reliable evidence that laughter directly benefits the immune system, the idea is provocative enough to have prompted a first-of-its-kind study focusing on sick children with depressed immune systems. In the ongoing study, "Rx Laughter," young cancer and AIDS patients at the University of California at Los Angeles Jonsson Cancer Center watch classic cartoons, television shows, and comedy films, then have their immune responses tested. If laughter turns out to boost their immunity, a daily dose of humor could become a routine part of cancer care.
◆ **What to do.** Read the comics every day, listen to funny audiotapes in the car, and spend more time in toy stores. If your schedule is overbooked, send yourself a message in big letters on your calendar: DON'T POSTPONE JOY!

Nature: A Soothing Path

Do your troubles seem to vanish when you gaze at waves breaking on sand? Does the sight of a fluttering butterfly give you cheer? Nature holds the key to health, believes Harvard naturalist and Pulitzer Prize winner Edward O. Wilson. Ancient warriors fled to sacred springs when they were injured or ill. By the Middle Ages, cloistered gardens with flowering trees and water fountains were being used to soothe the sick.

Modern research confirms that contact with plants, trees, and animals has special healing power. Just looking at nature photographs can help mend the body, as Texas A&M University environmental psychologist Roger S. Ulrich, Ph.D., found in a

The Power of Touch

Ahhh! Think how relaxing it feels to have someone rub your shoulders at the end of a trying day. Research examining the power of massage—the systematic application of pressure and movement to the skin, muscles, tendons, and ligaments—now shows that those feelings of release and pleasure deliver many health benefits, including an enhanced immune response. Just one example: HIV-positive men who received 15-minute massages twice a week for five weeks showed dramatically decreased levels of the stress hormone cortisol. Massage also can ease the inflammation that follows a physical trauma. For instance, when lymph nodes are removed during breast-cancer surgery, lymphatic fluid can collect in the arm, causing swelling. Other than massage, there is no good treatment.

In general, the best massage for you is the one you like best. Don't make the mistake of assuming that if it

hurts, it's good for you. Here are the most popular techniques.

1 Acupressure. The philosophy guiding acupressure practitioners is that injury or illness can block the flow of energy through the body, creating muscle tension and other types of discomfort. Unblocking the flow by pressing and holding specific "energy points" restores energy flow and health.

2 Craniosacral. This combination of head massage and acupressure is said to release tension and restore energy balance by relaxing the head and neck muscles and

promoting circulation to the brain.

3 Deep-tissue. This sometimes painful technique involves manipulating the fascia, a thin layer of tissue supporting and connecting the muscles. Past injuries may make the fascia tight.

4 Lymphatic drainage. This technique uses rhythmic touch and pressure on the lymph glands, supposedly to detoxify the body by speeding elimination of waste. It is said to ease water retention.

5 Reflexology. Proponents believe that certain spots on the feet,

hands, and ears provide direct pathways to various other body parts and organs. When these spots are pressed, rotated, grasped, and patted, the corresponding body parts benefit.

6 Shiatsu. Named by combining the Japanese words *shi*, meaning finger, and *atsu*, meaning pressure, shiatsu is an ancient form of acupressure massage. It traditionally is done on the floor with the client fully clothed.

7 Swedish. The classic massage technique, it relies on five basic strokes—kneading, rubbing, pressing, and light pounding—to work out muscle kinks, promote relaxation, and improve blood and lymph circulation.

8 Watsu. This new form of shiatsu massage, developed in the 1980s, is done in a small pool of warm water. Its free-flowing, relaxing, and meditative qualities are said to help those who experience it to recall soothing memories from early childhood.

landmark 1984 study. Ulrich found that surgical patients who looked out at a view of trees as they recovered had shorter hospital stays and needed less pain medication than similar patients who looked out at a brick wall. Other studies have found that looking at nature scenes can lower systolic blood pressure in five minutes or less.

After a stressful experience, gazing at nature can help the body return to its normal state more quickly, as measured by changes in muscle tension, respiration, and emotional state, all of which may be linked to better immune function.

And in a recent Swedish study, 160 post-operative heart patients looked at a landscape, an abstract art work, or, in a control group, no artwork. Those who looked at the landscape felt less anxious, required less pain medicine, and spent a day less in the hospital than the control-group patients. Abstract art, however, turned out to be worse than no art at all. Patients who viewed abstract works were more anxious than control patients, and they took more painkillers as well.

◆ **What to do.** To reap the healing benefits of nature, you don't have to take up hiking. Just hanging a beautiful nature poster on your wall will have a beneficial effect. So will hanging a bird feeder outside your window, putting plants in every room of your house, eating on a park bench instead of in the company cafeteria, or driving on quiet back roads instead of on busy highways.

Writing: Self-Exploration

If you've ever kept a diary, you know that putting pen to paper can help resolve problems. Now researchers at Southern Methodist University have confirmed that writing about your troubles can keep you healthy. One group of students wrote about their worries for 20 minutes three times a week, while the others wrote about ordinary events. In the months after the journal writing, those who wrote about their troubles were less likely to visit the doctor than the others.

Follow-up research found that jotting down stressful reactions to negative events helped bolster immunity. One group of adults wrote about their feelings regarding a personal trauma. Another group wrote about an emotionally neutral topic. Over the next four months, those in the group that had written about trauma exhibited heightened immune function, as measured by

---

And the Top 10 Are...

For adults in the workforce, the biggest sources of everyday stress are related to balancing the multiple demands of job and family, a recent survey reports.

STRESS INDUCERS

1. Time pressures
2. Feeling a lack of control
3. Worries about physical appearance
4. Job pressures
5. Health concerns
6. Lack of joy
7. Family relationships
8. Friends/social life
9. Lack of self-esteem
10. Worries about marriage/primary relationship

Source: Lahey Clinic.

GOOD QUESTION!
Is taking anti-stress supplements a good idea?

No. Some brands of stress-formula vitamins contain several times the RDA of vitamins C and B_6. The only proof that these products mitigate the harmful effects of stress comes from one study of a highly specific form of stress—the type caused by serious burns, major fractures, and general surgery. In fact, two major drug companies recently paid fines in the United States for overstating the benefits of their anti-stress supplement products.

More Than a Good Feeling

It's official: Making love is not only good for the heart, it's good for overall health—at least in moderation.

A study by a team of psychologists at Wilkes University in Wilkes-Barre, Pennsylvania, suggests that the right amount of sexual intimacy strengthens the body's defenses against colds, flu, and other diseases. The team studied 44 men and 67 women, collecting saliva samples and conducting interviews about sexual habits, frequency of sex, satisfaction with love relationships, and length of their current romances. The results showed that saliva samples of the group who made love at least once—but not more than twice—a week had 29 percent higher levels of immunoglobulin A

(IgA), an immune system protein in saliva and mucosal tissues that helps defend the mouth and upper respiratory tract against cold and flu viruses.

Does this means having sex more often is a route to an even more robust immune system? Sorry. By this study's measures, you really can get too much of a good thing.

Study participants who said they had sex three or more times per week had the lowest IgA levels of all—even lower than the people who had no sex at all.

Those results led researchers to speculate that frequent sexual activity could be a sign of unsatisfying, stressful, or obsessive relationships, which may generate anxiety and, in turn, depress the immune system.

levels of helper T-cells in their blood. They also went to the doctor half as often as they had in the four months before the writing exercise.

Also, a groundbreaking study published in the *Journal of the American Medical Association* examined how writing about emotionally charged versus emotionally neutral topics affected symptom severity in asthma and rheumatoid arthritis (RA). Both diseases result from hyperactive immune-system responses. A group composed of 39 asthma patients and 32 RA patients was asked to write for 20 minutes on three consecutive days about the most traumatic experiences of their lives. Asthma and RA patients in a control group followed the same writing schedule but were led to believe that

they were doing a time-management exercise. Therefore, they wrote about impersonal topics. Four months later, the patients who had written about traumatic events had significantly fewer disease symptoms than the control patients.

◆ **What to do.** Write in a journal for 10 to 20 minutes three times a week—and don't censor yourself. To enhance your health, your writing must explore your deepest anxieties. Don't worry about your spelling, punctuation, grammar, or style; you're writing to express your feelings and gain insight into yourself, not to communicate with others. If you're afraid someone will read your diary entries, rip them up—chances are you'll still feel better for having written.

The Importance of Friends

When you visit with your friends, you're not just getting updated on the TV shows you've missed or enjoying the chance to brag about your grandchildren. Sharing your thoughts with companions could very well save your life.

Many of us know intuitively that having friends keeps us healthy. You might not realize, however, that researchers have been exploring the connection for decades. People who frequently interact with others, whether face-to-face or by phone, mail, or e-mail, have lower death rates in any given time period than those who live in isolation. Sociable people get sick less often, and they recover faster when they do.

Why is friendship (or, as researchers call it, social support) such a positive and healing force? Answers are only now emerging. To start with, a friend can influence your perceptions and your behavior. A good friend might even point out health problems you haven't noticed. Friends can clue you in on symptoms, such as fatigue, weight loss, or less accurate hearing or sight. They might even insist that you go to the doctor for that checkup you keep putting off.

Play Your Cards Right

You and three of your friends sit around a card table and yak about your neighbors while you silently plot a strategy to trump your opponent's last bid. Fun, perhaps—but how could card playing possibly be good for your health?

It just might boost your immunity, says University of California at Berkeley biologist Marian Cleeves Diamond, Ph.D. In a small study, she found that contract bridge players have increased numbers of T-cells and other immune cells after a game of bridge.

Diamond interprets this preliminary study, along with earlier work she and other scientists have done, as evidence that an area of the brain shown to be active during bridge games stimulates the thymus gland, which produces T-cells. If more studies confirm Diamond's observation, it will be the first time the "thinking" part of the brain has been linked directly to the immune system.

Benefits you can measure. A central factor, though, is that simply staying connected to other people strengthens immune function, particularly in the elderly. How does social support provide that protection? It's an antidote to the poisonous effects of loneliness and isolation. Lonely people feel alienated even in the midst of congenial groups. Their sense of isolation may come in part from misperceiving what other people say and do. Loneliness feeds on itself because the less relaxed contact you have with others, the more likely you are to feel out of place when you try to mingle.

In time, you may feel so anxious that you avoid most socializing.

Elderly people, many of whom have outlived spouses and/or friends or have seen their loved ones become disabled, are especially vulnerable to loneliness. Relocation, which is more and more common after retirement, also leaves a substantial proportion of older people lonely, out of touch with old friends, and unable to replace them with new ones.

Loneliness is a fairly substantial medical risk factor. It elevates the chance of premature death about as much as high blood pressure, lack of exercise, and obesity do. Researchers estimate that, within a given time period, individuals who lack social networks are two to three times more likely to die from any cause than people who have lots of relatives and friends.

The impact of sadness.
How does loneliness exert a physical effect powerful enough to increase the risk of illness and death? Lonely people secrete an excessive amount of cortisol, a stress hormone that can cause immune system suppression. When loneliness is com-pounded by day-to-day difficulties, cortisol levels rise even higher and the risk of developing a stress-related disease, such as high blood pressure, climbs, too. Bereavement, which often leads to loneliness, is closely associated with suppressed immune function. In the first two years after being widowed, men and women (particularly men) have below-normal levels of immune system activity. Lonely people take longer to recover from minor illnesses and surgery and suffer higher rates of complications than people with many friends.

FRIENDS ARE ESSENTIAL for rich and meaningful life experiences, as well as for good health and strong immunity.

Reach out and talk to someone.
On the flip side, social support can stress-proof the immune system, according to a study of medical students. During finals, certain types of cells in the students' immune systems became ineffective. But those with strong ties to family and friends were spared.

Do you have an old college pal or a favorite cousin you haven't seen in years? Make contact. Renewing past relationships links you to your own history. Or turn a hobby, such as reading or golf, into an opportunity to meet new people who share your interests. Check your local library to find a reading group to join or get matched up with others who want to form a new group.

15 Ways to Create Calm

Want to achieve a more peaceful state of mind but not sure where to begin? Start here. Following even one or two of the suggestions will make a difference.

It won't take long to implement most of these soul-soothing strategies, so don't use lack of time as an excuse. Even just smiling more often can lift your mood and boost your immune system without costing you much more than a few minutes a day. Consider making a few of these small but potentially significant changes:

1. Go slow. When you have to go somewhere, start out 10 minutes early instead of waiting until the last possible moment. You won't have to rush, and you'll be less stressed. Also, make an effort to move and talk in a very relaxed manner and see if your stress doesn't ebb away. Drive within the speed limit; pause before you reply to a question; let the phone ring a few times before answering it. And sit back and do nothing for a few minutes every day.

PEN A DAILY TO-DO LIST, and don't forget to write in at least one fun activity like "Time for a manicure."

2. Grab some green. Practitioners of feng shui (an Eastern discipline that purportedly helps you fine-tune your environment for comfort and success) believe plants increase vitality, which is the first step toward achieving happiness.

3. Give yourself a break. You can't make everyone in your life happy all the time. And it's okay to make mistakes now and then.

4. Fit in time-outs. To avoid tension buildup, follow this rule: For every 50 minutes you work, take a 5-minute break. Don't feel guilty: Time-outs are proven to increase productivity.

5. Get a pet. A dog, cat, bird, or even a fish can play a vital role in stress relief. In a Johns Hopkins Medical Center study, 50 out of 53 pet owners were alive a year after their first heart attacks, while only 17 of 39 people without pets lived that long.

GET A PET: Even a fish can make you happier and healthier than a petless person.

6. Use your vacation time. Austrian researchers recently showed that a two-week vacation does more than just clear the mind and calm the spirit. It also improves health and reduces stress levels for up to five weeks. Both during and after a good vacation, we sleep better and enjoy better moods. For a vacation to be healing, however, it must be restful and not overly structured. People who didn't have any down time on their vacations didn't enjoy the same health benefits.

7. Take up a hobby. Do something for the sheer pleasure of it, whether it's knitting, collecting rocks, or bird-watching. Hobbies instill self-confidence and help you connect with others who share your interests. And being engaged in numerous pursuits will help shield you from depression, which has been linked to impaired immune function and increased risk for cancer and other diseases. In one key study, men and women were asked to rate their happiness on a moment-by-moment basis for six weeks. The results showed that overall happiness depended upon how much time each person spent doing something that made him or her feel good.

SHOWING YOUR APPRECIATION can deepen your connection to others.

8. Learn to love lists. Try making daily to-do lists if you tend to forget things or if it makes you feel more organized. Prioritize your goals for the day, then divvy them up into realistic chunks of available time. If something won't fit onto today's list, move it to tomorrow's.

9. Read. Nothing takes your mind off your worries faster than a good book. Since reading is a silent activity, it also lets you escape noise—a known stressor—for a while. For the quietest refuge, head to the library.

10. Play around. The next time you're feeling anxious or stressed, take a break and do something childish: Find crayons and draw a picture, rent a favorite childhood movie, blow bubbles, or search the attic for a few of your favorite old toys.

11. Ask for help. When you feel overwhelmed, enlist help. Don't be afraid to ask; it's one of the things family and friends are there for. Also, conquer the habit of saying yes to every request or

FIND YOUR INNER CHILD by cuddling with a favorite toy.

obligation when your energy is at stake. Remind yourself that your health comes first, and that taking on too much can compromise your immune system.

12. Cultivate kindness. Tell the checkout clerk that you appreciate the way your groceries were packed. Call or visit a homebound friend. Bake cookies for a child you know. Giving makes you feel more positive by raising your self-worth and connecting you to others.

13. Don't ignore negative feelings. Like a warning light on your car's dashboard, your feelings can alert you that something is amiss. If you're angry, jealous, frustrated, or just plain irritable, it's a sign you need to take a deep breath and find a way to change directions.

14. Force a smile. Surgeon Bernie Siegel, M.D., an expert in the field of mind-body medicine, says that if you pretend to be happy by forcing a smile or a laugh, your body will react by producing less of the stress hormone cortisol.

15. Reward yourself for your accomplishments. Take time to give yourself a pat on the back instead of immediately rushing to get the next task done.

"Stress Relievers" You Can Live Without

It's bad enough that our bodies become taxed and inefficient under stress. Too often, we make matters worse by trying to alleviate tension with unhealthy habits such as smoking, drinking, or using illicit drugs.

"Relaxing" with the help of alcohol, tobacco, and drugs can quickly snowball into a serious health problem. Tension by itself puts your immune system at risk. When you use such substances as alcohol, nicotine, marijuana, or prescription drugs to ease stress, your immune system suffers all the more. Before long, your worries will roar back, stronger and meaner than before. Should you light another cigarette? Pour another drink? Or do the hard work of rooting out whatever lies beneath your tension?

We all know that a quick fix can't solve a deep-seated problem. Don't let a momentary escape turn into a new problem that may be extremely difficult to solve.

Drinking Sensibly

People with high-pressure jobs often kick back with a drink at the end of a tough day. It's a common impulse, given alcohol's sedating effects. Though researchers don't yet fully understand what alcohol does to the brain, it seems to act on the hippocampus, a ridge-shaped structure deep in the brain, between the cerebral cortex and the brain stem. Stimulation of this structure is responsible for the euphoric feeling that occurs after one or two drinks.

Alcohol is not intrinsically bad. In fact, a daily glass of wine or another cocktail can be an effective immune stimulant and even increase life expectancy (see page 54).

DRINKERS AND SMOKERS, on average, have higher levels of stress.

But there's also ample evidence that drinking too much alcohol damages the immune system. Heavy drinkers have a higher than average risk of infection, cancer, and liver disease. Alcohol also weakens the immune system's response to invaders (such as viruses and bacteria) and vaccines by preventing a wide variety of white blood cells from working properly. One study found that alcohol decreases the efficiency of bacteria-fighting lung cells in animals, suggesting a possible explanation for the high rates of pneumonia among alcoholics.

Another danger is that when you get a little tipsy, your motivation for making healthy lifestyle choices wanes. Chances are that if you drink, you will exercise less and smoke and overeat more than you would otherwise.

Clear Smoke Away

Nicotine, one of many dangerous chemicals found in tobacco smoke, is a deadly drug. Yet it is one of the most seductive fixes for people under stress because it immediately makes you relax. Researchers believe that nicotine increases levels of dopamine, the chemical in the brain that induces feelings of pleasure. Therefore, a cigarette can be a kind of reward for enduring tension.

In truth, however, the calming effect is only short term. Nicotine actually is a stimulant that revs up the nervous system. And it's frightfully easy to become tolerant to nicotine, meaning you need to smoke more and more to get the desired effect. A smoker who is satisfied by four cigarettes a day for awhile can grow to need a pack a day over the course of one stress-filled week. The stress may dissipate, but the smoker will need a bigger dose of nicotine to feel normal.

Smoking does major damage to the immune system (see page 32), as well as to every other body system. It can also seriously harm your

> ### HEALTH HINT
> #### Cut the Coffee
> Many people do not realize that caffeine (in coffee, tea, chocolate, or cola) is a drug—a strong stimulant that generates a powerful stress reaction in the body. Don't believe it? Try giving up coffee for three weeks. You're almost sure to feel calmer. One warning, however: Gradually taper off your caffeine intake, or you may get migraine-like withdrawal headaches.

loved ones. Spending just half an hour in a smoke-filled room can cause a 33 percent drop in levels of health-promoting antioxidants such as vitamin C in the bloodstreams of nonsmokers, according to Finnish research published in the journal *Circulation*. The same team also discovered that secondhand smoke changed low-density lipoprotein cholesterol (the "bad" cholesterol) in a way that enhanced its uptake by immune system cells—a step thought to be important in the progression of heart disease.

Dangers of Drugs

Using cocaine or marijuana (the second most widely smoked substance after tobacco) can also suppress immunity. The most recent evidence: UCLA researchers evaluated the effects of marijuana and cocaine on a special type of immune cell—the alveolar macrophage—which is crucial in defending human lungs against infections. Samples of alveolar macrophages were taken directly from the lungs of drug users, smokers, and nonsmokers and placed in cultures of bacteria and tumor cells. The drug users' macrophages, in the words of the researchers, were "severely limited in their ability to kill both bacteria and tumor cells."

Many types of bacteria and fungi normally dwell in the human body and are held in check by healthy immune cells like the alveolar macrophages. The UCLA study and many others like it suggest that chronic drug use may damage specific types of immune cells. Such damage makes it easier for already-present or invading germs to gain a foothold and cause disease.

Beliefs, Attitudes, and Health

We've all heard about the power of positive thinking. Visit any bookstore and you'll see shelves overflowing with self-help books that promise to tell you how to turn your life around simply by envisioning yourself as a success.

A subgenre in the self-help category is aimed at people with catastrophic illnesses and chronic health problems. No matter how sick you are, these books claim, a can-do attitude and a sunny outlook will improve your odds of recovery. Religious belief and observance enter the picture as well; faith is not just a comfort when you're ill but a safeguard against poor health and a powerful healer when disease strikes.

Scientists have long been looking for proof that a cheerful heart and deep faith make for a more resilient immune system. In general, their findings raise far more questions than they answer. One thing they've shown for certain, though: Seeing the proverbial glass as half full—in other words, being an optimist—doesn't automatically lengthen your life, but being a pessimist almost certainly shortens it. And like stress, pessimism can take a huge toll on your immunity.

Adopt the Right Attitude

A recent Mayo Clinic study looked at 800 former patients of the renowned institution. In the course of their treatment at Mayo, these men and women, who had a wide range of medical conditions, had taken a personality test that measured their optimism (or pessimism). When researchers followed up on these patients 30 years later, they found that the optimists in the group had lived longer than expected, based on their age and sex. Even more telling, the pessimists had died earlier than expected. In the 30 years between testing and follow-up, the pessimistic patients were almost 40 percent more likely to have died than their more upbeat counterparts.

How can optimism affect health? In his classic book *Learned Optimism*, Martin Seligman, Ph.D., a professor of psychology at the University of Pennsylvania, outlines three theories:

1. Optimists may have a biological advantage. Studies with animals have shown that the helplessness and hopelessness that go along with a pessimistic attitude weaken the immune system. The same applies to humans: A study of healthy first-year law students found higher levels of disease-fighting NK-cells in optimists than in pessimists.

2. Optimists take better care of themselves. In general, they are more likely to do the things that promote health (for example, exercising) and to seek medical advice. Pessimists, on the other hand, tend to avoid preventive measures such as flu shots and to ignore medical advice, believing instead that nothing they do really matters. In a 35-year study of 100 university graduates, pessimists were less likely to give up smoking and much more likely to suffer illness.

3. Optimists are less likely to feel powerless. They manage stress more effectively and feel more in control of their lives. They're also more likely than pessimists to take action to avoid bad events. Pessimists, by contrast, are more passive about their life courses. One provocative study asked whether state of mind had any effect on disease progression and length of survival in a group of men with AIDS. The men who indicated that they had a "realistic"

> ### Quick Tip
>
> Next time you feel negative, try this quick reality check to snap yourself into a better mood. It's called "downward comparison." All you do is think of someone unluckier than you—not to gloat, but to help you recognize your good fortune.

viewpoint about the probable course of the disease died nine months sooner than those who were more hopeful about their long-term survival.

Optimists Are Made, Not Born

What if your natural tendency is to see the glass not just as half empty, but cracked and rapidly draining? Is there any way to change your point of view? Although experts estimate that at least 25 percent of your outlook on life is determined by your genes, the nature-nurture question is really beside the point. Here's why: Time and again, even the most die-hard pessimists have changed their thinking by imitating optimistic attitudes. In other words, if you train yourself to think like an optimist, you'll gradually become one—even if early experiences shaped your less-than-rosy viewpoint on life.

Consider the stark contrast between pessimists' and optimists' reactions to good times and bad times. Pessimists personalize their troubles ("It's all my fault"), while optimists minimize them ("This, too, shall pass"). When something goes right, pessimists give all the credit to chance ("I was just lucky"), but optimists pat themselves on the back ("I did good"). Optimists are also positive about the future and feel hopeful, not helpless. Since they expect to be happy, their fantasies focus on success and they seek out uplifting experiences. This kind of positive attitude crowds out any negativity, and it also improves health.

To counter pessimism, Seligman advocates a method called disputing—learning to monitor and argue against the poisonous messages you send yourself automatically. The technique is similar to cognitive psychotherapy, which has been proven to help depression-prone people beat back the blues.

The first step in disputing is to evaluate your negative thoughts as soon as they pop into your head. If you find yourself thinking that a setback is a catastrophe, search objectively for some evidence that your reaction is appropriate. Ask yourself whether there's an alternate, less gloomy way to look at what's happened. Then go further and make a realistic appraisal of the true nature of the event. Even if your assumptions are correct, is the situation really catastrophic?

Let's say today's difficulty is that your best friend has not returned your phone calls. Your first thought? "She really isn't my friend." Memories of past wrongs pop into your head one after another, so that when the poor woman finally does call, you may well be curt and dismissive. But if you had evaluated your first response objectively, your thoughts might have gone more like this: "I know she's working a lot of overtime this week. I'll send her an e-mail and find out how she's getting along."

Learned optimism also involves giving up overgeneralizations— blanket declarations that produce a sense of helplessness. Rather

SURROUND YOURSELF WITH UPBEAT PEOPLE: An optimistic outlook is contagious.

than declare "I'm ugly," "All bosses are unfair," or "I can't cook anything," recognize that you're experiencing an isolated negative event: "I'm having a bad hair day," "This boss is unfair," or "That recipe didn't turn out."

Don't Worry, Be Happy!

You don't have to be an all-out pessimist to be adversely affected by your outlook. The fight-or-flight mechanism Mother Nature gave us all manifests itself in modern life as a nagging sense of worry, something to which we're all vulnerable to a degree. Without the ability to anticipate adversity, we could never plan for it or take steps to avert it. Worry has helped our species to survive.

Unfortunately, though, the natural warning system goes haywire, producing not solutions, but constant anxiety. In addition to robbing you of joy and making you more likely to become depressed, too much worrying can take a toll on your physical health. The next time you find yourself brooding more than seems necessary, use these strategies to rein in your galloping thoughts:

◆ **Talk to someone.** A supportive friend can give you a much-needed reality check, pointing out which worries are well-founded and which are unrealistic. A pal who knows you well can also offer meaningful suggestions and encouragement.

◆ **Squelch it.** Allen Elkin, Ph.D., director of the Stress Management and Counseling Center in New York City, recommends a quick, modified form of disputing to nip a rising worry in the bud. He calls it the "stop" technique. When you sense a worry rising, distract yourself with the image of a big

A GREAT NUMBER of Canadians say prayer has helped them deal with or recover from an illness.

red-and-white stop sign. Interrupt your mind's amplification of your worry by silently commanding "Stop!". Now picture something that makes you happy to replace anxiety with comfort.

◆ **Take action.** If you're concerned about a cough that won't go away, make an appointment to discuss it with your doctor. If you're anxious about a mounting credit card debt, break the pattern by mapping out a budget—now. (An interesting aside: The more income you have tied up in debt—especially big credit card bills—the more likely you are to have medical problems, according to a U.S. study.) If you need help getting out from under a pile of bills, ask at your bank about a short-term, low-interest loan or make an appointment with a trained financial counselor.

Faith as a Healer

The next time you visit your doctor, don't be surprised if the talk turns to God. Although few physicians are likely to pull out a pad and write a prescription for prayer three times a day, many ask if you pray or attend religious services or if faith is an active part of your life. No, doctors haven't become faith healers, but they have become more aware of the research—much of it published in leading medical journals—that shows the positive impact faith can have on health.

What began as a trickle of offbeat studies in health psychology journals has, in recent years, become a torrent as medical researchers have applied science-based methods to exploring the relationship between religious devotion and health. Their preliminary results suggest that people who derive strength from faith are healthier and live longer than those who don't.

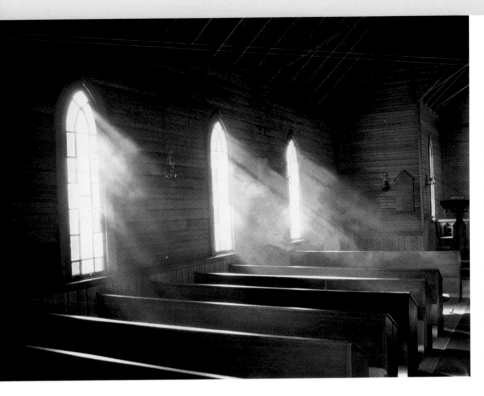

FAITH IN A HIGHER POWER can extend your life, thanks, in part, to its proven ability to strengthen the immune system.

Divine power?

Why do actively religious people live longer? The protective effect of religious faith appears to go well beyond its obvious benefits, such as the comfort of belonging to a community. When they undergo medical procedures, religious people report less pain than their nonreligious peers. They also tolerate treatments better and longer. They are less likely to have side effects from medications, and their rates of depression and anxiety during prolonged illnesses are lower.

One study even found that hip-fracture patients who were devoted to their faith could walk farther than their nonreligious counterparts when they were discharged from the hospital. And a 12-year study of over 2,000 older adults in New Haven, Connecticut, found that people who frequently attended religious services were significantly less likely than infrequent attendees to have physical disabilities, a finding that persisted after the researchers took into account health practices, social ties, and other factors affecting well-being.

A healthy dose of religion. Researchers suspect that faith helps people cope with stress and avoid depression. Coping protects the body from damage due to surging stress hormones; therefore, it boosts the immune system.

A considerable amount of research backs up the claim that faith positively influences immune function. One study, for example, found that

The association between longevity and belief in a higher power was first seen in a large study conducted in California and published in the 1970s. Financed by the Centers for Disease Control and Prevention, it tracked the health of thousands of randomly selected people in a California county over several decades.

Although the link between religion and longevity was far from the only thing researchers were looking for, its strength and significance made it one of the most notable findings of the study. The researchers took every precaution to make sure they were measuring the effects of religious faith (or lack thereof) instead of lifestyle habits that might distinguish churchgoers from the nonreligious. Reasoning that religious people would naturally tend to have lower overall health risks because they take care of their bodies and don't smoke, drink, or use illicit drugs, they found nonreligious people with equally healthy lifestyles to serve as a control group. Even when the poor health habits of the unchurched were accounted for, the same significant differences in longevity emerged. The consistent finding: Weekly attendance at a house of worship was associated with longer life. Churchgoers died at age 83, on average. Those who never went died at age 75.

open-heart surgery patients were three times more likely to survive if they looked to a higher power for support. Another study analyzed the habits of nearly 4,000 elderly people in North Carolina and revealed that those who attended religious services every week were 46 percent less likely to die during the six-year study period than those who attended infrequently or not at all.

The head of the North Carolina study, Harold Koenig, M.D., of the Duke University Medical Center, has made a career of unraveling the ties between religious faith and health. His work provides compelling evidence that faith not only promotes overall good health but also aids in recovery from serious illness. Koenig believes that by praying to a higher power, religious people acquire an indirect form of control over their illness. The reassurance that they're not alone in their struggles and that God takes a personal interest in their well-being buffers them from stress and helps them cope with illness.

But Koenig isn't satisfied with just documenting the beneficial outcomes of prayer and faith—he's hoping to uncover the biological pathway through which faith moves from the mind to the molecules that control the immune response.

Already, he has taken an extremely

DEVOUTLY RELIGIOUS PEOPLE are 46 percent less likely to die in any given year.

preliminary but provocative step toward that goal. Searching for a way to measure and demonstrate the biological effects of prayer and religion, Koenig checked church attendees' and nonattendees' levels of an immune system messenger chemical—interleukin-6 (IL-6)—that orchestrates the actions of different cells and organs involved in the immune response.

Koenig and his colleagues found that people who frequently went to church were less likely to have high levels of IL-6 than people who rarely or never went. Elevations in IL-6 are thought to occur when the immune system is weakened.

Although there are many lingering questions about this observation, professionals in the health field have clearly taken notice, as evidenced by their growing willingness to explore the possible

99 PERCENT OF FAMILY DOCTORS agree that "religious practices"—such as using Tibetan prayer beads (ABOVE), Jewish mezuzahs (RIGHT), or Catholic rosary beads (LEFT)—enhance treatment.

{ "I go to nature to be soothed and healed, and to have my senses put in order."

—JOHN BURROUGHS / NATURE WRITER (1837-1921)

preventive and curative powers of faith. Since 1995, Harvard Medical School has attracted nearly 2,000 health professionals each year to a conference called "Spirituality and Healing in Medicine." Nearly half of the United States' 126 medical schools now offer courses on spirituality and health. Canada's 16 medical schools are following the trend.

Keeping the faith. If the results of Koenig's studies and other work in the field are interpreted correctly, just showing up at church won't make you live any longer. The clear message, though, is that religious involvement—regardless of the faith you choose to follow—is a significant predictor of health and longevity. Seventh Day Adventists, whose doctrines (including vegetarianism) are highly focused on health, have a longer-than-average life expectancy. But so do people living in religion-oriented kibbutzim (communal settlements) in Israel compared with people in secular kibbutzim. In fact, the health differences between religious and secular kibbutz dwellers, who share very similar lifestyles and environments, are truly dramatic. Over the course of a 16-year study, death rates were 50 percent lower in religious kibbutzim.

Implications for nonbelievers. Faith clearly can't be faked. But if you're a confirmed agnostic or a sporadic churchgoer, you can still make spiritual practices a significant part of your life and get in touch with your own core beliefs.

Health psychology research suggests many ways to introduce the faith factor into everyday life. For example, a sense of hope for the long-term future,

an acceptance of the immutable circumstances of life, and the relaxed observance of prayer or Sabbath rituals are all characteristics of health-enhancing, faith-based living. Even if you don't subscribe to any particular doctrine, you could establish the tradition of meals that include giving thanks.

Other options: Form a book group centered around spiritual or ethical issues. Or set aside time for reflection, for pondering the big questions such as, "Why am I here?" and "What is my purpose?". Seeing yourself as part of a larger plan can help you put your problems into perspective. And that can go a long way toward making you happier, healthier, and alive to your fullest potential.

FOR MANY PEOPLE, NATURE is an abiding source of inspiration.

Unhealthy Emotions

Just as friendship and faith help build up your immune defenses, negative feelings and their destructive expression take a toll on them. Anger, hostility, and hopelessness do the most harm. So it pays to gain control over these emotions.

Bad to be mad? When we feel angry, stress hormones and other chemicals surge through our bodies, affecting almost every organ. In most ways, anger and stress have similar physical effects. But an added element of emotional arousal makes anger even more harmful. All the metaphors for anger—blazing mad, out for blood, seeing red—reflect its fierce, sometimes uncontrollable nature.

As children, many of us learn to be ashamed of our anger because we are punished for expressing it in unacceptable ways. What parents often forget is that anger is a normal emotion. When someone hurts or belittles you, it's in your nature to strike out and defend yourself physically and psychologically. When you acknowledge your anger, act assertively, and then move on, getting good and mad can actually be liberating.

Problems occur when people misdirect their anger. The classic example is the man who kicks his dog when he gets home because he's just had a fight with his boss. It's also common to react to anger by suppressing it—a poor choice in terms of your health.

Suppressed anger affects the body in much the same way as chronic stress. Your adrenaline level surges, with your cortisol level not far behind. If you don't express your ire, these levels remain elevated, opening the door to a variety of physical problems, such as high blood pressure, heart problems, headaches, skin disorders, and digestive conditions.

Suppressed anger also weakens our ability to fight off infection and disease and may lead to behavior that further damages health.

Anger and the immune system.

Anger's negative effect on the immune system is fairly well understood. In one study, investigators exposed a group of healthy men to a cold virus. The men who were depressed, angry, and frustrated when they inhaled the virus came down with colds. After viral exposure, a subgroup of study participants was asked to recall and discuss an anger-provoking event. These men, like the ones who started the study angry, were more likely to develop cold symptoms from the virus than those whose moods stayed neutral.

According to conventional wisdom, suppressed anger can even lead to cancer. This view may be oversimplified, but some evidence suggests that bottled-up anger is indeed a factor in cancer growth. One study found low numbers of cancer-fighting immune system cells near the tumors of skin cancer patients who held their anger in check.

The good news is that patients who learned how to express anger turned their prognosis around. The skin cancer patients who suppressed their anger and had reduced cancer-fighting immune system activity went through

UNCOMMON KNOWLEDGE
From Cradle to Grave

Childhood experiences can affect a person's ability to cope with stress. A Swedish study showed that family conflict increases the risk of developing insulin-dependent diabetes later in life, perhaps because stress affects some of the immune mechanisms thought to be responsible for damaging the pancreas. Researchers at the National Institute of Child Health and Human Development found that elevation of the stress hormone cortisol also predicts whether a child is likely to become an alcoholic in adulthood. On the other hand, events in early life can have a positive impact. A Canadian study demonstrated that when newborn animals are petted and gently handled, they produce lower amounts of cortisol in response to stress than other animals that have less physical contact.

Get a Handle on Anger

The next time you feel your ire rising, take a step back, and recognize and label your anger. Just saying the words "I'm really furious!" can help to defuse the fury. Remind yourself, "This, too, shall pass," then take a time out. Leave the room. Splash cool water on your face. It's also helpful to:

1 **Breathe easy.** It sounds overly simplistic, but it works: If you feel as if you're really going to explode, take two or three very deep breaths, and then count to 10. Slowly and intentionally wipe away your angry expression by clenching and relaxing your jaw, forehead, and mouth. These actions will help keep you from doing or saying something rash.

2 **Redirect your energy.** Doing something physical, like taking a walk around the block or doing a fast-paced 20 minutes on a treadmill, can help you use up the adrenaline in your bloodstream. Painting, drawing, clay modeling, and other things that provide satisfaction also can help to calm you.

3 **Heal your angry past.** Practice forgiveness. A grudge left to simmer can provide just enough irritation to maintain anger. Refusing to cling to resentment can provide long-term relief from your own negative emotions.

Hostility isn't fleeting. It's an attitude expressed in aggressive behavior, motivated not by a hurt or a slight, but by a more constant state of animosity and mistrust. Hostility comes from the Latin word *hostis,* which means enemy. Fittingly enough, hostile people expect to find enemies everywhere they go.

People with high hostility levels have a cynical, mistrustful, and doubting attitude. They express anger quite often, and the trigger is likely to be an issue that others find petty. Hostile behavior is usually threatening, and hostile people set themselves off from others, becoming isolated in their fury.

The combination of mistrust, anger, and isolation causes serious trouble in the body. A hostile brain sends out the same chemical signals as a stressed brain, producing the same detrimental effects. According to research at the University of Texas, adrenaline and other stress hormones completely block the ability of macrophages (immune system cells that "scavenge" for abnormalities) to kill tumor cells.

In addition, hostility weakens the branch of the nervous system designed to calm the body after stressful emergencies. In a study at the University of Michigan Emotion Lab, subjects with and without high levels of hostility were asked to describe events that made them so angry they "wanted to explode." Recollection of anger caused blood pressure to soar in both groups. Afterward, though, blood pressure took twice as long to return to normal in the high-hostility group.

training that helped them recognize and express their feelings. When they practiced venting in a healthy way, the growth of their tumors slowed.

Hostility—meaner than you think.

The words "anger" and "hostility" are often used interchangeably, but they're not the same emotions. Anger is temporary. It flares up, but if dealt with promptly, it subsides. The stress-like physical reaction eases off, too.

Getting a handle on hostility. Research demonstrates a strong link between hostility and heart disease. Hostile people are also more prone to asthma and arthritis. Fortunately, like anger, hostility can be overcome—it just may take a little more work because hostility involves a pervasive negative outlook.

Redford Williams, M.D., and Virginia Williams, Ph.D., who pioneered the study of hostility and

{ "Stand up to your obstacles and do something about them. You will find that they haven't half the strength you think they have." }

—NORMAN VINCENT PEALE/ MINISTER (1898-1993)

health, suggest that hostile people can relearn how to perceive their surroundings by reasoning with themselves when their negativity starts to mount. Before you let anger and resentment spiral out of control, ask yourself these questions: Is this matter worth my continued attention? Am I justified in my reaction? Do I have an effective response—in other words, will my expression of anger effect any change in the matter at hand?

If this doesn't defuse the situation, try distracting yourself—by listening to soothing music, working on a challenging puzzle or problem, or throwing your energy into a physical task such as pulling weeds or scrubbing the floor.

Depression: More than Sadness

Depression is more than just the blues. It's a state of utter hopelessness marked by chemical alterations in the brain and abnormal (usually sluggish) functioning of the entire body. Some depressed people feel listless, bored, and unwell. Others feel deep sadness and self-loathing, and many descend into suicidal despair.

The symptoms of depression (see page 108) are appetite loss or increase, insomnia or excessive sleep, inability to enjoy normally pleasurable things, irritability, guilt, sadness, hopelessness, anxiety, and thoughts of suicide and death.

Depression devastates the body as well as the mind. Depressed people are more likely to suffer from chronic diseases, and they take longer to recover from illness. Their chances of premature death are also increased.

How to get help. Medical treatment is essential for control of depression. But because self-blame is part of depression, many depressed people feel that their unhappiness stems from personal failings. Depression also saps initiative and motivation; if you can't get out of bed, you probably don't have enough drive to seek out help.

But thanks to the relatively recent discovery of many new antidepressant drugs that alter levels of different mood-controlling chemicals, most depressed people can be treated successfully. The first step is to contact your doctor and talk about how you feel. The doctor may prescribe medication immediately or refer you to a psychiatrist specializing in the treatment of depression.

STRESS AND DEPRESSION are not normal aspects of aging. Get help so you can enjoy life's pleasures again.

A closer look at... eating to beat stress

You know that what you eat can affect the way you feel—think of the rush you get after consuming a sugary snack. Now scientists have learned that certain foods, eaten in moderation, can help induce a calm, relaxed state. Reach for these edibles to take the edge off your anxiety.

WHOLE-GRAIN FOODS

Whole grains, found in whole-wheat bread and certain cereals such as shredded wheat and bran flakes, are rich in selenium, a mineral that can ease anxiety and lift you out of the doldrums, says USDA psychologist James G. Penland, Ph.D. Penland found that men who boosted their dietary selenium felt less anxious and more energetic, confident, and agreeable. The men who felt worst at the start improved the most.

COMFORT FOODS

The next time you crave security and reassurance, reach for foods that trigger happy associations, advises University of Illinois marketing professor Brian Wansink, Ph.D. His research shows that people subconsciously connect foods from the past with love: "My mom always gave me macaroni and cheese when I came home from school." Hint: If your favorite comfort food is high in fat, look for a low-fat recipe to follow for a healthier version.

MILK

Besides helping build bone, calcium is involved in regulating the tension and relaxation of blood vessels. Thus, it helps your arteries withstand the effects of the stress hormones cortisol and adrenaline. The old standby pre-bedtime soother, a warm glass of milk, provides a quick, easy, and substantial dose of calcium (300 mg), along with the nutrients that help you absorb it. Or enjoy a "cold one" with lunch.

TURKEY

When you need a mental edge without anxiety, eat a turkey sandwich on whole-wheat bread. The protein in turkey helps the body produce dopamine and norepinephrine, brain chemicals associated with alertness. Protein is also digested more slowly than carbohydrates, so you'll ward off hunger pangs longer. In addition, turkey contains high levels of tryptophan, an amino acid that raises levels of the brain chemical serotonin, which keeps the jitters at bay. Finally, the selenium in whole-wheat bread has its own anxiety-reducing properties.

What's Work Got to Do with It?

Built into our culture is the idea that those who work the hardest should be rewarded the most. And in today's economy, people are often encouraged to act like martyrs on the job. But what's the price we pay?

Some people "complain" about their grueling work schedules with more than a hint of pride. Others crave a vacation but simply can't get away from the office. While there's nothing wrong with hard work, being a workaholic can spell disaster to your relationships and your health.

Keeping your nose pressed to the grindstone creates adrenaline and cortisol surges in the body, and elevated levels of these stress hormones are clearly linked to coronary heart disease and other health problems. Even younger people are not immune. A close look at coronary patients under age 40 found that 70 percent worked more than 60 hours a week, while 25 percent held two jobs. Another analysis found that people who worked more than 48 hours a week were two times more likely to die from coronary heart disease than those who worked under 40 hours.

Another danger: Overwork is linked to several psychological conditions including, ironically, poor motivation to work. You may not even be getting as much done as you think because the more you work without rest, the more your efficiency decreases.

Unfortunately, more and more of us are on the workaholism treadmill. The numbers tell the story:

◆ **Two out of three Canadians work more than 40 hours per week.** And 1 in 12 reports working 60 or more hours per week.

◆ **44 percent of Canadians keep a computer at home.** It's not necessarily used for fun but as a means to stay in touch or catch up with business while out of the office.

◆ **Nearly half of all Canadian workers** complain of some symptoms of job burnout, such as interpersonal problems or alcoholism and other forms of substance abuse.

◆ **Stress is now the leading cause of absenteeism.** It has overtaken the common cold.

◆ **A full 40 percent of workers who leave their jobs cite job stress as the reason.** Compounding workers' usual problems with tight deadlines, unreasonable bosses, irritating coworkers, and rude customers, advances in technology have accelerated the transfer of

JOB STRAIN is defined as being in a job with high demands but low control over working conditions. So-called middle managers are especially susceptible.

information—and the pace at which we're now expected to work. Even our leisure time is affected: Hardly a play, movie, or ball game can be enjoyed without the interruption of someone's pager, cell phone, or beeper.

UNCOMMON KNOWLEDGE

Dying to Work

Western researchers have produced hundreds of studies documenting something Japanese researchers have known for many years: There's a significant relationship between high job strain and health problems. Every year, between 10,000 and 30,000 Japanese workers die at their desks from overwork, a specific type of death known as *karoshi*. The first *karoshi* victim, in 1969, was a 29-year-old man who suffered a fatal stroke while at work at Japan's largest newspaper. Today, the problem is so pervasive that there is a National Defense Council for Victims of *Karoshi*. No such epidemic exists in Canada—yet.

Are You out of Balance?

Though not officially a psychological disorder, workaholism is recognized as a compulsive behavior. Even in today's fast-paced workplace, there's a real difference between the conscientious employee who sometimes burns the midnight oil and the driven individual who never lets up.

Workaholics typically rationalize taking on more and more work for a variety of reasons, including pressure to earn money, get promoted, or please a superior. According to experts, workaholics find personal relationships stressful and are more easily angered than others.

They are also more likely to make themselves sick. The International Labor Organization estimates that health problems related to work stress cost employers worldwide more than $200 billion a year, and the World Health Organization reports that about 75 percent of people who seek psychiatric help have symptoms that relate either to lack of job satisfaction or the inability to relax.

From distress to de-stress. For better or worse, work is a huge part of our lives. But that doesn't mean overtime is obligatory. Most people who work too much wouldn't have to sacrifice a single necessity to cut back on their hours. As always, though, wanting to change and changing are two different things. The following pointers can help you get your life back on track.

◆ **Know your goals.** Some people never stop to question why they're doing the job they do. To what end are you working so hard? Are you on the career track you really want? If not, what do you want to be doing and how can you make it possible? One study of 8,000 people found that an essential key to human happiness is loving your everyday profession. Do you love what you do?

◆ **Slow down.** Force yourself to reclaim your personal life. Schedule dates with your friends and partner or spouse. Call family members just to say a quick hello or share an idea during the middle of the day. Plan social outings in advance and treat those commitments as seriously as you would a business meeting.

◆ **Use visual cues.** Keep a picture of someone you love in your wallet and on your desk. These can provide an instant "reality check" and help you relax in moments of stress.

◆ **Start an accomplishment journal.** At the end of each day, jot down one thing that you feel good about having accomplished at your job and one thing you feel good about having done for yourself or with friends or family. Reading this diary can help you figure out what is making you happy and what isn't. The patterns you discover will help you make better decisions in the future.

◆ **Get help.** Overwork that never ends can be serious stuff—a matter of life and death in some cases. So, if you have a hard time taking these steps on your own, seek help from a counselor,

Steer Clear of Road Rage

Tens of millions of commuters start and end their workdays with 30 to 90 minutes of noise, exhaust fumes, and slow-motion frustration, surrounded by others who are under just as much stress as they are. Unfortunately, a grueling commute can have a huge negative impact on your well-being and raise your stress hormones sky-high long before you get to the office. Ease the strain with these tips from Meni Koslowsky, Avraham N. Kluger, and Mordechai Reich, authors of the book *Commuting Stress: Causes, Effects, and Methods of Coping*:

1 Be prepared. Start by getting up at an hour that leaves you plenty of time for your morning routines, including a nice, leisurely breakfast and some family interaction. Waking up late, jumping in and out of the shower, and dashing out the door with a travel mug of coffee and a half-eaten donut is no way to start a stress-free day.

2 Relax behind the wheel. Before you turn on the ignition, take a few deep, slow breaths. Picture the tension flowing out of your body with each exhalation. Repeat this whenever heavy traffic or some insensitive road hog starts getting you hot under the collar. If your neck and shoulders begin to tense, consciously contract those muscles, then release them.

3 Get comfortable. Sit close enough to the pedals to keep your lower legs bent at a 45-degree angle to

your thighs and your elbows comfortably flexed. Set your seat as upright as possible; try a back support if your back gets tired.

4 Keep a safe distance. Leave adequate space between your vehicle and the one in front of you—in general, one car length for every 16 km/h you're driving. Tailgating is a sure prescription for accidents, and it only adds to the stress of the drive. When you're on someone's bumper, you have to constantly brake and speed up to

avoid a collision. When someone's tailgating you, just move out of the way.

5 Drive less or not at all. For some people, carpooling or taking a bus or train decreases the stress of commuting. The advantages are clear: less air and noise pollution, less traffic congestion, and, in many cases, a faster commute.

6 Stop being a 9-to-5-er. Speak to your employer about working flexible hours or telecommuting instead of being on the road at the same time as the rest of the working world. More than half of all companies now offer flexible working arrangements that can help you avoid at least a few maddening rush-hour journeys.

7 Distract yourself. If you absolutely must drive, try taking a new route along a side road that won't clog as much as a main thoroughfare. Bring along a book on tape or a CD of soothing music to help take the edge off the traffic jam.

psychotherapist, or your company's employee assistance program. Or contact Workaholics Anony-mous. Modeled after Alcoholics Anonymous, it's designed to help people stop working compul-sively. The program includes regular discussion meetings and emphasizes scheduling time for play and relaxation.

USE TECHNOLOGY TO YOUR ADVANTAGE. It should make your life easier—not harder.

Working Smarter, Not Harder

For many people, a major problem is having too much work and not enough time to do it. One solution: fine-tuning your time-management skills. By using your working hours more efficiently, you attack stress on several fronts: You'll feel more in control and be more productive and therefore more secure in your job. You'll get greater satisfaction from what you do. Perhaps most important, you'll give yourself more time to relax and enjoy life.

No matter how you juggle your schedule, the number of hours in the day will remain the same. But it is possible to adjust your habits to buy more time for the things that matter most.

1. Plan regularly. Every night, make a to-do list of all your unfinished business and projects. Review the list, prioritize, and decide how much time you need to get each activity done. Use a planner that shows you a full week at a time.

2. Prioritize at the office. Pareto's Principle, a well-known term in management theory, states that 80 percent of your accomplishments come from 20 percent of your efforts. So think strategically: What 20 percent of your work is the most valuable—to you and to your employer? Once you've identified it, try to focus the lion's share of your time and energy in that direction. Learn to say no to non-essential demands. And don't waste time perfecting every interoffice memo when you could spend the time more profitably on something else.

3. Delegate more. Pass projects on to subordinates at work, recruit your children to help with household chores, and hire a gardener or local teenager to maintain your lawn.

4. Set deadlines for major projects. Then focus only on starting to work on them—not finishing them. Instead of procrastinating, divide large projects into manageable pieces and attack only one piece at a time. Also, realize that many people who have trouble meeting deadlines have the unrealistic idea that their work should be perfect. Expect quality rather than perfection.

Interesting!

One study found that 87 percent of workers who volun-tarily cut back on their hours were happy with the decision, citing the top benefits as experiencing less stress and having more family time.

QUIZ: ARE YOU A WORKAHOLIC?

1   I rarely, if ever, dream about work.   ○ TRUE   ○ FALSE

2   I almost never work more than 40 hours a week.   ○ TRUE   ○ FALSE

3   Hobbies are an integral part of my life.   ○ TRUE   ○ FALSE

4   I rarely check my e-mail and voice mail while
     on vacation.   ○ TRUE   ○ FALSE

5   Missing important social events for work is
     usually unthinkable.   ○ TRUE   ○ FALSE

6   My work habits are not a problem for my family.   ○ TRUE   ○ FALSE

Count the number of times you answered false.

ONE OR LESS Congratulations! You're a balanced person who likes pleasure and gets satisfaction from many aspects of your life. Keep up the good work!

TWO OR MORE You probably push yourself too hard, and some might call you a workaholic. You need to get serious about making better use of your time or you could pay the price of poor health and strained relationships.

---

5. Schedule concentration time. Block out some time every day when you can't be disturbed except in an emergency. Use that time to get the most important tasks of the day done. If someone stops by your desk and asks for a moment of your time, you can honestly and politely reply, "No, I'm in the middle of something right now, and I can't give you my full attention." Close the door to your office if you can.

6. Organize throughout the day. Remember this rule: Tuck it, transfer it, or trash it. Quickly glance over every piece of mail and every memo or e-mail message you get. If it looks as if it's potentially important, file it right away in a folder marked PENDING, or delegate it to someone else to take care of. If it's not relevant or it's something you'll never look at again, trash it. Handle your mail the same way at home.

7. Make and return most phone calls at a set time. Set aside a portion of your day, perhaps a half hour in the late afternoon, as telephone time. Let people know that this is the best time to reach you by phone and that it's when you're most likely to return calls. People will come to expect to hear from you at certain times and won't bother you as much during the rest of the day.

8. Be social at work. Chitchat can be very important because it builds relationships and helps you stay plugged in to the office grapevine. Share a joke, anecdote, or personal story while standing at the photocopier or waiting for a meeting to start. Schedule a coffee break with an office buddy. Also consider joining your office softball team or helping organize the annual toy drive or basketball pool.

9. Stay flexible. All your careful planning will be of little use if you assume that you can't veer from the schedule you set. You may have to spend some time handling crises and putting out fires. Or you may get on a roll with a proposal you're writing, in which case it would be a mistake to stop just because you only scheduled an hour for it. Instead, practice effective procrastination. In other words, ask yourself, "Is putting off my next scheduled task and continuing what I'm doing an intelligent decision, or is it just a delay tactic?"

10. Start your workday right—at home the night before. After dinner, pack your lunch for the next day, while you're already in the kitchen. Lay out the kids' clothes and your own, and pack your briefcase. Then spend a pressure-free hour or more doing things you enjoy before bedtime.

On the horizon...new mood managers

If it seems as if your computer has taken over your life, just wait until these highly sensitive and—dare we say it?—intuitive communications devices hit the market. Don't be surprised if before long, your computer can tell when you're unhappy—and step in to help.

HIGH-TECH PSYCHOTHERAPY

Can a computer do what a professional therapist does—help you work through your troubles in a free-form, conversational style? It certainly can. Programmers have already developed Eliza, a program that simulates the responses a therapist might make when you talk about your feelings. A more sophisticated version of Eliza is now being developed; before long, she may find her way into clinical practice.

A MOUSE THAT FEELS

Remember the mood ring? Well, get ready for the mood mouse! Researchers at IBM are developing a computer mouse that can measure heart rate, temperature, perspiration, and pressure exerted by the user in pushing and clicking. If the mouse detects any signs of stress, such as clammy palms, it will automatically launch an anti-stress screen saver to help calm your nerves.

WEARABLE COMPUTERS

It may seem far-fetched now, but some electronics wizards predict that body- and mood-monitoring computers will eventually be hardwired into prescription eyeglasses, welded into jewelry, or sewn into textiles. These featherweight machines could continuously gather information about your state of mind and physiological functioning. Through wireless earpieces, they could also give you vital information about the world around you, helping you find your way around an unfamiliar city, for example, or supplementing your senses if they were impaired.

MONITORS THAT READ MOODS

Various researchers are trying to develop computer monitors that can track your facial movements and transmit the information to a program that will recognize whether you're happy or sad. How? While you work, specialized software will analyze which facial muscles are expanding and contracting. These patterns will enable it to recognize if you are happy, upset, or even bored. Depending on what the monitor detects, it might play a symphony, load a game, or signal that it's time for a nap.

Recharge Your Batteries

I f you've ever been to a spa, you probably remember how your tension melted away and time pressures seemed to vanish. You don't need to spend a bundle to enjoy these important wellness benefits. Here's how to treat yourself to a spa experience right in your own home.

Begin by getting into the right frame of mind. Don't equate taking time to relax with shirking your responsibilities. Busy people increase their productivity when they stop to reevaluate their daily priorities, engage in some healthy activities, and replenish their energy stores. In fact, health experts agree that as we age, it becomes more and more important to develop tools to minimize the impact of stress. According to Joan Borysenko, Ph.D., "Immunity takes a nosedive in those of us with poor coping skills, when we are faced with sudden stress as many people are later in life." So go ahead: Turn off the phone, turn on the answering machine, and explain to your family that you need a few minutes of solitude.

Get into hot water. Draw a bath that's warmer than body temperature and as hot as 38°C. (Check the temperature with a regular fever thermometer.) As the tub is filling, sprinkle in one cup of Epsom salts for a soothing, muscle-relaxing soak. Warm water will unknot your muscles and make your blood vessels dilate, lowering your blood pressure and improving your circulation. It will also promote the release of brain chemicals called endorphins, which relax

CREATING AN AT-HOME SPA is as easy as drawing a hot bath and indulging yourself.

you and put you in a euphoric mood even as they reduce the pain of sore muscles and stiff joints. Endorphins also are thought to lessen the negative effects of stress hormones on different immune cells.

Stay in the bath for as long as 30 minutes, adding hot water as needed to maintain the temperature.

USE SCENTED BATH OIL BEADS to take advantage of aromatherapy's purported benefits.

Five Senses Stress Relief

Engage all five of your senses with pleasurable stimuli during your spa experience. These sense soothers will enhance your warm, calming bath, but they're nice outside the tub, too.

Sight. Most bathroom lights are bright and glaring. To create a calmer environment, leave the overhead light off and place candles around the bathtub or on the vanity to cast a soft, glowing light. While you soak, close your eyes and picture a rolling ocean, sandy beach, or mountain vista. Another trick that works well is to focus on a candle flame to achieve a relaxed, meditative state.

Sound. Soothing music—anything from a Gregorian chant to a Bach concerto to soft jazz—has long been appreciated for its calming effects, but new research shows it also may help keep us healthy. According to Mitchell Gaynor, M.D., director of Medical Oncology and Integrative Medicine at the Strang-Cornell Cancer Prevention Center in New York, listening to meditative music raises levels of interleukin-1, an index of immune system strength, by up to 15 percent. It also significantly increases immunoglobulin levels. Listening to calming music has also been shown to reduce levels of the stress hormone cortisol by as much as 25 percent, lower blood pressure by up to 5 points, and slow the heart rate.

Smell. Scenting your bath with essential oils, especially lemon, chamomile, lavender, or sandalwood, may heighten the calming effect. When you take a deep breath of air imbued with these aromas, the hairs that line the nose pick up the scent. It then travels through the olfactory system on nerve impulses leading directly to the brain. Proof of the power: Patients at Memorial Sloan-Kettering Cancer Center in New York who breathed in vanilla fragrance while undergoing magnetic resonance imaging experienced 63 percent less anxiety than patients who did not. About 30 drops of essential oil should be enough to scent your bathwater. Alternatively, you can use a vaporizer to release the essential oil into the atmosphere.

Taste. During your bath, nibble on a half-ounce of dark chocolate, which is a known mood enhancer. Or savor fresh grapes, orange slices, or other fruits, which not only supply valuable nutrients but also help you replenish the fluids you lose by perspiring in the hot bath.

Touch. Ask your partner for a backrub, or give yourself a foot massage by grasping your right foot above the ankle with your right hand. Rotate your foot five times to the right, then five times to the left. Pull back your toes, then use your fist to lightly pound up and down your sole three times. Next, knead the sole from heel to toe. Finally, grasp your right big toe and rotate it around its joint. Squeeze it at its base, then pull it gently and slide your fingers up and off the end. Repeat with the next toe until you've done all five. Switch to the left foot.

After your bath, dry off with the softest towel you have, then slip into something soothing—furry slippers or a luxurious bathrobe—to sustain the sense of relaxation for just a little longer.

Love More, Live Longer

A wise person once observed that the real goal of living is to "die young as late as possible." There's persuasive evidence that you can improve your odds of reaching a ripe old age while you're still young at heart. The key is to make sure you stay connected to the world around you.

Cultivating a loving relationship with a spouse or partner is one way to increase your odds of having a healthy future. Numerous studies have documented the protective benefits of a good marriage and the negative effects of a marriage filled with strife or marred by indifference. But you need more than one central relationship to get the most from social connection.

It's equally important to cultivate friends whose interests and outlook on life match your own. Try also to find ways to connect with your community; it will enrich your life and elevate your sense of self-worth.

Researchers observed that retired people who devote about 40 hours of volunteer time a year to projects aimed at helping the disadvantaged (working at a local food bank, for instance, or mentoring a youngster) had a 30 percent lower risk of dying during the seven-year study than their less socially engaged peers. Clearly, doing good for others also does a lot of good for you.

Recreational activities will also expand your circle of friends. Whether you want to learn a computer program or need help perfecting a chocolate soufflé, you can probably find a class or club that will fulfill your need while introducing you to people with similar interests. If you live near a college, find out what continuing education classes they offer. Many public school districts offer community education programs as well. A walking club or a reading group will also lead you to people who want to make friends.

As John W. Rowe, M.D., and Robert L. Kahn, Ph.D., note in their book *Successful Aging*, humans "are hardwired, genetically programmed, to develop and function by interacting with others. Talking, touching, and relating to others is essential to our well-being. These facts are not unique to children or to older adults; they apply to all of us, from birth to death." Despite the difficulty of making friends, we must remember that we need them as much as we need food, water, and light.

That's What Friends Are For

Researchers say that social support is the key to a long and happy life. But what exactly is social support? The short answer is the degree to which a person's basic social needs are met through interaction with others. Social support fulfills the most basic human needs of:

- Being cared for and loved
- Sharing intimacy
- Being esteemed and valued; having your personal worth confirmed
- Companionship, communication, and a sense of belonging
- Easy access to information, advice, and guidance from others
- Material and financial assistance in times of need.

"There is no medicine like hope, no incentive so great, and no tonic so powerful as expectation of something better tomorrow."

—ORISON SWETT MARDEN / MOTIVATIONAL SPEAKER (1848-1924)

CHAPTER 7

Steer Clear of Harm

Can environmental factors such as chemicals, pollution, and airtight homes and offices make you sick? Some of the risks are imaginary— but a few aren't. The good news: Even when there is cause for concern, there is plenty you can do to protect yourself.

Are You Worrying Yourself Sick?

Not a day goes by without another TV exposé or newspaper article declaring that a particular health risk (such as contaminated water, food-borne germs, polluted air, or pesticide-laden produce) contributes to cancer and immune-system deterioration.

By the next day, there are new reports that dispute those "facts." This deluge of medical news has had a peculiar effect: Though as a nation we've never been healthier, our sense of well-being has declined. In the 1970s, 61 percent of North Americans said they were satisfied with their health. A decade later, the number was down to 55 percent. And today, over 11 percent of people between the ages of 45 and 54—a group not yet touched by the chronic diseases of old age—consider their health fair or poor. Why all the worry? Confusion, partly. We hear about new research all the time, but it's often contradictory and hard to interpret.

This chapter will help you evaluate real and potential health risks. You'll discover how to avoid the germs that will make you sick and find out which chemicals have and haven't been shown to be harmful to your health. You'll also learn about several well-documented ways to cut your risks.

Filtering the Flood of Information

But what if a report in next week's *Journal of the American Medical Association (JAMA)* suggests, for instance, that soy protein is bad for you? Should you immediately scramble to

MEDICAL NEWS can set off unnecessary anxiety unless you learn to tell fact from fiction.

revamp your diet? Take a tip from the editor of *JAMA,* Catherine DeAngelis, M.D., M.P.H. When she evaluates medical findings, she asks herself four key questions:

1. Where did the study appear? Was it published in a top-ranked journal, such as the *Canadian Journal of Medicine*? Was it publicized in a reputable newspaper, such as the *Globe and Mail*?

2. Where was the study conducted? Be wary if it isn't from a large university or research center.

3. How was the study conducted? For instance, were the subjects people or laboratory animals? While animal studies have value, what applies to animals does not necessarily apply to people.

4. Are the findings important to me personally? To decide if the study pertains to you, ask for

help from a doctor who knows you and your family medical history.

When reading media reports on medical studies, look for these terms. They refer to research methods that increase the reliability of the results.

◆ **Placebo controlled.** This means that one group of patients receives the treatment being studied while a control group of similar patients receives a placebo—often an inactive substance that looks like the medicine under study. A sugar pill is one example of a placebo.

◆ **Double-blind.** In this case, neither the patients nor the doctors involved in the study knows who's receiving the real treatment and who's getting an inactive treatment or placebo.

◆ **Randomized.** Patients are randomly assigned to different study groups (treatment A, treatment B, or placebo, for example), usually by computer.

VITAL STATISTICS: HEALTH CONCERNS

22 percent
Percentage of North Americans who say good health is the most important element of overall well-being

1 in 3
Number of North Americans aged 55 to 64 who rate their health as fair or poor

50,000 to 130,000
Number of premature deaths in North America associated with exposure to air pollutants

8 billion
Approximate Canadian dollars spent annually on organic foods in North America

When to listen up. If the findings of a major study seems plausible and they document a risk that applies to you, it may be worthwhile to change your behavior.

WHAT'S THE PROBLEM?

Smoking, poor diet, and physical inactivity cause at least 80 percent of all illness in Western nations. Even so, when North Americans evaluate threats to their own health, 90 percent think that environmental pollutants are the biggest menaces. Given eight environmental issues and asked whether each posed a "great" danger to health, here's what over 1,200 adults said.

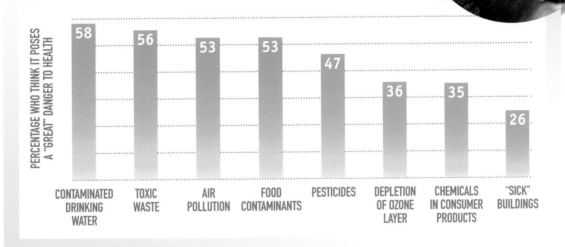

PERCENTAGE WHO THINK IT POSES A "GREAT" DANGER TO HEALTH

CONTAMINATED DRINKING WATER	TOXIC WASTE	AIR POLLUTION	FOOD CONTAMINANTS	PESTICIDES	DEPLETION OF OZONE LAYER	CHEMICALS IN CONSUMER PRODUCTS	"SICK" BUILDINGS
58	56	53	53	47	36	35	26

Source: Centers for Disease Control and Prevention.

Common Culprits

Mother Nature supplies plenty of challenges for the immune system every day—fungi, viruses, bacteria, solar radiation, harmful chemicals naturally present in foods, and more. But the modern world is rife with new health threats. Avoid them and you'll make fewer demands on your immune system—and be less likely to get sick.

A large part of strengthening your immune system involves minimizing the extra workload it has to manage. Some of the most obvious immunotoxins (substances or situations with the potential to poison your immune system), such as tobacco smoke and air pollution (see pages 32–33), have been discussed earlier. Others aren't as well known but still pose possible dangers.

Antibiotics in Food

Today's farming and animal-raising techniques introduce hormones, pesticides, and herbicides into the food supply. The food we eat, however, usually contains such small amounts of these toxins that the liver generally has no problem removing them before they cause harm.

But these foods pose other dangers. In an effort to fatten up farm animals and keep them free of harmful bacteria, most farmers add antibiotics to their feed. Ironically, these additives don't make for cleaner or safer meats. In fact, the overuse of antibiotics in livestock feed probably *raises* your risk of a food-borne illness.

Interesting!

More and more microbes are no longer vulnerable to the drugs that once vanquished them. For some infections, including certain strains of tuberculosis, physicians are running out of options. Drug makers, in response, are rushing to find new antibiotics. One newcomer, linezolid, appears to be effective against several resistant strains of bacteria.

Chickens, for instance, now harbor bacteria, such as salmonella, that are resistant to antibiotics. If you handle raw chicken or eat undercooked chicken contaminated with such resistant bacteria, the resulting illness could be especially hard to treat because standard antibiotics may not work. The situation could be life-threatening, especially to an elderly person, a child, or someone with a weak immune system.

Even if contaminated meat doesn't make you sick, ordinarily harmless intestinal bacteria that winds up on the meat of antibiotic-fed animals during processing may carry drug-resistant genes. When people ingest these bacteria, there is a risk of so-called "gene transfer" with existing human intestinal bacteria. Simply put, antibiotic-resistant genes can move into the genetic material of normal bacteria in the human gut, according to a study in the journal *Applied and Environmental Microbiology*. This results in increased chances of developing a treatment-resistant infection after surgery.

◆ **What you can do.** If you want antibiotic-free meats, look for labels that say "no added color or artificial ingredients." Free-range chickens are often (but not always) antibiotic-free.

Barbecued Meats

The blackened surface of grilled or charbroiled meat contains cancer-causing compounds called heterocyclic amines, formed when the amino acids and sugars in meat are exposed to high temperatures. When melting fat hits hot coals, it triggers formation of another group of carcinogens, called polycyclic amines, which are absorbed into food via smoke and flames.

◆ **What you can do.** Try grilling vegetables instead of meat. Vegetables don't create any carcinogens when

MARINATING MEAT before grilling may cut the formation of cancer-causing chemicals by as much as 99 percent.

Electromagnetic Fields

In 1979, the first study linking electromagnetic fields (EMFs) from power lines with some types of childhood cancer was published. Ever since, there has been some concern that electronic devices that emit electromagnetic radiation—from alarm clocks to computers—may pose a risk to our health. One worry is that exposure to some EMFs might raise the temperature in human tissues, setting the stage for disease or even altering cellular DNA.

So far, research on the health dangers of EMFs is frustratingly inconclusive. It is a field of study that is relatively new. Health Canada's Environmental Health Program (EHP) is in the process of working with provincial governments to jointly develop electromagnetic radiation safety codes.

grilled. Fish is also a better choice; since it contains less fat than meat, it produces fewer polycyclic amines. If you want to grill meat, reduce the time it spends on the barbecue by precooking it in a microwave or on the stove, then placing it over the flames just long enough to get a grilled flavor. Raise the grill as far from the coals as possible. If you're using a gas grill, simply lower the heat setting. Turn the meat with tongs rather than a fork to avoid releasing more fatty juices.

Scientists from the American Institute for Cancer Research also recommend marinating meat before cooking it. Studies show that it's the most effective way to cut the creation of carcinogens during grilling. If you use the marinade as a serving sauce, boil it for three minutes first.

◆ **What you can do.** To learn how strong EMFs are from a power line near your home or workplace, contact the utility that operates the line. If levels are below 2 mG (milligauss, a standard unit of measurement for EMFs), there is little cause for concern. Check the Yellow Pages under ENGINEERS, ENVIRONMENTAL to find a technician who will do the test for a fee.

ELECTROMAGNETIC FIELDS are present near power lines and plugged-in appliances.

{ "The human body has been designed to resist an infinite number of changes and attacks brought about by its environment." }

—HARRY J. JOHNSON, M.D. / PHYSICIAN, EDUCATOR

If you want to minimize your exposure to EMFs from appliances, keep your alarm clock at least an arm's length from your head. When possible, use a laptop computer instead of a desktop model. Hold your hairdryer away from your head, and use an old-fashioned razor instead of an electric shaver.

Plastic Menaces

Most of us take plastic for granted. We use plastic wrap to keep foods fresh. We drink from plastic bottles. And we buy and store all kinds of food in plastic containers. Yet a growing number of

Do You Need to Detoxify?

Detoxification is an amazingly popular health fad. The idea is that we take in so many toxic substances through food, drink, and air that our bodies become toxic and our immune systems get overloaded. To restore health, we have to remove toxins by fasting or flushing the colon. Sounds reasonable—but there's not a shred of fact behind the theory and not an ounce of evidence that any detoxification regimen does any good.

In fact, even though the idea that fasting can cleanse your body of toxins is thousands of years old, medical experts today say that drinking only water or juice for more than a day or so can be dangerous, especially for those with kidney or liver disease.

As for colonics— super-sized enemas that are supposed to remove bacteria and poisons from the colon and solve every health problem from allergies to chronic fatigue to pimples— they're risky even for people in the best of health. A pump pulses water—gallons of it— through one hose-like tube high into your colon. A second tube draws the water out. Within a 45-minute session, the colon is filled and emptied several times over.

While there are valid reasons to have an occasional enema (to cleanse the bowel before having a colonoscopy, for instance), getting rid of toxins is not among them. The cells lining the gastrointestinal tract turn over every two to three days, so toxins have no chance to build up. Finally, there are plenty of reasons not to have colonic cleansing.

1 The process may trigger irregular heartbeats. It also may slow the heart rate and lower blood pressure.

2 Colonics may worsen real bowel problems, such as diverticulitis (inflammation of small pockets in the wall of the colon) and irritable bowel syndrome.

3 There's a slight risk of bowel perforation or infection.

4 Habitual colonics can render the colon lazy. It is possible to become dependent on colonics to evacuate.

reports suggest that certain plastics aren't entirely safe. The biggest threat occurs when food is reheated in plastic containers that aren't microwave safe. This produces chemical by-products that can disrupt normal hormone secretion. In animals, these by-products can cause cancer, birth defects, and immune problems, but they may not in humans.

Years ago, the U.S. Environmental Protection Agency (EPA) gave American manufacturers the green light to make food containers using plastics that, when heated, give off the chemicals. But now the EPA has gone on record as being very concerned about the growing body of evidence that some man-made chemicals in the plastics may be interfering with normal endocrine system functioning in humans and animals."

◆ **What you can do.** It's considered safe to microwave foods in plastic containers designed for microwave use. But plastic take-out containers, as well as plastics meant for use only in the refrigerator or pantry, shouldn't be put in the microwave. If you must use clear plastic wrap in the microwave, don't allow it to touch the food. Avoid drinking hot beverages in poly-styrene (Styrofoam) cups; use a mug instead.

REPEATED EXPOSURE to latex—a natural rubber found in many types of plastic gloves—can result in allergic symptoms.

Interesting!

If you're allergic to latex, you may be more susceptible to allergies to bananas and certain other foods. Bananas, apricots, avocados, carrots, celery, figs, kiwis, papayas, passion fruit, peaches, tomatoes, and Brazil nuts may contain proteins that resemble latex. Allergies triggered by similar proteins in seemingly unrelated foods and plants are known as cross reactions.

Latex

Chances are, the rubber gloves you slip on your hands before diving into a sink full of dirty dishes contain latex, a processed rubber that causes immune-system reactions in millions of North Americans each year. The number of these allergic reactions has increased dramatically in recent years, spurred by the widespread use of latex gloves to prevent the spread of AIDS and hepatitis B.

Not surprisingly, health-care workers are most at risk. Up to 17 percent are already allergic. Some people have specific antibodies, called IgE antibodies, that make them hypersensitive to proteins in latex. Others are allergic to chemicals that are added to the rubber. Compounding the problem is the powder that is placed in latex gloves to make them easier to slip on. This powder absorbs allergens from the latex. Then, when the gloves are jostled or snapped onto the hands, the allergen-impregnated dust wafts into the air and onto instruments, sutures, and skin.

Latex can cause two different reactions in latex-sensitive people. The first, a poison ivy-like rash known as contact dermatitis, usually appears 12 to 36 hours after contact with latex and vanishes within a day or so. The second type of reaction can be more serious, causing hives, rashes, a runny nose, watery eyes, and difficulty breathing. In rare cases, there may be life-threatening symptoms—rapidly falling blood pressure, swelling in the throat, or constricted breathing. A handful of people have even died of latex-related allergies in the past 15 years.

◆ **What you can do.** The less contact you have with latex, the less likely you are to develop an allergy to it. Use synthetic gloves instead of the latex type, and avoid items that contain latex, including some types of chewing gum, rubber bands, balloons, tennis-racquet grips, and clothes made with Lycra. If you are in a monogamous relationship and you and your partner are HIV- and hepatitis B-negative, consider using natural skin or synthetic condoms instead of latex ones.

Ask your dentist, doctor, and any other health professionals who care for you to examine you with nonlatex gloves. If you need surgery, try to schedule it for early morning, when airborne latex allergen levels are at their lowest. Anyone who has had a severe reaction to latex should wear a MedicAlert bracelet or necklace and carry a prescription epinephrine pen and nonlatex gloves wherever they go.

If you think you have an allergy to latex, see your doctor or an allergist. For more information, go to www.latex-allergy.org.

Volatile Organic Compounds

Thousands of common products, including rug and oven cleaners, paints, paint thinners, lacquers, perfumes, hair sprays, and dry-cleaning fluids, emit volatile organic compounds, or VOCs—chemicals that transform quickly from liquid to vapor. These compounds also emanate from wood finishes, plywood, paneling, fiberboard, particleboard, carpeting, furniture, permanent-press fabric, draperies, and mattress ticking. VOCs that accumulate in airtight buildings contribute to what some people term "sick building syndrome."

One of the most widespread VOCs is formaldehyde, classified as a "probable human carcinogen." It causes nasal cancer in laboratory animals. In humans, it irritates the eyes, nose, throat, and lungs. Another common VOC, chloroform, is a by-product of the process used to sanitize drinking water in water-treatment plants.

◆ **What you can do.** Many items that contain VOCs carry labels that explain the risks and give instructions for safe use. When shopping for carpets, look for the Carpet and Rug Institute "Seal of Approval" sticker, designating lower-than-average VOC emissions. Have carpets tacked down rather than glued—adhesives often emit VOCs.

When you buy new cabinetry or furniture, ask the dealer to allow your goods to "off-gas" by airing them in an empty, well-ventilated room before delivery. And if you're painting indoors, open the windows, and consider using an environmentally friendly paint that is low in VOCs. When using varnish or solvents, move your project outdoors if possible.

If you live near a landfill, your tap water may contain higher-than-average levels of VOCs. If it does, consider bottled water as a safe alternative.

Side Step Sick Airplane Syndrome

"Sick building syndrome" has taken to the skies. Research is showing that the same volatile organic compounds (see opposite page), other toxins, and allergens that accumulate in airtight buildings and cause health problems can build up in the cabins of jet planes.

This wasn't always the case. Until the 1970s, aircraft cabins were well ventilated with fresh air drawn through the engine intakes and pumped into the cabins. Then major airlines decided to cut back on ventilation with fresh air as a way of reducing fuel costs. Ironically, the move to banish smoking from the skies contributed to the problem by reducing the need to refresh cabin air more frequently.

As a result, colorless and often odorless VOCs are left to linger in aircraft cabins. The VOCs emanate from people, cosmetics, perfumes, food, plastics, polymers, solvents, fuels, lubricants (especially

hydraulic fluids), exhaust gases taken aboard during ground operations, cleaning products, and other compounds.

Flight attendants say that in addition to VOC buildup, under-ventilated cabins also result in too little oxygen and too much carbon dioxide. They blame "sick plane syndrome" for a sky-high increase in complaints of headaches, fatigue, heart palpitations, dizziness, and breathing difficulties among both

crew and passengers. In one case, they've successfully pressed that claim: Alaska Airlines recently agreed to pay hundreds of thousands of dollars to settle a lawsuit brought by flight attendants who claimed noxious cabin fumes made them sick. To protect yourself:

1 Sit near the front. Air in most aircraft passes from front to back, so the freshest, most oxygen-rich air is found in front of the wings. Not only does the stale air in the back contain less

oxygen, it is also the ideal medium for the transmission of bacteria, viruses, and molds. Many long-haul passengers develop minor infections, such as colds, within 48 hours of flying.

2 Direct the overhead air vent away from your face. "Passengers think the air coming out of that little 'gasper' vent above them is all fresh air, when it's not," notes Martin Hocking, Ph.D., an expert on cabin air quality at B.C.'s University of Victoria.

3 Ask for the ventilation to be increased. The mix of fresh and recirculated air in the cabin sometimes can be adjusted if passengers request the change.

4 Bring your own clean air. Air Supply, the world's first wearable air purifier, which costs about $100, draws in and filters contaminated air. It then directs toxin-free, germ-free, clean air toward your mouth and nose. It's available online from Magellan's, at www.magellans.com or by calling 800-962-4943.

No Cause For Alarm

It's easy to be overwhelmed by the parade of information about new threats to our well-being. But these disturbing reports—many delivered in the form of e-mails—are often complete nonsense. The next time you hear or read about an imminent health catastrophe, don't accept it as the final word. Ask your pharmacist, doctor, or local librarian to help you find more information.

In the meantime, here are 10 unfounded scares you can safely put out of your mind.

1. Shampoo is hazardous to health. For years, the urban-legend underground has been rumbling with rumors that sodium laureth sulfate (SLS), a cleansing and lathering substance found in most

WASHING YOUR HAIR with shampoo containing sodium laureth sulfate is perfectly safe.

shampoos and tooth-pastes, causes cancer.
◆ **The truth.** Health Canada and the International Agency for Research on Cancer say that SLS is noncarcinogenic.

2. Antiperspirants cause breast cancer. Persistent e-mail warnings have proclaimed that antiper-spirants prevent sweat glands from ridding the body of toxins, which wind up in the lymph nodes and trigger breast cancer.
◆ **The truth.** It's a total falsehood, say American Cancer Society scientists. Most potential carcino-gens are processed by the kidneys and liver, not sweated out. Besides, although underarm sweat glands happen to be near some lymph nodes, they have no interaction with them.

3. Microwaves leak dangerous radiation. Myth mongers insist that using microwave ovens exposes people to cancer-causing radiation.
◆ **The truth.** Microwave ovens use electrical and magnetic energy—not radioactive waves—to vibrate water molecules in food and produce the heat that cooks food. The only major health danger they pose is that they may cook food unevenly, leaving cold spots where bacteria can survive. The remedy: Cover the food and stir it during cooking.

4. Using aluminum pots leads to Alzheimer's. The first warnings about the danger of cooking with aluminum pots surfaced more than 25 years ago, after studies of deceased Alzheimer's patients found abnormally high concentrations of aluminum in their brains. To some people, this signaled a direct link between the disease and cooking with aluminum pots.
◆ **The truth.** Aluminum is one of the most abundant elements in the environment. Therefore, exposure to this metal is unavoidable. But that exposure doesn't lead to Alzheimer's disease.

Instead, aluminum seems to build up in the brain as a result of the disease.

5. Pesticide-laden produce can kill.
A highly publicized Consumers Union report proclaimed that even a single serving of some fruits delivers "unsafe levels of toxic pesticide residues" to kids.
◆ **The truth.** After checking 4,500 scientific studies, the American Institute for Cancer Research declared that trace amounts of pesticides in food do not pose a risk of cancer. Inhaling pesticide fumes may affect health, however.

6. Sugar-free sweeteners trigger multiple sclerosis. This frightening fable holds that the widely used artificial sweetener aspartame breaks down in the body into methanol, a toxic substance said to trigger multiple sclerosis (MS).
◆ **The truth.** Both the Multiple Sclerosis Society and the FDA say there's absolutely no scientific evidence of a link between aspartame and MS.

7. Irradiated food is "Frankenfood." Critics charge that this method of safeguarding food, using minute amounts of radiation to disrupt the genetic machinery of microbes such as *Escherichia coli,* may

ASPARTAME, the sugar-free sweetener found in some candies and other foods, does not pose a health risk, according to the National Cancer Institute and the FDA.

DENTAL FILLINGS are so small that many scientists say the mercury in them is irrelevant.

create cancer-causing compounds, damage chromosomes, and sap foods of nutrients.
◆ **The truth.** Levels of radiation used are so low that the foods aren't harmed, chemically altered, or made radioactive, according to the FDA.

8. Mercury fillings are poisonous. This myth purports that the mercury in dental amalgam poisons the immune system and causes chronic fatigue syndrome, multiple sclerosis, and Alzheimer's disease.
◆ **The truth.** Contaminated fish and shellfish are the major cause of mercury poisoning—not dental fillings, say the National Institutes of Health, the FDA, the World Health Organization, and the American Dental Association.

9. Cell phones trigger brain cancer. Cellular phones—now used by nearly 90 million Americans—have been blamed for brain cancer, which strikes 16,500 Americans a year.
◆ **The truth.** Recently, several rigorous studies of brain-tumor incidence among cell-phone users found no evidence of a link.

10. Breast implants cause disease. The manufacturers of silicone implants have been mired in controversy and lawsuits claiming that their products cause systemic health problems.
◆ **The truth.** Despite the claims of thousands of women, no long-term scientific study has shown that breast implants cause any serious disease. That's not to say that they're risk free. The FDA acknowledges that silicone implants can rupture, causing pain and infections. Also, as with any surgery, there's an intrinsic danger of infection and complications related to anesthesia, internal bleeding, or scarring.

Healthy Home Checkup

R ecent studies show that indoor air—even in clean, well-ventilated country homes—can actually be more seriously polluted than the outdoor air in the largest cities.

The EPA counts poor indoor air quality as one of the five most urgent environmental problems facing the nation. Air—the invisible blend of oxygen, nitrogen, and other gases on which we depend—absorbs tobacco smoke, dust, pollen, molds, emissions from household products, and a host of other undesirable compounds. These substances can irritate mucous membranes (such as the eyes, nose, and mouth), aggravate allergies and asthma, and reduce resistance to cold and flu viruses. In the worst-case scenario, indoor air can contain a deadly level of carbon monoxide.

We may not be able to have a huge impact on the outdoor air we inhale, but we can control the quality of the air under our own roofs. Here is a list of where pollutants may be lurking in your home. Breathe easier by checking the following hot spots and implementing the suggested changes for making yours a healthier home.

1. Front door. Use a sturdy doormat to scrape off dirt from shoes before it gets tracked in. Place the mat vertically instead of horizontally so that everyone who enters will have to step on it several times.

LEAD PAINT may be lurking in any home built before 1980.

2. Lead paint. Over time, ingesting or inhaling dust and flakes from lead-based paint can cause brain damage. If you suspect that the paint in your home contains lead, have it tested. If it contains lead, don't remove it yourself. Hire a specialist, or cover it with wallpaper or paneling.

CLEANSERS AND SOLVENTS should always be used in well-ventilated areas.

3. Household cleansers, pesticides, paints, and solvents. To avoid potentially harmful chemicals, select detergent-based, biodegradable products on which the words "danger," "caution," or "flammable" do not appear.

4. Tightly closed windows. Keep a couple of windows cracked open year-round to remove fumes released by harsh cleaning products and chemical-laden furnishings, reduce mold-breeding moisture, and lower levels of unsafe gases. If you have allergies, consider buying a High Efficiency Particulate Arresting (HEPA) air cleanser. For tobacco smoke, consider an air purifier that uses an activated carbon filter.

5. Pressed wood products like plywood and particleboard. Construction materials, shelving, furniture, paneling, cabinets, and other products made with these woods are assembled using urea-formaldehyde glues and adhesives, deemed probable human carcinogens. Formaldehyde irritates the respiratory tract and can cause or exacerbate allergic reactions.

Opt for furniture and cabinetry made with hardwood or "exterior grade" pressed wood, which contains phenol resins, not urea resins, so the fumes they emit are less troublesome. Or opt for metal shelves and cabinets. Open the windows wide after bringing home new furnishings that might contain formaldehyde,

especially if you put the new items in the bedroom.

6. Woodstoves or fireplaces. In addition to producing toxic and irritating combustion by-products, these may fill the air with dangerous particles of ash if you burn anything other than commercial logs or hardwood—maple, oak, beech, elm, or ash. Avoid damp firewood, which may release mold spores.

7. Air conditioners. Both central and window air-conditioning units can harbor mold, especially when they're not being used. Empty water trays and change filters often.

FIREPLACES release carbon monoxide, nitrogen dioxide, and ash particles.

8. Closets. Patronize dry cleaners that minimize their use of perchloroethylene, a carcinogenic solvent also found in spot removers. Also, remove the plastic bags from newly dry-cleaned clothes before you leave the store so that the garments can air out on the way home. And keep your wool garments free of holes without mothballs, which emit toxic vapors. Instead, store woolens in a cedar-lined closet or with cedar chips or aromatic herbs, such as eucalyptus or bay leaf.

CLOSETS can be filled with toxic fumes from mothballs.

Healthy Home Checkup

9. Wall-to-wall carpeting. It can be a significant source of indoor pollution, trapping dust mites and dangerous fumes, particularly if anyone in the house smokes. These harmful agents are later released into the air. Carpeting also can be a hideaway for mold and mildew. Synthetic carpets may emit toxic volatile organic compounds (VOCs). The healthier alternative: hardwood, linoleum, ceramic tile, or any other hard-surface flooring.

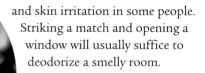

SHUT OFF THE STOVE if the flame won't stay lit. The pilot may need cleaning.

10. Air fresheners. Strong fragrances may mask the odors of chemicals such as formaldehyde, so you may be breathing dangerous fumes without realizing it. Spray air fresheners can emit VOCs and provoke asthma

and skin irritation in some people. Striking a match and opening a window will usually suffice to deodorize a smelly room.

11. Gas stove. Install an exhaust fan—preferably one that vents to the outdoors—over the stove to reduce exposure to combustion by-products, including carbon monoxide. Check the flame and pilot lights regularly—the flames should be blue, with a slight yellow tip at most. If the flame is too yellow or orange, have the utility company adjust it. If you have a gas stove, be sure to install a carbon monoxide detector in your home.

12. Kitchen trash can. Storing your garbage indoors may raise levels of airborne bacteria and fungi that could make you sick, according to one study. Samples of house dust from 99 homes in the Netherlands showed a significantly higher level of airborne microbes in households that stored remains of fruits, vegetables, and other foods indoors instead of outdoors.

13. Sink or toilet. Leaky fixtures can increase indoor humidity, promoting the growth of black mold *(Stachybotrys chartarum)*, identified as a health threat only in the last decade. Black mold isn't the stuff that grows on ceramic tile or the grouting in your shower, but it may grow on walls, ceilings, ceiling tiles, and carpets. In adults, it can cause fatigue as well as symptoms affecting the eyes,

SINKS AND SHOWER CURTAINS can harbor mold spores. Wipe them down weekly with bleach.

FLUSHING the toilet sprays droplets all over the room. Close the lid.

skin, lungs, and nervous system. Exposure to this mold has also been linked with fatal cases of bleeding lungs in infants. To keep moisture from building up, install and regularly use exhaust fans in all bathrooms, as well as in basements and kitchens, and fix water leaks promptly.

14. Showers, dishwashers, and washing machines. These appliances strip chemicals from the water and spew them into the air via heat and spray. University of Texas researchers found dishwashers to be among the worst offenders, releasing numerous chemicals including chlorine. Wait until the dishwasher has completely cooled before you open it. And turn on the exhaust fan or open a window during your bath or shower and for at least 10 minutes afterward.

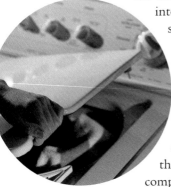

WASHING MACHINE water is often loaded with viruses and bacteria.

Other research found that fecal bacteria and viruses, including hepatitis A and *E. coli.* can survive the wash cycle and possibly infect you when you handle wet laundry. Minimize the risk by adding bleach to the first load to sanitize your machine. Wash underwear separately from other clothes using the hottest water setting.

HOME, SAFE HOME CLEANSER

Next time you need to clean house, consider using less toxic and less irritating alternatives to conventional household cleansers. Try scouring sinks, countertops, and appliances with baking soda and a damp sponge. Spritz a vinegar-and-water rinse on windows and tiles. For other washable surfaces, mix up this all-natural cleanser. Essential oils pump up its disinfecting power, making it especially appropriate for kitchens and bathrooms.

- 250 ml water
- 250 ml vinegar
- 2 tsp liquid castile soap (available in health-food stores)
- 25 drops essential oil of thyme, eucalyptus, lemon, orange, or tea tree

Add all ingredients to a large spray bottle (about 650 ml) and shake before using.

Where the Germs Are

You can't see, hear, or feel germs, but hundreds of billions of microorganisms —from bacteria to viruses to fungi and parasites—surround us 24 hours a day.

They are in the air we breathe and in the water we drink, and they cling to virtually every surface on the planet. Think the steering wheel in your new car is germ-free? It isn't. What about the sheets you just took out of the dryer? No again. And microorganisms positively flourish in wet spots, such as kitchen sponges. (One study found that more than a billion germs a day can grow in a damp sponge!) The good news: Fewer than one percent of these microbes are nasty enough to make us ill. And normally, when a

disease-causing germ gets into the body, the immune system is strong enough to fend off its advances. However, if a few particularly virulent germs come along, or if a large enough number of germs attack, they can overwhelm our defenses and make us sick. Fortunately, you can greatly limit your exposure. Here are some common germ havens, along with tips for stopping the spread.

Kids. Do you have children, grandchildren, nieces, or nephews? Then you certainly have germs. If prizes were given out for excellence in spreading germs, children would always be the winners. When they're not touching everything in sight, they're rubbing their eyes, noses, and

SMALL CHILDREN sometimes spread germs to their families and caregivers without getting sick themselves.

mouths, ensuring that any bugs they've picked up will have warm, damp places to grow. What's more, children who go to day care, play groups, or school every day are exposed to dozens of other youngsters, each ready to share his or her own germs. Small wonder that 36 percent of playgrounds and 46 percent of surfaces in day-care centers are contaminated by disease-causing microbes.

On the positive side, children who are exposed to lots of other kids (and their germs) develop exceptionally robust immune systems. Researchers at the University of Arizona College of Medicine followed more than 1,000 children from birth to age 13 to determine whether their exposure to other children affected their risk of asthma and allergies. Preschoolers who spent lots of time around siblings and playmates or in group day care had a 50 percent lower risk of developing asthma when they reached school age than kids whose contact with other children was more limited. Children in the high-exposure group were also 20 percent less likely to develop allergies.

While meeting up with a wide variety of microbes may ultimately be good for kids, it does result in illness on occasion. Besides colds, some of the infections most commonly transmitted from child to child (and then, as often as not, to one or more adults) include diarrhea and impetigo, a bacterial skin infection. Adults in families with children come down with at least twice as many colds each year as adults in families without kids.
◆ **What you can do.** Rather than keeping your children out of play groups and day-care centers, make sure the toys, telephones, doorknobs, counters, and other potentially germ-laden items and areas in your home and at your child's nursery school or day-care center get disinfected every few

PAPER CUPS are an excellent alternative to office coffee mugs, which research shows are often full of dangerous germs.

days with a solution of one part bleach to nine parts water.

Will it really help? Absolutely! A recent study of day-care centers found that the simple practice of cleaning toys with bleach three times a week slashed the number of respiratory infections the children had and pediatrician visits they made by more than one third.

Office coffee cups. According to microbiologists at the University of Arizona, most office coffee mugs are jumping with diarrhea-causing microbes. They found that 60 percent of the coffee cups office workers drank from every day were hosting *Escherichia. coli,* transmitted via the grimy sponges used to wash them.
◆ **What you can do.** Protect yourself by bringing your own mug from home, washing it thoroughly with soap and hot water after each use, and drying it carefully with a fresh paper towel. Or just use a disposable cup. Be careful when you order take-out coffee, too. Because harried deli workers tend to use and reuse dirty cleanup rags to wipe the counter, it's usually teeming with bacteria. Make sure the rim and lid of your cup don't come into contact with the countertop.

GOOD QUESTION!
Why do so many different germs cause diarrhea?

Mainly because all kinds of germs can easily find their way into your intestinal tract. When we eat with unwashed hands, we risk ingesting bacteria, some of which pass into the gut. There, they reproduce frantically, releasing toxins that impede water absorption. The result: diarrhea.

Doctors. In North America, more than 2 million infections and 90,000 deaths a year could be prevented if health-care workers washed their hands for 30 seconds between patients, estimates William R. Jarvis, M.D., chief of the Investigation and Prevention Branch at the Centers for Disease Control and Prevention (CDC) in Atlanta.

Yet in one study of an emergency room, doctors lathered up before or after examining a patient less than 20 percent of the time. But hands aren't the only germ-laden things that will touch you. Recent reports suggest that two standard tools of the trade, stethoscopes and pens, may also harbor more than a few microbes. When 150 stethoscopes used by medical staff at a community hospital in the United States were tested, researchers found that nearly 90 percent were teeming with staphylocci (staph) bacteria, which can cause abscesses, boils, and potentially life-threatening systemic infections. A similar analysis of pens belonging to doctors in Austria found that 71 percent had colonies of staph bacteria on their surfaces.

VIRUSES, IN THEORY, can survive in chlorine-treated swimming pool water, but you're much more likely to meet up with them when you use a pay phone.

◆ **What you can do.** Make sure your doctor washes his hands and swabs his stethoscope with alcohol before examining you.

Pay phones. You pay for the call, but the cold or flu is free. The receiver handle, mouthpiece, and buttons of any well-used pay phone can be loaded with influenza and cold viruses.
◆ **What you can do.** Handle the phone with a handkerchief or tissue and keep the mouthpiece a fair distance from your mouth.

Public rest rooms. It's a no-brainer: Public bathrooms are fertile grounds for germs. What may surprise you is where the danger is most likely to lurk. Another university investigation found that even rest rooms that appeared to be quite clean and tidy were actually dense with bacteria. Although the germiest bathrooms of all, as expected, were in high-traffic areas, such as airports and bus terminals, hospitals weren't far behind. Bathroom sinks harbored more bacteria than toilets did.
◆ **What you can do.** Choose the stall closest to the door; it is usually the least used and therefore the cleanest. Next, scrub your hands vigorously with hot water and soap. (See pages 254–255 for more on washing germs away.) If paper towels are available, use them instead of automatic hand-dryers—bacteria thrive inside hot hand-dryer nozzles. For more protection, don't touch the faucet directly when you turn it off; hold a paper towel over it while you turn it instead. Use the same paper-towel trick on the bathroom

On the horizon...new antibacterials

Although experts question their benefits, clothes, stationery, appliances, and auto parts sold as "germ-free" are already commonplace in Japan. Here's a peek at four innovations that you can expect to see soon on our shores.

GERM-KILLING RUBBER

The first antimicrobial rubber has been developed at Auburn University in Alabama. What makes the creation especially significant is that its germ-fighting powers do not wear out. In addition, the rubber kills not only bacteria, but viruses and fungi. Potential applications include medical supplies, such as gloves and catheters, and consumer goods, including baby bottles, nipples, and pacifiers, as well as condoms.

OH-SO-CLEAN STEERING WHEELS

First came anti-lock brakes. Then air bags. Now, another safety device—a germ-resistant steering wheel—may soon become standard auto equipment. These steering wheels, already offered in the Toyota Logo sedan sold in Asia, proved so popular that other antibacterial auto accessories are being introduced there, including heater-control and gear-shift knobs and inner door handles.

BUG-BATTLING UNIFORMS

German scientists are experimenting with ways to incorporate triclosan—the active ingredient in most antibacterial soaps and detergents—into clothing fiber. The goal of their endeavors: Fungus-, yeast-, and bacteria-repellant clothing for hospital and restaurant workers. That's good news: A Cornell University study recently found that everyday clothing, particularly cotton, often carries spores of Aspergillus fungus, which can be deadly in patients with weakened immunity.

KILLER ATM SCREENS

It's touched by thousands of fingers each day. Could your automatic teller machine (ATM) screen make you sick? Whether the worry is justified or not, a Methuen, Massachusetts, technology company has come up with a solution: CleanScreen, a touch-screen coated with a microbe killing substance (Microbe Shield) that bursts the cell membranes of bacteria and other microscopic germs, killing them on contact. In tests, Microbe Shield withstood more than 200 million touches.

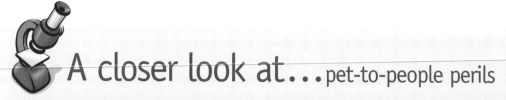

A closer look at…pet-to-people perils

Nobody likes to think about it, but the truth is that your beloved pets are potential disease carriers. In fact, each year about half a million Americans contract "zoonoses"—pet-to-people infections. The ones below are the most common.

PARROT FEVER

Humans are exposed to the bacterium *Chlamydia psittaci* (the cause of parrot fever, or psittacosis) when they inhale dust from the feathers or dried waste of infected parrots, parakeets, love birds, pigeons, finches, chickens, or turkeys. In humans, parrot fever causes flu-like symptoms; infected birds rarely get sick. A fecal test can detect infection in birds. Tetracycline is an effective treatment.

RINGWORM

Ringworm has nothing to do with worms. It's a skin disease caused by a fungus and carried by dogs, horses, cows, and cats. The infection, which is most common in small children, usually appears as an inflamed, scaly patch on an part of the body not normally covered by clothing. The scalp is a common ringworm site. An antifungal cream usually clears up the condition in both humans and animals.

ROUNDWORM

This parasite is common in dogs, though it can also live in the intestinal tracts of cats and horses. Roundworm eggs, excreted in infected animals' feces, may become embedded in their fur and transferred to human hands. About 10,000 human cases of roundworm are reported in North America annually. Most aren't serious, but rare cases of roundworm-related blindness have occurred. To be safe, test and treat your pets for worms, and wash your hands after petting any dog, cat, or horse.

TOXOPLASMOSIS

A majority of North Americans (60 percent) have been exposed to toxoplasma, a parasite usually spread to humans via cat feces. The resulting infection, toxoplasmosis, generally goes undetected, leaving most cat owners with antibodies that protect against repeat infection. But toxoplasmosis is a serious disease in infants and people with weakened immunity. If a woman contracts it during pregnancy, toxoplasmosis can also cause birth defects or fetal death. If you're pregnant, caring for a newborn, get someone else to change the litterbox.

doorknob when you leave. All the people before you who didn't wash their hands on their way out have handled that knob.

Swimming spots. Swimming is a fun, low-cost form of family recreation; that's why North Americans make 400 million visits to public pools annually. If you're squeamish about germs, the idea of getting into the equivalent of a big bathtub with scores of strangers carrying heaven knows what germs may be extremely unappealing.

While it's true that swimmers can contaminate pool water with germs that cause intestinal, skin, ear, and upper-respiratory infections, most public pools are a lot cleaner than ocean- or bayside beaches. Nearly 25 percent of North American public beaches harbor high levels of infectious organisms. The source of contamination: human and animal waste from sewage and storm-drain discharges. One of the areas hardest hit in Canada is the Great Lakes Basin.

A number of studies have found that people who swim in polluted beach water have an increased incidence of gastrointestinal illnesses. They may also contract ear, eye, nose, throat, and skin infections, as well as hepatitis or bladder infections, at higher-than-average rates. Some viruses are so hardy that they can survive for weeks in cool ocean waters and last even longer in bottom sediment. And runoff doesn't mix quickly into the ocean. It lingers on top near the shore, where swimmers are likely to encounter it. Ponds, lakes, and streams are not necessarily better places for swimming, since they, too, can harbor a wide range of parasites and other potentially dangerous microorganisms introduced by runoff from land-fills and sewage systems.

Not Worth the Worry

You may have heard that the following things are teeming with malevolent microbes, but they're not.

1. Money. Metal coins and paper bills are generally too dry to harbor organisms.

2. A peck on the cheek. Theoretically, you can transmit bacteria and viruses back and forth with a good-bye kiss, but even brushing lips together is a lot less risky than shaking hands.

3. Restaurant mints. Although unclean hands already may have dipped in the bowl, there's only a small chance that the mints next to the cashier at your favorite diner will make you sick—and certainly little or no chance if they are wrapped. The odds rise slightly, however, if you take an antacid after dinner. Antacids reduce the stomach acids that kill bacteria.

4. Urine on toilet seats. Truth be told, urine is sterile, so even though it's certainly off-putting, you don't have to worry that it harbors any germs besides the ones on the seat to begin with.

5. Garden dirt. Common soil bacteria tends to be harmless. It has so many beneficial and benign organisms (up to 6 billion in a teaspoonful) that disease-causing germs can't survive.

◆ **What you can do.** Instead of dry-docking yourself, ask the local health department to direct you to beaches that are monitored regularly for contamination. (Or visit the community or park web site, which may offer reports on beach water

{ *"Wisdom is to the soul what health is to the body."*
—FRANÇOIS, DUC DE LA ROCHEFOUCAULD / FRENCH WRITER (1613–1680) }

conditions. Also, avoid ocean swimming for 48 hours after a heavy rain, which can make sewage systems overflow. And since swallowing water of questionable quality is what makes most people sick, wherever you swim, keep your mouth closed as much as possible.

Your Mouth: A Hotbed of Hazards

Scrupulous dental habits will reward you with a brighter smile. But the benefits of regular brushing and flossing go way beyond the obvious. What happens in your mouth is irrefutably linked to your immune system and your overall health.

Skeptical? You're not the only one. Almost 20 years passed between the first research on the connection and its acceptance by the scientific community. But since then, several studies have confirmed that a number of illnesses are related to gum disease (also called periodontal disease), the most common chronic disease in the world, affecting 80 percent of adults at some time or another. Gum disease is caused by plaque, the sticky substance that is also responsible for tooth decay. When plaque-forming bacteria work their way below the gum line, gum disease starts to develop. Psychological stress can accelerate its progression by triggering the release of hormones that help bacteria thrive. Until it becomes severe, gum disease may have no obvious symptoms. In time, it can cause bad breath, loose teeth, and swollen gums that bleed easily, especially when you brush your teeth.

interesting!

A close look into the mouths of 128 people who used dry, toothpaste-free toothbrushes for six months suggests that dry-brushing is most effective at removing plaque. For the tidiest teeth in town, consider dry-brushing for the first 90 seconds, then using toothpaste for 30 seconds longer to remove stains, freshen your breath, and provide a dose of fluoride to strengthen and protect your enamel.

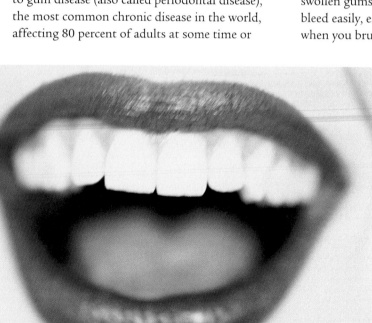

The trickle-down effect.

More than 400 species of bacteria can exist in plaque. Left unchecked, these bacteria carve out tiny pockets between gums and teeth. After growing for 8 to 12 weeks and extending the pockets more than one-eighth of an inch below the gum line, the bacteria become much more aggressive and destructive.

The germs themselves or the toxins they release then may enter the bloodstream, where they can

BACTERIA IN THE MOUTH can reduce immune protection from heart disease.

QUIZ: WHAT'S YOUR DENTAL I.Q.?

1 The more sugar you eat, the more plaque and decay-producing acid you'll have in your mouth.   ○ TRUE   ○ FALSE

2 Chewing sugarless gum creates more saliva—a natural antibacterial that neutralizes acid.   ○ TRUE   ○ FALSE

3 Flossing can injure your gums if not done properly.   ○ TRUE   ○ FALSE

4 Cheek and lip biting raise the risk of oral cancer.   ○ TRUE   ○ FALSE

5 Chronic bad breath is caused by oral bacteria.   ○ TRUE   ○ FALSE

6 Teeth and gums need exercise, such as vigorous chewing, to stay strong.   ○ TRUE   ○ FALSE

All are true. Count the number of times you answered correctly.

FOUR OR MORE Your smile must be beautiful—or at least you know what it takes to make it that way. Keep brushing twice a day and flossing at least once a day.

THREE OR LESS You need to brush up on techniques to protect your smile and your immune system from bacteria in your mouth. Ask your dentist for advice.

---

contribute to clogged arteries and raise the risk of heart attack and stroke. Plaque also contains types of bacteria that can infect the respiratory tract, causing bacterial pneumonia. A powerful immune system will usually repel these invaders. Such factors as recent surgery may lower your resistance, however, clearing the way for infection to spread.

Dental plaque has even been linked to miscarriage and premature birth. Researchers from a U.S. university found that women with gum disease are three to eight times more likely to give birth to undersized and premature infants. The suspected reason is that toxins from bacteria in plaque interfere with fetal development. Another possibility: Gum disease may stimulate the release of chemicals that can dilate the cervix and set off premature labor.

Plaque may cause another danger. Some evidence suggests that *Helicobacter pylori,* the bacterium that causes most stomach ulcers, takes root in plaque and goes from there to the stomach.

Preventive steps. Good dental hygiene helps keep the germs that attack gum tissue in check.

◆ **Brush your teeth properly.** It takes two to four minutes to brush all your tooth surfaces, yet most people spend 30 seconds or less brushing. As a result, they miss the same spots day after day.

◆ **Scrape your tongue daily.** It hosts more bacteria than any other part of your mouth does. Use an inexpensive plastic scraper (sold in a drugstore) to give the boot to these germs.

◆ **Floss.** Most periodontal disease starts between teeth, in areas that are out of the reach of toothbrush bristles. In fact, you miss nearly 40 percent of tooth surfaces when you brush without flossing. If you floss only once a day, the best time to do it is in the evening before bed. Use unwaxed dental floss. Slide the floss into the space between teeth, then move it gently under the gum line, first in the front of each tooth, then in the back.

◆ **Keep your mouth moist.** If you take any medication regularly, ask your doctor whether it may dry out your mouth. This side effect occurs with some antidepressants, antihypertensives, antihistamines, and decongestants. Restore moisture by chewing sugarless gum or using a saliva-replacement spray.

◆ **Use more than one soft-bristled toothbrush.** If you rotate brushes, each one has a chance to dry out, eliminating viruses and bacteria that thrive on moisture. Replace your brushes every few months or if the bristles start to splay.

The ABCs of Hand Washing

Roughly one-third of North Americans have forgotten one of the most basic lessons their mothers taught them: Wash your hands. Though 95 percent of North American adults say they scrub after using public rest rooms, researchers found that only 67 percent actually do.

At first it may seem ridiculous that serious scientists bothered to check on the matter. But hand washing is a serious issue. If, for example, you're sick and you don't wash your hands frequently, the warm, moist creases in your palms become perfect havens for disease-causing germs, making it easy for you to spread them directly to others or onto surfaces that others may touch. Soon, you'll have lots of sniffling company.

Within your control. The important thing to remember is that some pretty serious diseases, including hepatitis A, meningitis, and infectious diarrhea, can easily be prevented if people make a habit of washing their hands. Used the right way, soap and hot water can remove most of the danger in seconds.

Common sense tells us that hands should be washed when they are dirty. But it's also essential to wash them after coughing, sneezing, using tobacco, blowing into a handkerchief or tissue, using the bathroom or handling diapers, cleaning dirty surfaces, handling an animal, and before, during, and after preparing food. Studies have found that even when people wear gloves as a safety barrier, hand washing can significantly reduce transmission of infections.

Quick Tip

Keep your hands away from your face to reduce the chance of delivering bacteria and viruses directly to your eyes or nose. One study found that people typically touched their faces 15 times every hour.

GOOD QUESTION!
How good are waterless hand sanitizers?

Waterless, antibacterial hand sanitizers are marketed as a way to wash your hands when soap and water aren't available. But research shows that they do not significantly reduce the overall amount of bacteria on hands and, in some cases, may even increase it. A typical hand sanitizer is mostly alcohol, which strips the skin of natural oils that normally protect bacteria from penetrating below the surface.

Essential Tips for Health and Well-Being

Good hand washing requires three elements: soap, water, and friction. Although washing hands seems easy, these often-overlooked techniques make it more effective—and more likely to protect your health.

1. Get into hot water. A public opinion survey found that 3 in 10 North Americans don't know that warmer water (somewhere between 37.7°C and 42.2°C) is more effective in eliminating germs. You are in the right range if the water feels comfortably toasty.

2. Remove the jewels. When researchers compared bacteria counts on the hands of

4. Take your time. Once your hands are lathered up, timing is critical. One study demonstrated that a five-second rinse with water alone made essentially no difference in the number of certain bacteria on the fingertips. A 30-second wash with water plus soap, however, eradicated them all.

Forgot your watch? Vigorously rub your hands together for about as long it takes to say the alphabet slowly. Cover all surfaces: fronts, backs, and sides of hands and fingers, as well as spaces between fingers and under fingernails.

KEEP FINGERNAILS SHORT AND CLEAN. Bacteria like to hide under cuticles and nails.

50 ring-wearing health-care workers to those of 50 who did not wear rings, they discovered that ring wearers had higher counts of staph bacteria both before and after hand washing. Hand washing reduced staph counts by 46 percent for those without rings—but only 29 percent for those with rings.

The lesson: Before washing, remove your jewelry, then wash your jewelry and your hands.

3. Soap it up. Unless you or someone in your family is quite ill or has weakened immunity, avoid antibacterial cleansers. Wash with the mildest soap available, preferably one that contains a moisturizer. Germs from other people's hands can cling to bars of soap, so it is better to use a squirt of liquid soap. Liquid soap dispensers can become contaminated, so use disposable ones or clean reusable ones often.

5. Rinse thoroughly. Cold water is fine for rinsing. The physical force of the water is what carries dirt and germs down the drain.

6. Pick paper. Wipe your hands well after washing. The friction from drying rubs off most remaining microbes. One study found that when people with washed but still-wet hands touched skin and food, they transferred 68,000 microorganisms to skin and 31,000 microorganisms to food. The most effective way to dry? Use a clean paper towel to turn off the faucet. Then take a fresh paper towel and dry your hands with it for 10 seconds. Finally, let your hands air dry for 20 seconds. Cloth towels hold on to germs from previous users; paper towels are cleaner.

{ "Hand washing is the single most important means of preventing the spread of infection."

—CENTERS FOR DISEASE CONTROL AND PREVENTION }

Cooking Up Comfort

By now it's certainly clear: Germs are everywhere. And sooner or later you're bound to get sick. When you do, turn to this old-fashioned remedy to ease your symptoms.

The twelfth-century physician Moses Maimonides was the first to prescribe chicken soup for respiratory ailments. Eight centuries later, scientists finally began to understand why the medieval medic was so enthusiastic about such a simple remedy.

Modern proof of the immune-enhancing, cold-relieving benefits of chicken soup first appeared in 1978, when Florida pulmonologist Marvin Sackner, M.D., reported in the journal *Chest* that sipping hot chicken broth cleared up congestion better than hot or cold water.

More recently, Stephen Rennard, M.D., chief of pulmonary medicine at the University of Nebraska Medical Center in Omaha, reported that chicken soup can slow down several of the inflammatory processes that make colds worse.

Rennard found that chicken soup exerted a direct effect on the immune system, making neutrophils (white blood cells released in great numbers to attack viral infections) less likely to congregate in the bronchial tubes, where they trigger swelling and excess mucus production.

It turns out that chicken broth also contains drug-like compounds similar to those in modern cold medicines. One of these compounds, cysteine, an amino acid released from chicken during cooking, chemically resembles the drug acetylcysteine, which doctors prescribe for respiratory ills.

Making what's good even better.

Additional research suggests that adding these extras to your soup can boost its healing powers even more:

◆ **Cayenne pepper.** It's full of capsaicin, a compound that is similar in chemical makeup to guaifenesin, an expectorant found in such commonly used over-the-counter cold remedies as Robitussin and Tussi-Organidin.

CAYENNE PEPPER is a natural warming agent that clears the sinuses and helps make breathing easier.

◆ **Garlic.** It invigorates the immune system in several ways, notably by adding to the ranks of natural killer cells, which attack and remove virus-infected cells from the mucous membranes. Additionally, a compound in garlic called allicin has effects very similar to those of the European cold remedy S-carboxymethylcysteine, which is an ingredient in the decongestant Mucodyne and several other products sold there.

◆ **Ginger.** This sweet-and-hot Asian root spice helps shut down production of prostaglandins. Prostaglandins are inflammation-producing chemicals released by macrophages, the immune cells that poison and ingest disease-causing agents. The prostaglandins released in an immune response cause the aches and pains that accompany colds and flu. Ginger also helps quell nausea and vomiting.

IMMUNE-BOOSTING CHICKEN SOUP

Freeze the soup in 250-ml portions so you'll always have it ready for use as a cold-fighting medicine.

1   whole stewing chicken or hen (about 1.5 kg,
    see note), cut into eighths, neck and giblet
    reserved, liver discarded
6   large carrots, cut into slices
6   parsnips (about 800 g), cut into
    1-cm chunks, divided
4   medium onions, cut into 2.5-cm chunks
4   stalks celery, cut into 2.5-cm chunks
1   turnip (about 450 g), peeled and cut into
    1-cm chunks
2.5 liters water
3   whole peppercorns
60 ml loosely packed cilantro leaves, plus
    1 tablespoon chopped cilantro
60 ml loosely packed parsley leaves
2   tablespoons olive oil
2   tablespoons curry powder
4   cloves garlic, minced
2   teaspoons cayenne pepper flakes
1   tablespoon chopped fresh ginger
1   teaspoon salt
250 ml frozen peas
4   scallions, thinly sliced
2   tablespoons fresh lime juice (about 2 limes)

1. Heat the olive oil in a 7.5-liter Dutch oven or soup pot over medium heat. Add chicken, neck, and giblets and cook until browned, about 15 minutes. Remove with a slotted spoon and set aside.

2. Drain all but two tablespoons of remaining drippings. Add half of the carrots, parsnips, onions, celery, and turnip. Cook 15 minutes. Add chicken, water, peppercorns, 60 ml each cilantro and parsley. Cover and bring mixture to a boil, skimming off any foam that rises to the surface. Reduce heat and simmer for one hour or until chicken is cooked through.

3. Cool chicken in broth. When chicken is cool enough to handle, remove and discard skin. Tear chicken meat from bones and discard bones. Shred chicken and set aside.

4. Strain broth through colander and discard solids. Rinse Dutch oven and return strained broth to pot. Cover and store broth in refrigerator for 8 hours or overnight.

5. In a large skillet or saucepan, heat oil over medium heat. Add remaining carrots, parsnips, onions, celery, turnip, curry powder, garlic, cayenne pepper, ginger, and salt. Cover and cook, stirring occasionally, 15 minutes or until vegetables are crisp-tender.

6. Meanwhile, skim off any congealed fat from broth. Bring it to a boil, covered. Add sautéed vegetables, chicken pieces, and peas. Cover, and simmer 10 minutes or until vegetables are tender. Stir in remaining cilantro, scallions, and lime juice. Remove from heat and serve.

NOTE: If you can't find a stewing chicken (sometimes labeled "hen" in the poultry section of your supermarket), you can substitute a roasting chicken.

MAKES 16 SERVINGS
PER 250-ML SERVING: calories 143, total fat 6 g, cholesterol 15 mg, sodium 718 mg, protein 13 g, carbohydrates 9 g

Safeguard Your Kitchen

They're everywhere—on your hands, on the kitchen counter, in the air. They're the bacteria and other organisms that can cause food-borne illness if you don't handle, store, and cook food properly.

Generally, the food we buy in stores is very safe. If it weren't, we'd be sick most of the time. The danger of buying contaminated food is small, at least in terms of the quantity of food affected. Health inspectors keep close watch over food preparation in manufacturing plants and in restaurants. Their job is to make sure food handlers are preparing the the things we eat in the cleanest, safest way possible.

It takes more than cooking.

But who inspects food preparation in your home? It's up to you to make sure you're preparing food safely, whether you are fixing food for yourself, your family, or a large group of guests.

Make a Clean Start

◆ **Be sponge savvy.** What's the dirtiest item in your kitchen? Your sponge, thanks to the bits of food and moisture it holds onto day after day. Using the same sponge for several different tasks—washing dishes, cleaning counters, and wiping down oven knobs—simply spreads the germs around.

As a countermeasure, some experts advise cleaning your sponges in the dishwasher. But dishwashers are designed to lift debris from hard surfaces, not

ferret it out of tiny holes. Even if the water in the dishwasher gets very hot, there's no guarantee that germs deep in the interior of a sponge will be killed. Furthermore, a sponge will not dry fully in a dishwasher cycle, leaving leftover moisture that not only contains harmful bacteria but also drip onto clean dishes.

Instead, sanitize your sponges daily by microwaving them on high for one minute or soaking them for five minutes in a bleach solution. (See "An Ounce of Prevention," next page.) And if you find that a package of beef or poultry has leaked on your counter or refrigerator shelf, don't wipe up the drippings with a sponge. Use a dilute bleach solution and paper towels instead. Then wash your hands in warm, soapy water.

◆ **Do not let pets on kitchen counter tops.** Some of us would never dream of letting a cat lounge around on the kitchen counter. Many cat owners seem not to mind. They should; cats' feet, fur, and saliva harbor large numbers of bacteria.

Shop Wisely

◆ **Check the "use-by" date.** If you eat food after the use-by date, it may be unsafe, and its fresh flavor will certainly be lost.

◆ **Size it up.** Make sure cold food is cold and frozen food is free of ice crystals (freezer burn). Choose only cold, tightly wrapped packages of meat, fish, and seafood. Pass up any

EACH AVERAGE-SIZED SPONGE can harbor one billion bacteria.

Is it hot enough?

Use a food thermometer to make sure your cooked food reaches these safe temperatures.

FOOD/ TEMPERATURE
Whole cuts of beef, veal, and lamb 65°C
Ground beef, pork, and casseroles with eggs 70°C
Leftovers or take-out food 75°C
Ground poultry 75°C
Chicken breasts 80°C
Whole poultry and thighs 80°C

product that is leaking. Canned goods should be free of dents, cracks, and bulging lids.

◆ **Pick up perishables last.** Make the meat, seafood, and dairy counters your last stops at the grocery store, and—especially in hot weather—refrigerate your purchases quickly. If you have a long drive home, put perishables in a cooler for the trip.

Store Properly

◆ **Check cooling power.** Keep your refrigerator as cold as you can without letting anything freeze. Check the accuracy of the temperature setting from time to time by placing a thermometer in a container of food and setting the fridge for 4°C. At that setting, hot food should take about six hours (and room-temperature food, about four hours) to cool down to 4°C. If it takes longer, lower the thermostat to 3°C. Always keep the freezer temperature at –18°C.

◆ **Handle with care.** To keep raw meat, fish, and poultry from spreading bacteria, wrap it well (in a zip-lock bag, for instance) and place it on a plate.

◆ **Never thaw frozen food at room temperature.** Bacteria multiply rapidly in meat and poultry left on the kitchen counter to thaw. It's safer to put frozen meat in the refrigerator overnight.. Normally, it will be ready to use the next day. For faster thawing, put the frozen package in a watertight plastic bag under cold water. Change the water often. The cold water temperature slows bacterial growth in the outer, thawed portions of the meat while the inner areas are still thawing. To safely thaw meat and poultry in a microwave oven, follow the microwave manufacturer's directions.

Be a Cautious Cook

◆ **Wash, wash, wash.** Carefully scrub all fruits and vegetables—even organic ones—especially if you intend to consume them raw. Herbs and lettuce leaves should be rinsed individually under cool tap water. Root vegetables should be scrubbed, even if you plan to peel them later. After all, they were grown underground. Rinse delicate fruit, such as strawberries, in a colander, and remove leafy stems, which provide good hideouts for bacteria. Also wash dishes, utensils, and work surfaces with soap and water after each use. It's especially important to clean equipment and work surfaces used in preparing raw meat, poultry, or seafood before you allow any cooked food to come into contact with them. This prevents your meal from becoming contaminated with bacteria that may have been present in the raw food.

STORAGE SMARTS

Wondering how long you can store canned soup before eating it? Whether the cheese that's been in your refrigerator since last week can still be a candidate for your morning omelet? Here's the rundown on what to eat and what to toss.

FOOD CATEGORY	STORAGE LIMIT
BABY FORMULA AND BABY FOOD	Toss after its "use by" date.
HIGH-ACID CANNED FOODS These include tomato sauce, fruits, and sauerkraut.	Can be used for 12–18 months after purchase.
LOW-ACID CANNED FOODS These include fish, meat, stews, soups (other than tomato), corn, carrots, beans, peas, and pumpkin.	Can be stored for 2–5 years if the cans are in good condition and kept in a cool, dry place.
LUNCH MEATS AND BACON (UNOPENED)	Refrigerated for up to two weeks, but no more than one week after the "sell by" date. Opened packages of lunch meat should be used within 3–5 days; opened bacon within a week.
GROUND POULTRY AND GROUND MEAT	Use within 2 days after purchase. Or freeze for up to 4 months.
MEAT, BEEF, PORK, AND LAMB	Must be used within 3–5 days from the day of purchase if kept in the refrigerator. You can freeze meat for up to a year.
POULTRY	Should be used within 2 days after purchase, or you can freeze it for up to 9 months.
EGGS	Eggs bought before their expiration date (which refers to the last date they can be sold) will stay fresh in your home refrigerator for 3–5 weeks.
HARD CHEESE	Can be kept refrigerated for several months.
SOFT CHEESE	If stored in an airtight container, can be kept 1–3 weeks after opening the package.
MILK	When stored at 4°C, milk should stay fresh for up to a week after the "sell by" date stamped on the carton.

COOKING GUIDELINES

Almost everyone has experienced a food-borne illness at some point. But do we get sick only from restaurant food? No. Many more cases of food-borne illnesses occur when food is prepared at home. One common cause is undercooking food. Use this guide to keep yourself and your family safe.

FOOD	SAFE APPROACH
EGGS	• Cook eggs until they are firm and not runny. • Do not eat raw or partially cooked eggs. • Avoid eating foods that contain raw or partially cooked eggs.
POULTRY	• Cook poultry to an internal temperature of 82°C. • It is done when the juices run clear and the meat is white in the middle. • Never eat rare poultry.
FISH	• Cook fish until it is opaque or white and flaky.
MEAT	• Cook ground meat to 71°C. • It is done when it's brown inside. This is especially critical with hamburger meat.

Source: Centers for Disease Control and Prevention.

◆ **Take care with cutting boards.** Studies show that cutting boards are another top bacterial hot spot. In fact, the average cutting board carries 200 times more fecal bacteria (primarily from raw meat) than a toilet seat. If possible, run your cutting board through the dishwasher after each use. Also opt for a plastic board; the more porous wooden ones have too many places for bacteria to survive and thrive. If your cutting board has deep, difficult-to-clean slashes on its surface, replace it. For maximum cleanliness, have two cutting boards on hand: one for raw meats and a second for chopping produce and cooked foods.

◆ **Cook through and through.** Do not partially cook meat or poultry one day and complete the cooking the next day.

◆ **Read labels.** Follow directions on the packages of commercially prepared and partially prepared frozen foods precisely. Heating for the specified time ensures that the food is safe.

Serve Up Safety

◆ **Keep hot foods hot and cold foods cold.** Serving tuna salad at your next backyard picnic? Remember this: Food that lingers in tepid temperatures creates a perfect breeding ground for bacteria. To stop most germs, keep cold items, like salads, chilled to 4°C or below. Keep hot foods, like casseroles, in an oven set at 90°C to 120°C or in a chafing dish or slow cooker that's been preheated to 60°C.

◆ **Watch the clock.** Whether you're having a picnic, a party, or regular weekday dinner, follow this rule of thumb: Let no food sit out for more than two hours. Limit its sitting time to no more than one hour on hot days or in very warm rooms.

Handle Leftovers with Care

◆ **Divide and conquer.** Store leftovers in several small containers instead of one big one. The food will cool down more quickly, reducing the rate of bacterial growth.

◆ **Wash your hands—again.** You washed your hands well before handling food. And you always wash after you handle meat. But consider this: Researchers have found that active baking yeast can be transferred from the hands to mucous membranes, such as those in the vagina, and causing yeast infections. It's one more reason to wash your hands after any kind of cooking.

Food-Borne Foes

North Americans enjoy the safest and most varied food supply in the world. But this variety, along with greater importation of foods, changes in eating habits, and the growth of high-risk population groups— especially the elderly—has resulted in a number of serious and sometimes fatal episodes of food poisoning in recent years.

In fact, experts say, contaminated food presents a far greater threat to the health of North Americans than pesticide residues and environmental contaminants. The illness most commonly contracted is an acute gastrointestinal infection, which usually subsides after a day or two as the immune system battles back against the bacteria.

Who is most at risk?

But for infants, the elderly, pregnant women, and those with compromised immunity, food-borne microbes can be especially dangerous and stubborn, evading treatment and flaring up repeatedly.

The result: Some 350,000 North Americans are hospitalized each year, and about 5,000 die, as a result of unsafe food.

Here's a closer look at seven of the leading culprits.

HEALTH HINT

Grab Some Mayo

Think mayonnaise is a cause of food-borne illness? Wrong! The acid (vinegar or lemon juice) and salt in commercially prepared mayo actually slows bacterial growth. Cooked, unrefrigerated eggs, potatoes, and other low-acid foods are less likely to make you sick if they're mixed with mayon- naise than if they're left out plain.

BAD BUGS THAT THRIVE IN FOOD

MICROBE

SALMONELLA
Typically, it is found in undercooked meat, poultry, eggs, and unpasteurized dairy products.

CAMPYLOBACTER
Contaminated water, raw milk, and raw or undercooked meat or poultry can all carry it into the human intestinal system.

ESCHERICHIA COLI 0157:H7 (E. COLI)
Most illness from E. Coli has been associated with eating undercooked, contaminated ground beef. Person-to-person contact in families and child care centers is also an important mode of transmission. Infection can also occur after drinking unpasteurized milk or swimming in contaminated water.

HEPATITIS A VIRUS (HAV)
Water, shellfish, and salads are the most frequent sources, but cold cuts, sandwiches, fruits, fruit juices, milk, milk products, vegetables, and iced drinks are also often implicated in outbreaks.

LISTERIA
This bacteria is found in soil and water, which means vegetables can become contaminated while growing. It also has been detected in a variety of raw foods, such as uncooked meats and fish, as well as in foods that become contaminated during processing, such as soft cheeses, franks, and cold cuts.

NORWALK VIRUS (VIBRIO VULNIFICUS. E)
Raw oysters, cake frosting, and salads, as well as drinking water, have been implicated in outbreaks.

SYMPTOMS OF INFECTION	YOUR RISK
Symptoms of *Salmonella* infection include diarrhea, fever, and abdominal cramps that develop after 12–72 hours. The illness usually lasts 4–7 days, and most people recover without treatment.	Moderately high. You face a 1 in 144 chance of getting sick from it. Contaminated foods usually look and smell normal. **Protect yourself:** Avoid sunny-side-up or soft-boiled eggs. Eat only well-cooked poultry and meat, including hamburgers, which should not be pink in the middle. Thoroughly wash all produce.
Campylobacter infection, which usually occurs within 2–10 days after the bacteria are ingested, may cause fever, headache, and muscle pain, followed by diarrhea, stomach pain, and nausea. In some cases physicians prescribe antibiotics when diarrhea is severe.	High. *Campylobacter* is the leading cause of bacterial diarrhea in North America. With about 2 million cases each year, you have about a 1 in 130 chance of getting sick. **Protect yourself:** The bacteria are easily destroyed by thorough cooking. If there is a chance that your water may be contaminated with this organism, boil it before drinking.
Severe abdominal cramping and watery, bloody diarrhea are the most prevalent symptoms. Usually little or no fever is present, and the illness resolves in 5–10 days. In some people, particularly children under age five and the elderly, the infection can cause hemolytic uremic syndrome, in which the red blood cells are destroyed and the kidneys fail.	High. It takes less than 10 *E. coli* organisms to cause a problem. **Protect yourself:** Cook ground meat to a temperature of 70°C at its thickest part (a meat thermometer is a must for this), avoid unpasteurized milk, cider, or juices, rinse produce—especially sprouts—thoroughly, and wash hands carefully.
It may take a month after infection for symptoms to develop. These can include fever, fatigue, nausea, jaundice, poor appetite, and abdominal pain.	High, if you dine on raw shellfish. About one in every 1,000 oysters is contaminated. **Protect yourself:** Wash your hands after using the toilet and before preparing or eating food. Cook shellfish thoroughly.
Infection may cause influenza-like symptoms, including persistent fever and stiff neck, sometimes preceded by nausea, vomiting, and diarrhea. Symptoms usually appear 3 weeks after infection but can emerge as early as 11 days or as late as 70 days from exposure. Miscarriage and stillbirth are risks for pregnant women.	Generally low, with less than 2,000 cases a year. Almost exclusively strikes pregnant women, newborns, young children, the elderly, and people with weakened immune systems. **Protect yourself:** If you're in a high-risk group, buy only pasteurized dairy products, cider, or juices. Avoid eating any foods after their use-by dates. Heat hot dogs and cold cuts to 75°C before eating. Warm up dips like hummus, too. Wash vegetables thoroughly. Refrigeration does not prevent the bacteria from multiplying.
Most common are mild and brief nausea, vomiting, diarrhea, and/or abdominal pain; headache and low-grade fever may also occur. Severe illness requiring hospitalization is very rare.	High, especially if you eat raw oysters from warm, Southern waters. Only the common cold is reported more frequently than Norwalk virus as a cause of illness in North America. **Protect yourself:** Eat only cooked shellfish and throw away any shellfish that does not open during cooking.

Source: Centers for Disease Control and Prevention.

Allergies: Nothing to Sneeze At

A healthy immune system usually reserves its ammunition for dangerous invaders, such as viruses and bacteria. But sometimes our fighting forces, overly eager to do battle, confuse the good guys with the bad. That's the case with one of the most common immune disorders: allergies.

An allergic reaction is the immune system's version of a panic attack—an extreme response to something that's totally harmless. If someone who is sensitive to pollen sniffs the wrong flower, his or

her immune system reacts by sending protective antibodies to the scene to seize the offending pollen proteins. Next, the body releases potent chemicals that cause blood vessels in the nasal passages to swell.

Regardless of the site of an allergic reaction— the respiratory tract, skin, or gastrointestinal system—the basic mechanisms are the same. The most common allergic reactions are:

◆ **Hay fever.** Also known as allergic rhinitis, this type of allergy tends to occur when weeds and grasses are releasing pollen. The reaction takes place in the nose, where specialized cells (mast cells) release the chemical histamine in response to the pollen. The linings of the nose and eyelids swell, producing sniffling, sneezing, and itching.

◆ **Hives.** Also called urticaria, this allergic skin reaction shows up as a crop of raised, red, itchy bumps from one to several centimeters across, appearing anywhere on the body. Allergies to foods such as eggs and nuts frequently cause hives.

◆ **Asthma.** Allergens can cause spasms of the smooth muscles surrounding the small tubes through which air enters and carbon dioxide exits the lungs. The result is allergic asthma, marked by difficult breathing, especially exhaling.

◆ **Anaphylaxis.** This most severe allergic reaction, characterized by rapid throat swelling that can cut off all air, is usually triggered by insect stings, foods, latex, or drugs. It can be fatal unless it is halted with a shot of adrenaline (epinephrine).

So much sniffling. No doubt about it: The number of allergy sufferers in North America is growing. Up to 30 percent of adults and 40 percent of children now have hay fever. That's roughly twice as many sufferers as there were 20 years ago. Experts aren't sure what accounts for the increase. Nor do they know why some

PENICILLIUM (LEFT) is a mold and common allergen that grows on water-damaged walls and in rotten food. It is often found in house dust.

people develop multiple allergies early in life while others are totally spared. Heredity plays a role, but genes can't explain the sharp increase over the past 30 years, particularly in North America.

There are many suspected culprits, including everything from pollution to food additives, but the most provocative possibility is the "hygiene hypothesis," which poses that a squeaky-clean modern lifestyle doesn't challenge the immune system enough early in life. Therefore, the immune system doesn't know how to distinguish harmful from harmless substances, attacking both with the same chemical weapons.

Although there's no sure cure for allergies, the problem consistently appears in the top-10 list of reasons for visits to doctors' offices. Medications can reduce symptoms. The newest ones, which belong to a class called anti-leukotrienes, were originally developed to treat asthma. These drugs, including zafirlukast (Accolate) and montelukast (Singulair), combat certain inflammation-causing chemicals—leukotrienes—produced by white blood cells and responsible for allergy symptoms. New treatments to block a broader range of leukotrienes, as well as IgE (the so-called allergy antibody), are in the works.

Know Thy Enemy

Some substances are especially likely to set off allergic reactions. If you have unexplained bouts of sneezing and wheezing, the culprit may be:

◆ **Animal dander.** A clingy compound known as Fel d1, found in the saliva, dander (skin flakes), and urine of cats, dogs, and other furry and feathered beasts, provokes allergies in 15 percent of people. Dander can haunt a house even after the

Good-Bye Dust Mites

Want to rid your bed of dust mites (BELOW, ORANGE), those ubiquitous allergens that live by the thousands in each pinch of dust? Experts have long known that washing sheets, pillows, and blanket covers weekly—and blankets and quilts monthly—in hot (54°C) water helps kill off most of the bugs. But that's tough on bedding.

Now, there's an easier way to be rid of these unwanted bedfellows. A study from the University of Sydney in Australia found that adding eucalyptus oil (available at most health-food stores) to your wash cycle—whether hot, warm, or cool—will vanquish the vast majority of dust mites. The recipe: Mix one part liquid dish soap with four parts eucalyptus oil. Once mixed, the solution should remain opaque for at least 10 minutes. If it separates, try a different kind of dish soap. Fill the washer, pour the mixture in, and soak bedding for 30 minutes before laundering as usual. For best results, repeat weekly on sheets and every other month on blankets and other large bedding. In addition, use a dehumidifier in your bedroom. Be sure to empty the collection pan daily.

creatures who shed it are long gone. One study found that it took six months of daily scrubbings to rid a home of feline allergens.

What to do. If you are severely allergic to animal fur, you probably can't have a pet unless it's a fish. To get rid of animal dander, replace rugs, carpets, and draperies; steam clean upholstered furniture;

"Healing is a matter of time, but it is sometimes also a matter of opportunity."

—HIPPOCRATES / GREEK PHYSICIAN, FATHER OF MODERN MEDICINE (460–375 B.C.)

Stopping Allergies Before They Start

1 Shut the windows. It's fine to leave one or two open a crack to let gases out and fresh air in. But otherwise, turn on the air conditioning to clean, cool, and dry the air. High humidity encourages the growth of molds and can attract cockroaches.

2 Limit outdoor excursions when the pollen and mold counts are high. Peak pollen times usually fall between 2:00 P.M. and 4:00 P.M. Avoid long periods outdoors on windy days, too, when dust, mold, and pollen are blown about. Keep allergens out of your eyes by wearing wrap-around sunglasses.

3 Vacation in low-allergen areas. The seashore is a good choice. Although the breeze is damp, levels of allergy-causing pollen tend to be low.

4 Shower and change your clothing (including shoes) after being outside. It's yet another way to exile outdoor allergens, which can easily collect on your skin, hair, and clothing,

then be transferred to your hands, face, and pillowcase.

5 Get someone else to do the yard work. It can expose you to high levels of pollen and mold. Have trees and bushes pruned regularly to cut down on vegetation near doors and windows. Don't use a leaf blower. These noisy yard tools spurt mold into the air at full force.

6 Keep indoor plants dry. Wet soil encourages mold growth. Top pots with

small pebbles or stones to help avoid this.

7 Get your child a pet. Having an animal around in childhood seems to steer an immature immune system away from overreactions to animal dander. Studies of European children show that those who live on farms and are in regular contact with animals are four times less likely to have hay fever or asthma than city-dwelling kids.

8 Encase the beds. Cover the mattress, box spring, and

pillows with allergen-proof covers to keep dust mites in check.

9 Choose feathers. Research from the University of Manchester in Great Britain found that synthetic fiber and foam pillows contain more dust mites and pet dander than feather-filled pillows. The densely woven covers designed to keep the feathers in also help to keep allergens out.

10 Dust less often. For your children's sake, leaving an occasional dust bunny under the bed could be a wise move. Doctors at the National Jewish Medical and Research Center in Denver say that a molecule called endotoxin, found in ordinary house dust, appears to protect youngsters against allergy and asthma.

11 Roll up the rugs. Dust mites can't live on bare wood. If you must have carpeting, vacuum often.

12 Bag stuffed animals. Keep them in the freezer during the day to kill dust mites.

Children with severe allergies are about 10 percent more likely to have significant behavior problems, such as irritability, aggressiveness, and depression, than children with no allergies, according to research at the National Jewish Medical and Research Center.

and vacuum the underside of every sofa, upholstered chair, and box spring in your house. Also scrub and vacuum the areas behind and beneath all your furniture.

◆ **Dust mites.** According to a U.S. study, the bedding in approximately 50 million homes in North America harbors enough dust mites to create full-blown allergies in susceptible people. Teeny as they are, spider-like dust mites and their droppings pose a significant risk for the development of allergies and asthma.

What to do. Follow the instructions in "Good-Bye Dust Mites" (see page 265) to get these critters out of your bedding. A similar approach might work for washable draperies. Cut down on household clutter, plush toys, and even books on open shelves to reduce dust accumulation.

◆ **Mold.** Any damp area—your heating or air-conditioning system, or the walls or flooring next to a leaky pipe—offers a friendly haven for mold. Indoor molds can thrive year-round, constantly sending microscopic spores into the air.

What to do. Fix leaky pipes, windows, and roofs at the first sign of dampness. Choose dry heat instead of steam. If your basement is humid, use a dehumidifier, and make sure to clean it often.

◆ **Pollen.** Pollen—the powdery reproductive cells of trees, grasses, and weeds—isn't only a spring or fall phenomenon. In some climates, it abounds all year. Plants produce great quantities of pollen (one ragweed plant can put out a million grains a day), and pollen grains are lighter than feathers, so they travel great distances with ease. In fact, pollen has been found 400 miles out at sea!

What to do. The same things that will help protect your children from becoming allergic to pollen (see opposite page) will also minimize your pollen exposure if you already have hay fever.

Asthma: The New Epidemic

Since 1980, rates of this chronic lung disease have increased by 75 percent, now affecting more than 20 million North Americans. Asthma experts from around the world suspect that rising levels of air pollution and decreased resistance to bacteria are the main reasons. Modern children encounter less bacteria than children a generation ago, so their immune systems overreact to more foreign substances.

The allergy connection. Although young children have been hit the hardest by the asthma epidemic, you can develop asthma at any age, especially if you have allergies. Both conditions

Asthma Red Flags

Allergic reactions, infections, exercise—even laughing or crying—may trigger asthma attacks. But many people ignore mild attacks or attribute them to colds or allergies. If you persistently have the following symptoms, you may have asthma.

- A nagging dry cough that won't go away
- A wheezing sound when you breathe
- Frequent episodes of rapid breathing or inability to catch your breath
- A feeling of tightness in your chest
- Symptoms that sometimes get worse at night or after vigorous activity.

are tightly intertwined with the immune response, particularly with reactions mediated by the immune system protein IgE, also known as the allergy antibody. These allergic reactions trigger asthma attacks in 90 percent of children and in about half of all adults with asthma.

The immune system, to a large extent, determines how much inflammation will accompany an allergic reaction. Thus, it controls the severity and duration of asthma attacks. Whether you're at risk for asthma depends on a number of factors, including your genetic susceptibility to allergies in general. If other members of your family have allergies and asthma, you're more likely to develop it,

too. Living in an urban environment, particularly in an old building, also seems to increase risk.

Pointers on prevention. Even if you are at high risk for asthma, there are things you can do to avoid it. Here are some steps you should take.

◆ **Ban secondhand smoke.** Cigarette smoke is a serious asthma trigger. Do not let anyone smoke in your home or car, and try to avoid smoke in restaurants, offices, and the homes of family and friends. Toxins from cigarette smoke can linger in furniture, carpets, and clothing long after the smoker has left.

◆ **Detox your furniture.** Formaldehyde is a source of irritating vapors. Seal unfinished surfaces of new cabinets and furniture with a formaldehyde sealant, available at any hardware store. (Although "formaldehyde sealant" sounds like something that's made of formaldehyde, its function is to lock formaldehyde fumes into cabinetry.) Unfinished pressed-wood surfaces, including the undersides of counters and the insides of drawers, can emit potent formaldehyde fumes.

◆ **Develop an action plan.** If you suspect that you may have asthma, get a proper diagnosis. You'll need to describe your symptoms and, if possible, see your doctor while they are occurring. All asthma patients should work with their health-care providers to develop an asthma-management plan. It should tell you how and when to use preventive and "rescue" medications (for short-circuiting attacks once they've started). Your management plan should also tell you when to take peak-flow measurements. This self-monitoring activity involves using a hand-held device to measure how much air you are pushing out of your lungs. Done regularly, it can help you detect a developing attack before it gets worse.

NATURAL AIR FILTERS

Plants shield against indoor air pollution. **So says the National Aeronautics and Space Administration (NASA). NASA scientists measured the filtering capacity of specific plants by putting them into sealed chambers with toxic chemicals, then checking at 12-hour intervals to see how much of each chemical remained. The best performers: the areca palm, lady palm, bamboo palm, and rubber plant.**

Having a Bad Air Day?

Experts agree that air pollution is a key contributing factor to the increasing prevalence of asthma. Bad air also promotes chronic bronchitis, lung cancer, and other respiratory diseases. Although some strides have been made in cleaning up smog and soot in our cities, outdoor air pollution is still a major health threat.

A U.S. study demonstrates how harmful air pollution can be. It found that children with asthma were 40 percent more likely to suffer asthma attacks on high-pollution summer days than on days with average pollution levels. Environment Canada attributes 5,000 deaths in Canada each year from the effects of air pollution. In Canada's largest city, Toronto, the number of deaths is 1,000, according to the Toronto Public Health Department. The Ontario

CARBON MONOXIDE in car exhaust reduces your blood's ability to carry oxygen.

Medical Association estimates that air pollution costs the province of Ontario health care system more than one billion dollars annually in "hospital admissions, emergency room visits, and absenteeism."

Following is a primer on the three types of air pollution that affect the largest numbers of people in North America, along with precautions to help you avoid them. But no matter how careful you are while you're outside, air pollutants and irritants may create or worsen respiratory problems. If you ever have trouble breathing, consult your physician. You need a thorough medical assessment along with advice on what to do about the harmful effects of air pollution.

Carbon Monoxide

Automobile emissions are the main source of carbon monoxide (CO) in the air. Invisible and odorless, CO invades your red blood cells and displaces life-giving oxygen. Consequently, less oxygen is carried to the cells in your body. Some 10 million North Americans live in areas with air that regularly exceeds federal CO limits. Also, about 3 million people who suffer congestive heart failure (a life-threatening chronic condition

---

AIR POLLUTION: HOW DOES IT HURT?

Even at low levels, air pollution can damage your health in several ways.

Irritation
Burning eyes, cough, and chest tightness

Reduced lung function
Difficulty breathing deeply and vigorously, more rapid and shallow breaths than normal

Aggravated asthma
Increased hospitalizations and ER visits to treat severe symptoms

Increased susceptibility to infections
Reduced ability to fight colds, flu, bronchitis, and pneumonia because protective membranes in the nose and throat dry out and immune function is impaired

DIESEL FUEL spews microscopic particles into the air that may escape the body's defenses and go deep into the lungs.

in which the heart cannot pump out all the blood that enters its chambers) may be extremely vulnerable to the effects of CO. Studies show that even permissible levels of CO could intensify heart-failure symptoms enough to require hospitalization, and that high exposure to CO for even a short period can lower the amount of exertion it takes to induce chest pain (angina) in people with coronary artery disease.

◆ **What you can do.** Regular car maintenance can help reduce your exposure. Because CO can escape from gasket leaks, holes in the muffler, or holes in the pipes, it's critical to get your car's combustion and exhaust systems checked out regularly. Even normal CO emissions can make you sick if your car is standing still with its motor running and there is no wind.

If you work on your car in your garage, make sure the garage door is completely open and that exhaust fumes from the garage do not enter your house (see pages 242–245). Also, keep vehicle windows closed in tunnels and enclosed parking garages. If you're a smoker, quit—tobacco smoke contains high CO levels.

Ozone

Ground-level ozone (or smog) forms when sunlight reacts with chemicals emitted by cars and various commercial and industrial sources. Ozone is a powerful respiratory irritant. In high concentrations, it can severely limit your ability to take a deep breath, causing coughing, throat irritation, and discomfort on breathing. There is also evidence that ozone can lower resistance to respiratory disease (such as pneumonia), damage lung tissue, and aggravate chronic lung diseases (such as asthma or bronchitis). The severity of

these effects increases with the concentration of ozone in the air, the length of exposure, and the amount inhaled.

When you exercise, you breathe faster. In high-ozone environments, this means that more ozone gets into your airways and lungs. Even healthy people may suffer breathing difficulties if they exercise outdoors when there's an ozone alert. Ozone is at its worst on hot, stagnant summer afternoons in areas with large volumes of motor vehicle traffic. More than 50 million North Americans live in cities and towns that don't meet government standards for ozone.

The harmful ozone in the lower atmosphere (troposphere) should not be confused with the protective layer of ozone in the upper atmosphere (stratosphere), which screens out harmful ultraviolet rays.

◆ **What you can do.** If possible, stay indoors in a cool, well-ventilated place on days when the air quality index (see opposite page) is unhealthy. Children tend to be more sensitive to ozone pollution than adults because they breathe faster. During peak smog months (May to September), plan "must-be-outside" activities for early in the morning, when air pollution is lowest.

Particulate Matter

A wide range of man-made and natural pollutants—pollen, road dust, diesel soot, and wood smoke to name a few—are suspended as particles in the air. These particles are a mixture of visible and microscopic solids and liquid droplets known as aerosols, which are easily inhaled.

The danger is significant, according to a seven-year study from the Harvard School of Public health. The study, which followed 552,138 people in 151 U.S. cities, found that residents of areas with the highest concentration of particulates had a 16 percent higher risk of death from all causes than those who lived in the least polluted areas. Death rates from heart and lung diseases were particularly high in polluted locales. Interestingly, the findings were consistent for smokers and nonsmokers alike. Even smokers who lived in nonpolluted areas were less likely to die.

◆ **What you can do.** You cannot choose the air you breathe, but you can choose cleaner and more efficient energy sources for home heating and cooling, transportation, and appliances. Carefully maintaining your automobile and carpooling whenever possible are also good ideas. Finally, limiting the use of fireplaces and wood-burning stoves will make your indoor air safer.

AIR QUALITY INDEX

The best way to protect yourself from the adverse health effects of polluted air is to keep tabs on the Air Quality Index (AQI) in your area. Every day, cities across Canada measure the concentration of ozone in the air. Many convert the reading to an AQI number on a scale of 0 to 500. The higher the number, the more unhealthy the air quality is that day.

INDEX RANGE	WEATHER CONDITIONS	HEALTH ADVISORY
GOOD 0–50	Cool summer temperatures; windy and/or cloudy; recent rain or cool front	None
MODERATE 51–100	Mild summer temperatures; light/moderate winds; high pressure system, or partly cloudy skies	Unusually sensitive people, especially children or older people with respiratory disease, should limit outdoor activities.
UNHEALTHY FOR SENSITIVE GROUPS 101–150	Temperature upper 80s or above; light winds; sunny skies	Sensitive people should limit prolonged outdoor exertion. Children may be more affected by high ozone levels than adults because their lungs and immune systems are still developing; they also breathe more rapidly and deeply than adults do, so more pollutants enter their lungs. Older people also must be careful because they tend to have heart and lung conditions and may be at higher risk for respiratory infections, such as the flu, bronchitis, and pneumonia.
UNHEALTHY 151–200	Hazy, hot, and humid	Active children and adults as well as people with respiratory diseases such as asthma should avoid prolonged outdoor exertion; everyone else, especially children and older adults, should limit prolonged outdoor exertion.
VERY UNHEALTHY (ALERT) 201–300	Continuous hot, stagnant weather	Active children and adults should avoid all outdoor exertion; everyone else, especially children, should minimize outdoor exertion and stay indoors with air conditioners running and windows and doors closed.

Source: Environmental Protection Agency, Office of Air Quality Planning & Standards.

When Eating Is Risky

Have you ever landed in the hospital, covered with hives and gasping for air, because of something you ate? If you haven't, you probably don't have a food allergy.

In surveys, about 33 percent of North Americans say that they have food allergies. For most of them, the real problem is what experts call a food intolerance or sensitivity. True food allergy—an adverse immune reaction to a component of a particular food—affects less than two percent of adults. But for that unlucky few, even a taste of a problem food can be dangerous. In one tragic case, a college student who was allergic to peanuts died after eating two bites of chili that contained peanut butter.

The gang of eight.

Amazingly, just eight foods are responsible for 90 percent of all food allergies in North America: peanuts, tree nuts (such as almonds, cashews, pecans, and walnuts), fish, shellfish (crab, shrimp, lobster, and crayfish), eggs (especially the whites), milk, soy, and wheat. Most food allergies develop during childhood, but a few— to fish, shellfish, and tree nuts, for instance— sometimes appear the third or fourth decade of life, or even later.

What's happening?

In the case of a food allergy, the immune system perceives a compound in food (usually a protein) as an enemy. The immune system manufactures an antibody known as immunoglobulin E (IgE) to fight the specific allergen. If you're allergic to peanuts, for example, when your immune system first was exposed to those legumes, it created an IgE to attack peanut protein. The next time you ate just a fraction of one peanut, your immune system went into action to protect you from what it mistakenly perceived as danger. Within anywhere from two minutes to two hours, symptoms of the immune reaction appeared, in the form of hives, nausea, diarrhea, vomiting, runny nose, stomach cramps, tingling, or swelling in the mouth or throat. In some cases, an allergic reaction to food creates a sense of impending doom—much like that which often occurs in heart attacks.

Fortunately, the vast majority of food allergies are not life threatening. But unlike pollen and animal allergies, which

Interesting!

Since the foods we are most likely to react to are the ones we eat often, other food allergies are more common in other countries. In Japan, for example, rice allergy is more widespread. People in Scandinavia are more likely to have codfish allergy.

HEALTH HINT

Learn the Lingo

If your doctor tells you that you have a food allergy, be sure to ask for the names of by-products you must also avoid. If you are allergic to milk, for instance, you'll also need to check food labels for casein, caseinate, nougat, and whey. If you're allergic to eggs, you'll need to avoid lecithin, and if you react to wheat, you must look out for gluten, too.

ALTHOUGH COMPLETELY UNRELATED, peanuts (technically legumes) and tree nuts are equally prominent on the list of common food allergens.

OLIVES and other pickled foods sometimes cause reactions in people who have mold allergies.

sometimes can be lessened with allergy shots that retrain the immune response, the only safe treatment for food allergies is avoidance of the food. In what may prove to be a medical breakthrough, however, researchers at Mount Sinai Medical Center in New York City are conducting trials of a peanut vaccine in people who have previously had an allergic reaction. After identifying and isolating the peanut protein responsible for the reaction, the researchers altered the protein so that IgE antibodies couldn't bind to it. If successful, their vaccine could become a prototype for tackling other food allergies.

When It's Not an Allergy

There are several ways to have an adverse reaction to food without being allergic to it.

Food intolerance. Most food intolerances are simply digestive problems: gas, bloating, or diarrhea. High-fiber foods, such as bran, beans, and cruciferous vegetables (including broccoli, brussels sprouts, cabbage, and cauliflower), often cause those problems in susceptible people.

Another food intolerance, lactose intolerance, occurs in people who do not manufacture enough of an enzyme called lactase, which is necessary to digest the carbohydrate in milk (called lactose). Therefore, lactose remains in the intestines, causing cramping and diarrhea. People with lactose intolerance can avoid these problems by not drinking milk or by drinking only small amounts at a time. (Most people produce enough lactase to handle tiny amounts of lactose.) You can also avoid symptoms by choosing foods such as yogurt, in which bacteria have already broken down some of the lactose, or drinking milk with lactase added, such as Lactaid-brand milk.

Food sensitivities. Sometimes naturally occurring substances or food additives trigger reactions that seem as if they are related to allergies—sneezing, headache, or nausea, for example. But these reactions are not true allergies because the immune system plays no role in their occurrence. Hundreds of substances can cause such reactions in sensitive people. Some of the most common offenders are tyramine in aged cheese; sulfites in red wine, beer, and dried fruits; phenylethylamine in chocolate; nitrites in hot dogs, salami, and pastrami; pickled products such as olives and sauerkraut; and fructose (fruit sugar) in sweetened soda, fruit juices, and other drinks.

Food-borne illness. Eating improperly cooked or handled foods, especially undercooked meats (see pages 260–261), also can cause severe gastro-intestinal symptoms such as nausea, abdominal pain, and diarrhea. Sometimes, these symptoms are mistaken for food allergies.

Get the Right Test

To confirm or rule out a food allergy, consult an allergist. The visit should start with a physical examination to check for medical problems other than allergies. Since allergies are hereditary, the allergist will want a family medical history. This part of the workup, as well as the scratch and radioallergosorbent (RAST) tests described on the following page, is the same regardless of the type of allergy you might have—hay fever, hives, asthma, or food allergy.

ORAL ALLERGY SYNDROME

If you're allergic to pollens, you may experience mouth itching when you eat certain fresh fruits, raw vegetables, nuts, or seeds. This phenomenon, known as oral allergy syndrome, is due to a cross-reaction between nearly identical allergens present in both fresh fruit and pollen. The immune system reacts to these allergens when the food touches the mouth, causing itching or swelling of the lips, tongue, roof of the mouth, or throat. Luckily, the allergens are usually destroyed in cooking. Even if, for instance, you're unable to eat fresh apples, it may be harmless for you to eat applesauce, apple pie, or an apple heated briefly in a microwave oven.

POLLEN ALLERGY	FOODS THAT MAY CROSS-REACT
ALDER	Celery, pears, apples, almonds, cherries, hazelnuts, peaches, and parsley
BIRCH	Apples, pears, almonds, peaches, apricots, cherries, plums, nectarines, prunes, kiwi, carrots, celery, fennel, parsley, coriander, parsnips, peppers, potatoes, and (in rare instances), hazelnuts, almonds, and walnuts
GRASS	Melons, tomatoes, and oranges
MUGWORT	Celery, fennel, carrots, parsley, coriander, sunflower, and peppers
RAGWEED	Watermelon, cantaloupe, honeydew, zucchini, banana, and cucumber. Even tea made from dandelion or chamomile can cause a reaction because they belong to the same plant family as ragweed.

Source: Canadian Food Inspection Agency.

If you suspect a food allergy, you'll be asked to describe the symptoms you experience when you eat specific foods. Keeping a food diary for a few weeks can help pinpoint the relationship between different foods and your symptoms. Such a record is often the most useful tool in distinguishing true food allergies from the more common conditions, food sensitivities and intolerances.

One or more of the following tests will confirm the diagnosis of an allergy.

◆ **Scratch or skin-prick test.** A drop of a commercially prepared extract of a suspected allergen is placed on the skin, and a thin scratch is made in the skin at the same site. If a red bump (called a wheal) appears, you may have an allergy to the substance used in the test. In 60 percent of cases, though, false-positive results occur—a wheal forms when there is no real allergy. A negative test (no visible bump) usually means that you don't have the allergy for which you are being tested.

◆ **RAST.** This blood test measures immuno-globulin E (IgE) antibodies to particular allergens. The RAST is less accurate than the scratch test, so it's used mainly when scratch testing isn't feasible.

◆ **Double-blind, placebo-controlled challenge.** Both scratch and RAST can give false-positive results, so a firm diagnosis of a food allergy may require a challenge test. In this test, the patient ingests both a suspected allergy-causing food (disguised) and a placebo that looks and tastes the same. Neither doctor nor patient knows which mouthful contains the allergen. This test should be conducted in a doctor's office where emergency help is available in case of an extreme reaction.

Are You Allergic to Your Makeup?

The European cosmetic ceruse was used from the second to the nineteenth century, mainly by wealthy women who sought the fashionable alabaster-like cast it gave their faces, hands, and arms. Made with white lead, it was toxic—even fatal.

Today's beauty potions are far safer. Still, some ingredients, especially certain fragrances and preservatives, can cause contact dermatitis (an itchy rash that breaks out where an allergen has touched your skin) or itchy red eyes, tearing, and puffy lids.

Even if you've used a cosmetic for years with no problems, one or more ingredients can still trigger an allergic reaction. Your body may build up sensitivities to these ingredients, causing your immune system to overreact suddenly, producing allergy symptoms.

If you develop a rash or other reaction that seems linked to makeup, stop using all of your cosmetics until the symptoms have abated. Then try reintroducing them one at a time to see which one is causing the problem. If the irritation continues, consult your dermatologist.

Makeup is safe for most people, but do observe these common-sense rules.

1 Wash your hands and your face before applying makeup. It's a basic precaution.

2 Never use anyone else's cosmetics. Sharing cosmetics means sharing germs, whether the makeup belongs to your best friend or sits on a store counter for any customer to test.

3 Don't apply eye makeup if you have an infection, such as conjunctivitis. Throw away all products you were using when you first discovered your eye infection.

4 Toss old cosmetics. Every time you open a bottle of foundation, micro-organisms in the air have an opportunity to rush in. Most cosmetics have enough preservatives to kill off the bugs for about one year.

5 Test new cosmetics. If you tend to have allergic reactions to cosmetics, ask for free samples before buying. Products labeled "allergy-tested," "dermatologist-tested," "nonirritating," or "hypoallergenic" may or may not help you avoid the ingredients that bother you. No federal regulations govern the listing of cosmetic ingredients.

6 Apply mascara with care. Use it only on the outer two-thirds of the lashes; Do not start at the roots. And never apply eyeliner to the inner eyelid margins. Use it only above the eyelashes of the upper lid and below the eyelashes of the lower lid. Contact lens wearers should avoid frosted eye shadow. The iridescent particles can flake, get in the eyes, and attach themselves to the contact lens, causing enough friction to scratch the cornea.

7 Don't be misled by the word "natural." If you have an allergy to the "natural" ingredient, you could have an allergic reaction. For instance, lanolin, extracted from sheep wool, is an ingredient in many moisturizers and a common cause of contact dermatitis.

A Sensible Back-Up Plan

Cancer. You probably try not to think about it, and in truth, the chance that you'll face it is less than fifty-fifty. An average woman's lifetime risk of cancer is 35 percent; an average man's is 40 percent. You can reduce your odds even further by taking the best possible care of yourself.

The strategies you've been learning about in this book—eating a low-fat diet rich in fruits and vegetables, enjoying close relationships with friends and family, exercising regularly, and racking up enough sleep time—will help strengthen your immune system and provide a powerful line of defense against cancer.

But don't stop there. Since so many cancers are now curable when found at early stages, having regular physical exams and screening tests is critical. In fact, the availability of new and better detection methods is the main reason that deaths from all cancers have been dropping by 6 percent each year since 1992. Here's the rundown on the tests you need.

Current Screening Guidelines

Screening guidelines are for healthy adults. People with risk factors, such as a family history of cancer or ongoing exposure to potential carcinogens, may need to be tested more frequently.

Breast Self-Examination

◆ **What it is.** Using your fingers, check for lumps, swellings, nipple discharge, skin irritation or dimpling, and other irregularities, and do a visual check of your breasts in the mirror. If you notice anything unusual, consult your doctor as soon as possible for evaluation.

◆ **How often.** Begin practicing breast self-examination every month by the age of 20 and continue it throughout your life, even during pregnancy and after menopause.

◆ **Why it's important.** By examining your breasts regularly, you'll become familiar with what your breast tissue normally feels like. This may help you detect any abnormality at a very early stage.

◆ **Points to remember.** Perform this five-minute test during the week after menstruation, so that breasts aren't swollen or tender. Postmenopausal women should choose a date that's easy to remember each month.

BREAST SELF-EXAMS (LEFT) are the number one way that breast tumors are detected.

BREAST CANCER RISK

Probability of developing breast cancer in the next five years:

AGE...	CASES
80	15.5 per 1,000
70	15.4 per 1,000
60	12.9 per 1,000
50	9.2 per 1,000
40	4.8 per 1,000
30	1.5 per 1,000

Source: Health Canada.

Clinical Breast Examination

◆ **What it is.** A physician or other trained health-care professional performs a physical breast exam that is very similar to the procedures used for breast self-examination.

◆ **How often.** Women ages 20 to 39 should have one every three years; women 40 and over should have the exam annually.

◆ **Why it's important.** Most cancer experts advocate clinical breast examination, breast self-examination, and mammography (see below) together to give you the best chance of detecting breast cancer in an early stage.

◆ **Points to remember.** Schedule the test for the week after your period, when breasts are least tender and when abnormalities are easiest to detect.

Mammogram

◆ **What it is.** Each breast is compressed between two plastic plates, then X-rayed to detect cancer or other problems.

◆ **How often.** All cancer experts agree women should have mammograms on a regular basis (every one to two years) when they're in their 40s. However, many recommend that starting at age 40, women should have a mammogram every year.

Cancer specialists suggest that women who may be at increased risk for breast cancer should consider mammograms at an earlier age.

◆ **Why it's important.** Mammography can detect cancer before a lump becomes large enough to feel. It can also help identify other breast problems.

◆ **Points to remember:** For the most accurate results, schedule the test for the week after your period. Don't wear body lotion, powder, perfume, antiperspirant, or jewelry on the day of the test.

Fecal Occult Blood Test

◆ **What it is.** A sample of your stool is tested for hidden (occult) blood.

◆ **How often.** Every year after age 50 for both men and women.

◆ **Why it's important.** Microscopic amounts of blood in the stool can signal colorectal cancer, the second leading cause of cancer death in Canada. When colorectal cancer is detected early, it is 95 percent treatable.

◆ **Points to remember.** To help ensure accuracy, consume plenty of high-fiber fruits (especially apples, pears, and raisins), cruciferous vegetables (broccoli, brussels sprouts, spinach), beans, and bran cereal. To reduce the chance of a false-positive result, avoid red meat, vitamin C, and aspirin for three days before submitting samples.

Flexible Sigmoidoscopy

◆ **What it is.** A painless exam to detect cancer of the large bowel (the colon and the rectum). It involves inserting a slender, lighted tube through the rectum into the colon so that the rectum and about half the colon can be checked. The sigmoid-oscope is connected to a video camera and monitor, permitting a thorough visual exam.

◆ **How often.** Every five years after age 50 for both men and women.

◆ **Why it's important.** It can pinpoint polyps, precancerous growths that may not be detectable with a fecal occult blood test. Having both the fecal occult blood test and sigmoidoscopy may be the best bet: Harvard researchers estimate that annual fecal occult blood tests, in combination with sigmoidoscopy every five years, would reduce colorectal cancer deaths by 80 percent.

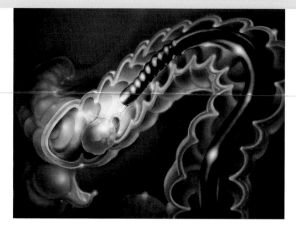

PRECANCEROUS COLON POLYPS (REDDISH ORB, ABOVE) can be easily and safely removed if detected early.

◆ **Points to remember.** You may be asked to use a strong laxative or enema prior to the exam to cleanse the colon and rectum so that the doctor can get a clear view of the tissue lining the colon.

Colonoscopy

◆ **What it is.** Colonoscopy is an examination of the entire colon with a slender, flexible, lighted tube to check for precancerous growths.

◆ **How often.** Every 10 years beginning at age 50 for men and women. It is most valuable when combined with a yearly fecal occult blood test and a sigmoidoscopy every 5 years.

◆ **Why it's important.** If everyone had a colonoscopy at age 55, colorectal cancer death rates would drop by 30 percent. Colonoscopy finds many potential cancers that sigmoidoscopy by itself would miss.

◆ **Points to remember.** Surgical instruments can be passed through the colonoscope to take tissue samples (biopsies) for laboratory analysis and remove suspicious growths immediately.

Prostate Specific Antigen Test

◆ **What it is.** A blood test to measure prostate spe-cific antigen (PSA), a protein made by prostate cells. High levels can be a sign of prostate cancer.

◆ **How often.** Annually for men 50 and older.

BIOPSY involves closely studying tissues taken during screening tests for signs of cancer.

Building a Better Pap Test

The Pap test has been a winner ever since its introduction more than 50 years ago. But like most things in life, it is imperfect, yielding a fair number of so-called false negatives, which are ambiguous or abnormal results that are mistakenly termed normal.

Enter several high-tech approaches that may help reduce the error rate. You might want to ask your doctor about them.

1 ThinPrep. This provides lab technicians with a bigger, better sample to examine, letting them detect 65 percent more abnormalities than they could using conventional Pap smears.

Traditionally, doctors smear a few cervical cells onto a glass plate, then toss the swab (and thousands more cells that cling to it) into the medical-waste bin. With ThinPrep, the whole sample, including the swabbing instrument, is preserved, then filtered using centrifugal force (spinning) to remove any obscuring material. The result is an easier-to-read sample with more distinct cells.

2 PapNet and AutoPap. These methods use computers to zero in on potentially suspicious cells in a particular sample. PapNet is employed to recheck Paps that have been declared normal, in case any problems have been missed. If the computer finds potentially suspicious areas, it snaps a photo, then sends a magnified image to the lab for a closer look.

AutoPap, which uses a video microscope to examine slides and red-flag any that appear to have abnormalities, can be used in place of a conventional Pap or to follow up on an abnormal Pap result.

3 Pap Plus Speculoscopy. This device shows possible abnormalities of the cervix during an office visit. The doctor swabs the vagina and cervix with vinegar, then shines the special speculoscopic light on it. Normal and abnormal cells have different chemical reactions to vinegar, so they show up as blue (normal) and white (abnormal) under speculoscopic light.

◆ **Why it's important.** The cure rate for early-stage prostate cancer is 80 percent.
◆ **Points to remember.** The test isn't foolproof. Sometimes men who have a benign enlargement of the prostate may also have high PSA levels. A false positive PSA can lead to needless diagnostic tests and anxiety.

Pelvic Exam and Pap Test

◆ **What it is.** In a pelvic exam, the uterus, vagina, ovaries, fallopian tubes, bladder, and rectum are felt to check for abnormalities. An instrument called a speculum is used to widen the vagina so that it can be examined in its entirety, along with the cervix (the neck of the uterus). During the Pap test, the doctor collects a sample of cervical cells with a small brush or cotton-tipped swab. The specimen (or smear) is sent to a laboratory, where it is checked for infection, inflammation, and abnormal (cancerous or precancerous) cells.
◆ **How often.** Sexually active women and those age 18 and over should have annual exams. Regular exams are a must for women with human papilloma virus infections, which can lead to cancer. Otherwise, after three consecutive tests are normal, less-frequent Paps are safe. Women who have had hysterectomies should ask their doctors whether they still need Pap tests.
◆ **Why it's important.** In the decades since Pap tests became a routine part of women's health care, the number of deaths from cervical cancer has tumbled more than 70 percent.
◆ **Points to remember.** For maximum accuracy, schedule Pap tests and pelvic exams for two weeks after your period, and avoid douching, vaginal medications, and sexual intercourse for at least 24 hours before the exam.

The Big Picture

This book has introduced you to a vital part of your body that's easy to neglect—your immune system. You've read summaries of research supporting the fairly new idea that your diet, your exercise habits, and even your mental outlook can make it easier for the various components of your disease-fighting defenses to save your life every day.

Putting It All into Practice

What's next? How do you put all this information together into an action plan for daily living? Turn to Chapter 8, "Spring into Action." It will provide you with a day-to-day agenda for bringing your immune system up to its optimum strength. Bolstered with all the important nutrients and appropriate supplements, buffered from stress and negative emotions, protected from many of the traumatic effects of pollution—and, yes, loved—it is

your best ally and your most powerful weapon against premature aging, disability, and disease.

Your Doctor, Your Partner

There's one more step to take to truly maximize the healing potential within you: to cultivate a good relationship with your health-care provider.

Your doctor or nurse practitioner is the person best suited to helping you use the information in this book. To be sure you're getting the care you need, take these steps:

◆ **Be open.** Ask your doctor for advice and help the way you would ask a friend, assuming that he or she will be eager to accommodate you. Don't be afraid to discuss any alternative treatments you may be thinking of or already trying. Doctors feel frustrated when patients withhold information about their health practices.

◆ **Do your homework.** The more you know about the health issues you face, the better you can ask the right questions and make the best decisions. Show your doctor the health articles you've been reading and ask his or her opinion about them. Patients who take an active role get better results.

◆ **Switch.** If your doctor is unwilling to consider you a partner in your medical care, find someone else. Patient-advocacy groups, medical educators, and medical associations today place great emphasis on communication, and practicing doctors have taken the message to heart. In some medical groups and managed care organizations, patients are regularly asked to rate their doctors' communication skills. Those with low ratings are urged to get professional help to become clearer and more direct in their conversations with patients, as well as to become better listeners.

UNCOMMON KNOWLEDGE
No Such Thing as a Zero Risk

Risk is involved in everything you do. If you drive to work, you can get in a car accident. If you fly, your plane can crash. Even at home, you're never 100 percent safe; household accidents kill many thousands of people each year.

Because there is no such thing as a zero risk, the best we can do is figure out which risks are worth taking (such as risking a sports injury in exchange for getting fit) and which are truly foolhardy (smoking, for instance). One goal of this book has been to help you put your risks in perspective. Another has been to prepare you to make the behavior changes needed to reduce them. These changes will reward you with greater stamina, a more optimistic outlook, a stronger immune system—and, by extension, a longer and healthier life.

"One learns by asking one's self questions, then going out and finding the answers."

—EUGENE A. STEAD, JR., M.D. / PROFESSOR EMERITUS, DUKE UNIVERSITY COLLEGE OF MEDICINE

CHAPTER 8

Spring into Action

You want to live a healthier life. You know you should make every single day count. But how many times have you vowed to change, only to give up before you really got started? Turn the page to see how to progress from intention to action and never slide back again.

12 Weeks to a Stronger Immune System

Now you know that the antioxidants in fruits and vegetables can fend off cancer-causing molecules, that herbs can help keep you well, and that regular exercise can revitalize your body and mind. So what's stopping you from having a robust immune system?

Chances are, it's your own comfort with the status quo. Most of us cling stubbornly to routines we've fallen into almost by accident, even if they're clearly feeding into long-term problems such as insomnia, hostility, and constant fatigue. One change—revamping your sleep schedule, for instance—can threaten to upset the whole wobbly apple cart. And if you're looking at a complete lifestyle overhaul, you're bound to feel overwhelmed. What you need now is a plan.

As any pro will tell you, the best way to take a major leap forward is to break it down into smaller steps. Eager to learn a language? Start with basic words, then phrases, and then sentences. Want to paint a masterpiece? Begin with sketches before you move to a canvas.

The action plan on the following pages suggests simple, day-by-day steps you can take to incorporate a full range of immunity enhancing habits into your lifestyle. Each two-week block has a specific focus and is full of practical advice. At the end of the 12 weeks, you should feel truly great and have a revitalized, protective army of immune cells at your service, ready to meet all the challenges you face each day.

The essential steps. By picking up this book, you've already taken the first important step toward supercharging your immunity. That step is to contemplate change. Next, following the "stages of change" model developed by behavior-change expert James Prochaska, Ph.D., comes preparation—getting ready to alter habits and making plans for following through. (We've done some of the planning for you in this chapter.) After preparation comes action— really doing what you've planned, keeping tabs on your progress, and dealing with inevitable setbacks. A setback can actually be a chance to learn.

"People who take action and fail within a month," says Dr. Prochaska, "are twice as likely to succeed over the next six months as people who don't take any action at all."

Maintenance is the next and probably the hardest

E IS FOR EATING RIGHT AND EXERCISE: A healthy immune system thrives on fruits, vegetables, and an active, limber body.

stage of change. It's the time when new behavior should become established habit. Because the excitement of the challenge may have worn off, however, the temptation to slide back into old ways can be great. It takes at least six months to move from the maintenance to the termination stage, when you can consider the change completed. As long as you have to remind yourself to take a lunch-time walk or distract yourself when you're about to reach for a donut, you are still in maintenance.

In time, though, you should reach termination, leaving the past behind you for good. If you started as a couch potato, for instance, you'll see yourself as a true fitness enthusiast.

12-Week Lineup

Weeks 1 and 2: **Revamp your diet.** The best way to fortify your immune system is to eat a nutritious and diverse diet. If you're careful, you can still eat the foods you like. "Think of calories as dollars," says Stephen Gullo, Ph.D., author of *Thin Tastes Better.* "Don't spend them recklessly."

Weeks 3 and 4: **Ease into exercise.** "If packed into a pill," says Robert Butler, M.D., former director of the U.S. National Institute on Aging, "it would be the single most widely prescribed, and beneficial, medicine in the nation." By "it," he means exercise—and not a huge amount. Try to fit in 20 minutes of moderate activity most days.

Weeks 5 and 6: **Be smart about stress.** Up to 80 percent of visits to primary-care physicians are related to stress, a nasty little stealth bomb that raises blood pressure, quickens heart rate, and sends potent hormones coursing through your bloodstream. Since no one can live without stress, it's time that you found a way to live with it.

STRESS ADDS UP FAST: It often comes from over-scheduling. Limit the tasks you take on so that you have time to unwind.

Weeks 7 and 8: **Sleep soundly.** Fewer than 40 percent of us get the recommended eight hours of shut-eye every night. By the end of the year, we've missed out on two full weeks of rest. For the sake of your immune system, remember—your waking hours aren't the only ones that matter.

Weeks 9 and 10: **Play it safe.** With all the pollen, smog, and germs outdoors, it's a wonder we aren't afraid to leave the house. But plenty of things can make you sick indoors, too. As clean as you keep your house, and as clean as you think it is, it is not. How can we stay healthy in this environment? That's the job of the immune system, and here are some ways to help it.

TIME FOR A NAP? Tired people get sick more often than well-rested people.

Weeks 11 and 12: **Coast to the finish line.** Your mission for the next two weeks is to keep doing what you've been doing, while adding in a few more positive steps. Already, you should feel more energetic and have a brighter outlook.

That's the program. Now, to get started, turn to page 298 to record a few baseline statistics. Only by knowing where you began will you be able to recognize how far you've come when you have completed the 12 weeks.

WEEK 1: Revamp Your Diet

MONDAY

Start a food diary.
Beginning today, write down everything you eat, along with the calorie and fat counts. And be honest. (Yes, every M&M matters!) Recent research shows that would-be losers (weight losers, that is) who record what they eat shed twice as much as those who don't. Keep your record as a list and note how you feel. As your habits improve in the coming weeks, you'll have an inspiring record to reread.

TUESDAY

"Food is an important part of a balanced diet."
—**FRAN LEBOWITZ**
HUMORIST

WEDNESDAY

Read food labels.
Researchers at the Fred Hutchinson Cancer Research Center surveyed 1,450 people and found that those who read labels ate significantly less fat than those who didn't bother.
◆ **One word: Tomatoes.** Eating tomatoes—including pizza and pasta sauce—cuts your risk of prostate, lung, stomach, cervix, pancreas, colon, esophagus, mouth, and breast cancer.

THURSDAY

Know your BMI.
Do you really need to lose weight? Don't go by outdated weight charts. Find out for sure by calculating your BMI, or body mass index, using the simple formula on page 56.

WEEK 2: Get More Nutrients for Optimum Immunity

MONDAY

Go bananas over fruit. Any fruit that you enjoy is going to be a healthy alternative to the cakes and cookies most of us are used to snacking on.
◆ **Hint:** Add nutrient-dense fruits to salads.

TUESDAY

Take a daily multivitamin with minerals. No doubt about it—food should be your main source of the B vitamins you need to feed your T-cells and the zinc required to power up your antibodies. But even the best diet won't give you all the nutrients you need.
◆ **Important:** Most supplements are easier to absorb if you take them with food.

WEDNESDAY

Vary your menu.
Don't eat the same meals every day, no matter how nutritious they are. To get all the nutrients you need and satisfy your taste buds, consume many different types of foods each week.

THURSDAY

Eat protein at every meal. More than half your caloric intake should come from whole grains, vegetables, and fruits. But if you add some protein to each meal, you won't feel ravenous the rest of the time. Try less traditional protein sources, such as *edamame* (green soybeans) or tofu.

FRIDAY

Eat dinner for breakfast.
Rather than having your big meal just before you plop down to watch TV at night, have it for breakfast or lunch. Sometimes all you need to do to lose weight is eat more in the first half of the day and less in the second half when you are not as active.

◆ **Hint:** Use smaller dinner plates so that servings appear larger.

SATURDAY

Bring home nature's bounty.
You can't eat well unless you have the right ingredients. Whenever you can, shop at farmers' markets.

◆ **Hint:** In general, select the most colorful fresh fruits and vegetables that you can find. Color = nutrients.

SUNDAY

Give yourself a reward.
Your first week is over and you deserve one. When you set out to make major lifestyle changes, it's important to set interim goals—like making it through each week of this plan. Put more fun into it by planning rewards, too! An example of a great reward: Buy a hardcover best-seller that you're eager to read today instead of waiting for it to come out in paperback. Now take a moment to jot down a reward for each of the 11 weeks ahead.

NOTES

....
....
....
....
....
....
....
....
....
....

FRIDAY

Cook your carrots.
Think raw veggies pack the biggest nutritional punch? Surprise! Cooking vegetables breaks down their tough cell walls, releasing more anti-oxidants.

SATURDAY

Seek out C.
Recent evidence makes clear that vitamin C is critical to immune function because it is involved in antibody production and white blood cell activity.

◆ **Hint:** Take advantage of calcium-fortified orange juice. For the same price as the old standby, you get 100 mg of vitamin C and 350 mg of calcium per cup—more calcium than is in a cup of milk.

SUNDAY

Put a cork in it.
Recent studies show that wine drinking maintains immunity. The key is moderation. Just as it would be unhealthy to eat a pound of chocolate a day, drinking more than one or two glasses of wine a day is overdoing it. Too much will dehydrate you, disrupt your sleep, and add excess weight.

NOTES

....
....
....
....
....
....
....
....
....
....

WEEK 3: Ease into Exercise

MONDAY

A doctor's OK.
Check with your doctor before starting any exercise program, especially if you've been sedentary, if you're taking medication, or if you have health problems. Ideally, your physical exam should include a resting and a stress electrocardiogram. Repeat these tests every three years or as often as your doctor recommends.
◆ **Motivation:** People who start exercising later in life gain many of the same health benefits that lifelong exercisers enjoy.

TUESDAY

Get in gear. To get in shape safely, you need the right equipment. Head to a sporting-goods store and buy a new pair of sneakers, some cotton-poly–blend socks, a sports bra, and a water bottle. Got a portable stereo, plus some CDs that get your energy flowing? If not, add those to your list.

WEDNESDAY

Don't overdo it.
A modest 20 minutes of moderate exercise, four or more days a week, provides significant health and longevity benefits.
◆ **Important:** With exercise, what makes the biggest difference to overall well-being is consistency.

THURSDAY

Stre-e-etch it out.
One of the healthiest habits you can adopt is stretching. It loosens muscles before you exercise and improves flexibility. For a quick stretch, lie flat on your back. Point your toes and extend your arms above your head. Hold for 10 seconds, then relax. Repeat three times.
◆ **Important:** Always cool down for five minutes or so by walking around slowly after working out.

WEEK 4: More Moves for Optimum Immunity

MONDAY

Try something different. To prevent boredom, switch activities. Try jumping rope for 10 minutes, working out to a fitness tape, or taking a new class at the gym or Y.
◆ **One word: Innovation.** New workout trends: kickboxing—aerobics with a punch; recess—run around like a kid; and spinning—stationary bike riding to a rhythmic beat.

TUESDAY

Start the day off right. More than 90 percent of people who exercise on a regular basis work out in the morning. It revs up your metabolism and makes it easier to stick to your regimen.
◆ **Important:** Don't exercise within two hours of bed; fast-paced activities can interfere with sleep.

WEDNESDAY

Work out at work.
Don't just sit there. Do a desktop pushup: Stand a few feet away from your desk. Place your palms flat near the edge of the desktop, shoulder width apart. With your back straight, lower your chest toward the desk, then push out. Don't rush. Repeat 10 times.

THURSDAY

"An early-morning walk is a blessing for the whole day."
—**HENRY DAVID THOREAU**
ESSAYIST (1817-1862)

FRIDAY

Envision the future. Being specific about goals helps you achieve them. Imagine the clothes you'll wear, the energy you'll have, the confidence you'll gain from your fitness routine. Page through magazines to find inspiring pictures that evoke what you are seeking.

SATURDAY

"Good habits are as easy to form as bad ones."

—TIM McCARVER
SPORTSCASTER

SUNDAY

Create time. Write exercise into your weekly schedule, then stick with it. Be creative about finding time. Set up a baby-sitting or meal-making co-op with friends and neighbors so you can earn extra time for your workouts.

NOTES

....
....
....
....
....
....
....
....
....
....
....
....

FRIDAY

Take the long way. Exercise options are wide open. Try parking a few blocks from the mall and walking, then taking the stairs instead of the elevator (you'll melt nearly 100 calories in 10 minutes). Exercising on your way to do errands is a great way to add physical activity to a busy schedule. Over time, as you burn calories and tone muscles, small efforts add up. And pretty soon they won't seem like any effort, but simply part of your new, improved, active lifestyle.

SATURDAY

Pump it up. Although we lose muscle mass as we get older, a now-famous Tufts University study shows that muscles can be rebuilt with strength training at any age. Choose a weight you can lift 8 to 12 times—no more. Once you can do 12 reps without struggling, add additional weight.

SUNDAY

Keep moving. Although your body needs regular rest from vigorous training, try to fit in an enjoyable activity, such as a stroll or a bike ride, on your days off. Consistency is key.

NOTES

....
....
....
....
....
....
....
....
....
....

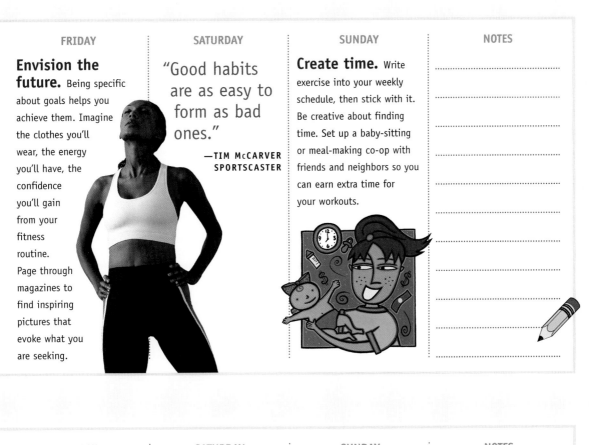

WEEK 5: Be Smart about Stress

MONDAY

Take 20. Study after study shows that 20 minutes a day of calm can stave off anger and anxiety. Sit still and focus on a sound, phrase, or the name of your God. Or fit in several mini-meditations, just closing your eyes and focusing or five minutes on breathing.

TUESDAY

Breathe deeply. Inhaling slowly is one of the quickest ways to relax mentally and physically. Make it easier by gently stretching the skin along the bottom of your rib cage. This stimulates your diaphragm, prompting you to take deeper breaths. As you get used to the feel of "belly breathing," make it a habit and enjoy the benefits that fresh, oxygenated air brings.

WEDNESDAY

Think positive. Pay attention to how your mind works—and teach it to stop thinking in self-defeating ways. When you're upset, your body is more likely to overproduce stress-related hormones that are damaging to the immune system. Instead, practice telling yourself, "It's not as bad as it seems." Repeat positive thoughts often enough, and they'll become automatic.

THURSDAY

"It's the moment you think you can't that you realize you can."

—CELINE DION
POP SINGER

WEEK 6: More Coping Strategies for Optimum Immunity

MONDAY

Phone a friend. U.S. researchers found that the more different types of relationships you have (marriage, work buddies, friendships, gym partners, etc.), the less susceptible you are to viral infections, specifically colds.

TUESDAY

Don't expect tension. If you anticipate stress, you'll have it. Get into the habit of assuming that a new situation will work out just fine.

◆ **One word: Pleasure.** Instead of focusing on what makes you stressed out, focus on what makes you happy, such as frequent sex within a loving relationship, artistic activities, volunteer work, nature walks, or hobbies.

WEDNESDAY

Laugh it up. A good laugh activates key immune system components, increases circulation, and boosts energy. Have lunch with a funny friend or pop in a Marx Brothers video. You'll feel better for it—fast!

THURSDAY

Try yoga. This ancient form of exercise strengthens and tones your body, increases flexibility, and calms your mind. Plus, studies show it reduces blood pressure and eases insomnia, asthma, migraines, diabetes, arthritis, and back pain, if practiced daily for several months. Rent a yoga video or try a class at a nearby yoga center.

FRIDAY

Take a spa break.
To reduce anxiety and relax muscles, pamper yourself with a long soak in a hot bath (see pages 226–227). Or just spend 10 minutes in a soothing shower. Start with very warm water and gradually make it cooler, then warm it up again. The changing temperatures and massaging action of the water will soothe your body while refocusing your mind.

SATURDAY

Play that funky music. Listening to music for 30 minutes raises the production of immunity-boosting proteins an astounding 30 percent, according to one study. And music stimulates the brain's production of endorphins—nature's pain-killers—so much that some hospitals are piping in patients' favorite tunes before surgery and during childbirth. It matters less what the music is than that you like it. Crank up the CDs you like most right now.

SUNDAY

Praise your partner. In strong, loving relationships, couples give ego-boosting compliments to each other every day. They also air and resolve disagreements fast.
◆ **Motivation:** Married people tend to enjoy better immune function than the unwed—if they don't feud often or bear grudges.

NOTES

FRIDAY

Plan a trip.
One study found that people who never take vacations are up to 32 percent more likely to die from a heart attack. You don't have to go far—or anywhere, for that matter—as long as you spend your time off relaxing and doing things you enjoy, not cleaning the garage or catching up on other chores.

SATURDAY

"Don't put off for tomorrow what you can do today, because if you enjoy it today you can do it again tomorrow."
—JAMES A. MICHENER
NOVELIST
(1907-1997)

SUNDAY

Pray tell. A U.S. study on aging found that the two most important predictors of "successful aging" were the frequency of visits with friends and family...as well as the frequency of attendance at religious services.

NOTES

WEEK 7: Sleep Soundly

| | MONDAY | TUESDAY | WEDNESDAY | THURSDAY |

MONDAY

"Sleep is that golden chain that ties health and our bodies together."

—THOMAS DEKKER
DRAMATIST (1570-1632)

TUESDAY

Wind down. People who have trouble falling asleep commonly complain of feeling mentally alert when they should be snoozing. To solve that problem, wind down before bed by engaging in an enjoyable activity, such as jotting down today's accomplishments in a journal, reading favorite poems, or listening to soothing music.

WEDNESDAY

Make your bedroom a haven. Banish computers and other reminders of work from your bedroom. Be sure that your pillow, blanket, and mattress are comfortable, and set the temperature to about 18°C.

THURSDAY

Get a bathroom night-light. You won't have to turn on a bright light if you get up during the night. Exposure to light, however brief, stops the secretion of the sleep-inducing hormone melatonin.

WEEK 8: More Fatigue-Fighters for Optimum Immunity

MONDAY

Consider valerian. Approved as an insomnia treatment in many European countries, valerian can make you feel drowsy without any addictive potential. Use a standardized extract (0.8 percent valeric acid) and follow label directions. But you may have to wait weeks before you notice an improvement in your sleep.

TUESDAY

Be scents-ible. Scenting your bedroom with an aroma that you find relaxing can ease the way to dreamland. Effective smells include lavender, vanilla, and baby powder, according to Alan R. Hirsch, M.D., neurological director of the Smell & Taste Treatment and Research Foundation.

WEDNESDAY

Set aside worry time. Worry has a way of descending at bedtime and preventing sleep. To keep that from happening, spend 15 minutes or so in the early evening thinking up rational solutions to your problems.

THURSDAY

Snack on cereal. Nutritionist Judith Wurtman, Ph.D., recommends high-fiber, whole-grain cereal with milk for better sleep. Carbohydrates release insulin, helping sleep-inducing chemicals in the bloodstream quickly reach the brain.

◆ **One word: Ritual.** Doing the same things each night before bed cues your body to get set for slumber.

FRIDAY

Is it drug-induced insomnia? Many medications, including some antidepressants and heart drugs, can make it harder to fall asleep. If you take a medicine regularly, ask if it could interfere with your sleep and find out if an alternative is available.

SATURDAY

Warm up. Fall asleep faster by donning soft socks and mittens 30 minutes before turning in. As the body prepares to sleep, the added layer of warmth helps blood vessels dilate in the hands and feet. This speeds the transfer of heat from the body's core to its extremities and lowers body temperature—a vital trigger for sleep. You can leave the socks and mittens on all night.

SUNDAY

Your dream mate. Ask your bed partner to observe your breathing during sleep for signs of sleep apnea—snoring or pauses in breathing. If you have either sign, losing weight, sleeping on your side, and avoiding alcohol near bedtime may help. Should these strategies fail, talk to your doctor.

NOTES

FRIDAY

Neutralize noise. If you find yourself waking up to different noises (obnoxious neighbors, barking dogs, airplanes, or traffic), you may want to try:
- earplugs
- thick rugs
- heavy draupes
- relaxation tapes
- white noise (sounds that come from a fan or special machine)
- a legal remedy. Some communities have local ordinances that impose fines on noisy people or businesses.

SATURDAY

"The time to relax is when you don't have time for it."

—SYDNEY J. HARRIS
SYNDICATED COLUMNIST
(1917–1986)

SUNDAY

Take a catnap. Sometimes it's the only way to feel more alert. Prime siesta time worldwide: midafternoon. Limit naps to 30 minutes to avoid the deeper stages of sleep.
- **Important:** A nap is not a substitute for a good night of sleep.

NOTES

WEEK 9: Play It Safe

MONDAY

Know where the germs are. Minimizing exposure to germs in your life can leave you less vulnerable to infectious diseases like colds. Research shows that we tend to pick up these illnesses from the most contaminated surfaces in public places:

◆ public phones
◆ public rest-room counters
◆ bank pens
◆ chair armrests
◆ elevator buttons
◆ escalator handrails
◆ shopping-cart and grocery refrigerator handles.

TUESDAY

Set your hot water heater to 55°C. That's the minimum temperature water must be to kill microscopic dust mites in linens and clothing. Laundering in cool water, then drying for 15 minutes at a high temperature, also kills mites.

WEDNESDAY

"You cannot escape the responsibility of tomorrow by evading it today."

**—ABRAHAM LINCOLN
16TH U.S. PRESIDENT
(1809-1865)**

THURSDAY

Freshen the air. Certain plants, not just green ones but flowering ones like the gerbera daisy (ABOVE), are especially powerful living filters that purge the air of dangerous chemicals. Other "eco-friendly" flowers include mums and wax begonias. Try to have at least two plants for every nine square meters.

WEEK 10: More Ways to Avoid Toxins for Optimum Immunity

MONDAY

Stay out of the sun. Ultraviolet solar rays weaken the function of special immune-system cells in the skin. So slather on sunscreen, such as a moisturizer with built-in sun protection, year-round. An SPF of 30 is plenty; going over 30 doesn't add much.

TUESDAY

Appliance protection. Hot, moist air expelled by dishwashers, washing machines, and dryers can be laden with toxins. Ventilate the laundry room and kitchen with exhaust fans or open windows.

◆ **One word: Mold.** Household molds can produce substances that are toxic to the immune system. Always switch on an exhaust fan when showering.

WEDNESDAY

Cut down on virus transmission. Wash your hands thoroughly and often (see pages 254–255).

◆ **Motivation.** This year, North American adults will each catch 2 to 4 colds, and kids 6 to 10. The result: 15 million workdays and 22 million school days will be missed.

THURSDAY

Bypass benzene. Found in everything from room deodorizers to gasoline, it poisons your white blood cells. Don't use spray air fresheners, and avoid inhaling gasoline fumes when you're filling your tank. Use pumps with vapor-control nozzles, and stand upwind of the nozzle with your face turned the other way.

FRIDAY

Stock up on slippers. Minimize the amount of dirt, chemicals, or other substances tracked into your home by not walking around inside in your outdoor shoes— especially on carpeted surfaces. Give family members and guests slippers and ask them to remove their shoes at the entry. Another good idea: Place mats in front of doors.

SATURDAY

Declare your home a smoke-free zone. Passive, second-hand smoke inhaled regularly paralyzes cilia, the hair-like cells in the nasal and lung passages that help keep them clear of viruses and bacteria. If you smoke, quit now.

SUNDAY

Take inventory. Improve the quality of the air you breathe inside your house. Make sure you have:
◆ pillows with dust mite–proof coverings
◆ mattress covers
◆ a good vacuum cleaner
◆ windows that open
◆ a cold-air humidifier
◆ air conditioners with clean filters
◆ a HEPA air filter

NOTES

FRIDAY

Anger trap. Be aware of the high price you pay for anger (see pages 215–218). When you're just upset and tense—not raging out of control—you still have a choice. Ask yourself, "Do I want to blow up?"

SATURDAY

Remember to drink. Not getting the recommended eight 250-ml glasses every day? Consider this: By the time your body sends the signal that it's thirsty, you're already in the early stages of dehydration. Need a bigger incentive? Proper hydration may curb your appetite and reduce chronic discomfort, such as lower back pain, headaches, arthritis, and muscle cramps.

SUNDAY

Open wide. The mouth can harbor hidden infections that take a toll on the immune system. Brush twice daily (tongue, too!) and floss at least once a day. Schedule professional dental exams at least twice a year.

NOTES

WEEK 11: Coast to the Finish Line

MONDAY

Root for the home team. A recent study showed that ardent sports fans felt less fatigue, tension, and depression—and they had higher self-esteem. So, get out the schedule for your local sports team and catch the next game.

TUESDAY

Dance! What better way to burn calories—200 to 400 an hour? Log onto www.bustamove.com for your own private swing, salsa, waltz, or fox-trot lessons. Or get in the groove with group lessons at a local community center.

WEDNESDAY

Boost your outlook. Put daily annoyances into perspective. Next time you catch yourself wallowing in pessimistic thoughts, ask, "Is it really the end of the world?"
◆ **Hint:** Adopt emotional role models. If you know people who always seem upbeat, listen closely to what they say, and watch what they do.

THURSDAY

Spend time with a child. Children are wonderful reminders of how playful and fun life can and should be.
◆ **One word: Happy.** Avoid people who leave you frustrated and angry.

WEEK 12: More Good-Health Habits for Optimum Immunity

MONDAY

Learn to say no. Conquer the habit of saying yes to every request or obligation when your energy is at stake. Remind yourself that taking on too much can pose a risk to your health.

TUESDAY

Practice your excuses. All it takes to gain a pound is to consume 3,500 extra calories. So don't be a pushover. Next time Aunt Edna tries to force another piece of pie on you, say, "I couldn't eat another bite, but I'd love to have your recipe." If she insists, go to Plan B: "Thanks. I'll wrap it up and take it home for later." With practice, you'll be prepared when you're put on the spot.

WEDNESDAY

Screen tests. At www.yourcancerrisk.harvard.edu, you'll find step-by-step instructions for calculating your risk levels for 12 cancers, plus preventive tips. At the Heart and Stroke Foundation of Canada's website, www.heartandstroke.ca, you can examine a health profile to learn your current risk of heart attack and stroke, with advice on how to improve your health.

THURSDAY

Ax heartburn. Steer clear of foods known to cause heartburn, such as fatty meats, spearmint, peppermint, and coffee (regular and decaf). Why? Overusing antacids or acid blockers to quell heartburn reduces stomach acid. Since stomach acid kills unfriendly bacteria, this can put you at risk for ulcers and other gastrointestinal infections.

FRIDAY

Pursue meaningful connections.

Volunteering is good for the body as well as the soul. Want to volunteer but not sure what to do? Why not...

◆ train for and join the local rescue squad?

◆ lead a bicycling club at a senior center?

◆ provide business counsel to a budding entrepreneur?

◆ conduct tours of a museum you know?

◆ mentor a youngster who needs guidance?

SATURDAY

Go to the dogs.

A furry friend can be a great exercise companion and a never-fail social icebreaker. Pet owners live longer and recover from illness faster than people without pets.

SUNDAY

Bounce back after a binge.

If you've overindulged:

◆ **Don't beat yourself up.** Negating your past successes makes you more likely to binge again.

◆ **Eat something.** If you compensate by skipping a meal, your appetite will soar.

◆ **Burn it off.** A good workout the day after gets you back on track.

NOTES

FRIDAY

Eat less sugar. Each day, the average American consumes more than 20 teaspoons of sugar added to food, twice the amount health experts recommend. Sugar added for flavor contributes to obesity.

◆ **Important:** Eat at regular intervals to keep blood sugar stable and cravings at bay.

SATURDAY

Share your success. Tell your friends and family about your progress over the past several weeks. Do you have more energy? Are your clothes looser? Have your candy cravings vanished? Don't brag, but do try to sell them on this plan.

SUNDAY

"If you wait, all that happens is that you get older."

—**LARRY MCMURTRY**
NOVELIST

NOTES

Your Record of Accomplishment

Way to go! You're ready to begin 12 weeks of basic training to fortify your immune system. Here's a glimpse of some of the things that might change over the next several weeks. Fill in your starting points (BELOW, LEFT) now, and report back again when you complete the plan. You'll be able to see what you've lost—and what you've gained.

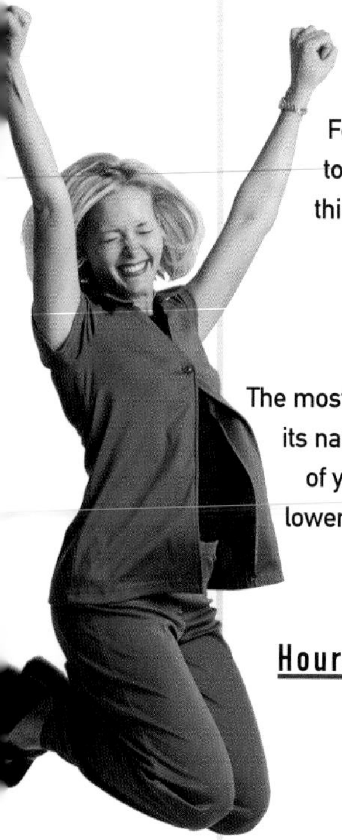

VITAL STATISTICS: TODAY

Body Mass Index

Body Mass Index (BMI) is considered the most accurate gauge of whether you are overweight, obese, or underweight. To calculate your BMI, see page 56.

_____

Weight

Few of us can give up the scale. Just be sure to use it right. Always weigh yourself first thing in the morning to get your true weight.

_____

Waist Measurement

The most accurate place to measure your waist is at its narrowest point—usually at the navel. One of your goals over the next 12 weeks is to lower this number through diet and exercise.

_____

Hours of Exercise in the Past Week

_____

Resting Heart Rate

Your resting heart rate (RHR) is taken just as you wake up (see pages 118–119), while you are still lying in bed. As your fitness level increases, your RHR will go down.

_____

VITAL STATISTICS: IN 12 WEEKS

Body Mass Index

If your BMI is between 18 and 24.5, your life expectancy is longer than average. Men are usually satisfied with a BMI of 23 to 25, women with 20 to 22.

_____

Weight

No matter what the numbers say, don't give up! The people who succeed in life often fail many times along the way. Keep trying! Your health is worth it.

_____

Waist Measurement

The location of fat on your body affects your health. If you've lost inches around your waist, you've decreased your risk for diabetes, coronary heart disease, and high blood pressure.

_____

Hours of Exercise in the Past Week

_____

Resting Heart Rate

Why not measure your resting heart rate every day from now on? If you're overtraining or coming down with a cold, your RHR will rise a few beats per minute, and you'll know to take it easy that day.

_____

{ "One never knows what each day is going to bring. The important thing is to be open and ready for it." }

—HENRY MOORE / SCULPTOR (1898-1986)

Appendix: Immune Disorders and Tests

Disorders of Immunity

Over the ages, the immune system has evolved into a fantastically intricate and sensitive network of checks and balances that can be influenced by the foods we eat, the supplements and medications we take, and the stresses to which we are exposed.

Sometimes, though, despite our best efforts to maintain balance, the immune system does not function adequately. It can attack normal tissues it perceives as foreign invaders. It may react to something harmless—pollen, for example—and harm healthy tissue in the process. Or it can fail to respond to real threats. Here is a guide to a few of the hundreds of immune disorders.

◆ **Addison's disease.** In most cases, this disease occurs when the immune system gradually destroys the outer layer of the adrenal glands, rendering the glands unable to produce hormones (specifically cortisol) in the necessary amounts. Symptoms include weight loss, weakness, fatigue, and low blood pressure.

◆ **Alopecia areata.** This autoimmune disease results in the loss of hair, usually on the scalp or beard. It starts when the immune system mistakenly attacks groups of hair follicles, drastically slowing production of new hairs.

◆ **Allergy.** This abnormal immune system reaction to ordinarily harmless substances manifests itself in many symptoms, including watery, itchy eyes, sneezing, and a constant runny nose. One of the most common allergic responses—seasonal allergic rhinitis or hay fever—occurs in response to various plant pollens.

◆ **Aplastic anemia.** A rare and often fatal blood disorder, it occurs when the bone marrow stops making enough healthy blood cells. In most cases the cause is idiopathic (unknown). There are a number of suspected triggers, however, including radiation, street drugs, benzene-based compounds, viruses such as hepatitis, environmental toxins, some medications, and other industrial chemicals.

◆ **Asthma.** This is an inflammatory lung disease that causes narrowing of the airways and recurrent breathing problems. Allergies, respiratory infections, exercise, cold air, and other factors can trigger attacks.

◆ **Autoimmune hepatitis.** In this condition, the liver becomes chronically inflamed because of an immune reaction directed against some of its cells. Symptoms include fatigue, abdominal discomfort, achy joints, and itching.

◆ **Celiac disease.** People with this disease cannot tolerate a protein called gluten found in wheat, rye,

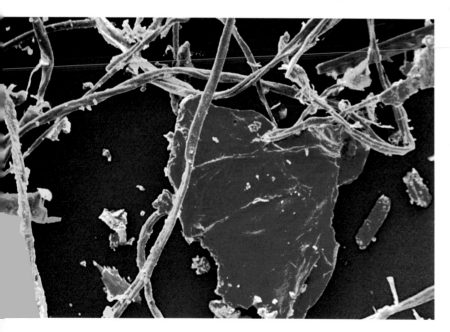

HOUSE DUST (LEFT), magnified more than 400 times, contains flakes of cat skin or dander (PINK), cat hairs (YELLOW), and insect droppings (BLUE). Tiny dust mites (not shown) also trigger symptoms.

barley, and possibly oats. When they eat foods that contain gluten, their immune systems respond by attacking the small intestine. Because the immune system causes the damage, celiac disease is considered an autoimmune disorder. However, it's also classified as a malabsorption disease because it keeps the body from absorbing nutrients.

◆ **Chronic fatigue immune dysfunction syndrome.** This debilitating and complex disorder, which is characterized by profound fatigue and is often accompanied by tender lymph nodes, is suspected of being an immune disorder. However, its true cause has not yet been found.

◆ **Crohn's disease.** In this autoimmune disorder, the intestinal walls are chronically inflamed. The symptoms are recurrent diarrhea, severe abdominal cramps, fever, loss of appetite, and weight loss.

HASHIMOTO'S THYROIDITIS, in which immune cells attack the thyroid gland (LEFT), is diagnosed with a simple blood test (ABOVE).

◆ **Goodpasture's syndrome.** In this rare auto-immune disease, the immune system makes antibodies that attack the lungs and kidneys. Several factors, including an inherited or genetic predisposition, are probably involved in the initiation of the syndrome.

◆ **Graves' disease.** Caused by an immune-system attack on the thyroid gland, it results in overproduction of thyroid hormone. Typical symptoms are nervousness, diarrhea, sweating, insomnia, and weight loss with increased appetite. In severe cases, a goiter (an enlarged thyroid gland) may form, and the eyes may bulge out.

◆ **Guillain-Barré syndrome.** The immune system, which may be activated by a previous viral infection, attacks part of the nervous system. The first symptoms include weakness or tingling sensations starting in the legs and sometimes spreading to the arms and upper

body. Paralysis can quickly overtake the legs, arms, breathing muscles, and face.

◆ **Hashimoto's thyroiditis.** The leading cause of hypothyroidism, in which the amount of thyroid hormones in the body is below normal, it is caused by an immune-system attack on the thyroid gland.

◆ **Human immunodeficiency virus (HIV) and acquired immunodeficiency syndrome (AIDS).** HIV is a retrovirus that takes over a cell's own genetic material. Once HIV infiltrates a cell, the virus uses the cell's reproductive mechanism to make more and more new copies of itself. These viruses then attack the immune system. The process causes no symptoms for some time; a person who is infected can look and feel perfectly well for years. Therefore, the disease may not be detected until the infected person develops illnesses (so-called "opportunistic" infections and cancers) that a normally

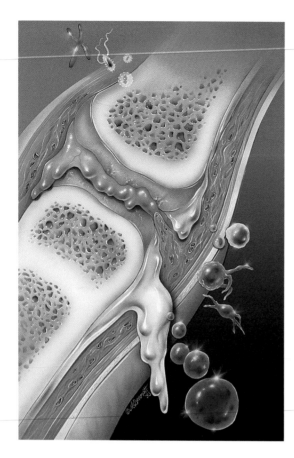

functioning immune system would fight off before symptoms could even occur. AIDS is a constellation of these opportunistic illnesses. Sexual contact (anal intercourse, vaginal intercourse, and oral sex) and sharing of needles are the usual routes of HIV transmission.

◆ **Idiopathic thrombocytopenia purpura.** Characterized by an antibody attack on platelets (disk-shaped components of the blood needed for prevention and control of bleeding), this disease may cause abnormal bleeding, unexplained bruises, bleeding from the gums and nose, and blood in the stool.

◆ **IgA nephropathy.** This autoimmune disease appears to be caused by accumulation of the antibody (immunoglobulin) IgA in the kidney.

◆ **Lupus.** An autoimmune disease, lupus can affect the joints, skin, kidneys, heart, lungs, blood vessels, and brain. Although individual cases of lupus vary greatly in symptoms and severity, extreme fatigue, painful or swollen joints (arthritis), unexplained fever, skin rashes, and kidney problems are characteristic of the disease. Systemic lupus erythematosus is the most common and serious type of lupus. Other types include discoid lupus erythematosus and subacute cutaneous lupus. Skin rashes and sun sensitivity are the primary symptoms in both these forms of lupus.

◆ **Lymphadenitis.** Lymphadenitis occurs when an infection anywhere in the body spreads to the lymph and the lymph nodes, leading to a painful buildup of immune and inflammatory cells. Causes include bacteria, viruses, fungi, or parasites.

◆ **Lymphedema.** An accumulation of lymphatic fluid in the tissues outside the lymph system, lymphedema is characterized by swelling, most often in the arm and/or leg. It can develop when lymphatic vessels are missing or impaired, when lymph vessels are damaged, or when lymph nodes are removed.

◆ **Lymphoma.** This is a general term for a group of cancers that results when a lymphocyte (a type of white blood cell) undergoes a malignant change and multiplies, in time crowding out healthy cells and creating tumors that enlarge lymph nodes.

◆ **Multiple sclerosis (MS).** An autoimmune disease of the central nervous system, MS gradually destroys the covering of the nerves. This damage interferes with signals from the nerve cells to the brain, resulting in loss of sensation, vision problems, and difficulty walking or performing fine motor tasks, such as writing. Most commonly, MS is relapsing and remitting, which means that from time to time the condition flares up and then calms down and symptoms come and go.

◆ **Myasthenia gravis.** This autoimmune neuromuscular disease makes certain muscles become weak during activity. Muscles of the face and throat, including those that control eye movement, expression, chewing, talking, and swallowing, are most often involved.

◆ **Pernicious anemia.** This form of anemia occurs when an overactive immune system attacks stomach cells, preventing the absorption of vitamin B_{12}. Symptoms include weakness, nerve damage, and pallor.

◆ **Primary immunodeficiency (PI).** A PI disease is the result of a genetic defect that keeps one or more essential parts of the immune system from functioning properly.

◆ **Psoriasis.** This common skin disease is marked by scaly, raised patches of skin. Researchers theorize that psoriasis is caused by abnormal T-cell activity in the skin.

◆ **Reiter's syndrome.** Marked by three seemingly unrelated symptoms (arthritis, red eyes, and urinary tract irritation), Reiter's syndrome is also referred to as reactive arthritis because it occurs in reaction to an infection elsewhere in the body. The triggering bacteria are usually sexually transmitted, such as chlamydia, or intestinal, such as salmonella. The syndrome develops in only a small proportion of people who have these infections.

◆ **Rheumatic fever.** Rheumatic fever is a delayed consequence of an untreated upper respiratory infection with group A streptococci ("strep throat"). It occurs in no more than 0.3 percent of all people who have untreated strep infections. The disease can permanently damage the heart.

◆ **Rheumatoid arthritis (RA).** This autoimmune disease, which causes pain, swelling, stiffness, and loss

of function in the joints, differs dramatically from other kinds of arthritis in that it affects multiple joints in a symmetrical pattern and causes general fatigue and malaise. Doctors suspect that RA develops in two steps. First, there is a genetic tendency to develop RA; then an environmental factor, such as a virus, sets the disease process in motion.

◆ **Scleroderma.** The term scleroderma means "hard skin." In this disease, an autoimmune reaction leads to increased deposits of collagen (a fibrous material that gives skin shape and elasticity), leaving the skin thick and stiff. There are two types: localized scleroderma, which affects limited areas, and systemic sclerosis, which can cause widespread damage to the lungs, heart, or kidneys.

◆ **Selective IgA deficiency.** One of the most common primary immunodeficiencies, this disease is marked by the total absence or severe deficiency of the IgA class of immunoglobulins in

X-RAYS are among the basic tests used to monitor bone and joint damage from autoimmune diseases.

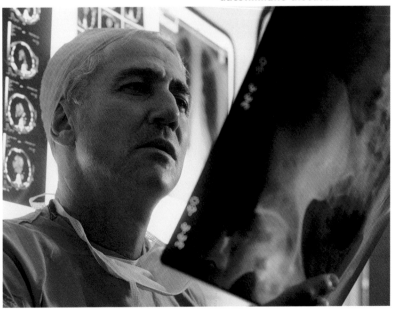

the blood. While it may cause few noticeable problems, chronic respiratory infections, allergies, and asthma sometimes occur.

◆ **Severe combined immunodeficiency (SCID).** People with this complete absence of a functional immune response suffer from one infection after another. The disease is ultimately fatal.

◆ **Sjögren's syndrome.** In Sjögren's, white blood cells invade moisture-producing glands, such as the tear glands, salivary glands, and Bartholin's glands in the vagina, destroying them and depriving the mucous membranes of lubrication. Sjögren's syndrome can also cause problems in the joints, lungs, muscles, kidneys, nerves, thyroid gland, liver, pancreas, stomach, and brain. Contributing factors may include viral infections, heredity, and hormones.

◆ **Type 1 diabetes.** This form of diabetes (also called insulin-dependent diabetes mellitus or juvenile diabetes) is an organ-specific— actually, even a cell-specific—autoimmune disease. It occurs when the immune system attacks the insulin-producing cells of the pancreas. The destruction of these cells usually begins months or even years before the first symptoms appear. Although genetic factors

INCREASED BLOOD SUGAR LEVELS trigger the release of insulin (TINY BLUISH DOTS, ABOVE) into the bloodstream (RED) by specialized cells (YELLOW) within the pancreas.

interesting!

You have four to five quarts of blood in your body, and most blood tests require only about a teaspoon of blood in each test tube. The body rapidly replaces the few teaspoons of blood you lose each time blood is drawn for a test. Even when you donate a pint of blood, the body replaces it so quickly that you can donate an additional pint after waiting about two weeks.

....

clearly determine one's risk of developing type 1 diabetes, an environmental agent—possibly a virus— seems to trigger its onset.

◆ **Ulcerative colitis.** This disease causes inflammation and sores in the top layers of the lining of the large intestine. The inflammation usually occurs in the rectum and lower part of the colon, but it may affect the entire colon. People with ulcerative colitis have specific abnormalities of the immune system, but doctors do not know whether these abnormalities are a cause or a result of the disease. Ulcerative colitis is not caused by emotional distress or sensitivity to certain foods. Many patients, however, say that these factors may trigger symptoms.

◆ **Vitiligo.** As a result of an immune reaction, people with this disorder lose pigment or color cells (melanocytes) in the skin, mouth, nose, genitals, rectum, and retinas, the vision-processing areas at the backs of the eyes. As a result, patches of white skin appear on different parts of the body. Although the cause is not fully understood, researchers theorize that autoantibodies are somehow directed to destroy the melanocytes.

◆ **Wegener's granulomatosis.** This rare vascular disease is characterized by immune-system activation resulting in blood-vessel inflammation. Inflamed blood vessels are unable to carry enough oxygen-rich blood to keep all the body's cells functioning smoothly. Over time, oxygen deprivation damages vital organs and destroys normal tissue, primarily in the respiratory tract. Wegener's granulomatosis occurs mainly in older people. Many patients are between the ages of 70 and 80 when the disease is diagnosed.

Evaluating Immune Function

You've been feeling tired, achy, dizzy, and generally unwell off and on for some time. Could your problems stem from an immune system disorder? Should you see a particular type of doctor? How will he or she determine the cause of your symptoms? Will you need lots of tests?

Start with a visit to your primary physician, not a specialist. Be prepared to give a complete medical history and discuss your lifestyle habits, past and present, in detail. You'll need to answer truthfully when asked about your sex life and drug use, even if you've taken no risks in these areas for years.

Describing symptoms will be easier. For example, do you have repeated infections? Do your infections clear up rapidly or slowly? If antibiotics are necessary, do you need more days of treatment than predicted? Have you recently had shingles, a painful skin condition caused by reactivation of the virus that causes chicken pox? (Although anyone who has had chicken pox can develop shingles, in a relatively young, healthy person, it often indicates immunosuppression.) Have you lost weight recently for no obvious reason?

If your answers suggest that your immune response may be either too aggressive or too weak, your doctor will most likely run a series of blood tests. Depending on your symptoms and on results of initial blood tests, laboratory tests may also be done on samples of stool, urine, or sputum.

Discovering what's gone wrong. Screening for most immune system problems starts with two simple tests: a complete blood count (CBC) and quantitative immunoglobulins (measurements of the basic antibodies or immune system proteins— IgA, IgD, IgE, IgG, and IgM). Your doctor also may order a measurement of the number of T-cells in your blood (CD4 count). These tests are usually performed in an offsite medical laboratory to which your doctor sends patients' blood samples. Test results are faxed or e-mailed to the doctor's

office. The laboratory also mails the doctor an official report.

A brief guide to the most commonly used screening tests for the immune system appears on the following pages. The guide begins with the three tests mentioned above, then lists the next two most widely used screening tests—blood chemistry and urinalysis. More specific or specialized tests are listed in alphabetical order. One patient rarely needs all these tests at once.

Bear in mind that in medical tests, as in most things, more is not always better. Unnecessary tests can lead to more unnecessary tests or even to needless treatments, as well as to errors. Tests should only be done when the results will guide diagnosis or treatment. Don't hesitate to ask what tests you are having and why. Also find out what your test results reveal about your health.

YOUR DOCTOR will order a series of blood tests if you are suspected of having an immune disorder.

GUIDE TO IMMUNE-SYSTEM TESTS

These are some of the most common tests performed to evaluate immune function. The information they provide can help your doctor rule out some diseases, confirm the diagnosis of others, decide what additional tests you need, or measure the effects of treatment. Medications can interfere with results, so you should always tell your doctor about any drugs you are taking.

TEST	PURPOSE
COMPLETE BLOOD COUNT (CBC) including white blood count (WBC), red blood count (RBC), hemoglobin, and hematocrit; differential blood count (DIFF); platelet count	A basic evaluation of the blood that checks for signs of disease or infection. A computerized analyzer performs this test in less than a minute on a drop of blood. Results show levels of red blood cells, white blood cells, platelets, and ratio of red blood cells to the total blood volume. DIFF, a more detailed version of the same test, itemizes the percentages of different types of white blood cells (neutrophils, lymphocytes, monocytes, eosinophils, and basophils). Often used as a general health screen. A low count signals immunodeficiency; high signals infection.
QUANTITATIVE IMMUNOGLOBULINS (including IgG subclasses)	Measures the different immunoglobulins (antibodies) in the blood to help detect immunodeficiency. Often used to check for inability to make antibodies.
CD4 COUNT	Counts the number of active helper T-cells (CD4 cells), which decline throughout the course of any infection. Can also be used to count the number of CD8, or suppressor T-cells. Often used to monitor the course of HIV infection.
BLOOD CHEMISTRY	Measures the amount of certain chemicals dissolved in the blood to help determine how well the organs and muscles are functioning. Often used as a general measure of liver, kidney, and other organ function.
URINALYSIS AND CULTURE	Uses a dipstick with reagent chemicals to analyze a sample of urine. Often used to check for kidney disease, diabetes, infection, or autoimmune disease.
ALLERGY TESTING	Tests the blood or skin to determine if you have IgE antibodies to common allergens, such as pollen and dust mites. Often used to diagnose hay fever.
AUTOANTIBODIES	Checks for autoantibodies, a sign that the immune system is fighting the body's own tissue. Often used to diagnose autoimmune diseases such as lupus.
BLOOD CULTURE	Examines a sample of blood over several days. Often used to determine if bacteria are in the blood.

TEST	PURPOSE
COMPLEMENT ACTIVITY	High activity of the blood serum proteins known as complement indicate inflammation. Low levels may indicate the presence of a so-called immune complex disease, which frequently develops into an autoimmune disease. A complete absence is sometimes found in the case of genetic diseases. Often used to monitor the severity of certain disease or to determine the effectiveness of treatment.
DELAYED HYPERSENSITIVITY SKIN TESTS	A small amount of antigen is injected into the skin or applied to the skin's surface to see if an allergic reaction occurs. Often used to check for contact dermatitis.
ELISA OR WESTERN BLOT	Detects the presence of specific antibodies to viruses and other infectious agents. Mainly used in research, but also used to confirm diagnosis of Lyme disease and to diagnose HIV.
ERYTHROCYTE SEDIMENTATION RATE	Checks for inflammation in the body, which may be the first sign of an immune system problem. Often used to diagnose hidden infection or autoimmune disease.
HEPATITIS VIRUS SEROLOGY (ANTI-HCV TEST)	Determines if you have hepatitis C, a chronic liver disease.
HIV TEST	Determines if you carry the HIV virus.
IMMUNIZATION (A specific antigen used to measure immune response)	A so-called "challenge test" in which you are immunized with a common vaccine (for example, a flu shot) to see if your body can recognize and make an antibody. Often used as a general test of immune function.
MICROSCOPIC STOOL EXAMINATION	Examination of a small amount of fecal material under a microscope to check for the presence of worms or the eggs of worms. Often used to determine the cause of severe diarrhea and stomach cramping.
SERUM PROTEIN ELECTROPHORESIS AND IMMUNOFIXATION	Checks for the presence of abnormal antibodies. Often used to determine if you have multiple myeloma, a cancer of the body's blood-forming and immune systems.
SPUTUM CULTURE	Phlegm is collected from your sputum (mucus ejected from the lungs, bronchi, and trachea, through the mouth). It then is stained and placed in a specially prepared dish that encourages the growth of whatever bacteria may be present. Often used to pinpoint the cause of a lung infection.
WHITE CELL FUNCTION TESTING	A series of rarely performed, sophisticated tests of different groups of white blood cells. Used primarily in children with recurrent bacterial infections.

Source: Centers for Disease Control and Prevention.

Credits

ILLUSTRATIONS

Art Explosion 286, 287, 288 (MIDDLE RIGHT, BOTTOM LEFT), 289, 291, 293, 295, 296, 297. Linda Holt Ayriss/Artville 297. Andrea Brooks 94. Teri McDermott/Phototake 302, 304. Debra Spina Dixon/Artville 289. Carol Donner/Phototake 278. linda Fong 25. Sandy Haight 165. Keith Kasnot 20-21 (PHOTO: Gio Barto/Image Bank), 196-197 (PHOTO: Fotomorgana /The Stock Market.) Jennifer Knaack/Artville 292. Rob Porazinski 6, 43. Robert L. Prince/Stockart 15, 27, 55, 61, 94 (TOP LEFT), 97, 137, 149, 179, 183, 219, 225, 242, 244, 249, 250, 288 (BOTTOM). Kevin A. Somerville/Phototake 301. Susy Pilgrim Waters/Artville 287. Dave Winter/Stockart 65.

PHOTOGRAPHS

COVER FRONT: CLOCKWISE FROM TOP LEFT Nick Rowe/PhotoDisc; Dynamic Graphics; Ken Scott/Tony Stone Images; Nancy R. Cohen/PhotoDisc; SPINE Kathleen Finlay/Masterfile; BACK Klaus Lahnstein/Tony Stone Images. 2 Kathleen Finlay/Masterfile. 4 Quill Telegraph Colour Library/FPG Intl. 5 John Neitzel. 6 TOP Robert Becker, Ph.D/Custom Medical Stock Photo; MIDDLE Dr. Dennis Kunkel/Phototake; BOTTOM Beth Bischoff. 7 TOP Pete Saloutos/The Stock Market; MIDDLE Super Stock; BOTTOM John Neitzel. 8 TOP Steve Mason/PhotoDisc; BOTTOM Siede Preis/PhotoDisc. 9 Neil Michel/Axiom Photo Design. 10-11 Klaus Lahnstein/Tony Stone Images. 12 TOP LEFT CNRI/Phototake; TOP RIGHT Dr. Dennis Kunkel/Phototake; BOTTOM LEFT CNRI/Phototake; BOTTOM RIGHT Institut Pasteur/ Phototake. 13 Nigel Hillier/Tony Stone Images. 14 Peter Nicholson/Tony Stone Images. 15 TOP Carolina Biological Supply Company/Phototake; MIDDLE LEFT Dr. Gopal Murti/Phototake; MIDDLE RIGHT Dr. Dennis Kunkel/Phototake; BOTTOM Dr. Dennis Kunkel/Phototake. 17 Robert Becker, Ph.D./Custom Medical Stock Photo. 18 John W. Banagan/Image Bank. 19 Walter Smith/FPG Intl. 22 LEFT Zack Burris, Inc.; MIDDLE David Scharf/Peter Arnold, Inc. 24 Comstock. 25 Microworks/Phototake. 26 Kevin Dodge/Masterfile. 27 TOP Institut Pasteur/Phototake; MIDDLE LEFT Eurelios/Phototake; MIDDLE RIGHT Jean Claude Revy/Phototake; BOTTOM CNRI/ Phototake. 28 TOP Linda S. Nye/Phototake; BOTTOM Comstock. 29 MTPA Stock/Masterfile. 30 Comstock. 31 TOP RIGHT Comstock; MIDDLE Comstock; BOTTOM RIGHT Andy Cox/Tony Stone Images; BOTTOM MIDDLE Spielman/CNRI/Phototake. 32 LEFT Paul Cherfils/Tony Stone Images; MIDDLE Bruce Forster/ Tony Stone Images. 33 TOP Schlowsky/Workbook Co./Op Stock; MIDDLE Ron Chapple/FPG Intl. 34 Spencer Jones/FPG Intl. 35 John Neitzel. 37 Kevin Dodge/Masterfile. 38-39 Ian O'Leary/Tony Stone Images. 40 LEFT Andrea Monikos/Tony Stone Images; MIDDLE Eric Tucker/Tony Stone Images. 41 Jeff Burke/Lorraine Triolo/Artville. 42 C Squared Studios/PhotoDisc. 44 Judd Pilossof/FoodPix. 45 Burke/Triolo/FoodPix. 46 Ann Stratton/FoodPix. 47 Eising/ StockFood. 48 Burke/Triolo/ FoodPix. 49 MIDDLE Digital Vision/Eyewire; BOTTOM C Squared Studios/PhotoDisc. 50 Eising/StockFood. 51 Amy Neunsinger/ Tony Stone Images. 52 TOP Eising/StockFood; BOTTOM C Squared Studios/PhotoDisc. 53 MIDDLE RIGHT Eising/StockFood; BOTTOM LEFT Carrier/ StockFood; BOTTOM RIGHT Burke/ Triolo/FoodPix. 54 TOP Mariani/StockFood; MIDDLE John Neitzel. 55 TOP Mastri/ StockFood; MIDDLE LEFT John A. Rizzo/ PhotoDisc; MIDDLE RIGHT Eyewire; BOTTOM Susan Kinast/FoodPix. 56 Eyewire. 57 Rubberball/The Stock Market. 59 TOP PhotoDisc; MIDDLE Eyewire. 60 TOP John A. Rizzo/PhotoDisc; MIDDLE Raymond Allbritton/Tony Stone Images. 61 TOP Schlowsky/Workbook Co/Op Stock; MIDDLE LEFT Eisenhut & Mayer/FoodPix; MIDDLE RIGHT Comstock; BOTTOM Jean Claude Revy/Phototake. 62 BOTTOM Eyewire; BACKGROUND Eising/StockFood. 63 Jeff Burke/Lorraine Triolo/Artville. 64 TOP Jeff Burke/Lorraine Triolo/Artville; BOTTOM The Stock Market. 66 TOP Paul Poplis/FoodPix; BOTTOM Steve Cohen/FoodPix. 67 LEFT Gentl & Hyers/FoodPix; MIDDLE John E. Kelly/FoodPix; RIGHT Eising/StockFood. 68 Karl Petzke/FoodPix. 69 Gentl & Hyers/FoodPix. 70 Shaun Egan/Tony Stone Images. 71 Eyewire. 72 Burke/Triolo/FoodPix. 73 John Neitzel. 74 John Manno Photography. 76 LEFT Lawrence Lawry/PhotoDisc; MIDDLE Digital Vision/Eyewire. 78 Eyewire. 79 Dennis O'Clair/Tony Stone Images. 80 Rubberball/The Stock Market. 81 Artville. 82 Monica Stevenson/FoodPix. 84 Hohnen/StockFood. 85 Digital Vision/Eyewire. 86-87 Barbara Bellingham/FPG Intl. 88 Brian Hagiwara/FoodPix. 89 Lisa Koenig. 90 TOP Mariani/StockFood; MIDDLE Siede Preis/PhotoDisc. 91 MIDDLE Monica Stevenson/FoodPix; BOTTOM Eisenhut & Mayer/FoodPix. 92 LEFT Monica Stevenson/FoodPix; MIDDLE Maximilian Stock, Ltd./FoodPix. 93 Mariani/StockFood. 95 Monica Stevenson/FoodPix. 96 TOP Monica Stevenson/FoodPix; BOTTOM Carol Conway/FoodPix. 97 Meredith Parmelee/Tony Stone Images; MIDDLE LEFT Elizabeth Simpson/FPG Intl.; MIDDLE RIGHT Artville; BOTTOM John Neitzel. 98 John Neitzel. 99 Brian Hagiwara/FoodPix. 101 Burke/Triolo/FoodPix. 102 Worrell/StockFood. 103 Meuth/StockFood. 104 BACKGROUND Siede Pireis/PhotoDisc; RIGHT Nancy R. Cohen/PhotoDisc. 105 Mariani/StockFood. 106 MIDDLE Brian Hagiwara/FoodPix; RIGHT Paul Barton/The Stock Market. 107 Kathleen Finlay/Masterfile. 108 PhotoDisc. 109 TOP LEFT A/Z Botanical; TOP RIGHT Matthew Donaldson/Pictor; MIDDLE ZEFA/Index Stock; BOTTOM MIDDLE Dr. Dennis Kunkel/Phototake; BOTTOM RIGHT Dean Ripa/courtesy Ripa Ecologica. 110 Siede Preis/PhotoDisc. 112 Comstock. 113 Quill Telegraph Colour Library/FPG Intl. 114-115 Stuart McClymont/Tony Stone Images. 116 MIDDLE Ronnie Kaufman/The Stock Market; LEFT Lori Adamski Peek/Tony Stone Images. 118 Eyewire. 119 Eyewire. 120 John Henley/The Stock Market. 121 Alan Thornton/Tony Stone Images. 122 Jane Hurd/Phototake. 123 Comstock. 124 Comstock. 125 Eyewire. 126 Chuck Savage/The Stock Market. 127 TOP Digital Vision/Eyewire; BOTTOM Andre Perlstein/Tony Stone Images. 128 TOP Paul Cherfils/Tony Stone Images; MIDDLE Melanie Dune/Emme Modeling, The Emme® Collection . 129 Andre Perlstein/Tony Stone Images. 130 John Neitzel. 131 TOP CNRI/Phototake; BOTTOM Comstock. 132-136 Beth Bischoff. 137 TOP Comstock; MIDDLE LEFT Nick Vedros/Tony Stone Images; MIDDLE RIGHT Kent Knudson/Weststock; BOTTOM John Neitzel. 138 John Neitzel. 138-139 Comstock. 140 Nancy Ney/The Stock Market. 141 Gary Ochner/FPG Intl. 142 Philip & Karen Smith/Tony Stone Images. 143 Stephen Simpson/FPG Intl. 144 LEFT Philip & Karen Smith/Tony Stone Images; MIDDLE Bill Losh/FPG Intl. 145 Jose L. Pelaez, Inc./The Stock Market. 146 Ryan McVay/PhotoDisc. 147 Christopher Bissell/Tony Stone Images. 148 TOP Rob Lewine/The Stock Market; BOTTOM Ralf Schultheiss/Tony Stone Images. 149 TOP Comstock; MIDDLE LEFT Comstock; MIDDLE RIGHT Eyewire; BOTTOM Jason

Reed/Ryan McVay/PhotoDisc. 150 Digital Vision/Eyewire. 151 Stephen Simpson/FPG Intl. 153 Michael Keller/The Stock Market. 154-155 Marcelo Coelho/FPG Intl. 157 TOP RIGHT Pete Saloutos/The Stock Market; MIDDLE S.P.L./Custom Medical Stock Photo; 158 Mark Tuschman/The Stock Market. 159 Digital Vision/Eyewire. 160 Comstock. 161 Andrew Brookes/The Stock Market. 163 Patrick Cocklin/Tony Stone Images. 166 Steve Krongard Inc./Image Bank. 167 Spike/PhotoDisc. 168 TOP Ryan McVay/PhotoDisc; BOTTOM Nancy R. Cohen/PhotoDisc. 169 TOP Image Club Photography/Eyewire; BOTTOM LEFT Comstock; BOTTOM RIGHT Comstock. 171 Beth Bischoff. 172 TOP Victoria Blackie/Tony Stone Images; BOTTOM Ian O'Leary/Tony Stone Images. 174 LEFT Gandee Vasan/Tony Stone Images; RIGHT Digital Vision/Eyewire. 175 Geoff Brightling/FPG Intl. 176 Michael Segal/Super Stock. 177 Dick Patrick/Workbook Co/Op Stock. 178 Paul Poplis/FoodPix. 179 TOP Eyewire; MIDDLE LEFT Steve Cole/PhotoDisc; MIDDLE RIGHT Comstock; BOTTOM Nancy R. Cohen/PhotoDisc. 180 David de Lossy/Image Bank. 183 TOP Dr. Dennis Kunkel/Phototake; MIDDLE LEFT Eddie Soloway/Tony Stone Images; MIDDLE RIGHT Comstock; BOTTOM David de Lossy/Image Bank. 184 The Stock Market. 185 Eyewire. 186-187 Karen Moskowitz/Tony Stone Images. 188 Eyewire. 189 Stephen Johnson/Tony Stone Images. 191 Rubberball/The Stock Market. 193 Thomas Hoeffgan/Tony Stone Images. 194 LEFT Comstock; MIDDLE C Squared Studios/PhotoDisc; RIGHT David Chasey/PhotoDisc. 195 Dr. Dennis Kunkel/Phototake. 198 Anthony Redpath/The Stock Market. 199 Koji Kitawawa/Super Stock. 200 John Neitzel. 201 V.C.L./FPG Intl. 202 Super Stock. 203 Joe Polillio/Tony Stone Images. 204 Francisco Cruise/Super Stock. 205 Ariel Skelley/The Stock Market. 206 LEFT Duncan Smith/PhotoDisc; RIGHT Eyewire. 207 TOP Randy Allbritton/PhotoDisc; BOTTOM C Squared Studios/PhotoDisc. 208 LEFT Nicholas Eveleigh; MIDDLE Comstock. 210 CMCD/PhotoDisc. 211 LWA/Stephen Welstead/The Stock Market. 212 Jerry Atnip/Super Stock. 213 Will & Deni McIntyre/Tony Stone Images. 214 MIDDLE LEFT CMCD/PhotoDisc; BOTTOM LEFT CMCD/PhotoDisc; MIDDLE CMCD/PhotoDisc. TOP RIGHT Chris Salvo/FPG Intl.; 215 Pete Saloutos/The Stock Market. 216 Eyewire. 217 Myron J. Dorf/The Stock Market. 218 Francisco Cruise/Super Stock. 219 TOP Eyewire; MIDDLE LEFT Susan Kinast/FoodPix; MIDDLE RIGHT Milton Montenegro/PhotoDisc; BOTTOM Gerald Zanetti/The Stock Market. 220 Jon Riley/Tony Stone Images. 221 John Lund/Tony Stone Images. 222 Alistair Berg/FPG Intl. 223 Paul Barton/The Stock Market. 224 Harry Bartlett/FPG Intl. 225 TOP Eyewire; MIDDLE LEFT Comstock; MIDDLE RIGHT George B. Diebold/The Stock Market; BOTTOM Comstock. 226 Dan Bosler/Tony Stone Images. 227 David Loftus/Tony Stone Images. 228 Comstock. 229 Colorstock/FPG Intl. 230-231 Thatcher/Fisher/Tony Stone Images. 232 Lisette Le Bon/Super Stock. 233 Paul Grebliunas/Tony Stone Images. 235 TOP Ricardo Elkind/PhotoDisc; BOTTOM A.L. Sinibaldi/Tony Stone Images. 236 Randy Allbritton/PhotoDisc. 237 Comstock. 238 S. Achernar/Image Bank. 239 Klaus Lahnstein/Tony Stone Images. 240 Rick Rusing/Tony Stone Images. 241 TOP Comstock; BOTTOM Steven Mark Needham/FoodPix. 242 BOTTOM Comstock; RIGHT Eyewire. 243 TOP Eyewire; MIDDLE Janis Christie/PhotoDisc; BOTTOM Ryan

McVay/PhotoDisc. 244 TOP Emanuele Taroni/PhotoDisc; BOTTOM LEFT Nancy R. Cohen/PhotoDisc; BOTTOM MIDDLE Nancy R. Cohen/PhotoDisc. 245 TOP LEFT Eyewire; TOP RIGHT Siede Preis/PhotoDisc; MIDDLE Ryan McVay/PhotoDisc. 246 Florian Franke/Super Stock. 247 Siede Preis/PhotoDisc. 248 TOP Anton Vengo/Super Stock; MIDDLE The Stock Market. 249 TOP The Stock Market; MIDDLE LEFT courtesy of American Honda Motor Co., Inc.; MIDDLE RIGHT Chip Simons/FPG Intl.; BOTTOM Eyewire. 250 TOP James Gritz/PhotoDisc; MIDDLE LEFT Edmund Van Hoorick/PhotoDisc; MIDDLE RIGHT Jack Daniels/Tony Stone Images; BOTTOM Alan & Sandy Carey Tony Stone Images. 251 Comstock. 252 Daniel Arsenault/Image Bank. 253 TOP John Neitzel; BACKGROUND Comstock. 255 Eyewire. 256 Burke/Triolo/FoodPix. 257 Burke/Triolo/FoodPix. 258 TOP Russell Kaye/Tony Stone Images; BOTTOM CMCD/PhotoDisc. 259 Spike/PhotoDisc. 260 TOP Comstock; BOTTOM Ernie Friedlander/Cole Group/PhotoDisc. 261 The Stock Market. 262 LEFT Ryan McVay/PhotoDisc; RIGHT C Squared Studios/PhotoDisc. 263 Comstock. 264 Dr. Dennis Kunkel/Phototake. 265 Dr. Dennis Kunkel/Phototake. 266 Laurence Monneret/Tony Stone Images. 267 Spike Mafford/PhotoDisc. 268 John Neitzel. 269 Terje Rakke/Image Bank. 270 Tommy Ewasko/Image Bank. 271 Comstock. 272 LEFT C Squared Studios/PhotoDisc; RIGHT CMCD/PhotoDisc. 273 Eyewire. 274 Burke/Triolo/Artville. 275 J. P. Fruchet/FPG Intl. 276 LWA/Dann Tardif/The Stock Market. 277 ADAMSMITH/FPG Intl. 278 Digital Vision/Eyewire 280 Don Farrell/PhotoDisc. 281 David Arky. 282-283 BACKGROUND Gary Hunter/Tony Stone Images. 282 TOP LEFT Corbis; BOTTOM LEFT Peter Cade/Tony Stone Images; TOP MIDDLE Z & B Baran/Tony Stone Images; BOTTOM MIDDLE Steve Taylor/Tony Stone Images; RIGHT Eyewire. 283 BOTTOM Terry Doyle/Tony Stone Images. 284 TOP C Squared Studios/PhotoDisc; MIDDLE Artville; BOTTOM Jurgen Reisch/Tony Stone Images. 285 TOP Digital Vision/Eyewire; BOTTOM V.C.L./FPG Intl. 286 TOP RIGHT Eyewire; BOTTOM LEFT John A. Rizzo/PhotoDisc; BOTTOM RIGHT C Squared Studios/PhotoDisc. 287 TOP (2) Jeff Burke/Lorraine Triolo/Artville; BOTTOM Craig Brewer/PhotoDisc. 288 Jeff Maloney/PhotoDisc. 289 TOP LEFT Paul Barton/The Stock Market; BOTTOM Comstock. 290 TOP LEFT Jules Frazier/PhotoDisc; TOP RIGHT Chet Phillips/Artville; BOTTOM LEFT Digital Vision/Eyewire; BOTTOM RIGHT Michael Keller/The Stock Market. 291 MIDDLE C Squared Studios/PhotoDisc; BOTTOM Comstock. 292 TOP LEFT CMCD/PhotoDisc; TOP RIGHT Kim Steele/PhotoDisc; MIDDLE Lawrence Lawry/PhotoDisc; BOTTOM LEFT Lisa Koenig. 293 TOP Ryan McVay/PhotoDisc; MIDDLE Siede Preis/PhotoDisc; BOTTOM Harry Sims/Image Bank. 294 TOP C Squared Studios/PhotoDisc; MIDDLE Eyewire; LEFT Digital Vision/Eyewire; BOTTOM Comstock. 295 TOP Janis Christie/PhotoDisc; MIDDLE Nancy R. Cohen/PhotoDisc; LEFT Digital Vision/Eyewire; BOTTOM Comstock. 296 TOP LEFT PhotoLink/PhotoDisc; TOP RIGHT Steve Mason/PhotoDisc; MIDDLE Rubberball/Eyewire; BOTTOM Doug Menuez/PhotoDisc. 297 TOP Ryan McVay/PhotoDisc; BOTTOM Doug Menuez/PhotoDisc. 298 Rubberball/The Stock Market. 299 Michael Segal/SuperStock. 300 Dr. Ryder/Jason Burns/Phototake. 301 Nick Rowe/PhotoDisc; 303 Digital Vision/Eyewire. 305 Photo Disc. 306 MIDDLE Don Farrall/PhotoDisc; BOTTOM Comstock. 307 Comstock.

Index

Page numbers in **bold type** refer to photographs or illustrations.

Page numbers in **bold type** refer to photographs or illustrations.

Page numbers in **bold type** refer to photographs or illustrations.

Page numbers in **bold type** refer to photographs or illustrations.

Page numbers in **bold type** refer to photographs or illustrations.

Page numbers in **bold type** refer to photographs or illustrations.

Page numbers in **bold type** refer to photographs or illustrations.

Page numbers in **bold type** refer to photographs or illustrations.

Page numbers in **bold type** refer to photographs or illustrations.

Page numbers in **bold type** refer to photographs or illustrations.